Domestic Animals, Humans, and Leisure

Domestic animals are an integral component of human leisure experience and can enhance the physical, social, and mental wellbeing of humans. The interplay of human and animal experiences of justice, wellbeing, rights, and roles within leisure is the central theme of this book. Research explores the position of domesticated animals in human leisure experiences, in a wide array of leisure settings. Chapters question whether domestic animals may have a desire for leisure that is different from human leisure, whether animals have and wish to fulfil needs for meaningful leisure or non-leisure, and whether human leisure needs and desires may coincide or contradict wellbeing interests of animals.

This book provides a venue for the dissemination and exploration of research, which champions the welfare and rights of these animals to have their needs and interests in leisure recognised. It moves the debate about animals in leisure beyond the current limits which have seen research mainly confined to the exotic 'other' rather than more mundane, everyday domestic animals. This book will be of interest to individuals in the fields of tourism ethics, zoology, animal behaviour, and leisure studies.

Janette Young lectures in health policy, politics and promotion at the University of South Australia. Her research interests hub around the human–animal intersection, salutogenesis or what creates health and wellbeing, social justice and public policy. She has a background as a social worker in ageing, and project and policy work across a diverse range of human interest areas. It was working as a social work student many years ago that she learned that seeking to holistically meet the needs of some people has to encompass caring about the animals these people care about.

Neil Carr is head of the Department of Tourism at the University of Otago and the editor of *Annals of Leisure Research*. His research focuses on understanding behaviour within tourism and leisure experiences, with a particular emphasis on children and families, sex and animals. He has authored and edited several books, including *Dogs in the Leisure Experience* (2014) and *Domestic Animals and Leisure* (2015).

Routledge Ethics of Tourism
Series edited by Professor David Fennell

This series seeks to engage with key debates surrounding ethical issues in tourism from a range of interdisciplinary perspectives across the social sciences and humanities. Contributions explore ethical debates across socio-cultural, ecological and economic lines on topics such as: climate, resource consumption, ecotourism and nature-based tourism, sustainability, responsible tourism, the use of animals, politics, international relations, violence, tourism labour, sex tourism, exploitation, displacement, marginalisation, authenticity, slum tourism, indigenous people, communities, rights, justice and equity. This series has a global geographic coverage and offers new theoretical insights in the form of authored and edited collections to reflect the wealth of research being undertaken in this sub-field.

1 **Animals, Food, and Tourism**
   Edited by Carol Kline

2 **Tourism Experiences and Animal Consumption**
   Contested Values, Morality and Ethics
   Edited by Carol Kline

3 **Wild Animals and Leisure**
   Rights and Wellbeing
   Edited by Neil Carr and Janette Young

4 **Domestic Animals, Humans, and Leisure**
   Rights, Welfare, and Wellbeing
   Edited by Janette Young and Neil Carr

5 **New Moral Natures in Tourism**
   Edited by Kellee Caton, Lisa Cooke and Bryan Grimwood

For a full list of titles in this series, please visit www.routledge.com/Routledge-Ethics-of-Tourism-Series/book-series/RET

Domestic Animals, Humans, and Leisure

Rights, Welfare, and Wellbeing

Edited by Janette Young
and Neil Carr

LONDON AND NEW YORK

First published 2018
by Routledge
2 Park Square, Milton Park, Abingdon, Oxon OX14 4RN

and by Routledge
711 Third Avenue, New York, NY 10017

Routledge is an imprint of the Taylor & Francis Group, an informa business

© 2018 selection and editorial matter, Janette Young and Neil Carr; individual chapters, the contributors

The right of Janette Young and Neil Carr to be identified as the authors of the editorial material, and of the authors for their individual chapters, has been asserted in accordance with sections 77 and 78 of the Copyright, Designs and Patents Act 1988.

All rights reserved. No part of this book may be reprinted or reproduced or utilised in any form or by any electronic, mechanical, or other means, now known or hereafter invented, including photocopying and recording, or in any information storage or retrieval system, without permission in writing from the publishers.

Trademark notice: Product or corporate names may be trademarks or registered trademarks, and are used only for identification and explanation without intent to infringe.

British Library Cataloguing-in-Publication Data
A catalogue record for this book is available from the British Library

Library of Congress Cataloging-in-Publication Data
A catalog record for this book has been requested

ISBN: 978-1-138-20927-5 (hbk)
ISBN: 978-1-315-45745-1 (ebk)

Typeset in Times New Roman
by Apex CoVantage, LLC

Contents

List of figures vii
List of contributors ix
Acknowledgements xi

1 **Introduction** 1
   JANETTE YOUNG AND NEIL CARR

2 **Behind bars: contradictions in the expectations and experiences of life with marginalised companion animals** 12
   RUTHANN ARLETTA DRUMMOND

3 **Dog shows as casual leisure: asymmetry of human and animal experience** 32
   MAGDALENA DĄBROWSKA

4 **Dog showing and training: enjoyable hobbies or destructive practices that reinforce speciesist ideologies?** 47
   SCOTT HURLEY

5 **Off-leash recreation in an urban national recreation area: conflict between domesticated dogs, wildlife and semi-domesticated humans** 63
   JACKSON WILSON, AIKO YOSHINO AND PAVLINA LATKOVA

6 **Walking the dog – chore or leisure?** 82
   LISEL O'DWYER

7 **Recentring companion species wellbeing in the leisure experience: towards multispecies flourishing through dog walking** 98
   KATRINA MYRVANG BROWN AND PETRA LACKOVA

8	**Domesticated dogs and 'doings' during the holidays** BODIL STILLING BLICHFELDT AND KATARÍNA LECI SAKÁČOVÁ	113
9	**From labour to leisure: the relocation of animals in modern Western society** JANETTE YOUNG AND AMY BAKER	128
10	**Post-humanistic insight into human-equine interactions and wellbeing within leisure and tourism** PAULA DANBY	146
11	**Pampered prisoners: meeting the ethological needs of the modern sport horse to enhanced equine welfare** ANTONIA J. Z. HENDERSON	165
12	**Human-initiated animal fights** ERIK COHEN	190
13	**Domestic animals' leisure, rights, wellbeing: nuancing 'domestic', asymmetries and into the future** JANETTE YOUNG AND NEIL CARR	209
	Index	223

Figures

1.1	Highland cow, or perhaps bull	5
1.2	Jersey cow	5
2.1	Koi are commonly kept in garden ponds for their ornamental beauty	14
2.2	Baby red-eared and yellow bellied turtles waiting to be sold at a Texas warehouse	16
2.3	Clara was a classroom pet injured by students tossing her hamster ball while she was inside	17
2.4	Inadequate housing and care can cause parrots to exhibit self-mutilating behaviours	20
2.5	Many commercially-available enclosures provide only enough room for rabbits to turn around and lie down	23
2.6	Snakes are often housed in barren enclosures without room to stretch their bodies entirely	24
2.7	Smokey was surrendered when his incisors became grossly overgrown due to inadequate care	25
2.8	Parrots kept in human homes often display destructive and property damaging behaviours	27
2.9	Rabbits enjoying a free-range lifestyle, integrated into a family home	29
6.1	Frequency of dog walking by dwelling type	88
6.2	Distribution of dog owners' attachment to their dogs (Johnson et al. 1992)	89
9.1	Animal facilities in Adelaide, SA, past and present	130
9.2	"A day out" sculpture by Marguerite Derricourt	131
9.3	Preparation for tram tracks, King William Street, Adelaide, SA (1909)	133
9.4	Rundle Street, Adelaide, SA (c1930s)	135
9.5	Horses pulling dual level trams, Grenfell Street, Adelaide (1896)	136
11.1	Equine Prisoners Model; based on Fraser et al. (1997) and Henderson (2007)	167

viii *Figures*

11.2	Allowing horses to interact between stalls	179
11.3	Weanling practising cribbing	180
11.4	Cribbing station installed around water bowl	181
11.5	Cribbing on a portable cribbing station	182
11.6	Horses engaged in allogrooming	182

Contributors

Amy Baker is a Lecturer in the Occupational Therapy Programme at the University of South Australia. Her research interests include mental health and suicide prevention, human flourishing and physical and social environmental issues that influence health and wellbeing, such as community gardening and pets.

Bodil Stilling Blichfeldt has a PhD in marketing and is an Associate Professor at University of Southern Denmark. She has authored around 50 journal articles and her key research areas are tourist studies, consumer behaviour in tourism, destination branding and tourism methodologies.

Katrina Myrvang Brown (Senior Researcher, James Hutton Institute) is experienced in using mobile video methods to investigate how the values, norms and experiences of outdoor recreationists shape wellbeing and abilities to share space, most recently on the much neglected role of haptic senses.

Erik Cohen is the George S. Wise Professor of Sociology (emeritus) at the Hebrew University of Jerusalem, where he taught between 1959 and 2000. He has conducted research in Israel, Peru, the Pacific Islands and, since 1977, in Thailand. He is the author of more than 200 publications and of several books, including *Contemporary Tourism: Diversity and Change* (Elsevier 2004) and *Explorations in Thai Tourism* (Emerald 2008). Cohen is a founding member of the International Academy for the Study of Tourism. He was awarded the UN World Tourism Organisation's Ulysses Prize for 2012. He presently lives and does research in Thailand.

Magdalena Dąbrowska (PhD) is Assistant Professor at the Institute of Culture Studies, University of Maria Curie-Skłodowska in Lublin. She was a researcher for the European Commission's project "QUING" (Quality in Gender + Equality Policies) (2007–2009). She studied in the ERSTE Stiftung (Patterns Lectures programme), Institut fur die Wiessenschaften vom Menschen, and at Central European University (MA studies). Her recent research interests include human-animal relationships in contemporary culture, especially dog shows.

Paula Danby is a Lecturer in International Tourism Management at Queen Margaret University, Edinburgh, UK. Her research focuses on human-animal relations within leisure and tourism environments, particularly equestrian tourism.

Interests include animal tourism, ecotourism, leisure and wellbeing. Paula's work explores human-animal interactions for mutual wellbeing.

Ruthann Arletta Drummond, Contract Faculty at York University, Canada, holds a Master's in Environmental Studies. Ruthann's research focuses on human-animal relationships. Her Master's research, Think Outside the Cage: Moving Towards New Understandings of Companion Rabbits, appears in York's Faculty of Environmental Studies Outstanding Graduate Paper Series.

Antonia J. Z. Henderson is a psychology professor at Langara College in Vancouver, BC. Her research focuses on interpersonal relationships, the human-animal bond and the psychology of equine behaviour. Her writings on equine welfare have appeared in both academic (*JAWWS*) and lay journals (*Horse Sport*).

Scott Hurley is Associate Professor of Religion at Luther College. His research interests include critical animal studies, intersection of oppressions, human-canine relations and Buddhist and Daoist perceptions of nonhuman animals. He is the author of "Engendering Empathy for Nonhuman Suffering: Using Graphic Narratives to Raise Awareness about Commercial Dog Breeding Operations" and "Human-Canine Relationships in China."

Petra Lackova is a conservation social researcher with background in collaborative, video (film) and mixed methods research on wildlife management. She is currently a PhD researcher developing a new approach to respond to wildlife conflicts, combining conflict resolution and adaptive management principles on the conflict around white-tailed sea eagles in Scotland.

Pavlína Látková is an Associate Professor in the Department of Recreation, Parks and Tourism at San Francisco State University. Her research interests include community-based tourism, destination image and resident attitudes towards tourism development.

Lisel O'Dwyer has a background in social policy, public health, ageing, human-animal studies and animal behaviour. Recent work addresses attitudes towards chickens and cattle, pets and mental health and pet attachment in bushfire preparation. She is based at Central Queensland University and Flinders University, South Australia.

Katarína Leci Sakáčová has a Master's degree in tourism from Aalborg University. Her main research area is tourist studies. She teaches consumer studies in tourism and supervises tourism students at a Master's level.

Jackson Wilson is an Associate Professor and Graduate Coordinator in the Department of Recreation, Parks and Tourism at San Francisco State University. His research focuses on the health impacts of recreating in natural environments, including the impact of leash use on dog walkers' physical activity.

Aiko Yoshino is an Assistant Professor in the Department of Recreation, Parks and Tourism at San Francisco State University. Her research areas are health and nature, youth development and psychological resilience in outdoor education.

Acknowledgements

An edited book is a collective undertaking and labour, even when about leisure!

Both of us (Neil and Janette) have human and animal companions and colleagues to thank.

For Janette, the two small dogs who snoozed their way through the days spent locked in my study have been living breathing companions in the solitariness that comes with solid writing opportunities. Thanks for breaking up my days with greeting the postage, brief garden explorations (greeting the birds, listening to the magpies chortle) and confirmation that the mantra that "dogs should be walked every day" definitely was not your sentient individual position on leisure. Confirmed as I carried *two* dogs back from the park on several occasions. Leisure for them, like some people, consists more in the pleasures of home and hearth than exploring even the not-so-great unknown (the park being less than 5 minutes' walk away).

For Neil, the original cause of an interest in animal-related research was his first dog, Snuffie. While she alas, has "crossed the rainbow bridge", without her this book would never have come to be. Gypsy, her follower, has worked tirelessly to place herself at the centre of life. Ten days before writing this acknowledgements segment, Gypsy left us as well. Ebony, snoozing on my lap as I type this (as a Mastiff cross puppy this is unlikely to continue as she enters adulthood!) will never replace those who have gone before her but she has helped to begin the healing process and to push my work onwards (and often upwards out of reach of her mouth). Yet these acknowledgements cannot centre only on dogs. The Carr household cat (currently dealing with a pup after 8 years of blissful and total dominance of Gypsy and 3 years prior to that of a respectful truce with Snuffie) deserves a mention. While she may have a tendency to write gobbledegook as she stomps across the keyboard, she serves as a reminder that the world of animals is not restricted to dogs, something reinforced by the ducks and chickens that exist on the Carr property as well. They offer the reminder that all animals can be capable of demonstrating sentience and a desire for leisure.

As always, mention must also be made of our human families who keep us on the straight and narrow. For Neil thanks go to Sarah, long suffering wife, Ben, stoic 17- year-old, Tat, absent 15-year-old daughter off chasing her ballet dancing dreams, and Gus, the unstoppable force of nature. Greg, Janette's human partner in life (and dogs) has brought cups of tea, and even meals as she laboured over a keyboard especially in the final push to get a book ready for the publisher.

Thanks are also due to our work colleagues and friends. Caroline Adams and Richard McGrath have been great to debrief with and have been tolerant of an absent and distracted Programme Director (Janette) for much of 2017. We are both indebted to everyone in our departments and beyond who directly and indirectly have helped to support us, meaning that we have time to get on with research and writing. Particular thanks to Neil's departmental administrator Trudi, and to Brent for always being willing to take on the role of acting Head.

As co-authors we would like to acknowledge all the authors of the chapters in this book and thank you all for your patience and good humour as you worked with us as editors. Thank you for joining us on this journey exploring the leisure of domestic animals. Thank you to Faye Leerink from Taylor & Francis who originally picked up on the call for papers to the 2015 Australian and New Zealand Association for Leisure Studies Conference and suggested that our session focus could become a book. An exciting opportunity. We look forward to the future in this space as the welfare, wellbeing and leisure of animals continues to deservedly receive attention.

Janette and Neil
June 2017

1 Introduction

Janette Young and Neil Carr

Introduction

Domestic animals are an integral component of many human leisure experiences and in this position can enhance the physical, social and mental wellbeing of humans (Brooks et. al. 2016, Rijken and van Beek 2011; Wood et. al. 2007). At the same time it is increasingly recognised that as sentient beings these animals have their own rights, welfare and wellbeing needs (Kymlicka and Donaldson 2014; Garner and O'Sullivan 2016). The interplay of human and animal experiences of justice, wellbeing, rights and roles within leisure is the central hub of this book. Here authors explore the position of domesticated animals in human leisure experiences, and the position of leisure in the lives of these animals. Within this context the book, and the individual chapters within it, explore whether domestic animals may have a desire for leisure that is distinct from human leisure, whether animals have and wish to fulfil needs for meaningful leisure or non-leisure, and whether human leisure needs and desires may coincide or conversely contradict domesticated animal leisure and wellbeing interests.

Our aim in compiling this book has been to provide a venue for the dissemination and exploration of cutting edge research on domesticated animals and leisure. Such an opportunity enables forwarding of knowledge in this area while championing the welfare and rights of domesticated animals in relation to their own leisure needs. Within this context, this book is not an 'end'. Rather, it is intended to build on the work in the field that has gone before it[1] and help to push for further research on domesticated animals and leisure.

Why domesticated animals?

Domestic animals have received far less attention in the leisure field than their binary other – 'wild animals'. Carr (2015a) documents the relative wealth of books that have encompassed wild animals in explorations of predominately touristic leisure spaces. Why might this imbalance be the case though? Four core arguments are noted in this chapter, and these carry through to the conclusion of the book. Firstly, it may be suggested that domesticated animals are largely overlooked as part of the unequal power relationship that exists between humans and animals. By and large humans make decisions and control domestic animals' leisure experiences and opportunities. It is humans who decide the what, where and with who of domesticated animals lives. When these animals' leisure is considered, it is usually as an adjunct to human leisure experiences; animals' own needs, wishes or desires are rarely considered a legitimate factor. This imbalance of power weaves through the book and is explored in more detail in the conclusion. Secondly, domestic animals may be overlooked because in general we tend to give little or no conscious thought to, and even at times despise, the domestic. It is every day and mundane. This fits with the notion forwarded by Edward Said (2003) that the foreign and largely unknown is seen as far more attractive and inspiring than one's own culture and environment. In this way, domestic animals may be seen to lack the appeal of the exotic. Thirdly, the relative lack of attention paid to some domestic animals by leisure researchers may be due to an inherent tension across the spectrum of domesticated animals. This tension exists between the domesticated animals we see ourselves as sharing our human lives with (the dominant focus of the chapters in this book), and those animals (also domesticated) overtly utilised for human purposes; be this animal to animal fighting (see the chapter by Cohen) or simply feeding one domesticated animal (the factory farmed) to another (the pet cat or dog). In this way, it may not be surprising that the domestic animals most studied are the ones we love the most. Finally, related to the mundane and the notion of domestication is the argument that domestic animals, particularly pets, are not 'real' animals but instead have been bred into existence by humans. Indeed, Miklósi (2007, 1) notes that dogs, probably the ultimate domesticated animal, have often been identified as "artificial animals". As such, they may be identified as human constructs less worthy of investigation than the 'real' wild animals (Bradshaw 2011).

These issues are intertwined, and glimpses of them can be discerned across the chapters as the complexities and at times contradictions inherent within and across understandings of human and animal 'leisure' are explored. We return to them in the conclusion. For now though, neither editors of the book nor the other contributors would agree that domestic animals are less worthy of attention than wild animals nor that they are somehow less real than their wild counterparts. As such, domestic animals are as deserving of study in general, and with specific reference to leisure, as wild animals.

Defining domestic and domesticated animals

So what exactly are 'domestic' or 'domesticated' animals? What do the terms 'domestic' and 'domesticated' mean of themselves?

Online searching readily reveals several definitions of 'domestic' including (www.dictionary.com): "of or relating to the home, the household, household affairs, or the family" and "no longer wild". Hence 'domestic' or 'domesticated' can be seen as a contrasting or negative binary to the notion of 'wild'. Certainly there is a position in the animal studies field that domestic animals are somehow corruptions of the 'natural order', that humans have interfered with nature creating un-natural, domesticated animals (Francione 2009; Hall 2006). The definition provided by Clutton-Brock (1989 in Eddy 2003) encompasses this notion of human control or interference in domesticated animal lives in general and with specific reference to reproduction. Domesticated animals are: "[a] species of animal which has been artificially selected by humans over a number of generations to possess specific traits and over which humans have reproductive control" (100). In other words, domestic animals experience a level of control by humans that is in contrast to that experienced by wild animals. These animals are kept from making the most basic of choices (who they will reproduce with) by humans.

Carr (2015a) suggests that animals can be seen as fitting into a continuum from domestic through to wild with dogs and cats often seen as the exemplars of domesticated animals. A common terminology for these exemplar animals is "pets". It is estimated that more than half of households globally have pets (GfK 2016). There are many definitions of pets but generally they tend to hinge on the notions that pets are animals with which we share our domestic spaces, they are named, they are not readily eaten and humans have them predominately for reasons of companionship. Pets have faced a paradoxical treatment in the academic literature. On one hand they have been construed as privileged for the close relationships they may have with humans and the benefits that this may offer individual animals and even species (Carr 2014). On the other hand they have been critiqued as 'not real' animals (Francione 2009; Hall 2006), and seen as frivolous and extraneous to serious human experiences (Young and O'Dwyer 2015).

Aside from pets, there are other species that have also been domesticated in the manner defined by Clutton-Brock (1989) but these animals do not generally share our homes and lives in the same way. Species such as sheep, cattle, horses and camels are animals that are generally de-personalised, seen as utilitarian means to fulfil human interests and agendas such as transport, and human consumption of food and other 'products'. In other words, not all domesticated species are equally domestic. To complicate things further, individual animals may be treated in quite different ways. For example, there is the house lamb who becomes the family pet sheep, the dog who is released to guard at night and locked in an outdoor pen during the day, and as revealed in the chapters in this book that focus on horses (Danby, and Henderson), whilst fulfilling a utilitarian role of recreational transport, some humans and horses may feel a unique sense of bonding. But their relative size means that in general horses do not share human domestic spaces.

The domestication of species and individual animals, and human and animal experiences of leisure occur within and are shaped by the diversity of human cultures. Most of the species discussed as domestic in this book are killed and devoured by humans somewhere on the globe. Eating dogs is still seen as an integral part of some cultures, including those where dogs are also seen as pets (Podberscek 2016, 2009). Guinea pigs are on the menu in some South American and African countries (Yiva et al. 2014, Graham, Vascon and Trueba 2016), and horses are eaten by humans in some European countries (Belaunzaran et al. 2015).

Hence concepts of 'domesticated' and 'domestic' animals can be seen as broad and flexible. However, these animals have a common connector in their relationship to humans either individually (kept contained or reliant upon humans) and/or generationally (products of human reproductive management). This is distinct from the relationship that exists between animals considered wild and humans, who may be impacted by human behaviours but have a less direct connection to human society.

Domesticated animals and human leisure

A key argument for seeking to explore the leisure needs and positions of domestic animals in human leisure is the sheer scale of this population. A current indication of domesticated animal numbers is that there are now around three chickens and one bovine per person worldwide (Huffpost 2011). In addition, 57 percent of households globally are estimated to have pets, with dogs (33 percent) and cats (23 percent) being the dominant species of choice, although significant numbers of households have fish (12 percent) and pet birds (6 percent) as well (GfK 2016).

Domesticated animals play a diverse variety of roles in human leisure experiences. There are people who breed animals as a leisure pursuit, and there are those who engage in sport with their domesticated animals. For example, Hultsman (2015) provides a detailed look at a range of sports that utilise pet dogs, while domesticated dogs have also been widely used in human leisure pursuits such as hunting and racing (see Carr (2015b) for a discussion of greyhound racing and Carr (2014) for an examination of dog sledding as both a sport and holiday attraction). While dog agility is well known, attempts have also been made to create a cat agility sport (www.catagility.com/). It is, of course, not just dogs that are utilised in human-constructed sport. Horses, camels (Khalaf 2000), cows (www.compasscup.com.au/) and hamsters (Holmes 2017) amongst others, have all been raced for human entertainment. Horses are also widely ridden as a leisure experience (see chapters by Danby, and Henderson), while riding the donkey at the beach was a Victorian innovation for tourists in the UK that can still be found in various parts of the world today (Blakeway and Cousquer, forthcoming). Other animals, including mules, lamas and alpacas, are utilised as beasts of burden for tourists while dogs, proving once again their adaptability within human society, are now utilised to meet and greet holiday visitors and calm nervous or stressed individuals at airports (Carr 2014).

Domesticated animals may also form an integral component of the leisure and holiday landscape. For example, Herdwick sheep, whose fleece is virtually worthless for farmers are, today, a prominent feature of the rural landscape of the Lake District National Park in the UK. They are not there for agricultural purposes as much as they are there because visitors to the Park expect them to be there. Similarly, when visiting Scotland we expect to be able to see the hairy Highland cow depicted in Figure 1.1 (is it a bull or a cow – arguably, to the average tourist it does not matter as long as it is appropriately shaggy and horny), not just some 'ordinary' cow. Likewise, when visiting Jersey we expect to see a Jersey cow (Figure 1.2) (not unlike the issue of the sex of the Highland cow, how many people can tell the difference between the Jersey and Guernsey cow?). Domesticated

Figure 1.1 Highland cow, or perhaps bull
Photograph: Neil Carr

Figure 1.2 Jersey cow
Photograph: Neil Carr

animals are not just part of the expected leisure landscape; they are also increasingly visitor attractions in their own right. More and more farms are diversifying their activities away from traditional agricultural activities to offer visitors the opportunity to pet, touch, feed and even milk, domesticated animals such as cows, sheep and goats (Adam 2001; Ollenburg 2008; Wilson 2007). This industry both helps to provide for the leisure needs of people and generates significant revenue and employment in servicing these needs (Veeck, Che and Veeck 2006). This is yet another reason why domesticated animals should not be overlooked in leisure research.

Chapters in this book focus on a range of human-designed leisure spaces that ostensibly bring together human and animal leisure – dog shows (Dabrowska), dog training (Hurley and O'Dwyer), pet-friendly holiday locales (Blichfeldt and Sakacova) and horse riding establishments (Henderson, and Danby). A further reason for suggesting more research needs to be conducted on domestic animals and leisure relates to the changing position of at least some of these animals in society in general and individual families in particular. While this shift is most clearly seen in relation to dogs, it has, and still is, arguably occurring in relation to other animals as well. With specific reference to dogs, Carr (2014) has discussed how they are becoming an increasingly central component of many human families. They are shifting from having been an animal, to being a pet, to being a companion or member of the human family. This shift is leading to changing demands from humans no longer willing to leave their pets at home while they go on a leisure experience. It has also led to the rise of leisure services ostensibly aimed at the leisure desires of pets.

Leisure, rights and welfare

The definition of leisure employed within this book is broad, incorporating notions of activity and time spent by humans in non-labour, with some sense of "enjoyment, pleasure, self-fulfilment, and identify construction" (Carr 2015a, 6). Leisure has been defined as a human right (Veal 2015) and this book starts to take us into the space of considering animal rights to leisure. As a right for humans, the benefits of leisure have been well documented. It is seen as offering the opportunity to increase physical and emotional wellbeing (Symons, O'Sullivan and Polman 2016; Denovan and Macaskill 2016), and facilitating individuals in search of themselves (Kelly 1981; Clarke and Critcher 1985; Bammel and Bussus-Bammel 1996). In addition domestic animal-related tourism (including the examples mentioned previously in this chapter) creates significant income and employment for humans.

If it is widely agreed that humans have basic rights, including a right to leisure as enshrined in various legal and UN documents (e.g. Article 24 of the UN Declaration of Human Rights), the rights of animals are far more contested. The core issue regarding animal rights, even their right to welfare, is whether animals are sentient beings. Are they cognizant, able to feel pain and experience pleasure? Until relatively recently the widely held view amongst scientists, and even more broadly by those who ever gave the issue conscious thought, was 'no' (Carr 2014). Instead, animals were best portrayed as automated objects incapable of the sentience displayed by humans (Griffin 2001). More recently, academics and society in general have shifted away from this view as the evidence of sentience in a diverse array of animals has been identified, ironically beginning to prove what many who engage with animals regularly had long known, that animals have feelings and are very capable of independent conscious thought.

If we see animals as sentient beings rather than objects, then the question of animal rights becomes important and their welfare needs to be refocussed away from the notion of taking care of objects, akin to how we care for our houses and cars, and towards the idea of emotional and physical wellbeing for a thinking, feeling individual, irrespective of species. This does not mean that there are no differences between species, but rather that the historic desire of humans to completely differentiate themselves from nonhuman animals is erroneous. Detailed discussions of animal rights and welfare have been undertaken elsewhere (see Bekoff 2007; Horowitz 2009; Rudy 2011) and rather than repeat them here it is sufficient to recognise that welfare concerns for animals are increasing and legal positions are increasingly being adopted to ensure the wellbeing of animals, though none have yet gone so far as to give any animals the same rights as humans. It is important to note here the point made by Broom (2010) that rather than focussing on 'rights' or 'welfare', we should instead think about our obligations to animals. In doing so, it is incumbent on humans that animals own 'definitions' of notions such as leisure, work, enjoyment, be explored before simply assigning them rights and human-centric definitions of animal welfare. Consequently, rather than creating legislation and arguments that assuage human guilt (and other agendas) we actually need to ensure animals have what they might identify as needed. This is akin to understandings of including and responding to self-defined and identified needs and rights for a diverse spectrum of human beings who may be unable to participate on an 'equal' basis in human society (Kymlicka and Donaldson 2011).

It is within this emerging context of seeking to understand animals' own interests in leisure (their own and that of humans) that this book explores issues of the wellbeing of animals within human leisure, and begins to address the question of the leisure needs of animals. It is the latter that seeks to break new ground as we seek to explore whether domesticated animals need access to leisure opportunities, and what such opportunities might look like.

Book structure

The chapters presented in this book examine the intersection of human and animal leisure in a variety of settings. This includes holiday villages, public recreation parks, dog shows, as ex-labourers and in human competitive environments. This diversity is complemented by the range of countries in which authors are situated, including Canada, the USA, Poland, Scotland, Australia and Israel.

The major species focussed on in the book are dogs and horses. Having the opportunity to include a chapter (Drummond) that focusses on a range of other animals who are generally kept caged in domestic spaces (birds, small mammals, reptiles, fish) was exciting and offers new and challenging insights. The focus on dogs in leisure studies (and more broadly) can be seen to somewhat reflect previously noted global patterns of pet ownership. The role of the horse in human history, including the recent past, is well documented (e.g. Clutton-Brock 1992; Mitchell 2015) and as expressed in the chapters on horses (Danby, and Henderson) they are an animal that emotes strong responses from many humans, in a way that is more akin to the emotions felt for dogs and cats compared to perhaps reptiles and birds.

We would encourage readers to look beyond species to the broader issues and analyses that each chapter offers. All of the chapters focus, in differing ways, on issues of domestic animals' sentience, rights and wellbeing and how this relates to human rights and wellbeing within leisure.

In Chapter 2, Drummond explores the experiences, issues and complexities of keeping commonly smaller, usually caged, animals. She entitles these animals (including hamsters, guinea pigs, rabbits, parrots and reptiles), "marginalised companion animals". This terminology reflects the relative status that these species hold in comparison to other companion animals in terms of human interaction, concern, understanding and interests in their wellbeing.

Two chapters use dog showing as vehicles for exploring understandings of animal leisure and rights. Dabrowska explores the world of dog shows and showing in Europe. She provides rich descriptions that enable high level analysis and exploration of whether dog shows really are such great fun and leisure for the animals involved in comparison to the humans. Following on from Dabrowska, Hurley provides a theoretical exploration of several well regarded models of dog training, and the notions of "breed standards". He exposes the speciest power relations overtly embedded and proactively endorsed within these.

In Chapter 5, Wilson, Yoshino and Latkova track the intensity of public debate and interactions between conservationists, National Park authorities and dog walkers in the San Francisco Bay area. Their analysis puts a spotlight on the topic of domestic, 'private place' animals, within public spaces. They argue that despite the levels of passion and length of these debates, there has been little intellectual discussion that could progress both human and animal rights to leisure in natural environments.

O'Dwyer's research in Chapter 6 presents findings from an online survey exploring the common human and animal domestic leisure activity of 'dog walking'. Within the post-modern framework of seeing pets, in particular dogs, as 'family', dog walking is seen as being caring and responsible, addressing animal needs. Walking the dog is presumed leisure for both humans and animals. But is it? For whom, how and when, and with what implications for both humans and animals is the focus of O'Dwyer's analysis. Brown and Lackova (Chapter 7) also explore understandings of dog walking. Their approach is complementary to O'Dwyer's, exploring understandings of animal agency and engagement in leisure seeking to deepen our understandings of the relational natures of dog walking for both species (human and canine). Blichfeldt and Sakáčová continue the exploration of dogs as family in Chapter 8. Their chapter presents research with Danish campers who holiday with dogs. Blichfeldt and Sakáčová's interviewees describe the intersections of human and close domestic animal lives, and the lengths to which considering and seeking to encompass animal family members needs can shape, and even constrain, the planning and undertaking of family holidays. Incorporating cross-species needs for leisure and holiday making leads to compromise and adaptation in much the same way as responding to the diversity of human family members.

The next chapter, by Young and Baker (Chapter 9), shifts attention to horses (with some small notes regarding other species). The authors explore the notion that domestication aimed at supporting human labour created animals that have an inherent need for 'non-leisure' or labour. Has removal of opportunities to labour with humans over the last 100 years actually lead to a loss of meaningful engagement in non-leisure for some of these animals? Has this engendered harm akin to overlooking needs for meaningful occupation that are recognised as crucial in human wellness and wellbeing?

Chapters 10 and 11 complement each other. Danby (Chapter 10) presents an emotive picture of how one group of humans (older female horse riders and owners) see and feel themselves to be involved in the creation of a cross-species interface. An interface and environment that Danby coins 'equiscapes'. Equiscapes exist only when both species are present and engaging with the other in leisure. In the following chapter (11) Henderson explores the manner in which lack of recognition and/or knowledge of the needs of another species (horses) can lead to significant and demonstrable harm and trauma to animals that are ostensibly well cared for, even 'pampered'. Mirroring Young and Baker's questions with regard to domesticated animals needs for non-leisure, Henderson explores how equine evolutionary adaptations may be out of sync with the current constrained experiences of some of these domesticated animals. But as Henderson demonstrates, awareness of these evolutionary mis-matches can mean that humans adjust and adapt horse environments to better meet the needs of these animals that, at least partly due to their domestication, are no longer able to live 'wild' lives.

The penultimate chapter, by Cohen (Chapter 12), presents the dark side of human's animal-related leisure. Cohen explores the worlds of human-initiated animal:animal fighting. Domesticated but not domestic – these animals are exploited in the interests of human leisure and profiteering, revealing a savage face of cross-species power relations. Dogs, cocks, camels and buffalo are entrapped in fighting their own in the interests of human profit and ego.

Our concluding chapter seeks to draw together the mega-themes and learnings that emerge from all the chapters, seeking to chart some ways forward for understandings of domesticated animals – their welfare, rights and wellbeing, especially with regard to leisure – and the intersection of these issues for the humans with which they share 'domestic' environments.

Note

1 See Carr's (2015) edited volume on domesticated animals and leisure and his 2014 work that was focussed exclusively on dogs, as arguably two of the main foundations in this field.

References

Adam, K. 2001. "Entertainment Farming and Agri-Tourism." Appropriate Technology Transfer for Rural Areas. USA: The National Center for Appropriate Technology. Accessed June 14, 2017. www.agmrc.org/media/cms/EntertainmentFarmingAgriTourismATTR_8681C2E7FDC64.pdf.

Bammel, G., and L. Bussus-Bammel. 1996. *Leisure & Human Behavior*. 3rd ed. Madison: Brown & Benchmark Publishers.

Bekoff, M. 2007. *Animals Matter*. Boston: Shambhala.
Belaunzaran, X., R. Bessa, P. Lavín, A. Mantecón, J. Kramer, and N. Aldai. 2015. "Horse-Meat for Human Consumption – Current Research and Future Opportunities." *Meat Science* 108(October): 74–81.
Blakeway, S., and G. Cousquer. 2018. "Donkeys and Mules and Tourism." In *Animal Welfare and Tourism*, edited by N. Carr and D. Broom. Wallingford, UK: CABI.
Bradshaw, J. 2011. *In Defense of Dogs*. London: Allen Lane.
Brooks, H., K. Rushton, S. Walker, K. Lovell, and A. Rogers. 2016. "Ontological Security and Connectivity Provided by Pets: A Study in the Self-Management of the Everyday Lives of People Diagnosed with a Long-Term Mental Health Condition." *BMC Psychiatry* 16(1): 409–22. doi:10.1186/s12888-016-1111-3.
Broom, D. 2010. "Cognitive Ability and Awareness in Domestic Animals and Decisions About Obligations to Animals." *Applied Animal Behavior Science* 126(1): 1–11. doi:http://dx.doi.org/10.1016/j.applanim.2010.05.001.
Carr, N. 2014. *Dogs in the Leisure Experience*. Wallingford, UK: CABI.
Carr, N. 2015a. "Introduction: Defining Domesticated Animals and Exploring Their Uses by and Relationships with Humans." In *Domestic Animals and Leisure*, edited by N. Carr, 1–13. Basingstoke: Palgrave Macmillan.
Carr, N. 2015b. "The Greyhound: A Story of Fashion, Finances, and Animal Rights." In *Domestic Animals and Leisure* edited by N. Carr, 109–126. Basingstoke: Palgrave Macmillan.
Clarke, J. and C. Critcher. 1985. *The Devil Makes Work: Leisure in Capitalist Britain*. Basingstoke: Palgrave MacMillan.
Clutton-Brock, J. 1989. *The Walking Larder: Patterns of Domestication, Pastoralism, and Predation*. London: Unwin Hyman Ltd.
Clutton-Brock, J. 1992. *Horse Power: A History of the Horse and the Donkey in Human Societies*. London: Natural History Museum Publications.
Denovan, A., and A. Macaskill. 2016. "Building Resilience to Stress Through Leisure Activities: A Qualitative Analysis." *Annals of Leisure Research* (online) doi:10.1080/11745398.2016.1211943.
Eddy, T. 2003. "What Is a Pet?" *Anthrozoös* 16(2): 98–105. doi:10.2752/089279303786992224.
Francione, G. 2009. *Animals as Persons: Essays on the Abolition of Animal Exploitation*. New York, NY: Columbia University Press.
Garner, R., and S. O'Sullivan. 2016. *The Political Turn in Animal Ethics*. London: Rowman and Littlefield International.
GfK. 2016. "Pet Ownership: Global GfK Survey." Accessed June 14, 2017. www.gfk.com/fileadmin/user_upload/country_one_pager/NL/documents/Global-GfK-survey_Pet-Ownership_2016.pdf.
Graham, J.P., K. Vasco, G. and Trueba. 2016. "Hyperendemic Campylobacter jejuni in guinea pigs (Cavia porcellus) Raised for Food in a Semi-Rural Community of Quito, Ecuador." *Environmental Microbiology Reports* 8(3): 382–387.
Griffin, D. 2001. *Animal Minds: Beyond Cognition to Consciousness*. Chicago: University of Chicago Press.
Hall, L. 2006. *Capers in the Churchyard: Animal Rights Advocacy in the Age of Terror*. Darien, CT: Nectar Bat Press.
Holmes, T. 2017. "Have You Heard About Hamster Racing?" *Wide Open Pets*. Accessed June 14, 2017. www.wideopenpets.com/heard-hamster-racing/.
Horowitz, A. 2009. *Inside of a Dog: What Dogs See, Smell, and Know*. New York, NY: Scribner.

Huffpost. 2011. "Domesticated Animal Populations Skyrocket: Chickens Outnumber People Three To One." *Huffpost*, September 29, Accessed June 6, 2017. www.huffingtonpost.com/2011/07/29/domesticated-animal-populations_n_913464.html.
Hultsman, W. 2015. "Dogs and Companion/Performance Sport: Unique Social Worlds, Serious Leisure Enthusiasts, and Solid Human-Canine Partnerships." In *Domestic Animals and Leisure*, edited by N. Carr, 35–66. Basingstoke: Palgrave Macmillan.
Kelly, G. 1981. *Leisure in Your Life: An Exploration*. Philadelphia: Saunders College Publishing.
Khalaf, S. 2000. "Poetics and Politics of Newly Invented Traditions in the Gulf: Camel Racing in the United Arab Emirates." *Ethnology* 39(3): 243–261.
Kymlicka, W., and S. Donaldson. 2011. *Zoopolis: A Political Theory of Animal Rights*. New York, NY: Oxford University Press.
Kymlicka, W., and S. Donaldson. 2014. "Animals and the Frontiers of Citizenship." *Oxford Journal of Legal Studies* 34(2): 201–219. doi:10.1093/ojls/gqu001.
Miklósi, Á. 2007. *Dog Behaviour, Evolution, and Cognition*. Oxford: Oxford University Press.
Mitchell, P. 2015. *Horse Nations: The Worldwide Impact of the Horse on Indigenous Societies Post-1492*. Oxford: Oxford University Press.
Ollenburg, C. 2008. "Regional Signatures and Trends in the Farm Tourism Sector." *Tourism Recreation Research* 33(10): 13–23.
Podberscek, A. 2009. "Good to Pet and Eat: The Keeping and Consuming of Dogs and Cats in South Korea." *Journal of Social Issues* 65(3): 615–632.
Podberscek, A. 2016. "An Appetite for Dogs: Consuming and Loving Them in Vietnam." In *Companion Animals in Everyday Life*, edited by Michał Pręgowski, 111–127. New York: Palgrave Macmillan.
Rijken, M., and S. van Beek. 2011. "About Cats and Dogs . . . Reconsidering the Relationship between Pet Ownership and Health Related Outcomes in Community-Dwelling Elderly." *Social Indicators Research* 102(3): 373–388.
Rudy, K. 2011. *Loving Animals: Toward a New Animal Advocacy*. Minneapolis: University of Minnesota Press.
Said, E. 2003. *Orientalism*. New pref. ed. London: Penguin.
Symons, C., G.O'Sullivan, and R. Polman. 2016. "The Impacts of Discriminatory Experiences on lesbian, Gay and Bisexual People in Sport." *Annals of Leisure Research* (online). doi:10.1080/11745398.2016.1251327.
Veal, A. 2015. "Human Rights, Leisure and Leisure Studies." *World Leisure Journal* 57(4): 249–272. doi:10.1080/16078055.2015.1081271.
Veeck, G., D. Che, and A. Veeck. 2006. "America's Changing Farmscape: A Study of Agricultural Tourism in Michigan." *The Professional Geographer* 58(3): 235–248.
Wilson, L. 2007. "The Family Farm Business? Insights into Family, Business and Ownership Dimensions of Open-Farms." *Leisure Studies* 26(3): 357–374.
Wood, L., B. Giles-Corti, M. Bulsara, and D. Bosch. 2007. "More Than a Furry Companion: The Ripple Effect of Companion Animals on Neighborhood Interactions and Sense of Community." *Society and Animals* 15(1): 43–56. doi:10.1163/156853007x169333.
Yiva, C., E. Fon Dorothy, F. Meutchieye, A. Niba, Y. Manjeli, and A. Djikeng. 2014. "Cavies for Income Generation, Manure for the Farm and Meat for the Table." *Scholarly Journal of Agricultural Science* 4(5): 260–264.
Young, J., and L. O'Dwyer. 2015. "Pets and Our Health: Why We Should Take Them More Seriously." *The Conversation*, December 2. Accessed June 14, 2017. https://theconversation.com/pets-and-our-health-why-we-should-take-them-more-seriously-47774.

2 Behind bars

Contradictions in the expectations and experiences of life with marginalised companion animals

Ruthann Arletta Drummond

Introduction

Humans bring caged pets into their homes for many reasons, all of which aim to contribute something beneficial to people's daily lives. From entertainment to ornaments, companions to children's toys and even as teaching tools, caged pets are expected to fulfil their roles in the human sphere from within the confines of their compact and minimalist spaces; real-life TV shows that can be tuned in or out at human leisure.

Whilst claiming connection and even kinship with the animals we keep in our homes, the care we provide them often refers very little to their own natural histories and behavioural needs, and instead seeks to satisfy human desires and aesthetics (DeMello 2012). It may be more appropriate, therefore, to refer to these animals not as caged pets, but as marginalised companion animals. Animals who, because of their relative minority in the realm of pets – which results in a significant discrepancy in the amount of accessible information, qualified veterinary care and overall resources available to their caretakers – tend to be caged, subjected to lower standards of care and limited by impoverished human conceptions (Drummond 2014). The term nods to the many discordant ways we live with these creatures while acknowledging at least some intention to seek even minimal connections with the caged animals kept in our homes.

Ultimately, marginalised companion animals are captive wild or semi-wild animals (Livingston 1994). The human-constructed environments containing them cannot come close to replicating the physical, mental and social freedoms of their natural habitats. This is justified by the misrepresentation that they are provided with everything they need when given food, water, shelter and some degree of interaction. However, these animals are biologically geared up to forage, reproduce, interact and engage with their environments, and these needs are not eradicated through meagre provisions (Spinka and Wemelsfelder 2011).

Toys for caged pets are big business. Every hamster has a wheel, every bird a swing, every rabbit a chew toy. These are an implicit acknowledgement that the animals confined in cages want or require activity or entertainment. While thus admitting that they have complex needs for occupation and engagement with their surroundings, human caretakers deny marginalised companion animals all but the most rudimentary of existences.

It is generally believed that people receive some benefit from the pets they keep (Friedmann and Son 2009), but are there reciprocal benefits the animals may claim? There are many tensions inherent in the lives of marginalised companion animals that must negotiate living within the human sphere. These animals are usually under-stimulated in their caged environments and can become inactive, antisocial and even physically ill. To humans, they often become boring to watch, difficult with which to interact and a burden for which to care. It may be that, by denying marginalised companion animals their own leisure and enjoyment, we effectively nullify their very purpose or expected contribution to our own. We will explore what all of this means to humans, the animals we keep and our relationships with one another.

Purposes of marginalised companion animals in human lives

Humankind has a long history of caging animals for our pleasure. Ancient civilizations as diverse as the Aztec and Roman empires kept collections of wild animals as symbolic demonstrations of their mastery over the natural world. At the end of the seventeenth century, wealthy Europeans were building extensive private menageries of exotic species as symbols of their wealth and status to exhibit to the socially elite (DeMello 2012). However, it was the beginnings of the Industrial Revolution that saw a major shift in the way caged animals were integrated into Western people's daily lives.

With a middle class that had increasing access to unprecedented disposable income, keeping caged animals was no longer restricted to the aristocracy. Average families began to bring animals as diverse as birds, tortoises and squirrels into their households, even though the creatures brought them no financial benefit (Thomas 1983). From this point forward, pets in cages became common features in Western family life.

Philosopher Yi-Fu Tuan (1984) believes that our attitude towards pets is a blend of affection and condescension – a protective sense of power over another being. In order for this to be successful, pets must be completely obedient to their caretakers and thus "be as unobtrusive as a piece of furniture" (107). Wild or semi-wild animals that cannot be controlled through this type of coerced compliance must instead be confined to cages or enclosures, but Tuan calls these "admissions of failure" (168), prosthetics that are used in place of the obedience he believes is essential to the nature of a pet.

If, as Tuan suggests, marginalised companion animals are not pets in the same way as are more traditional dogs and cats, what are they and why do we keep them?

Hal Herzog (2010) cites many theories that have been put forth to explain why humans bring animals into their homes, from biophilia, to misfiring of parental instincts, to social contagion, to emulation of the upper class, to the desire to teach children responsibility. In reality, just as marginalised companion animals do not fit neatly into categories such as "pet," "object," or "family," the reasons for keeping them overlap and interweave in messy ways. Herzog justly concludes that while the reasons for keeping such animals ultimately remain unclear, what

14 *Ruthann Arletta Drummond*

is clear is that companion animals of all kinds are vitally important in the lives of many people.

Historian Keith Thomas (1983) notes three features that distinguish a pet from other animals: they are allowed into the house; they are named; and they are never eaten. Of the most interest in this chapter is the first feature: pets are allowed in the house. While this could be interpreted as a physical location, in which case most marginalised companion animals easily qualify, it could also be considered a way of living – that animals are integrated into household activities and routines, and allowed relative freedom within the home – in which case, the majority would not. Again, there is some haziness around the "petness" of marginalised companion animals; a tension that belies a discordant relationship between humans and the many other animals with which we live.

What contributions do humans perceive marginalised companion animals make in their lives? While there are an infinite number of nuanced possibilities here, we will highlight four common umbrella reasons that people identify as their chief motivations: animals as ornament, novelty or oddity; as toy, entertainment or diversion; as teaching tool; and as companion or family member.

Animal as ornament, novelty or oddity

Some marginalised companion animals are kept primarily as objects of beauty or rarity, making their purpose in human lives one of aesthetics and/or novelty. Often, species that have specialised habitat requirements combined with minimal handling potential will fall into this category, as it can be more difficult for humans to conceive of them fulfilling other major roles.

Fish are a prime example, and are often kept as ornaments (see Figure 2.1). They cannot be held, cuddled or pet without endangering their health, so interaction is typically restricted to observation. As such, they are often displayed for

Figure 2.1 Koi are commonly kept in garden ponds for their ornamental beauty
Photograph: Paul C. Wye

their pleasing beauty and variation, rather than being kept for more interactive purposes or for companionship. Since fish are predominantly treated more akin to decorative objects than to living beings, the level of research and knowledge of their physiology, the veterinary care they receive and their legal protection all reflect their perceived objectivity and is minimal at best (Iwama 2007).

Reptiles and amphibians are also frequently kept as spectacles of oddity or exoticism. Caretakers of these species often refer to the animals they keep as being in their "collections," a term that postures them as being curated rather than cared for. Some species, such as chameleons, are even acknowledged as having better welfare if their constructed habitat allows for them to be almost entirely visually protected (Wilson 2003). Such an animal can surely provide little contribution to humans' lives, other than through a feeling of pride or accomplishment for the act of keeping such an exotic species in the home.

Parrots, as well, are often considered novelties. While their known intelligence and over-emphasized ability to mimic human speech often sees humans acquire them more as a source of entertainment than as ornaments, their beautiful and brightly-coloured plumage can sometimes lend them to be viewed as mere objects of decoration (AWC, Born Free USA and ASPCA 2006).

Animal as toy, entertainment or diversion

Many marginalised companion animals are acquired primarily to provide entertainment or diversion for their human caretakers or their children. While similar to the animals used for ornament or novelty in that they are grossly objectified, they are different in that they are meant to be interacted with, at least minimally, to provide for human enjoyment.

Baby red-eared slider turtles are commonly used as toys or diversions for children in this way. Only 3 cm in diameter they are cute, fit easily in the palm of your hand, and fit into tiny enclosures. However, three quarters of these animals will not survive the first year in the human home due to lack of appropriate environment, diet and medical care (Toland, Warwick and Arena 2012), and they are treated as disposable commodities (see Figure 2.2). Those who do survive will grow to be the size of a dinner plate, and their requirements end up exceeding what most of their caretakers are able or willing to give. Many of these turtles are abandoned in outdoor ponds and wetlands only to die in unsuitably cold environments or wreck ecological havoc in more tropical ecosystems as invasive species (Warwick 1990).

Many people acquire parrots based on the much-touted misconception that they will all talk and mimic human speech, without previously researching what it means to live with an intelligent, wild bird. As only a small percentage of parrots actually can or do "talk," humans can be disappointed in their new objects of fascination, and these birds often end up severely neglected (Tweti 2008). Those who do mimic human speech are often coerced into talking and performing tricks for their caretakers and their friends (AWC, Born Free USA and ASPCA 2006), while their own needs and desires often go unconsidered.

Figure 2.2 Baby red-eared and yellow bellied turtles waiting to be sold at a Texas warehouse
Photograph: PETA - People for the Ethical Treatment of Animals

Rabbits are marketed as ideal children's pets due to their relatively small size and perceived gentle natures (Dickenson 2014). This assumption is only strengthened by myriads of canonic children's literature, such as *The Tales of Peter Rabbit*, *The Velveteen Rabbit* and even *Winnie the Pooh;* tales in which rabbits cross the boundaries of animal, child and toy. Companion rabbits are usually "put away" (put back into their cages) when we are done playing with them, effectively designating times when it is unacceptable (or inappropriate) for them to interact with the family, in much the same way that a child is asked to turn off a video game or clean up their Lego before coming to dinner (Drummond 2014). While many rabbit caretakers intend the animals to be teaching tools for their children, a topic which we will look at next, in truth most are treated as toy objects that are taken out and played with when this suits the child or their parents.

Animal as teaching tool

A study conducted by Fifield and Forsyth (1999) illustrated that one of the most popular reasons for acquiring a pet for a child today is "to teach them responsibility and care," and that this outcome is seen by parents as the primary benefit of pet ownership. Ironically, the children of the parents in this study who acquired a pet specifically for this purpose were actually *less* likely to participate in caring for the pet, than those who acquired the pet because the child wanted one, or for the purpose of companionship.

Hamsters are often acquired for this purpose, because their typical enclosures fit easily on a small desk or table in a child's room, and their care is perceived to be minimal. Parents believe that their children will learn to be responsible, empathetic and to care for others by carrying out the basic husbandry needs of the hamsters. However, their logic is flawed. In their natural habitats, hamsters live largely solitary lives. They dig out extensive burrows and run long distances back and forth with foraged food (RSPCA 2016). In the child's room, the hamster lives in a cage as small as one cubic foot of space, is provided with a shallow layer of substrate and a laboratory wheel for exercise. They are then "socialised" at the child's whim. In attempting to teach children to be "responsible," no consideration is given to actually fulfilling the needs of the hamster, providing them with appropriate care for their species, or empathising with their position within the human home. The lesson the child learns has nothing at all to do with the hamster, and everything to do with fulfilling anthropocentric preconceptions.

Another common venue for animals as teaching tools is within the classroom. Classroom pets are used in an attempt to teach children anything from compassion, to a love of nature, to scientific inquiry (Daly and Suggs 2010). Unfortunately, the reality of many classroom pets is that their behavioural needs are all but ignored; they are largely unsupervised and receive erratic care and handling (see Figure 2.3). Many of them are acquired for a particular school year, and end up in shelters when there is no one to care for them over the summer months (WSPA 2011). In these situations, children do not learn what it means to be a certain species or even what it means to care for that species and can often unintentionally learn that animals are disposable and do not require compassion or particular attention to their care.

Animal as companion or family member

Many marginalised companion animals are perceived as companions – friends or family members – who fulfill a certain relationship with a developed concept of

Figure 2.3 Clara was a classroom pet injured by students tossing her hamster ball while she was inside

Photograph: Ruthann Arletta Drummond

subjectivity, rather than being actively objectified as novelties, playthings or tools. While this role has traditionally fallen to the prototypical symbolic pets – cats and dogs (Herzog 2010), it has also been extended to many less common species living in the human home.

Most often, larger species such as rabbits and some parrots will fall into this category. Their physical size enables them to interact with humans in particular ways and to gain some freedom of movement within the home, even if highly supervised and restricted. While by no means exclusive (many rats, geckos and innumerable other species have been considered by their caretakers to be companions), most small, and/or environmentally-sensitive species spend too much time physically isolated from their caretakers for a companion relationship to form.

The greatest contradiction for marginalised companion animals lies in the human expectation that they fulfill their role as companions from within the confines of their cages. When and how they are interacted with is almost entirely human-driven, as are almost all aspects of their lives – what they eat, what activities to which they have access or in which they are allowed to participate, and what behaviours are considered appropriate for them to express within the home. It is worth asking if such a one-sided relationship is truly companionable.

In the next section we will take a closer look at the contradictions that exist between the human-perceived and the actual lived experience of marginalised companion animals who are navigating the human sphere, and what the implications of these contradictions are for our relationships with one another.

Contradictions in the perceived life experiences of marginalised companion animals within the human sphere

Anthrozoologist Hal Herzog (2010) believes that when people consider the idea of "pet," their minds conjure up images of cats and dogs. These two species have become symbolically "pet," and their characteristics have turned into prototypes of "petness": universal representations of all companion species. But these generalisations are misleading. While dogs and cats are indeed domesticated, marginalised companion animals are, in fact, wild or semi-wild animals who have found themselves living in the human domestic sphere. The significance of this distinction is profound when it comes to how we understand, relate to and care for the animals in our lives. Wild animals undoubtedly have different needs and are subject to different stressors than their domesticated contemporaries, and classifying them or thinking of them, as is so often done, as "domesticated" ignores these differences. Over time, the integration of this incongruous terminology (and way of thinking) into marginalised companion animal discourse has changed the way we consider these creatures and has virtually eliminated any recognition of the tensions created when animals are appropriated from the wild for the purpose of becoming "pets."

Living in the human home as a domesticated animal is materially different from living in the home as a captive, wild animal. While domesticated animals have been bred specifically with adaptation to the human environment in mind

(DeMello 2012), wild animals have to contend with a natural distrust of humans, strong instincts they do not have the freedom to obey, and hypersensitivity to human environmental stimuli. While domesticated animals tend to have longer life expectancies than their wild counterparts, due to their removal from the strains of natural selection (Livingston 1994), captive animals, such as parrots and reptiles, often have much shorter life expectancies than the same species living in their natural habitats (i.e. Mason 2010; Warwick 2014). The quality of life of animals is tightly bound to their state of captivity, as well as the degree to which they are socialised and accustomed to their new environments. Julie Ann Smith (2003, 91) notes that "[d]omestication is not a pure state of which animals are in or out. Rather, animals must manage the disconnection between their natures and their human surroundings."

Annamaria Passantino (2008), a member of the Federation of European Companion Animal Veterinary Associations, suggests that domestication exists on a continuum. It must balance the natural histories of the animals, the history of involvement they have had with humans and each individual's history of socialisation. Nor is each animal's place on this continuum a fixed point. In some cases, a wild animal may be socialised to a degree that gives them entry into domestic life, while some domesticated animals may undergo processes of de-socialisation or be born into situations where they enter a feral way of life. With such a nuanced spectrum of meaning, the fact that the title "domesticated" has been used as an umbrella term over all animals living in human homes is problematic. This type of use alienates those who do not fit into the static mould and perpetuates their marginalisation.

In his detailed history of modern humanity's relationship with the Syrian Golden Hamster, Michael Murphy (1985), writes that the species was first captured for the purpose of research by scientists at the Hebrew University of Jerusalem, in 1930. In 1938 they were exported to the USA for the same purpose, and soon after were introduced to North America as ideal pets. An image of the hamster socialisation process is painted by Murphy: "After only three days of handling, the wild hamsters I captured in Syria were tame and females produced litters" (18). Murphy believed that the laboratory hamster "has changed very little from the wildtype, especially with regards to its behaviour, because the wildtype was originally so well suited to the laboratory" (18). These hamsters were not domesticated. Instead, they naturally fit into an acceptable level of sociability and were easily controlled through the use of small cages – traits that made them easily transferable to the human home.

Like hamsters, most marginalised companion animals have become the target of human domestic interest through their sociable (or tractable) natures and their conveniently-caged and controllable sizes. Animals who live with humans and who are "socialised" (but not "domesticated") are inevitably kept captive. The very definition of "socialise" is "(t)o make fit for companionship with others" (ITP Nelson 1997, 1297). Unlike domestication, which is understood to be a process of naturalisation that is the consequence of controlled breeding over thousands of years (Williams and DeMello 2007), the idea that an animal must be naturalised to a new situation is not implicit in socialisation. The animals do not have to *feel* as though they fit in to domestic life; they just have to meet society's standards of sociability and *seem* as though they do.

Parrots exemplify this difference. All parrots commonly kept as pets are, in fact, wild animals in captivity. Like many other marginalised companion animals, these birds are also prey animals in their natural habitats, and their behaviours are moulded by a natural vigilance to avoid predation. In the human home, where they are almost always caged, fed inadequate diets, often immobilised by clipped wings, and never have adequate space in which to fly or the natural habitat coverage they need to feel safe from predators (in this case, humans), parrots suffer great amounts of stress (AWC, Born Free USA and ASPCA 2006) (see Figure 2.4). While modern breeding of domestic dogs and cats has had a tremendous impact on the behaviours of these traditional pets (DeMello 2012), selective breeding of parrot species has been almost entirely limited to aesthetic traits that produce visually appealing colour morphs, rather than behavioural traits that make them more suited to human domestic life (AWC, Born Free USA and ASPCA 2006). Unfortunately, one of the results is that most captive parrots have a truncated life expectancy – sometimes only half that of their wild counterparts.

Like the majority of hamsters and parrots, most other marginalised companion animal species are prohibited from freely associating with their human families by the physical boundaries of their enclosures. Some are never afforded the opportunity to leave their confines at all, spending their entire lives in an enclosure that is the tiniest fraction of their natural territorial space. Reptiles are especially prone to live their lives in this kind of profound isolation, usually walled in by glass vivariums and afforded little, if any, time outside of their enclosures. As

Figure 2.4 Inadequate housing and care can cause parrots to exhibit self-mutilating behaviours

Photograph: Ruthann Arletta Drummond

a result, reptiles display many captivity-stress-related behaviours, including persistent climbing of transparent (glass) walls, hyper- and/or hypo-activity, atypical aggression and consuming non-food materials such as bedding or substrates (Warwick, Frye and Murphy 2004). In fact, the enclosures, diets and other considerations provided for reptiles within the human home are generally so far from meeting their behavioural, biological and psychological needs that 75 percent of all reptiles brought into home settings die within the first year (Toland, Warwick and Arena 2012).

Fish, although the third most popular household pet, are largely ignored as subjects for welfare concerns. Their caretakers tend to be extraordinarily ignorant of their anatomy and physiology, and are unable or unwilling to provide them with appropriate medical care. Instead, these animals are largely treated as disposable commodities that can be easily replaced at fairly low costs. However, as costs rise (as in ornamental carp or koi), so too does the level of concern and care their caretakers afford them (Iwama 2007). For obvious reasons, fish must remain in complete physical isolation from their caretakers for the entire duration of their lives with humans and can never have increased access to the home, or their health and welfare would be immediately compromised. However, the pet industry has worked to frame extreme isolation as a positive action in the welfare of most non-aquatic species as well – something we will investigate next.

Constructions created by the pet industry

Companion animals

While it is clear that many tensions exist in the lives of marginalised companion animals, and that these tensions pose obstacles for truly companionable relationships with humans, the pet industry works very hard to disappear these difficulties. Ironically, the wide success of the term "companion animal" (rather than "pet") has been highly dependent not on a disassociation from traditional animal objectification, but on their commodification within the pet industry. Here, animals are being framed as consumers themselves, and for that they require plausible personhoods. With this framing, animals have been *branded* as "companion animals," making it conceptually conceivable that these animal-people want and deserve the same things as their caretakers: from the latest toys, to rain boots, to gourmet organic foods, to designer jackets, to spa treatments (Herzog 2010).

While thus believing that companion animals desire objects of enjoyment and leisure comparable to human consumer goods, we simultaneously ignore their biological and psychological needs that stem from their natural histories. We buy multicolour, futuristic spaceship-like cages for our gerbils that still only provide them with minimal space and practically no opportunities to burrow, and we give our cockatiels toy cell phones and bowling pin games to occupy their time, while taking away their ability to fly. Through these actions, we truly believe that we are giving our animals things that they will enjoy, without ever having considered what enjoyment might mean to these species.

Labels

The ways marginalised companion animals are labelled in the pet industry also has a profound impact on how they are perceived. Small mammals are often labelled "pocket pets," a title that can include anything from a dwarf hamster only an inch in size to a 16 kg Flemish Giant rabbit. This term brings to mind a particular object-making image of a toy, as well as certain assumptions: that they are small (and will stay that way), easy to care for, and good pets for children. However, as we have seen, caring for a wild animal (no matter how large or small) is more complicated than this title implies, and thus, many marginalised companion animals purchased under these assumptions experience inadequate care and possibly even neglect.

"Exotic" is also a title often given to these animals and can encompass any animal kept as a pet that is neither a domestic cat nor dog (Ballard and Cheek 2003). This label adds a certain appeal to species who have become fairly common in the pet industry, and brings with it connotations of rarity and excitement – characteristics that can be used to turn these animals into living status symbols. To define something as "exotic" implies that we know little about it – an apt admission of the truth in the case of marginalised companion animals. "Exotic" validates the higher prices paid for marginalised companion animals' supplies and care, while simultaneously excusing the poor quality and access they have to either. It turns them into objects for display, idolising their rarity and the difficulties inherent in keeping them. To remove these obstacles would be to de-exoticise them – something undesirable in the pet industry. "Exotic pets" is a self-fulfilling prophesy.

Pets for small spaces

Pet stores seem to emphasise the convenience of animals who can be kept in small spaces that do not infringe on our human lives (rather than looking to meet animal needs), allowing us to create modern private menageries in our homes (Drummond 2014). Inadequate equipment and accessories continue to be on the market and, with no education mandatory for private pet ownership, insufficient housing conditions are perpetuated by a widespread lack of knowledge or research, on an international scale (Steiger 2006).

The pet industry has been able to use this to their advantage, and rabbits exemplify this. The idea of the "pet rabbit" has been sculpted into an ideal apartment pet, because their captivity ensures they need minimal space to meet current standards of care (Davis and DeMello 2003). Closely contained in enclosures, they require little supervision and manageable clean up (see Figure 2.5). The caged rabbit has been conceived to fit a busy lifestyle – the perfect pet for the twenty-first century.

What is most interesting is that the standards that have been adopted to suit human desires have also been reframed as stemming from animal needs. Many sources declare that the human home is too dangerous for a rabbit who is not closely supervised, and suggest offering exercise in an enclosed pen that protects the rabbit, rather than modifying the human home to eliminate risks (Drummond

Marginalised companion animals 23

Figure 2.5 Many commercially-available enclosures provide only enough room for rabbits to turn around and lie down

Photograph: Ruthann Arletta Drummond

2014). We are taught that the extreme level of control we exercise over the animals is *necessary* to their wellbeing, thus relieving us of any feelings of guilt we may harbour over keeping them captive. The pet rabbits who endure these "standard" housing conditions, promoted in the industry, must tolerate exceptionally close confinement. When outfitted with the recommended litter box, food bowl, hay rack and toys (e.g. Harkness et al. 2010; Quesenberry and Carpenter 2012), there is little space remaining in the cage for the rabbit to hop, and they are lucky if they are able to stretch out fully.

Mason and Burn (2011) explain how these kinds of captive conditions prevent animals of all species from performing natural, motivated behaviours (as simple as moving about naturally), leading to behavioural deprivation. Such a state of being leads to frustration, negative emotions and ultimately compromises welfare. Stifled by their hyper-restrictive and regulated environments, these animals are never able to realise their potential as individuals, let alone as companions. As we will see in the next section, this situation has a profound impact on the human experience of living with marginalised companion animals.

Contradictions in expectations and experiences of caretakers

Not typical pets

While individuals of any companion species can be marginalised and mistreated, marginalised companion animals, as a designation, are not cats or dogs. While this seems blatantly obvious, it is nevertheless a frustrating realisation for those who acquire a different species as a substitute for a more traditional pet. Oftentimes, marginalised companion animals are recommended or marketed to people who, for one reason or another, are unable to keep a dog or cat. For example, the Canadian Veterinary Medical Association (2013) recommends adopting an "exotic pet" (aka marginalised companion animal) when owning a dog or cat is not possible due to allergies, lack of space, landlord rules, long work schedules or the inability to put in the time a dog or cat requires. This type of thinking not only sets up expectations of comparable relationships, it also positions marginalised companion animals as something lesser than dogs or cats – poor substitutes who should only be considered when circumstances preclude the more common animals. These conflicting messages set the caretaker/marginalised companion animal relationship up for failure. When the relationship is not what was hoped for, it is attributed to the animals' presumed inferiority as a companion, rather than being due to the fact that these species have entirely different needs, both physically and psychologically.

While lamenting the inability to feel the companionship with marginalised companion animals for which they were hoping, caretakers nevertheless continue to perpetuate the strained circumstances which keep them from knowing these animals better. Perhaps the single greatest obstacle to companionable relationships between humans and marginalised companion animals is the standard manner in which they are kept in the human home – enclosed behind bars or panes of glass in cages and vivariums. The impacts of the isolation such a way of living creates are twofold. Firstly, they create a physical and symbolic divide between human and animal, stifling opportunities for spontaneous interaction. Second, they form closely confined, stagnant and unvarying environments (see Figure 2.6) that subdue the animals themselves, causing boredom and atypical behaviours (Mason and Burn 2011).

Figure 2.6 Snakes are often housed in barren enclosures without room to stretch their bodies entirely

Photograph: Liam Grin

By nature, guinea pigs are nomadic creatures that live in small herds – spending their entire lives on the move with their family groups, in constantly changing surroundings. As highly vulnerable prey species, they are masters of finding shelter in rock crevices and other nooks to protect themselves from predation (Yamamoto 2015). In many human homes, guinea pigs are kept by themselves in cages no bigger than a few square feet, with little or no shelter to speak of. Devoid of the social interactions and environmental variety that their species are meant to have, guinea pigs kept as pets often become inactive and unengaged. Without adequate shelter from perceived threats, guinea pigs and other animal species can remain nervous and feel constantly stressed (Jones and Boissy 2011).

Like the guinea pigs, other animals kept in small enclosures are not themselves. They are often prone to boredom and inactivity (Mason and Burn 2011), and a great number of them develop health issues such as obesity, digestive issues, heart conditions and arthritis due to the nature of their sedentary lives, inadequate housing environments and poorly balanced diets (Ballard and Cheek 2003). The friendly, engaging and entertaining animals their caretakers were expecting turn into shadows of themselves. Their inactivity and lack of interest in their surroundings renders them boring to watch, which in turn causes caretakers to approach them less often. When the rare approaches do occur, the animals often become nervous or defensive, making interactions a challenge. Any health conditions that result from their restrictive environments become expensive to manage and a hassle to treat. In effect, the animals themselves become burdens on their caretakers, and any perceived value they had as novelties, entertainments, teaching tools or companions is dissolved, leaving many owners to ignore, neglect, abandon or surrender their pets (see Figure 2.7).

Figure 2.7 Smokey was surrendered when his incisors became grossly overgrown due to inadequate care

Photograph: Ruthann Arletta Drummond

Not low-maintenance objects

Even without behavioural issues or the added obligation of caring for medical concerns, the degree of daily responsibility a marginalised companion animal entails can be an unwelcome shock to caretakers. Due to the clever marketing of the pet store industry that frames these animals as ideal pets for small spaces and busy lifestyles, there is a prevailing myth that they are, in turn, easy to care for. However, this is anything but true. As wild animals, these creatures depend on very specific environmental conditions, particular and varied diets, immense sensitivity to their psychological positions as captive animals, and specialised knowledge of their ethology, physiology and health.

Even when a caretaker dedicates the time needed to research their species of interest, the resources they require for the proper maintenance of their animal can be extremely difficult to access. Appropriate housing, supplies, food and medical care can be problematic or impossible to locate, compromising the welfare of the animal by default. These resources, when found, can also be exceedingly expensive – much more than comparable resources for cats and dogs – because the pet industry is able to exploit the "exotic" label and associated expectations. These difficulties and expenses often come as a surprise to caretakers, since many of the animals themselves are inexpensive and readily available for purchase. Typically speaking, a veterinary exam conducted on a CAD $5 mouse, a $25 budgie or a $40 gecko will cost more than a veterinary exam on a $3000 purebred dog, because of the specialised knowledge and skills involved. However, this incongruity is not usually discovered until the animal is already ensconced in the home.

Not domesticated

Erica Fudge (2002) argues that by inviting pets to live with us in our homes we can see them both as animal and human. She believes the special status of pet supersedes animal natures, rendering them a different class of being altogether: "a pet first, an animal second" (32). However, Fudge notes that when pets openly display their *animal* nature (by peeing on the carpet, scratching the couch, chewing up a favourite shoe etc.), the tranquillity of the relationship is lost and the mirage of an animal/human hybrid being disappears. It is in these moments that we are reminded that we are living with another creature that has needs that are divergent from our own, who has their own sense of agency, and who is not entirely in our control. Looking back to Tuan's (1984) theory of what makes an ideal pet, these reminders may be unwelcome indeed.

Unfortunately for marginalised companion animals living in the human home, their animal natures are always present and on display. Probably the biggest shock to caretakers is the discovery that their animals are not domesticated, but are actually wild, with wild animal behaviours that like and need to be expressed. Whether loud vocalisations, destruction of human property through chewing, digging, scratching or shredding, messy eating habits, marking territory with urine or faeces, or any number of natural tendencies, the animalness of these creatures

Marginalised companion animals 27

cannot be disappeared (see Figure 2.8). These behaviours, which stem from animals' natural instincts and needs, are not usually considered positive pet qualities and often clash drastically with human desires and ways of life (Tweti 2008).

These same instincts and behaviours can also put up relational barriers. While the perception of pets giving one "unconditional love" is pervasive in Western culture, this is not always the experience of caretakers. Working hard to tame, socialise and acclimatise wild animals to the human domestic sphere does not guarantee they will show love to their caretakers or acceptance of their circumstances. Many animals remain reluctant, stressed and anxious their entire lives, often presenting with physical illness and irregular behaviours that are indicators of their poor overall welfare (Jones and Boissy 2011), despite their caretakers' best efforts. This can be a difficult reality to accept, and an uncomfortable reminder of the discordant lives these captives lead.

Parrots are extremely intelligent animals, and the cognitive abilities of some species have been compared to those of a young human child (Pepperberg 2009). What does this mean for a parrot living in a cage in the human home? While remaining conscious of the dangers of anthropomorphisations, it may do us well to use our imaginations and try to place ourselves in the bird's shoes. Highly intelligent and social beings, these birds spend much or all of their life in tiny cages that allow for very limited movements when everything about their bodies is built to fly, often significant distances, each day. If they are let out of their cages, their mobility is often drastically restricted due to clipped wings, leaving them feeling vulnerable to predation from the main predators – the humans – in their environments. Often, their environment varies very little, providing almost no novelty or opportunity to exercise their cognitive abilities, and their highly social, flock-based tendencies are left to wilt in social isolation from others of their species (Tweti 2008). If you were a parrot living in a human home, how would you feel?

Figure 2.8 Parrots kept in human homes often display destructive and property damaging behaviours

Photograph: Ruthann Arletta Drummond

Conclusion – a way to move beyond this paradigm/type of relationship

Throughout this chapter, we have spent a lot of time pondering what about marginalised companion animals challenges our expectations of pets, and what these challenges mean in terms of fulfilling their human-intended purposes – most notably, as companions in our leisure pursuits, in the many nebulous manifestations of such relationships. However, rather than using our final thoughts to contemplate how these animals could be better companions to humans, serving our leisure, desires and expectations more effectively, it would perhaps be a more valuable exercise to turn that question on its head and ask how humans can be better companions to these animals and their own leisure needs.

As it stands, the current accepted and promoted practices of marginalised companion animal care employed in human homes – and in particular, caging – limit, stifle and prejudice our relationships with these animals, so that neither animal nor human is given a chance to know the other in a less impoverished way. How can humans be better companions to these animals? That is the question most worth asking.

In writing of one of the more common marginalised companion animals, Margo DeMello (2010) has written that "the human-rabbit relationship [has been] hampered and defined by the lack of sustained, intimate contact between human and rabbit" (238). This must be true of any species where cages and enclosures play a primary role. Before we can hope to meet animals as companions, we must tear down the barriers that block our way. Yi-Fu Tuan (1984) believes that cages signify human failure to make a pet, but the failure actually goes deeper than that. Cages are echoes of exploitive traditions that demonstrate our close-mindedness to possibilities of meaningful relationships with these animals, or the idea that animals have desires of their own that are worth consideration. They are a way of satisfying our own whimsies to own a particular species of fancy while they blatantly ignore the needs, or leisure interests of those they contain. They promote human laziness, ensuring that minimal effort needs to be put into knowing animals through researching, observing and/or interacting with them, and instead their choices and agency are largely denied them as they are treated like animated toys whose main purpose is to provide for human enjoyment. Even fish, who could never safely live outside of an aquarium while in the human home, are given only the most minimal of habitats that cannot come close to meeting their natural needs.

Humans, in our relationships with these animals, are providing them with what is necessary to exist, rather than what is necessary to live an existence that allows for any leisure of their own. With human aesthetics, preferences and convenience in mind, we fail to consider the same for the animals – or even to acknowledge that they may have such desires. Although we cannot escape the reality that the human-marginalized companion animal relationship does contain a relationship of power and a certain degree of human control, considering the interests and desires of the animals in our lives alongside our own can begin to destabilise these dynamics (DeMello 2010). As animals in human homes perforce forfeit certain freedoms and abilities, so too can humans make considerable compromises in their homes and ways of life, in order to provide the animals with as much

Figure 2.9 Rabbits enjoying a free-range lifestyle, integrated into a family home
Photograph: Paul C. Wye

freedom as possible to be the animals they are meant to be (Smith 2003) (see Figure 2.9).

One small shift in thinking that could have a large impact on our interactions with marginalised companion animals is a shift to considering them as participants in relationships, rather than subjects to have relationships *with*. The acknowledgement of participation nods to a desire to work together in the navigation of this nebulous territory of human-marginalized companion animal relations. Erica Fudge (2002) eloquently wrote:

> The choice, as I see it, is a simple one: we acknowledge the limitations of our own perspective, but simultaneously accept that what we can achieve within those limitations is important and worthwhile, even if it is only the best we can do (159).

We have a lot to offer animals before we can claim that what we are doing is our best effort, but we can make a start by truly considering them for who they are and what they may desire, and not only what they can be within our own leisure experience.

References

AWC (Avian Welfare Coalition), Born Free USA and ASPCA (American Society for the Prevention of Cruelty to Animals). 2006. *Captive Exotic Bird Care: A Guide for Shelters*. Avian Welfare Coalition, Born Free USA and ASPCA: St. Paul, MN.

Ballard, Bonnie, and Ryan Cheek, eds. 2003. *Exotic Animal Medicine for the Veterinary Technician*. Ames, IA: Blackwell Publishing.

CVMA (Canadian Veterinary Medical Association). 2013. "Recommendations for Adopting an Exotic Pet." Accessed March 17, 2013. www.canadianveterinarians.net/documents/recommendations-for-adopting-an-exotic-pet#.UWuQY1fYzD8.

Daly, B., and S. Suggs. 2010. "Teachers' Experiences with Humane Education and Animals in the Elementary Classroom: Implications for Empathy Development." *Journal of Moral Education* 39(1): 101–112.

Davis, Susan E., and Margo DeMello. 2003. *Stories Rabbits Tell: A Natural and Cultural History of a Misunderstood Species*. New York, NY: Lantern Books.

DeMello, Margo. 2010. "Becoming Rabbit: Living with and Knowing Rabbits." *Spring: A Journal of Archetype and Culture* 83(Spring): 237–252.

DeMello, Margo. 2012. *Animals and Society: An Introduction to Human-Animal Studies*. New York, NY: Columbia University Press.

Dickenson, Victoria. 2014. *Rabbit*. London: Reaktion Books Ltd.

Drummond, Ruthann Arletta. 2014. "Think Outside the Cage: Moving Towards New Understandings of Companion Rabbits." *Faculty of Environmental Studies Outstanding Graduate Student Paper Series* 20: No. 6. York University.

Fifield, S.J., and D.K. Forsyth. 1999. "A Pet for the Children: Factors Related to Family Pet Ownership." *Anthrozoos* 121): 24–32.

Friedmann, Erika, and Heesook Son. 2009. "The Human-Companion Animal Bond: How Humans Benefit." *Veterinary Clinics of North America: Small Animal Practice* 39(2): 293–326.

Fudge, Erica. 2002. *Animal*. London: Reaktion Books Ltd.

Harkness, John E., Patricia V. Turner, Susan VandeWoude, and Colette L. Wheler. 2010. *Harkness and Wagner's Biology and Medicine of Rabbits and Rodents*. 5th ed. Ames, IA: Wiley-Blackwell.

Herzog, Hal. 2010. *Some We Love, Some We Hate, Some We Eat: Why It's So Hard to Think Straight About Animals*. New York, NY: Harper Collins Publishers.

ITP Nelson. 1997. *Canadian Dictionary of the English Language: An Encyclopedic Reference*. Toronto: ITP Nelson.

Iwama, George K. 2007. "The Welfare of Fish." *Diseases of Aquatic Organisms* 75: 155–158.

Jones, Bryan, and Alain Boissy. 2011. "Fear and Other Negative Emotions." In *Animal Welfare*, edited by Michael Appleby, Joy Mench, Anna Ollson, and Barry Hughes, 78–97. Wallingford, UK: CABI.

Livingston, John. 1994. *Rogue Primate*. Toronto: Key Porter Books Limited.

Mason, Georgia J. 2010. "Species Differences in Responses to Captivity: Stress, Welfare and the Comparative Method." *Trends in Ecology and Evolution* 25(12): 713–721.

Mason, Georgia, and Charlotte Burn. 2011. "Behavioural Restriction." In *Animal Welfare 2nd Edition*, edited by by Michael Appleby, Joy Mench, Anna Ollson, and Barry Hughes, 98–119. Wallingford, UK: CABI.

Murphy, Michael R. 1985. "History of the Capture and Domestication of the Syrian Golden Hamster (Mesocricetus auratus Waterhouse)." In *The Hamster: Reproduction and Behaviour*, edited by Harold Siegel, 3–20. New York, NY: Plenum Press.

Passantino, Annamaria. 2008. "Non-Domesticated Animals Kept for Companionship: an Overview of the Regulatory Requirements in Italy to Address Animal Welfare and Human Safety Concerns." *The European Journal of Companion Animal Practice* 18(2): 119–126.

Pepperberg, Irene M. 2009. *The Alex Studies: Cognitive and Communicative Abilities of Grey Parrots*. Cambridge, MA: Harvard University Press.

Quesenberry, Katherine E., and James W. Carpenter. 2012. *Ferrets, Rabbits, and Rodents: Clinical Medicine and Surgery*. St. Louis, MO: Elsevier.

RSPCA (Royal Society for the Prevention of Cruelty to Animals). 2016. "Hamster Behavior." Accessed May 25, 2016. www.rspca.org.uk/adviceandwelfare/pets/rodents/hamsters/behaviour.

Smith, Julie Ann. 2003. "Beyond Dominance and Affection: Living with Rabbits in Post-Humanist Households." *Society and Animals* 11(2): 81–97.

Spinka, Marek, and Francoise Wemelsfelder. 2011. "Environmental Challenge and Animal Agency." In *Animal Welfare*, edited by Michael Appleby, Joy Mench, I. Anna Ollson, and Barry Hughes, 27–43. Wallingford, UK: CABI.

Steiger, Andreas. 2006. "Pet Animals – Housing, Breeding and Welfare." In *Ethical Eye – Animal Welfare*, edited by Council of Europe, 111–133. Belgium: Council of Europe Publishing.

Thomas, Keith. 1983. *Man and the Natural World: Changing Attitudes in England, 1500–1800*. London: Allen Lane.

Toland, Elaine, Clifford Warwick, and Phillip C. Arena. 2012. "Pet Hate:The Exotic Pet Trade." *Biologist* 59(3): 14–18.

Tuan, Yi-Fu. 1984. *Dominance and Affection: The Making of Pets*. New Haven: Yale University Press.

Tweti, Mira. 2008. *Of Parrots and People*. New York, NY: Penguin Books.

Warwick, Clifford. 1990. *Reptiles: Misunderstood, Mistreated and mass-Marketed*. Worcester, UK: Trust for the Protection of Reptiles.

Warwick, Clifford. 2014. "The Morality of the Reptile 'Pet' Trade." *Journal of Animal Ethics* 4(1): 74–94.

Warwick, Clifford, Frederic L. Frye, and James Bernard Murphy, eds. 2004. *Health and Welfare of Captive Reptiles*. London: Chapman and Hall.

Williams, Erin E., and Margo DeMello. 2007. *Why Animals Matter: The Case for Animal Protection*. Amherst, NY: Prometheus Books.

Wilson, Brad. 2003. "The Lizard." In *Exotic Animal Medicine for the Veterinary Technician*, edited by Bonnie Ballard and Ryan Cheek, 31–80. Ames, IA: Iowa State University Press.

WSPA (World Society for the Protection of Animals). 2011. "Keep Pets Out of the Classroom." *WSPA*. Accessed June 4, 2011. www.wspadonations.org/pages/2147_leave_animals_out_of_the_classroom.cfm.

Yamamoto, Dorothy. 2015. *Guinea Pig*. London: Reaktion Books.

3 Dog shows as casual leisure

Asymmetry of human and animal experience

Magdalena Dąbrowska

Introduction

The chapter investigates both human and animal experiences of dog shows as leisure activity. Shows are casual leisure for many of human participants, who perceive them as opportunity to recreate or socialise with other dog fanciers. They provide attractions, emotions and excitement absent in everyday life. I argue that although dog shows are perceived as leisure by its human participants, only few aspects of leisure can be applied to animal experience.

The first section explores dog shows as casual leisure for human participants. Stebbins' concept of leisure is applied. Stebbins (1997) mentions eight types of casual leisure: play, relaxation, passive entertainment, active entertainment, sociable conversation, sensory stimulation, casual volunteering and pleasurable aerobic activity. Three seem to be particularly useful in context of dog shows: play, sensory stimulation and sociable conversation. Senses are hedonistically stimulated while travelling to new places for a show, and by consumption of food and alcohol. Sociable conversations during and after the show are an important aspect of leisure. They are not only entertaining, but also sustain coherence in the dog show community.

The second part explores the leisure of the dogs during a show. Cognitive ethology is used to understand animal experience of dog shows. Stebbin's outline of casual leisure is applied to a dog's experience of shows. Two aspects of leisure are analysed: sensory stimulation and pleasurable aerobic activity. It is argued that although some dogs may derive pleasure from participation in shows, many do not feel comfortable in an overstimulating environment and their body language reveals stress.

Examination of the parallel experiences of dogs and humans at dog shows allows one to develop a concept of leisure from both human and nonhuman points of view. While we know what leisure is for humans, animal experience is more problematic. Although animals can derive some joy from participation in a dog show, the event is often stressing and overwhelming. Human and animal experiences of leisure barely intersect.

Dog shows – past and present

It is almost impossible to imagine (human) leisure without animals. Animals have been a part of human life as companions, they provided protection, were used for transport, hunting, herding and entertainment. Historically hunting was one of the first leisure activities of high classes. Animals were used as equipment (horses, dogs) and prey (foxes and other animals). The pleasure of killing was enhanced by utility (food), although foxes were killed merely for sport (Dunning 1989). Social and cultural changes enhanced new forms of leisure involving animals. Animal exhibitions gained popularity when concern of animal welfare and animal advocacy influenced cultural changes, and bloody sports, such as dog- or bullfighting, were forbidden (Derry 2003). Scientific discoveries, including Darwin's theory of evolution, resulted in selective breeding. It became possible to influence nature and create a variety of animal breeds. Dog shows provide an example of a modern approach to animals, where pleasure is achieved by looking and observing while violence is invisible. Animal shows (including animal exhibitions and zoological gardens) provide entertainment for the masses and become leisure destinations.

Dog shows are a product of social, economic and scientific transformations of the nineteenth century. The growing middle class was looking for new forms of leisure activities. Although it is claimed that the first dog show was organised in Brussels in 1680, dog shows become really popular in the second half of the nineteenth century in Great Britain. One of the first modern dog shows, held in 1859 in Newcastle-upon-Tyne, was an added attraction to the annual cattle show (Pemberton and Worboys 2007). The first National Dog Show occurred in Birmingham, England in 1860; 267 dogs of 30 breeds entered and it was seen as an enormous success. At the end of the 1860s, the National Dog Show was attracting over 700 dogs and 20,000 visitors. In 1863, during a week-long event that took place at Cremorne Gardens in Chelsea, London, over 100,000 visitors, including celebrities such as the Prince of Wales, came to admire the purebreds. Purebred dog fancy spread rapidly. Numerous shows were organised in Great Britain, and the number of dogs entered at the shows as well as number of breeds grew rapidly. Cruft, an entrepreneur selling dog food, perceived dog shows as an opportunity to promote his business. He organised the first Crufts show in 1878 in Paris, as part of the L'Exposition Universelle, followed by similar events in Glasgow, Edinburgh and Brussels. In 1873 the Kennel Club was founded under the leadership of Sewallis Evelyn Shirley. Among its aims was the regulation and organisation of dog shows (Pemberton and Worboys 2007). The Kennel Club established a Stud Book, where all purebred dogs were registered. The Stud Book became an important marketing strategy, as proof of origin increased an animal's value (Pemberton and Worboys 2007; Derry 2003). Dog show fancy soon spread over Europe and reached the USA. Purebreds provided not only pleasure, but also profits.

Dog shows exemplify an important transformation in modern culture and illuminate our paradoxical relationships with companion animals. Not only are these shows about ambition and superficial beauty, but they also reveal deeply grounded paradoxes of contemporary culture and the ambiguous status of animals. Dogs gain special status and they become a significant element in a dense network of power relations, interaction rituals, disciplinary practices and beauty canons. At the same time the dogs are prone to physical and symbolic violence; their welfare and safety in some situations is questionable. Overtly shows are about dogs, whose confirmation is evaluated according to the breed standard, a text describing characteristic features of a particular breed. In fact, shows are about people, networks of social relations, power relations, emotions and scandals. Thus, canine and human participants are equally important and their role should be analysed in parallel.

Nowadays dog shows are still popular and attract participants and spectators. According to Federation Cynolgique Internationale (FCI), in 2015 there were 4586 shows worldwide awarding CAC certificates[1] (so called "national shows" granting title of champion of a given country) and 798 shows awarding CACIB certificates[2] ("international shows" allowing dogs to achieve the title of International Champion) (FCI 2017). Another important organisation, the American Kennel Club, organises over 16,000 events every year (Carr 2014). For comparison, every year the Polish Kennel Club (part of FCI) organises over 150 dog shows of various levels of prestige in major cities (Monikiewicz 2012). On average, between 400–900 dogs participate in national shows, while international shows can attract as many as 2000–4000 participants. Dog fanciers are not limited to shows taking place in their country. They often travel abroad, broadening the definition of leisure that can be applied to this focus on "dog shows".

Dog shows constitute an under-researched area of human-animal interactions. In popular culture, dog shows are likely to be represented ironically. Christopher Guest's (2000) movie *Best in Show* portrays dog show participants as emotionally disadvantaged neurotics, ready to do anything to achieve their ultimate goal: the "Best in Show" title. A BBC documentary *Pedigree Dogs Exposed* (Harrison, 2008) presents British dog shows as a "parade of mutants," a "freakish, garish, beauty pageant that has nothing to do with health and welfare." In one of the very few books on dog shows, sports journalist Josh Dean (2012) follows the show career of Jack, an Australian shepherd, and the engagement of the handlers, breeders and caretakers supporting him. Of the very few publications on dog shows, most refer to the history of breeding and the showing of dogs (Derry 2003). Dabrowska (2014) examines dog shows in Poland, paying special attention to the concept of "deep play" – that is, a situation when the financial and emotional engagement of showing a dog reaches far beyond potential gains (Dabrowska 2014). Dog shows are analysed in the wider context of leisure experience of humans and animals (Carr 2014; Gillespie, Leffler and Lerner 2002). This chapter fills a gap in academic research providing detailed analysis of dog shows as leisure.

Research methodology

The research presented in this chapter is based on the results of field research conducted at dog shows in Europe, particularly in Poland, and is a part of a wider project on dog show culture. It uses ethnographic methods of participant observation and interviews. Participant observation was conducted at two major locations: the local branch of the Polish Kennel Club, and at dog shows. Between 2012 and 2016 I conducted numerous field studies at dog shows in Poland and abroad. I observed and engaged in interactions and conversations with participants. In addition, over

40 interviews with show participants, breeders and judges provided more detailed information on social identities arising from engagement in dog shows.

Showing my West Highland White Terrier Szanti (Gorwin Libusza, according to her pedigree) allowed me to get deeper into show culture. I bought Szanti for personal reasons. My two dogs were getting older so I wanted a puppy to add fresh energy to our lives. I decided to show her in order to add another perspective to my research – that is, to better understand the emotions and social relations that accompany dog shows. Although I enjoyed Szanti's wins, I considered dog shows to be more work (field study) than leisure.

Cognitive ethology is "the study of cognitive abilities of animals and the psychological and evolutionary processes underlying these abilities" (Wilder 1996, 29). It is an interpretive discipline, in which animal behaviour is systematically observed leading to theoretisation of such behaviours to animals themselves. Cognitive concepts can be used to describe and explain behaviour and social worlds in which animals participate. Understanding animal behaviour gives insights into their inner worlds, their cognitive and emotional lives. In the chapter the approach is used to interpret dogs' perspective on shows and leisure.

The attempt to understand canine experience of dog shows was based on two sources. The first was information received from human caretakers, who were interpreting dog's feeling and attitudes towards dog shows. People, who knew dogs and share their life with them, acted as agents giving voice to animals. Caretakers were able to comment on dog's individual preferences, behaviours and characteristic interactions with people and animals. It should be noted that many participants of dog shows have experience with dog training and sometimes they have significant knowledge of animal cognition. Thus, their account seems to provide reliable sources of information. The second approach built on more general knowledge of canine behaviour (Horowitz 2009, 2014; McConnell 2003, 2007). Dogs have universal codes of communication that make it possible to understand their intentions or emotions. Body posture, ways of carrying ears or tail, calming signals – all these gestures seem to be shared by the species. During field studies I was observing and interpreting dogs' behaviour, hoping to understand their inner-worlds. Observation sometimes confirmed caretaker's opinions about dog's feelings, but it also allowed me to verify some statements and add aspects that were not mentioned.

Dog shows and human leisure

Dog shows combine elements of casual and serious leisure, and the division between the two is not always clear. Leisure is an "activity – apart from the obligations of work, family and society – to which the individual turns at will for either relaxation, diversion or broadening his knowledge and his spontaneous social participation, the free exercise of his creative capacity" (Rojek 1989, 1). Leisure is often contrasted with work. It is associated with positive experience: fulfilment, choice, growth, relaxation, recuperation, triviality, frivolity and freedom from obligation. Leisure may be considered the reward for labour, as it provides pleasure which derives from freely chosen activity.

Dog shows may be considered an example of what Stebbins (2007) calls "serious leisure". Serious leisure is

> the systematic pursuit of an amateur, hobbyist, or volunteer core activity that people find so substantial, interesting, and fulfilling that, in the typical case, they launch themselves on a (leisure) career centered on acquiring and expressing a combination of its special skills, knowledge, and experience.
> (Stebbins 2007, 5)

Participating in dog shows requires specialist knowledge regarding preparation of a dog. Some participants build their position in a career-like way, treating showing dogs as an important element of their social identity. In some cases, they receive additional income grooming or handling dogs of less experienced participants. For many, dog shows are both: serious and casual leisure. Although this chapter examines dog shows from the perspective of casual leisure, I would like to stress that the experience of leisure associated with shows is more complex.

Casual leisure is typically contrasted with serious leisure. Casual leisure can be defined as "immediately, intrinsically rewarding, relatively short-lived pleasurable core activity, requiring little or no special training to enjoy it" (Stebbins 1997, 18). Casual leisure can be understood as all leisure falling outside the realm of serious leisure and work. Stebbins (1997) claims that all forms of casual leisure share at least one central property: all are hedonistic. Participants experience significant levels of pleasure. Casual leisure is usually accompanied by other rewards: recreation (or regeneration), and social attraction that is the appeal of being with other people while participating in leisure (Stebbins 1997, 21).

Dog shows as casual leisure for humans

Stebbins (1997) initially suggested six types of casual leisure: play, relaxation, passive entertainment, active entertainment, sociable conversation and sensory stimulation. Later (Stebbins 2004, 2007) he added casual volunteering, and pleasurable aerobic activity. Although the types of casual leisure are distinct, participants can experience two or three of them while engaging in a particular activity (Stebbins 1997). The most relevant types of casual leisure in the context of dog shows are: play, sensory stimulation and sociable conversation.

Play

Play has three important elements. It includes lightness of behaviour, intrinsic motivation and "nonserious suspension of consequences, a temporary creation of its own world of meaning which often is a shadow of the 'real world'" (Stebbins 1997, 19). Dog shows contain an element of play. A show is similar to a temporally created world, with its own rules, structures and social relations.

The central aim of dog shows – the selection of the most beautiful dog – is a complex and multi-level procedure. Even if judges are supposed to use the breed standard as their reference point, interpretation is always subjective and based on judge's individual aesthetic preferences. Dogs are divided into classes depending on sex, age and achievements. Usually all animals of a given class enter the ring. They are evaluated while moving and standing, individually and in comparison to each other. Dogs are not only given places, but a judge provides a brief description commenting on particular features of the dog's anatomy and movement, pointing to what s/he considers to be animal's advantages and failures. Class winners compete for title of "Best of Breed". Breed winners are eligible to take part in "Best of group" competition at the show finals. Winners will compete for "Best in Show" title.

The event combines predicable elements (rules of selecting the most beautiful animal) with unpredictable elements (judges' preference for particular types; quality of dogs entered; and other factors that may influence a judge's decision). A win is always desired, but never sure. As play, shows provide entertainment and joy. The game-like character of events provides all kind of emotions and allows escape from everyday routine.

Sensory stimulation

Casual leisure can include activities undertaken to provide sensory stimulation. Humans are aroused by various things and activities. They "relish their creature pleasures by engaging in activities where they have sex, eat, drink, touch, see, smell, hear, or feel coolness or warmth" (Stebbins 1997, 20). To stimulate their senses humans may use alcohol or drugs, admire natural or human-made beauty or engage in activities that provide thrill or excitement.

Visiting foreign countries, tasting local cuisine stimulates senses. Tourism is a leisure activity that provides a departure from everyday experiences and contrasts with daily routine. Dog shows are associated with the necessity to travel. Participants may travel a few kilometres for local, nearby shows or hundreds of kilometres when they attend shows abroad. Travelling to dog shows (especially abroad) provides opportunities to visit tourist attractions and taste local cuisine. One of the participants recalls: "I went to Lithuania with a group of people. The show was not far from Vilnius. After the show a driver took us to Vilnius. We walked around the Old Town and we had dinner in local restaurant. On (the) second day, we visited another city. It was my first visit to Lithuania, so I wanted to see as much as possible. I'm not sure if I'll ever have chance to visit it again" (Field research 2015). Trips to dog shows are perceived as brief holidays, and they provide time for recreation and sightseeing.

Some dog fanciers incorporate dog shows into their holiday plans. One of the participants describes her strategy: "I spend holidays with family and we always travel with dogs. When planning holidays, we always check dog shows nearby. We like Italy and we frequently go there, so my dogs are already Italian champions. They got Croatian championships during one of our holidays trips" (Field research 2014). In this case, passion for dog shows influences the organisation of family free time. This participant admits she would never travel so far only to attend the dog show. Holidays provide opportunities to pursue her hobby.

For many women with family obligations, it is one of the few moments of freedom and independence. J. sees dog shows as an escape from family life: "I go to dog shows and I leave my kids with a husband. There is so much excitement at the dog show, so much emotions . . . you meet people, you prepare your dog for a ring. So much is going on, so I don't have time to think about what's going on at home. If I were on holidays, sipping a drink at a swimming pool, I'm convinced I would be constantly thinking about family and home" (Field research 2014). Travelling to distant destinations requires staying in a hotel, so attending a dog show often allows a "girls' night out".

Sensory stimulation is also provided by participation in dog shows. Intense emotions, social interactions, sociable conversations: all engage the senses and allow individuals to forget about mundane life. Sometimes dog shows are so exhausting that participants are too tired for sightseeing. Participants arrive at the show venue early in the morning. During the summer most of the shows are organised outdoors, so it takes some time to put up a tent and prepare all the necessary equipment. Some dog breeds need a lot of time for grooming. Participants spend their time preparing dogs, watching other dogs being evaluated at the ring, socialising, gossiping, consuming food and sometimes alcohol. Some stay at the show venue until the late evening if their dogs are selected for group finals. Experience of another country is limited to local food and alcohol served in the hotel restaurant and available at the show venue. Despite limited contact with local culture and lack of time for sightseeing, participants who were successful at the show are often very satisfied with the trip.

Dog shows abroad, although organised under the auspices of FCI, may differ due to local approaches. M. mentions wine tasting accompanying dog shows in Moldova.

> There were three dog shows in one day. In between there was wine tasting for show participants. I befriended waiters pouring wine, so I got countless refills. Finally, I got so drunk that I could barely show my dog. I wasn't worried, because the judge who was evaluating my dog also got countless refills.
> (Field research 2015)

Alcohol may also be used as a tranquilliser.

> When I was a novice at dog shows, I was extremely stressed. I needed a drink or two in order to relax before entering a ring. If you are nervous, (your) dog feels the emotions and is nervous too. After a drink I was relaxed and happy. My dog felt the emotions, was relaxed and able to show nicely.
> (Field research 2013)

Extreme emotions associated with winning (or losing) are also soothed with alcohol. It is not unusual that participants share food and alcohol during the show. Invitations to drink at someone's show "camp" indicate close relations or temporal alliance.

Social meetings before shows are often accompanied by consumption of food and alcohol. During the Club Show of Polish Lowland Shepherds in Łeba (2016) a contributive table with food and drinks was prepared. The night before the show participants organised a grill, where they brought food they cooked at home and they shared home-made liquors. While consuming, they were talking about dogs and their people. The event was accompanied by an informal dog show with funny contests for dogs and their handlers. The event contained all three aspects of casual leisure: play, sensory stimulation and sociable conversation. It provided joy and possibility to socialise and recreate.

Sociable conversation

Sociable conversation provides joy, relief and vivacity (Stebbins 1997). Shows, where people gather together to watch dogs being evaluated, provide the perfect environment for sociable conversations. Participants derive pleasure from interpersonal relations, conversations and gossiping during shows, and while travelling together to and from the event. Opportunity to meet friends and acquaintances is described by many participants as the biggest attraction of shows. There are numerous topics show participants talk about: they gossip about other people, talk about show news and "scandals", exchange opinions about judges, and first of all talk about dogs. Sociable conversation supports the coherence of dog show community.

When friends and acquaintances meet at a dog show, they talk not only about dogs, but also about people. Numerous aspects of biography, behaviour or even appearance of others are being discussed. Sometimes malicious and untrue information is shared. They speculate about sexual orientation ("is he gay or not") or discuss sexual life of judges and show participants ("who sleeps with who and why"). Sometimes participants talk about people they do not know, for example commenting on clothes or movements of people showing their dogs whilst conversations are ensuing. They discuss the general atmosphere of the show, behaviour of a judge, his or her opinion about their dog, reactions of other participants; winners receive congratulations, losers get supported.

Gossiping is one of the forms of sociable conversation. Both men and women gossip as part of their leisure. Gossip is defined as idle talk, based on the personal lives of others (McKeown 2015). According to Epstein, gossip carries various functions and meanings. It "can be mean, ugly, vicious, but also witty, daring, entirely charming. It can be damning, dampening (of the spirits), dreary, but also exhilarating, entertaining, highly educational" (Epstein 2011, 9). It is "informal personal communication about other people who are absent or treated as absent" (Bok 1982, 91). Gossip is entertaining and relational, as it builds (or destroys) trust and friendship. It creates networks of informal knowledge about people and their dogs. Sociable conversation allows the collection of knowledge about people and their dogs, enables the construction and maintenance of social hierarchies, and positions individuals including oneself within a network of social relations.

It is not surprising that show participants talk about dog shows, results and "scandals". It is particularly exciting if show results were surprising; that is, an unexpected dog won or usual winner lost. When a winning dog loses, it creates gossips about his/her hidden faults that were finally noticed by a judge. Behaviour and comments made by participants are analysed in details. "Scandals", real or imaginary, are discussed. When talking about show or judging scandals, participants refer to situations or behaviours that differ from routine. When a dog was disqualified and removed from ring for growling while being examined, some participants considered the event to be a scandal (Field research 2016). They commented on the rightness of the judge's decision and handler's reaction. When a handler shows familiarity with a judge before a show and later wins when their dog is judged by this person, some participants consider it to be a "judging scandal" (Field research 2015). Participants not satisfied with results share their disappointment and often accuse other participants, judges or organisers for violating rules.

Participants exchange opinions about judges and their preferences. This knowledge is valuable as it can increase or decrease chances for winning. Participants share experiences of being judged by a particular person, commenting on their aesthetic preferences regarding dogs, and attitude towards dogs and people.

Dogs are one of the main topics of conversations. "You meet people, who are as dog crazy as you are. No one is surprised that you want to talk only about dogs. You talk for hours and everyone is happy about it" (Field research 2014). Buying a puppy from a particular breeder or using his or her dog for breeding is interpreted as sign of alliance. Pedigree and anatomy of recently bought dogs are discussed, especially if the dog was imported from abroad or a well-known kennel. Real or imaginary faults or health problems carried by certain "bloodlines" are analysed. Discussion also includes the topic of breeding. What kennel is having or expecting puppies, what is their expected quality and what price has been set for a puppy are all discussed.

Conversations at shows have an educational dimension. Participants meet other dog fanciers and exchange formal and informal knowledge on dogs, shows, grooming and breeding. Conversations during and after dog shows are not necessarily trivial. On the contrary, quite often they are educational, sharing experiences or advice on breeding and other aspects of dog keeping. Learning during dog shows can be called edutainment, when knowledge is achieved not by serious study, but by playing and participating in leisure.

Sociable conversations are not restricted to in-person interactions (McKeown 2015). People also communicate in their leisure time outside of the dog show venue, through social media (Facebook being the most popular) or by telephone. Sharing experiences and exchange of opinions are important elements of post-show rituals. After the show, participants call (or text) friends to inform them of their dog's results (especially if these were satisfying). Post-show conversations contain elements of affective labour, as both sides of the exchange are supposed to express emotions when they deliver or receive information.

Dog shows as canine leisure?

While researching the human experience of a dog show is quite easy, reconstruction of animal perceptions of leisure is more challenging. Dogs cannot be interviewed, so they cannot express their opinions. However, despite difficulties we can – to some extent – know what animals feel. Commonly human caretakers speak on behalf of animal likes and dislikes, offering one form of insight into animal experiences. Cognitive ethology can help to understand animal points of view. Cognitive ethology not only treats animals as agents but it also believes that humans can understand animal behaviours, so mutual communication is possible. For many people, who share their lives with animals, there is nothing anthropomorphic in saying that one may exploit animal trust (Baier 1985) or that animals may be motivated.

Dogs are intentional creatures and "companion species" to humans (Haraway 2003, 2008). During eons of coexistence, communication skills that enabled mutual understanding and efficient communication across species by gestures and body language have developed. Human caretakers perceive their dogs as conscious individuals who are able to interact socially, and express their preferences, opinions, likes and dissatisfactions. They claim to understand a dog's thinking, emotions and unique personality. Sanders (1993) observes:

> (b)ased on routine, (and) intimate interactions with their dogs, caretakers come to regard their animals as unique individuals who are minded, empathetic, reciprocating, and well aware of basic rules and roles that govern the relationship. Caretakers come to see their dogs as consciously behaving so as to achieve defined goals in the course of routine social exchanges with people and other canines (207).

Moreover, caretakers attribute cognitive and emotional states, intentions and beliefs, to nonhuman animals. Usually, they grant at least limited mindedness to animals and define their interactions as being mutual and authentic (Sanders 1993).

Stebbin's definition of casual leisure has very limited application to a dog's experience of shows. From an animal point of view two aspects of leisure seem to be the most important: sensory stimulation and pleasurable aerobic activity. Dogs, like people, need sensory stimulation. They get excited about new smells, situations, people and dogs. Shows provide an entirely new environment, so some animals may derive pleasure from participation. After a show dogs are sometimes allowed to run or play with other dogs, so they may enjoy aerobic activity. It should be noted, however, that for some dogs show environments may be overstimulating and thus overwhelming. In addition, many show venues do not provide safe spaces for allowing animals to run and play.

Human participants claim that their dogs enjoy shows for similar reasons to humans: namely that shows provide excitement and allow escape from everyday routine. Caretakers claim that dogs enjoy shows.

> My dogs love going to shows. When they realise I am packing for a show, they wait in the car ready to be taken. It happened once that I didn't take one of them. He was sitting all day at the doorstep and crying. I have to sneak out in secret if I go to (a) dog show without one of them.
>
> (Field research 2013)

Her dogs are excited and eagerly jump into the car. They have usual places in the car, and they sleep calmly while travelling.

Based on observation of the abovementioned dogs, it is possible to provide more general characteristics of dogs who enjoy shows. At the show venue, they snooze in kennels for most of the time, except when being walked, groomed and presented in the ring. They do not show any symptoms that would indicate stress, even if they are surrounded by a noisy environment full of unknown smells. They do not get scared or overly agitated with the presence of other (strange) dogs. When allowed, they calmly approach another dog and smell each other. With similar calm interest they approach people. The dogs seem to be self-confident, despite an overly stimulating environment. They are accustomed to dog shows, since they have attend them from puppyhood. It seems that some dogs benefit from shows, as they may increase social skills and get familiar with new sensory stimulants. They become more resistant to stress and more open to unknown situations that they may face in everyday life.

Caretakers attempt to make dog's experience of the show as pleasurable as possible. Some make an attempt to make dog show a "dog's special day". Dogs get their caretaker's full attention, which is especially important if there are several dogs at home. Dogs are fed snacks and better food than when at home. Animals can do things that are not allowed at home. Participant says: "(w)hen we go to dog shows, my dog is allowed to sleep with me in (the) hotel bed. Normally she is not allowed to do it, so she is very happy" (Field research 2013). A show provides experiences that are significantly different from a dog's everyday routine.

Sensory stimulation continues when a show is over. It is not unusual that dogs are included in sightseeing. Some participants are reluctant to leave dogs alone in the hotel. Others want to spend as much time as possible with their dog, so they take them for a walk around the city. Dogs mark their presence in the city landscape. During the World Dog Show in Milan (2015), I noticed numerous purebred dogs being walked in the historic centre of the city. Some dogs in new places seem to be a little bit shy: they move with hesitation and carefully smell the ground. They move like human tourists who do not feel entirely safe in a new place. It is possible that dogs and people experience new places as exciting as well as intimidating.

Evaluating a dog's experience of the show is based on individual features of their character. "My dog loves to show, because she loves to be in (the) center of attention. She is excited when everyone is looking at her. That's why she loves to go to shows" one participant explains (Field research 2013). It is believed that a good show dog is a combination of excellent conformation and exceptional temperament. "Show temperament" means ability to cope with stress and willingness to joyfully perform in the ring. Dog shows are supposed to be about personality. "(A) Dog must like to show, otherwise s/he doesn't have any chance of winning" is a universally accepted statement. Dogs that do not enjoy shows look sad. They will be trembling, walking with their tail and head down or move without enthusiasm. Participants often anthropomorphise animals, saying that a dog "doesn't want to show". S/he may lie down in the ring, move slowly or quite the contrary – jump with overexcitement instead of running in trot. "Unwillingness" to show may mean that a dog does not feel comfortable.

Sensory stimulation is not always pleasant, and in some cases dogs may experience stress. A dog's wellbeing is particularly questionable during commercially organised group trips to shows abroad. A rented van usually accommodates approximately ten people and even more dogs. Usually there is no space for dogs to travel with caretaker in the car. All dogs are packed in crates piled up at the back of the van. They are accommodated near unknown mates and separated from their human caretaker. This may be a stressful experience. There are breaks in travel, so dogs may be walked, but the frequency of stops as well as responsiveness to dogs' behaviour differs. One participant reported:

> Once I went with X. There were frequent stops, we could walk the dogs and eat something. If a dog was squealing in a crate he stopped to check if s/he is fine. On another occasion I went with Y. They stopped frequently on the way to the show, but on the way back they wanted to get home as quickly as possible, so stops were very rare and short. A dog yelped in the crate. They did not want to stop. 'At least you know s/he is alive' they cynically told the caretaker.
>
> (Field research 2014)

While travelling by car, most caretakers attempt to make the trip as comfortable for animals as possible. They stop frequently so the dogs can walk and drink. They react immediately if an animal is showing signs of discomfort. Despite caretakers' efforts, some aspects of a dog's participation in shows may be unpleasant and stressful. Some dogs experience travel sickness. Long trips are exhausting for dogs, as their ability to move is limited and they are exposed to unfamiliar stimulants. For many dogs travel and show performance are stressful. The territory is new, they are surrounded by new smells, sounds and companions, so they may feel insecure. Some have diarrhoea or lack appetite. Those bodily symptoms indicate stress.

There are other aspects of dog shows that seem to be contradictory with the concept of leisure that it is a hedonistic time providing pleasure and opportunities to recreate. Coat preparation for shows may be time consuming and unpleasant. Dogs are usually forced to stay still during washing, brushing and drying. Some dog breeds require more preparation than others. I had the opportunity to observe preparation processes while attending the European Dog Show in Brussels (2016). A colleague with a long-haired dog woke up at 3 a.m. She bathed and conditioned her dog. Then she brushed, dried and straightened its hair. The dog was kept on the grooming table for at least 3 hours. At the show venue the dog was additionally groomed. He waited for his ring performance either on a grooming table or in his crate. In order to preserve his coiffure he was not allowed to move much.

Pleasurable aerobic activity, another aspect of canine leisure, "refers to physical activities requiring effort sufficient to cause marked increase in respiration and heart rate. The concept refers to aerobic activity in the broad sense, to all activity requiring such effort" (Stebbins 2004, 55). Pleasurable aerobic activity is a form of leisure equally enjoyable for people and dogs, and it may be partially proved by the growing popularity of canine sports, such as agility (Carr 2014). Performance combines physical activity with intellectual engagement, as it requires attention and concentration. Sometimes caretakers play with dogs before entering the ring, and presenting a dog in the ring requires some running. Although there are moments of activity, dogs spend most of their time in kennels, where their possibilities to move are limited.

Some dog shows, like a show in Wawrzkowizna in September 2016, provide opportunities for aerobic activity for dogs and people. The show was organised at the lake surrounded by a park. People and dogs had the opportunity to walk, run, recreate and even swim in the water (the latter was more attractive for dogs than for people). After the show, before going back home, many dogs were allowed to play at the lake and run with other dogs. Not all shows provide such good conditions for canine recreation. However, even in less stimulating environments, some dogs are let free to play and run when evaluation at the rings is over and most of participants leave the show venue.

Sensory stimulation and aerobic activity – both identified as leisure – are as important for dogs as people. One canine judge commented

> (p)eople come and tell me about problems they have with dogs. Most of the dogs eat too much, move too little and spend too much time alone, when caretakers are at work. I advise them to play with dogs, go for long walks, start basic training; but they are deeply disappointed, because the solution is so time consuming. (What) (t)hey want is a kind of "magic pill" they can give to a dog so s/he will lie happy on a couch.
>
> (Field research 2013)

It is obvious that dogs need leisure to relax and recreate. Of the forms of leisure enumerated by Stebbins, both dogs and their people would benefit from play, relaxation, active entertainment, socialising, sensory stimulation and pleasurable aerobic activity. Both dogs and people need leisure to add excitement to everyday life.

There are few things humans and non-humans can do together, and dog shows are one of the options. Unfortunately, although they contain elements that may be defined as "casual leisure" for dogs, negative aspects seem to prevail. For many canine participants shows are a stressful and exhausting experience; they hardly provide pleasure or possibilities to recreate. Responsible caretakers should look for leisure activities with canine companions other than dog shows.

Conclusions

There are numerous reasons why people enjoy dog shows. They provide entertainment, emotional stimulation, opportunities to socialise and to consume food and alcohol. Hedonism, that is pleasure or enjoyment, is a central property of casual (human) leisure. In general, such pleasure is derived from activities:

entertainment, meeting people, consumption. There are numerous benefits of casual leisure: creativity and the discoveries it sometimes engenders as well as serendipity (Stebbins 2001). Dog shows allow people to recreate and regenerate, as they provide escape from everyday routine. They stimulate senses. Experiences so absorbing that allow forgetting about mundane life and its problems. Participation in dog shows helps to develop and maintain human interpersonal relationships. Participants often mention satisfaction and intimacy that result from time spent together and sociable conversations during and after the show.

Dogs' experience of shows is more complex and interrelated with issues of animal welfare. While travelling to shows, dogs have limited ability to move. At the show venue, they spend most of their time in kennels or on grooming tables, while their coat is being prepared. Show ring performance requires skills and training. Dogs may derive pleasure from sensory stimulation and aerobic activity, but it seems that unpleasant aspects of shows in many cases may destroy an animal's experience of leisure.

Even if we are "companion species", it seems that human and animal needs in the context of leisure barely intersect. Dog shows constitute leisure time for many human participants, but would be probably considered as nuisance by their canine companions.

Notes

1 CAC is a French acronym for Certificat d'aptitude au Championnat: this is the national competence certificate for the championship of a given country.
2 CACIB is a French acronym for Certificat d'Aptitude au Championnat International de Beauté, that is, competence certificate for the international beauty champion.

References

Baier, Annette. 1985. "Knowing Our Place in the Animal World." In *Postures of the Mind*, Minneapolis: University of Minnesota Press.
Bok, Sissela. 1982. *Secrets: On the Ethics of Concealment and Revelation*. New York, NY: Vintage Books.
Carr, Neil. 2014. *Dogs in the Leisure Experience*. Boston: CABI.
Dąbrowska, Magdalena. 2014. "Głęboka gra? Wystawy psów rasowych w Polsce." [Deep Play? Dog Shows in Poland]. In *Pies też człowiek? Relacje psów i ludzi we współczesnej Polsce* [Relations of dogs and people in contemporary Poland] edited by Michał Pręgowski and Justyna Włodarczyk, 193–230. Gdańsk: Wydawnictwo Naukowe Katedra.
Dean, Josh. 2012. *Show Dog: The Charmed Life and Trying Times of a Near-Perfect Purebred*. New York, NY: HarperCollins.
Derry, Margaret Elsinor. 2003. *Bred for Perfection: Shorthorn Cattle, Collies, and Arabian Horses Since 1800*. Baltimore: Johns Hopkins University Press.
Dunning, Eric. 1989. "The Figurational Approach to Leisure and Sport." In *Leisure for Leisure: Critical Essays*, edited by Chris Rojek. Basingstoke: Palgrave Macmillan.
Epstein, Joseph. 2011. *Gossip: The Untrivial Pursuit*. New York, NY: Houghton Mifflin Harcourt.

FCI. 2017. "Statistics: FCI." *FCI*. Accessed May 5, 2017. www.fci.be/en/statistics/FCI.aspx.
Gillespie, Dair L., Ann Leffler, and Elinor Lerner. 2002. "If It Weren't for My Hobby, I'd Have a Life: Dog Sports, Serious Leisure, and Boundary Negotiations." *Leisure Studies* 21(3–4): 285–304.
Guest, Christopher. 2000. *Best in Show*. Directed by Christopher Guest. United States: Castle Rock Entertainment.
Haraway, Donna Jeanne. 2003. *The Companion Species Manifesto: Dogs, People, and Significant Otherness*. Chicago: Prickly Paradigm Press.
Haraway, Donna Jeanne. 2008. *When Species Meet*. Minneapolis: University of Minnesota Press.
Harrison, Jemima. 2008. *Pedigree Dogs Exposed*. UK. BBC One.
Horowitz, Alexandra. 2009. *Inside of a Dog: What Dogs See, Smell, and Know*. New York, NY: Scribner's.
Horowitz, Alexandra. ed. 2014. *Domestic Dog Cognition and Behavior: The Scientific Study of Canis familiaris*. Heidelberg: Springer-Verlag.
McConnell, Patricia. 2003. *The Other End of the Leash: Why We Do What We Do Around Dogs*. New York, NY: Ballantine Books.
McConnell, Patricia. 2007. *For the Love of a Dog: Understanding Emotion in You and Your Best Friend*. New York, NY: Ballantine Books.
McKeown, Janet K. L. 2015. "The Hens are Clucking: Women Performing Gossip in Their Leisure Lives." *Leisure Sciences* 37(5): 447–547.
Monkiewicz, Jerzy, Katarzyna Rogowska, and Jolanta Wajdzik. 2012. *Kynologia: Wiedza o psie* [Cynology. Knowledge of dogs]. Wrocław: Wydawnictwo Uniwersytetu Przyrodniczego.
Pemberton, Neil, and Michael Worboys. 2007. *Mad Dogs and Englishmen: Rabies in Britain 1830–2000*. London: Palgrave Macmillan.
Rojek, Chris. 1989. *Leisure for Leisure: Critical Essays*. London: Palgrave Macmillan.
Sanders, Clinton R. 1993. "Understanding Dogs: Caretakers' Attributions of Mindedness in Canine-Human Relationships." *Journal of Contemporary Ethnography* 22(2): 205–226.
Stebbins, Robert A. 1997. "Casual Leisure: A Conceptual Statement." *Leisure Studies* 16(1): 17–25.
Stebbins, Robert A. 2001. "The Costs and Benefits of Hedonism: Some Consequences of Taking Casual Leisure Seriously." *Leisure Studies* 20(4): 305–309.
Stebbins, Robert A. 2004. "Pleasurable Aerobic Activity: A Type of Casual Leisure with Salubrious Implications." *World Leisure Journal* 46(4): 55–58.
Stebbins, Robert A. 2007. *Serious Leisure: A Perspective for Our Time*. New Brunswick: NJ: Transaction.
Wilder, Hugh. 1996. "Interpretative Cognitive Ethology.". In *Readings in Animal Cognition*, edited by Marc Bekoff and Dale Jamieson. Cambridge, MA: MIT Press.

4 Dog showing and training
Enjoyable hobbies or destructive practices that reinforce speciesist ideologies?

Scott Hurley

Introduction

The Dog Fancy refers to the practice of breeding, showing and training dogs for both conformation dog shows and for dog sports such as agility and obedience. The American Kennel Club (AKC) frames these endeavours as opportunities for people to engage in fun and enjoyable activities with their dogs. For example, it describes Conformation dog showing as a pleasurable activity "that will bring many hours of enjoyment and education to every member of your family" (AKC 2016a). It states that agility – an athletic event wherein a dog-human team must navigate an obstacle course for time – is "a great form of exercise for both dog and handler and a fun way to bond" (AKC 2016b). It goes on to suggest that agility training itself is a gratifying activity that often leads to participation in competitive events: "And you don't have to compete to enjoy agility. Taking an agility class offers many other benefits. But many people start the sport just for fun, only to get bitten by the agility bug and become lifelong competitors!" (AKC 2016b).

While training and showing dogs can be entertaining activities, rarely are the structures and processes underlying these activities questioned. Social and cultural assumptions about the human-canine relationship exist that justify the use of the canine body and mind for entertainment. One such assumption is the notion that human animals always know better, and always have the power in the relationship. The power, for example, to decide what is good behaviour and what is not. This kind of power and control is clearly evidenced in the context of training, whether for basic manners or canine competitions. Another assumption espouses the view that the dog bodies that have the most value are those that are judged to be "beautiful" or determined to be "able-bodied." These assumptions reinforce human control and dominance over canines and lead to the manipulation, modification and regulation of their minds and bodies. They reify social and cultural constructions of beauty as well as perpetuate views that marginalise groups of nonhuman animals on the basis of their body shape and type and their abilities to successfully perform certain mental and physical tasks. Examining American Kennel Club breed standards and literature about how to train, breed and show dogs in both conformation and dog sports, I explicate the ways that the dog fancy contributes to canine exploitation and suffering.

Dog training: literature and practice

Dog training literature since the late twentieth century generally describes dogs as emotional beings that deserve respect and love. It emphasises the importance of understanding canine behaviour, focussing on the way dogs use calming signals and body language to communicate with one another and with their human companions. This literature also advocates for positive reinforcement rather than coercion for getting dogs to perform a variety of functions, including obeying house rules, doing dog sports, aiding the disabled and performing search and rescue operations. Contemporary dog training literature, then, emphasises the importance of cultivating a relationship with one's canine partner – one based on trust, integrity and understanding. Unfortunately, the literature does little to interrogate the hierarchical power dynamics that privilege humans over canines and thereby leaves intact a paradigm that allows for exploitation. While literature advocating positive reinforcement training, building relationships with canine companions and understanding canine ethology has done much to improve human-canine interactions, it has not contributed to a sustained critique of animal use that allows for the abuse of dogs in underground dogfighting rings, the existence of commercial dog breeding facilities (puppy mills) that operate with government sanction and the presence of millions of unwanted dogs languishing in shelters every year. Of course, dog training literature and methods are not directly responsible for these injustices, but they do not challenge them and thus conform to a view that nonhuman animal bodies (dog bodies) are objects to be used and exploited for work, entertainment and human-like companionship, and then discarded when they fail in these endeavours.

The dog training method most commonly practised in the early twentieth century up through the 1980s was compulsion training. Compulsion training is a method that "uses positive punishment, such as leash corrections, and negative reinforcement, such as ear pinches or an electric collar. The trainer manipulates the dog into a position by using physical placement or training equipment" (Family Pet 2013). In this method, when the dog performs the behaviour properly, the handler eliminates the discomfort applied to her. So, for example, if a trainer wants a dog to sit then he pulls up on a leash attached to a choke chain until the dog sits after which the choke is released. The most well-known representative of this type of training is the Koehler (1976) method (a method still used by some trainers today).

The 1980s also saw the concept of "dominance" appear – this came from research on wolves. Ethologists discovered that wolf packs adhere to strict hierarchies with clear leaders that dominate the other wolves in order to maintain pack cohesion. Research indicated that wolves that did not follow the rules were often disciplined by the "alpha" wolf, who occasionally used physical force to get the miscreants to submit to his authority (Steinhart 1995). In dog training, it became the norm to talk about the need for humans in dog-human packs to become alphas and thus dominate their dogs in order to gain their respect – only in this way, it was argued, could one get a dog to reliably do what was asked of him (The Monks of New Skete 2002). As a result of this emphasis on dominance, such practices as the "alpha roll" appeared, a technique in which one forcibly turns a dog onto his back and pins him to the ground until he submits to human authority and control by relaxing his body (76).

In the 1990s, trainers began to recognise that many dogs respond very poorly to compulsion training and alpha rolls. The language of "dominance" changes to the language of "leadership" and an emphasis on classical conditioning, positive reinforcement and marker training becomes common. The result of this change in training philosophy is the appearance of less coercive training methods which emphasise reward for desirable behaviour rather than punishment for undesirable behaviour. Here I will focus on this type of training philosophy for I see it as still contributing to a paradigm of dominance and control that ultimately causes suffering. While there are many well-known dog trainers who have authored books that encourage the use of positive reinforcement, I will focus on the work of Vicki Hearne and Patricia McConnell, both of whom are very well-known and respected dog trainers and authors.

Vicki Hearne was a writer, poet, professor and animal trainer. She trained dogs and horses for 25 years. In the course of her work with dogs, she taught basic manners classes as well as competition classes – that is, classes that teach people how to prepare their dogs for a variety of dog sports, including obedience and agility. She has written several books that explain her training methods and philosophy. Perhaps the most important of which is her book *Adam's Task* (Hearne 2007) wherein she argues that animals, particularly those with whom humans often share their lives, are highly intelligent, able to cultivate a sense of "the good" which influences their intentions and behaviours, and can enter into meaningful and reciprocal relationships with human beings. Though she has been credited for developing a unique training method, she is deeply indebted to the Koehler (1976) method of dog training.

Patricia McConnell is an adjunct professor of Zoology at the University of Wisconsin-Madison and a certified Applied Animal Behaviourist. She is a prolific writer who specialises in family dog training and treating aggression in dogs. She gives seminars about various issues related to dog training, has made a number of training videos and has written numerous training booklets and two very popular books – *The Other End of the Leash: What We Do Around Dogs* (2003) and *For the Love of a Dog: Understanding Emotion in You and Your Best Friend* (2006).

On anthropomorphism

Both authors/trainers have worked hard to correct views that interfere with people's ability to understand how companion animals engage their worlds. One concept that they address is anthropomorphism. McConnell and Hearne rightly point out that anthropomorphism has both a positive and negative side. On the one hand it is a type of exploitation, a means by which human animals appropriate nonhuman animals for their own purposes. For instance, people often use their canine and feline companions to satisfy their emotional desires; they refer to dogs and cats as their children and often expect them to provide the kind of emotional support and understanding that they need from other humans (Serpell 2005; McKenna 2013). About this kind of anthropomorphism, Patricia McConnell writes:

> Forgetting that other mammals are not furry people with paws is a mistake that dog lovers frequently make . . . humans hug as a sign of affection, while a dog's version of hugging is a display of social status. . . . Hugging is such an important part of expressing affection in our species, it's impossible for some people to imagine that their dogs don't necessarily like it.
>
> (2006, 16)

Such attitudes and practices are problematic because they betray a lack of recognition and therefore respect for the very real differences between human and nonhuman animals. Philosopher Erin McKenna notes that

> over-indulgence in anthropomorphism results in humans ignoring how the needs, interests, and intelligences of various other animal beings differ from those of human beings. This can lead to treating them as a kind of defective human – doted on but dependent.
>
> (2013, 9)

Dogs, McConnell would argue, are marvellous, wonderful living beings because they are dogs, not because they are humans with four legs. She seems to suggest that treating dogs as humans can cause them pain and suffering. Animal rights activist and scholar, Karen Davis, in her article "Procrustean Solutions to Animal Identity and Welfare Problems," contends that "in vivisection . . . the victim is also involuntarily made to appear as an aspect of the victimizer's identity, as when scientists call animals used in vivisection experiments 'partners' and 'collaborators' in the quest for knowledge" (2011, 44). The very real suffering that nonhuman animals experience in scientific research is masked by language that suggests they are colleagues in these pursuits – that they choose to undergo these painful experiments to aid the researcher in his/her search for "truth."

Similarly, when we regard dogs as humans, we erase their canine identities, applying human characteristics and desires instead – attributes that are completely irrelevant to their health and wellbeing. In other words, if we think or act as if dogs are four-legged human beings, we run the risk of ignoring (or, perhaps more accurately, not even recognising) their needs as canines. The act of shaping dogs' dispositions in the image of our own, then, is a kind of vivisection – a dissection, manipulation and reconfiguration of their natures according to our emotional and physical needs and goals.

While much dog training literature acknowledges the problems with ignoring important differences between humans and canines, it also recognises that we share much in common with them. From its title we can see that Patricia McConnell's book *For the Love of a Dog: Understanding Emotion in You and Your Best Friend* is about how dogs have many of the same emotions as humans do and express them in very comparable ways. For example, we learn from McConnell that dogs often communicate what they desire or need through facial expression, body language and vocal intonation (2006). Indeed, humans can understand these physical cues and what they mean because they express the same kinds of emotions in homologous ways. For example, a person knows that a dog has experienced pain when he cries out after stepping on a sharp object because humans also cry out when feeling pain like this. Similarly, human beings can recognise emotional states like anger in nonhuman animals from their faces. According to McConnell, "the face of an angry dog resembles the face of an angry human" (2006, 175). She continues by having readers conduct a kind of thought experiment. She says "Imagine being five years old again, and make an angry face right now. . . . You'll find that your mouth is closed, your lips pushed forward, and your eyebrows move together and downward. You can see a similar expression on the face of a confident dog warning that she's about to bite" (175). Thus, both humans and canines express rage with furrowed brow, the baring of teeth in an "offensive pucker" (lips forward, mouth open), tension in the cheek area and wrinkles on the bridge of the human nose and the canine rostrum. Again, humans can easily recognise this emotion in dogs because it manifests somatically in ways analogous to their own. From this example and others that McConnell describes in her book, we learn that the emotional lives of humans share much in common with those of nonhuman animals – a fact confirmed by work in evolutionary biology that has demonstrated the physiological, anatomical and genetic continuity between human and nonhuman animals (Bekoff 2007; Bekoff and Pierce 2009). In her work, Patricia McConnell regularly invokes evolutionary biology, ethology and work done by animal behaviourists to point out the similarities between humans and canines.

In this way, McConnell recognises that a certain kind of anthropomorphism is acceptable – in fact necessary for understanding dogs. Vicki Hearne, for her part, lauds the animal trainer for using anthropomorphic language when talking about nonhuman animals and criticises academics for failing to do so. Hearne writes,

> Trainers, for example, have no hesitation in talking about how much a mare loves or worries about her foal, a cat her kittens or a dog or a horse their work. But for philosophers and psychologists to speak of love was to invoke abilities that are, for reasons I am not still clear about, as rigidly restricted to *Homo sapiens* as some religious doctrines have restricted the possession of a soul to members of certain races, cultures and sometimes genders.
>
> (2007, 6)

By making such a comparison, Hearne suggests that disallowing the possibility that nonhuman animals feel emotions similar to humans indicates that academics are privileging the human species undeservedly. Currently there are a number of scholars who recognise that nonhuman animals indeed express emotions similar to human animals. For example, Marc Bekoff, Professor Emeritus of Ecology and Evolutionary Biology, has written about emotions in nonhuman animals. About love and courtship in canids, he says "(i)n many canids – that is, members of the dog family, which includes wolves, coyotes, foxes, jackals, and dingoes – males and females who have mated for years still greet one another like they're long-lost friends and court vigorously, even though they've done it before" (2007, 71). Moreover, primatologist Frans de Waal has written extensively on empathy in nonhuman animals (see de Waal 2008 for instance). Nevertheless, Hearne argues that the tendency to privilege human animals based on the ability to express emotion persists.

The work of Vicki Hearne and Patricia McConnell also professes to teach us how to read the body language of dogs that is not homologous with our own. They discuss what it means when a dog's tail is sticking straight up, when it is wagging, and when it is stuck between the legs as well as what ear positioning suggests (are the ears back, sticking straight up etc.). They indicate how to recognise certain actions as calming signals – the blinking of the eyes, the licking of the lips, yawning and turning the head, for example. McConnell even asks readers to become "field biologists," "making thoughtful, detailed descriptions" of their dogs' behaviour (2006, 29).

All of this, the authors of these texts hope, will help humans communicate better with their canine companions. Contemporary dog training literature then has come a long way in helping readers engender the condition that Karen Davis has called empathic anthropomorphism "in which a person's vicarious perceptions and emotions are rooted in the realities of evolutionary kinship with other animal species, in a spirit of good will toward them" (2011, 47). Knowing about dog behaviour and body language and understanding how we as a species share much in common with dogs in the way we express and experience our emotions allows us ultimately to act in kinder, more compassionate ways towards our canine companions and to respond appropriately to their needs.

On human-canine relationships

Finally, both Hearne and McConnell have done much to advance the notion that in order to live comfortably with our canine companions, we have to develop thoughtful and trusting relationships with them. Vicki Hearne was one of the first to talk about this idea. She criticises the behaviourist who studies animal behaviour in the laboratory because they do not allow that the animals under study can think, intend, believe or emote (2007, 58). She contends that teaching commands like "sit" requires a great deal of conceptual work on the part of both handler and dog. This work can only take place if there is a relationship between them. In other words, a dog can only understand what "sit" means if her person teaches her what it means; the presence of learning and teaching requires precise and clear communication and the existence of real communication implies a relationship. But communication and relationships are reciprocal. The dog must be able to communicate with the handler, just as the handler does with the dog. If the dog understands clearly what "sit" means, she can use it to communicate with her person (56).

Hearne believes strongly that dogs have intentions, make conscious decisions and communicate meaning. Moreover, she believes that it is the language of training that allows communication between human and canine to take place. In Patricia McConnell's work we likewise see a strong emphasis on relationship-building. She regards her efforts to elucidate canine behaviour as a means to improve communication between dogs and people, and in the introduction of her book, *For the Love of a Dog*, she remarks that she focuses on the emotions that are most relevant to dog-human relationships: namely fear, anger, joy and love. About her book, she asserts that

> (m)y goal is to be both interesting and helpful to those of us who are, quite simply, crazy in love with our dogs. I wrote this book as much for dogs as I did for us, in the hopes it will, albeit indirectly, help dogs to better understand us.
>
> (2006, xxxi)

Here, McConnell clearly recognises the reciprocal nature of the dog-human relationship.

Hearne and McConnell (as well as others) have done much to deconstruct the anthropocentric emphasis in the dog-human relationship. As I have pointed out above, their work underscores the importance of ethology, validates the similarities and differences between the species and entreats readers to develop deep and meaningful relationships with their dogs. In doing so, they intend to move us away from using overly coercive – even violent – systems of training. Thus, we might argue that their work in essence has amounted to a paradigm shift in the way humans work with canines.

Unfortunately, this is not the case because in fact there has been no substantive challenge to the underlying assumption that human animals are in control. Advocating for humane treatment, building connections and being sensitive to the emotional states of dogs do not obviate the reality that humans are making the rules about what dogs can and cannot do and are defining the parameters of what is an acceptable and unacceptable relationship. Dogs still must fit into human society, communities and families with little autonomy relative to human members of these social groups. Human hegemony is preserved despite compassionate training methods and positive relationships.

Human hegemony in dog training

Vicki Hearne, following William Koehler (1976) (of the Koehler method of dog training), insists that dogs have the right to the consequences of their actions. In other words, if they do something correctly they should be rewarded, but if they do something incorrectly they should be punished. Dogs of course must learn what is expected, but once they know then they get rewarded for adhering to the rules and punished for not (2007). This might seem reasonable, but the implication, here, is that people who share their lives with dogs define what is correct and incorrect behaviour. They establish what behaviours are appropriate and which ones are inappropriate. This is a relationship of dominance and control – in such a context a dog's independence and individuality is not recognised or respected and her ability to choose is severely truncated; that is, when told to "sit" the choice is to "sit" or suffer the consequences for not sitting so really there is only one acceptable choice.

Reflecting on the American legal system, comparative philosopher Jin Park writes

> (t)he law is there to protect citizens from violence. However, to exercise law, to 'en-force' law, the exercise of force is required, which limits an individual's freedom. As much as law protects people from violence, law is also violence – legitimized violence.
>
> (2015, 116)

Park points out that this two-sided nature of the legal system allows for its misuse which she argues is not completely fixed through creation of a better law (2015). Dog training systems operate in similar ways. Any system that defines what an obedient dog is and does assigns roles to all the actors: the human is the leader and the dog is the subordinate. The human rewards desirable behaviour and punishes (or at least withholds reward for) undesirable behaviour. This is the way one prevents unruly conduct (the house being soiled, property chewed up and hands bitten) or gets a dog to perform a desirable task (run through the weave polls or heel in place at one's side). Unfortunately, just as the law legitimises violence to keep order so too do dog training systems, which at times justify violence when a dog's conduct needs to be changed or controlled. Systems that establish this power differential always have the potential for this kind of cruelty – those that have authority can and do abuse their position which often results in tyrannical action. For instance, to stop her dogs from digging holes in her yard, Vicki Hearne fills the holes with water and shoves her dogs' heads in it. She finds this acceptable because it has the desired result – it prevents the dogs from digging holes in her yard. But clearly this is violence and a violence that she does not recognise. In fact, she justifies it:

> And [Salty] stops digging holes and devotes herself to preventing the very thought of holes from coming into my mind again. *This has nothing to do with either punishment or authority, and if it is corrupted by either, then it becomes cruel.*
>
> (2007, 68)

I would argue that she is wrong here – this has everything to do with both punishment and authority and it is cruel.

We find this attitude and approach in other contexts as well. For competition training, it is increasingly common for handlers to use deprivation techniques when preparing a dog for performance events like agility or obedience trials.

For example, a trainer might withhold a meal when a dog fails to perform a task correctly. That is, if the dog is being asked to heel for her food and she makes a mistake then she will not be fed right away. If she continues to make the mistake she may not get fed at all for that meal. In some cases, this can go on for more than a day (Fenzi 2012). Supporters suggest this approach has two benefits: firstly, not receiving the expected meal indicates to the dog that she did something wrong, and secondly, the hunger experienced serves to increase motivation for doing the task properly the next time. Handlers dismiss any question regarding the ethics of such a method by pointing to its effectiveness in helping them obtain the desired behaviour. Depriving dogs of basic life requirements, then, is justified primarily as a means for success in the performance ring: "(p)roponents [of deprivation training] argue that these dogs must receive all good things through work, lest they decide that work isn't very interesting if any other options are available" (Fenzi 2012, np). The immediate problem here is that the burden of responsibility falls completely on the dog, and the handler's efforts to communicate with her dog are not interrogated. Denise Fenzi, a well-known and well-respected competition obedience trainer, makes this point very clearly when she writes:

> Fully 90% of the problems I am asked to address are solved through a change to the handler's mechanical skills or personal interactions with their dog. If a dog lags and goes wide in heeling because the handler drifts about and walks slowly, then the solution is to teach the handler how to walk properly. . . . Holding the dog responsible . . . will not solve the problem if the handler's actions are maintaining the incorrect behaviour.
>
> (2012, np)

The underlying problem, however, that allows this kind of training method to persist is the perception that the dog is nothing more than a tool to be used to obtain a desired end – namely a successful run at a trial. In essence, the performance dog has no inherent value – her individuality and personality, and thus her desires and needs are in and of themselves irrelevant; she becomes an object or commodity to be exploited for human entertainment, prestige and recognition.

Park (2015) argues that this happens because of the fundamental nature of institutions (and I am regarding dog training and the kinds of relationships between humans and dogs it promotes as a system or institution). She writes:

> the problem is related to the nature of the institution, any institution, by virtue of the fact that a system always has an authorship and thus implements selected perspectives. However, comprehensive and objective the institution might be, the consolidation of power into a system becomes possible through exclusion and through promotion of what is included in the system (116).

The ways of interacting with and training dogs promoted in most dog training literature do not allow them to have their own opinions about what they should and should not do – to have their own perspectives as Park mentions. Instead, they consolidate power and control in the hands of human beings which unfortunately can result in them engaging in aggressive and destructive relationships with their canine companions.

Breeding and conformation

The American Kennel Club (AKC), the most well-known and respected registry for purebred dog pedigrees in the USA, supports and sanctions conformation dog shows (in the UK it is The Kennel Club; much of what follows applies to The Kennel Club as well). In these shows, judges assess the appearance and temperament of individual dogs according to standards written by breed clubs and endorsed by the AKC. These standards are a set of aesthetic criteria that describes in detail the ideal physical type for each breed. While they also describe the ideal temperament, the standards privilege physical appearance and ignore a dog's personality traits that form her distinctive character (Carr 2014). Each dog, then, is treated more as an object, than as a sentient being with a unique emotional life and psychological disposition. This objectification of dog bodies is strengthened by language found in the standards, such as the tendency to refer to dogs as "specimens". For example, in the section that addresses how the coat should look in the standard for the Cavalier King Charles Spaniel, one can read the following: "Coat: Of moderate length, silky, free from curl. Slight wave permissible. . . . Specimens where the coat has been altered by trimming, clipping or by artificial means shall be so severely penalized as to be effectively eliminated from competition" (AKC 1995). The "dog as specimen," reinforced by the fact that dogs in shows are referred to not by names but by numbers, becomes a representation of the breed that is valuable primarily for her contribution to a breeding programme that strives to produce canine bodies that exemplify the ideal body type. In addition to "specimen," words and phrases used in breeding and dog showing discourse such as "true to type" (showing desired breed characteristics), "linebreeding" (breeding of close relatives) and "an outcrossing" (breeding two dogs from different lines) as well as terms for father and mother like "sire" and "dam" further depersonalise individual dogs (Library Index 2016). They reinforce the perception that canine bodies are "things" that can be manipulated to create the perfect appearance as well as purchased and sold for profit. Breeding and conformation showing make individual dogs into abstract entities, mere embodiments of their breed.

The pursuit of the perfect canine body is concomitant with the Victorian era interest in eugenics and obsession with racial superiority. In his article, "The End of Identity Politics: On Disability as an Unstable Category," Lennard Davis (2013) points out that conceptions of race, gender and sexuality have their origins in the mid-nineteenth century, corresponding with both an interest in the scientific study of humans and the desire to create the "perfect" human – a desire that later became codified in the "field" of eugenics (266). Eugenics discourse encouraged the reproduction of people with desirable and inheritable mental and physical traits and discouraged and/or prevented the reproduction of people with undesirable, inheritable traits:

> (e)ugenics saw the possible improvement of the race as being accomplished by diminishing problematic peoples and their problematic behaviors – these peoples were clearly delineated under the rubric of feeble-mindedness and degeneration as women, people of color, homosexuals, the working classes, and so on.
>
> (Davis 2013, 266)

These groups, classified as mentally and physically deficient and understood according to a narrative of disability, needed to be managed and controlled. Eugenics was one way to accomplish this. Thus, oppressive practices, Davis argues, "were given scientific license through these medicalized, scientificized discourses" (2013, 266).

Canine breed classifications along with the first conformation dog shows of the modern era have their origins in the mid-to-late nineteenth centuries in England – the same time that the categories of race, sex and gender are used to classify human animals (McHugh 2004). With the rise of the conformation dog show, the focus of breeding was placed on a dog's physical appearance not on her behaviour or ability to perform certain tasks; that is, breeders began breeding dogs primarily to satisfy particular aesthetic criteria: "(b)ut their commitment to dog showing, which is often the breeders' primary objective and has become the chief means of regulating human interventions in dog breeding worldwide, exacerbates this problem of privileging appearance" (2004, 62).

The American Kennel Club states that the purpose of conformation dog shows "is to evaluate breeding stock" because the "dog's conformation – his overall appearance and structure – is an indication of the dog's ability to produce quality purebred puppies" (AKC 2016a). Genetic control of canine bodies is central to the creation of the ideal "breeding stock." Such genetic control is maintained and recorded in the construction of pedigrees that keep track of a dog's bloodlines. Knowing about the lineages of the dogs in one's breeding programme allows the breeder to make informed choices about potential mates that will ideally improve her breeding lines. For example, if the dogs in a breeder's kennels continue to produce puppies that have ears set too far forward on the head, the breeder will choose a mate that will correct this issue. In this way, the problem will be "fixed" in at least some of the puppies produced from the breeding. The practice of inbreeding or linebreeding serves a similar purpose: to pass on certain ideal physical features found in the parents or other close relatives to the puppies. Here, then, the improvement of the breeding programme is the priority and not the wellbeing or desires of individual dogs. In fact, dogs in breeding programmes have no control over their reproductive lives. Females in season are placed with males whether they want to breed or not and in some cases breeders will use physical force to hold the female in place while the male penetrates her (Dunayer 2001). In other cases, the male partner is eliminated altogether and instead a particularly invasive form of artificial insemination is used wherein a female is penetrated (again without any possibility of expressing consent or refusal) by "a long plastic or glass tube" during which "[a]ttempts are made to at least reach the level of her cervix which in large dogs may be several inches inside the animal" (Foster 2016).

Through genetic manipulation, various breeds of dog have been created out of the desire to produce "beautiful" animals. Because breeders control their health, physical characteristics and ability to reproduce, show dogs are literally engineered to produce a "beautiful body" that satisfies an aesthetic ideal. They are taken out of the context of their own reality and denied their own identity (Carr 2014). In this way, they are transformed into nothing more than fetishised art objects that represent and demonstrate human supremacy. Domination over living beings like this disempowers them, robbing them of agency, making them powerless over their own bodies. Such a relationship derives from a fascist discourse wherein those who have power completely control the lives and bodies of those who do not. Absolute power like this prevents breeders from turning a critical eye on their practices and instead allows them to engage in morally questionable breeding practices and, for some dogs, the willful mutilation of their bodies.

Many AKC standards encourage body modifications or cosmetic surgeries like ear cropping and tail docking – practices that have little to do with the ability of a dog to produce healthy representatives of the breed. Quite the contrary, ear cropping and tail docking are used primarily to shape a dog's body to produce a certain look that a breeder cannot get through breeding. Modifying a dog's body, then, reinforces the perception that dogs are aesthetic objects that can be manipulated to satisfy human definitions of canine beauty. Though there are no year to year records regarding the numbers of dogs that have experienced this kind of cosmetic surgery, in her article entitled, "Cropping and Docking: A Discussion of the Controversy and the Role of Law in Preventing Unnecessary Cosmetic Surgery on Dogs," Amy Broughton (2003) writes that in 2003 approximately 130,000 dogs experienced unnecessary cosmetic surgery in the USA. The American Kennel Club's official position on these surgeries supports the continuation of their practice: "The American Kennel Club recognizes that ear cropping, tail docking, and dewclaw removal, as described in certain breed standards, are acceptable practices integral to defining and preserving breed characters and enhancing good health. Appropriate veterinary care should be provided" (AKC 2014). That this statement stresses the importance of these practices for "defining and preserving breed characters" only reinforces the point that body modifications are performed to maintain a particular corporal aesthetic for certain breeds (note that this section, "Breeding and Conformation" is more fully treated in Hurley 2017).

Conclusion

Up to this point, I have argued that dog training, dog sports, breeding and conformation showing promote the view that dog bodies are objects (like tools or art pieces) that can be manipulated for entertainment purposes or for satisfying aesthetic criteria that delineate a "beautiful specimen." I have also argued that training literature and methods advocate – sometimes directly and sometimes indirectly – the view that dogs should submit to human hegemony – giving them limited (if any) opportunity to exercise agency over their own lives. Viewing dogs in this way leads to morally questionable training practices such as those associated with deprivation training or to the creation of breed standards and language about ideal body type that results in forced breeding and unnecessary cosmetic surgeries. Canines have been adversely affected by these discourses and practices because they objectify their bodies and take from them any sense of individuality, freedom and power.

While we need to interrogate and deconstruct practices like these that perpetuate suffering and exploitation, I do not think that we should stop living with dogs or interacting with them. We do, however, have to consider other ways of being in relationship with them (indeed, with nonhuman animals in general). We need to be open to the possibility that other ways of interacting with our dogs exist that are not based on hierarchy and control. Following philosopher and scholar Ralph Acampora, I would suggest that such a way is found in the common bodily experience of a shared life world (Acampora 2006).

In explicating what he means by corporal compassion, Acampora describes a concept he calls "symphysis" which he defines as a "somaaesthetic nexus experienced through a direct or systemic (inter)relationship" (2006, 76). It is symphysis that allows us to experience a shared life world with nonhuman animals – through our bodies, our senses – without colonising their consciousness. This is a kind of empathy but not, as Acampora points out, of the imaginative kind where we mentally visualise the self as other – where we become the other, taking on his/her identity and then . . . pretending to know the other's suffering, develop a moral sentiment that drives us to alleviate suffering and strive to prevent it from happening again. Complete identification is impossible, not desirable, and not the way real empathy works: "(c)ultivating a bodiment ethos of interanimality is not a matter of mentally working one's way into other selves or worlds by quasi-telepathic imagination, but is rather about becoming sensitive to an already constituted 'inter-zone' of somaesthetic conviviality" (Acampora 2006, 84). When a dog squeals because someone has stepped on its paw, we do not feel that pain the way the dog does – but we recognise it, flinch even in response to it because most of us have experienced a similar pain when someone has stepped on some part of our body. Acampora recognises that we share much in common with nonhuman animals. He writes, "(d)espite differences in some sensory modalities, members of various species retain enough somatic commonality to make sense of one another" (30).

But there is more. We also connect with other living beings in our experiences of certain ecological spaces. This can occur when we realise that we are experiencing the same climate or the same sounds (e.g. squirrel) as another animal like when we realise that during winter we don heavier clothing just as many nonhuman animals experience the thickening of their fur. In this way, we live together with nonhuman animals as neighbours because we share a similar space, a neighbourhood – like a patch of woods, park or city street. Sometimes these experiences, however, are recognised by both species as shared – as an experience between friends (those that live together). The idea of shared experience here is of key importance and it is this kind of interaction that needs to be reflected on when we consider alternative ways to engage other living beings – when we think about our life with dogs. Perhaps this is part of what Derrida's story about his cat in *The Animal That Therefore I Am* intends. He writes of the mutual gaze – meeting his cat (and being met by him) eye to eye, and of the subsequent recognition in that moment that each one had of the other's existence (Derrida 2008). No hierarchy, no domination, no control – equal in the recognition of the other. These experiences can happen with wild animals – when a deer for example meets one's gaze during a walk in the woods. But even more profound is the recognition of a shared experience with those nonhuman companions with which we spend our lives – an experience that is mutual and not governed by the language of domination and control. The question is can we note these experiences, recognise them for what they are and allow them to provide the foundation for a new way of conceiving of human and nonhuman animal (canine) relationships.

If the answer to this question is yes (and I think this indeed is the answer), then it would change the way we understand how canines and humans experience leisure time together. Both Neil Carr (2014) and Marc Bekoff (Bekoff and Pierce 2009) have indicated that dogs do play and have fun. They engage playfully with other canines as well as other species like humans and felines. Taking Acampora's notion of symphysis together with the understanding that canines enjoy playing with humans, we can and perhaps are ethically obligated to spend our leisure time playing together in such a way that minimises the power differential that privileges humans over canines. Surely, people showing dogs in dog shows or training them for sports like agility and obedience enjoy the activity. The question is whether such endeavours are pleasurable for the dogs involved. Are the dogs merely tools or objects in these activities (Carr 2014)? While surely it would be too facile to argue that dogs in every instance of human-dog interaction in these sports are regarded only as objects, I would, nevertheless, submit that these endeavours too easily lend themselves to the reification of hard and fast power distinctions between humans and canines as well as the idea that dogs are simply tools for human pleasure. Symphisis, instead, would insist on mutual interaction where the needs and desires of both human and canine are recognised – that both are equal participants in the game, walk or other activity, and each have the power to disengage if they so choose.

References

Acampora, Ralph. 2006. *Corporal Compassion: Animal Ethics and Philosophy of Body*. Pittsburgh: University of Pittsburgh Press.
American Kennel Club. 1995. "Official Standard of the Cavalier King Charles Spaniel." Accessed October 5, 2016. www.akc.org/dog-breeds/cavalier-king-charles-spaniel/.
American Kennel Club. 2014. "Summary Position Statements: Ear Cropping, Tail Docking, and Dew Claw Removal." Accessed May 4, 2016. www.akc.org/government-relations/position-statements/.

American Kennel Club. 2016a. "Conformation." Accessed May 3, 2016. www.akc.org/events/conformation-dog-shows/.

American Kennel Club. 2016b. "Agility." Accessed October 3, 2016. www.akc.org/events/agility/.

Bekoff, Marc. 2007. *The Emotional Lives of Animals: A Leading Scientist Explores Animal Joy, Sorrow, and Empathy – and Why They Matter*. Novato, CA: New World Library.

Bekoff, Marc, and Jessica Pierce. 2009. *Wild Justice: The Moral Lives of Animals*. Chicago: University of Chicago Press.

Broughton, Amy. 2003. "Cropping and Docking: A Discussion of the Controversy and the Role of Law in Preventing Unnecessary Cosmetic Surgery in Dogs." *Animal Legal and Historical Center*. Michigan State University College of Law. www.animallaw.info/article/cropping-and-docking-discussion-controversy-and-role-law-preventing-unnecessary-cosmetic.

Carr, Neil. 2014. *Dogs in the Leisure Experience*. Wallingford, UK: The Centre for Agriculture and Bioscience International (CABI).

Davis, Karen. 2011. "Procrustean Solutions to Animal Identity and Welfare Problems." In *Critical Theory and Animal Liberation*, edited by John Sanbonmatsu, 35–53. New York, NY: Rowman & Littlefield Publishers, Inc.

Davis, Lennard. 2013. "The End of Identity Politics: On Disability as an Unstable Category." In *The Disability Studies Reader*, edited by Lennard J. Davis, 263–277. New York, NY: Routledge.

de Waal, Frans. 2008. "Putting the Altruism Back into Altruism: The Evolution of Empathy." *Annual Review of Psychology* 59(1): 279–300. doi:10.1146/annurev.psych.59.103006.093625.

Derrida, Jacques. 2008. *The Animal That Therefore I Am*. New York, NY: Fordham University Press.

Dunayer, Joan. 2001. *Animal Equality: Language and Liberation*. Derwood: Ryce Publishing.

Family Pet. 2016. "What Is the Definition of Compulsion Training in Dog Behavior?" Accessed October 3, 2016. http://familypet.com/what-is-the-definition-of-compulsion-training-in-dog-behavior/.

Fenzi, Denise. 2012. "Deprivation." Accessed October 5, 2016. https://denisefenzi.com/2012/05/14/deprivation/.

Foster, Race. 2016. "Artificial Insemination (AI) in Dogs." Accessed June 13, 2016. www.pete3ducation.com/article.cfm?c=2+2109&aid=890.

Hearne, Vicki. 2007. *Adam's Task: Calling Animals by Name*. New York, NY: Skyhorse Publishing, Inc.

Hurley, Scott. 2017. "The Dog Fancy: A Site of Ableist and Speciesist Ideologies." In *Weaving Nature, Animals and Disability for Social Justice: From Theory to Experience in Eco-Ability*, edited by Amber George, Anthony Nocella II, and J.L. Schatz. Lanham, MD: Lexington Books.

Koehler, William. 1976. *The Koehler Method of Dog Training: Certified Techniques by Movieland's Most Experienced Dog Trainer*. New York, NY: Howell Book House, Inc.

Library Index. 2016. "Pets – The Purebred Dog Industry." Accessed June 13, 2016. www.libraryindex.com/pages/2207/Pets-PUREBRED-DOG-INDUSTRY.html.

McConnell, Patricia. 2003. *The Other End of the Leash: Why We Do What We Do Around Dogs*. New York, NY: Ballantine Books.

McConnell, Patricia. 2006. *For the Love of a Dog: Understanding Emotion in You and Your Best Friend*. New York, NY: Ballantine Books.

McHugh, Susan. 2004. *Dog*. London: Reaktion Books, Ltd.

McKenna, Erin. 2013. *Pets, People, and Pragmatism*. New York, NY: Fordham University Press.

The Monks of New Skete. 2002. *How to Be Your Dog's Best Friend: The Classic Training Manual for Dog Owners*. New York, NY: Little, Brown and Company.

Park, Jin. 2015. "The Visible and the Invisible: Rethinking Values and Justice from a Buddhist-Postmodern Perspective." In *Value and Values: Economics and Justice in an Age of Global Interdependence*, edited by Roger Ames and Peter Hershock, 109–124. Honolulu: University of Hawaii Press.

Serpell, James. 2005. "People in Disguise: Anthropomorphism and the Human-Pet Relationship." In *Thinking with Animals: New Perspectives on Anthropomorphism*, edited by Lorraine Daston and Gregg Mitman, 121–36. New York, NY: Columbia University Press.

Steinhart, Peter. 1995. *The Company of Wolves*. New York, NY: Vintage Books.

5 Off-leash recreation in an urban national recreation area

Conflict between domesticated dogs, wildlife and semi-domesticated humans

Jackson Wilson, Aiko Yoshino and Pavlina Latkova

Introduction

For the last 14 years, the National Park Service has led an effort to restrict dogs' recreation opportunities in the Golden Gate National Recreation Area (GGNRA) in the San Francisco Bay Area. Although the changes in rules do not exclusively deal with off-leash recreation, much of the focus has been on the reduction in opportunity for off-leash recreation in these public lands. In contrast to the unique off-leash opportunities in the GGNRA, the National Park Service generally restricts dogs to the inside of vehicles, or leashed in campgrounds, roads, parking lots or other developed areas (National Park Service 2016a). The GGNRA includes the redwoods of Muir Woods, the former federal prison of Alcatraz Island and many other natural and cultural national treasures including Crissy Field along the San Francisco Bay. The estimated 14.5 million annual visitors also make the GGNRA the most visited unit of the 413 units (e.g. national parks, battlefields, rivers, recreation areas, preserves) managed by the National Park Service in the USA and its territories (Industrial Economics Inc. 2016). Visitors to the GGNRA include international tourists, hang gliders, people on horseback, picnickers and 0.9 to 1.3 million annual visits by private parties walking dogs in the federal lands (Industrial Economics Inc. 2016).

The controversy over proposed restrictions to current off-leash recreation in the GGNRA is an example of the conflict between people that want to maintain public space free of off-leash dogs and those that feel that regulators must consider the recreation needs of domestic dogs and the people that enjoy recreating with canine companions. This is not the first analysis of controversies surrounding off-leash dog recreation in public space (e.g. Bowes et al. 2015; Matisoff and Noonan 2012; Sterl, Brandenburg and Arnberger 2008) and will likely not be the last considering the shifting role of domestic dogs in many modern societies (Olson and Hulser 2003). However, the controversy over off-leash recreation rights in the GGNRA is a particularly poignant instance of this debate because of the duration of the controversy and the vociferousness of the debate between the local community and the national agency managing the public land. This chapter contextualises the controversy and then uses media reports and scholarly research to illustrate the major arguments for and against the proposed restrictions to off-leash recreation in public space.

History

The GGNRA was created in 1972 as part of the Parks for People movement (Camhi 2014). A set of guidelines for dogs and other pets was developed in 1979, but apparently was not actively enforced (Camhi 2014). After an unsuccessful attempt to negotiate these guidelines with local interests (Lyman 2013), the National Park Service attempted to ban all off-leash recreation in 2001 (King 2013). However, a judge decided that such a ban could not occur before additional opportunities for public input were provided. In 2002, the National Park Service announced an Advanced Notice of Proposed Rulemaking and provided a 90-day comment period (National Park Service 2016b). In 2006, a negotiated rulemaking committee was formed to gather additional public input and develop a set of recommendations (National Park Service 2016b). The initial versions of a draught plan and environmental impact study were released at the start of 2011 (King 2013; Lyman 2013). Written comments and statements made at public hearings and rallies emphatically conveyed that many dog owners perceived the restrictions as unfairly limiting their recreation, while others, including environmental groups, wanted additional restrictions (Lyman 2013). At protests, politicians, such as the elected national official representing the San Francisco Bay Area, Representative Speier, promised to "unleash the forces of Washington against efforts to ban unleashed dogs from most of the Bay Area's string of federal parkland" (Lochhead 2015). The National Park Service released the Final Environmental Impact Statement on December 8, 2016 and explained that the rule would start being enforced after a period of education (National Park Service 2016 and 2016). The final rules have been characterised as a 90 percent reduction of space available for dog recreation (Stephens 2016).

Even though the National Park Service attempted to finalise the process in 2016, the process has been further delayed in response to requests by national political officials to allow review of National Park Service emails and other internal documentation released as part of a Freedom of Information Act. Representatives of dog activist organisations charged that the initial review of the materials suggest that the documents provide proof of anti-dog bias and misconduct by the National Park Service (Pershan 2017). A national elected official supporting the maintenance or expansion of dog recreation opportunities, Representative Speier, also requested the Inspector General of the federal department overseeing the National Park Service, the Department of Interior, to investigate the "improper and potentially illegal" actions taken by the National Park Service (National Parks Traveler 2017).

Contentious process

One of the reasons that this process has taken so long is the strong emotions involved. A GGNRA spokesperson stated, "Dog conflicts are among the toughest to deal with. Probably because of the passion of the constituency" (Lyman 2013). This is not the first off-leash dog issue that has proven to be challenging in San Francisco. In the process leading up to the adoption of new off-leash rules in San Francisco city parks, a park advocate commented on the process. "You would not believe the rancor that would go on at those meetings. . . . People would boo or hiss at speakers. Everyone was so politicized" (King 2013).

One challenge is that the National Park Service and dog advocates have different perspectives on the process. The National Park Service claimed that the dog management plan has been "subject to one of the most exhaustive outreach processes in the history of the National Park Service" (Kinney 2014). However, advocates for dog recreation claimed that the GGNRA was not following a democratic process, not being reasonable or simply acting arbitrarily (Bajko 2015; Stephens 2014). The elected national politician, Representative Speier, stated "This is not [the National Park Service's] fiefdom . . . They are sticking their feet in concrete, saying 'This is the way it is.' That's not the way this country is run" (Lochhead 2015). Similarly, dog advocates voiced doubts about the authenticity of the public input process. "The revised plan released last fall is essentially the same as the earlier plan, with only minor changes. The GGNRA ignored the substantive criticisms" (Stephens 2014).

Other than just being ignored, dog advocates claimed that the current regulation is the first step to a complete ban on dogs (Lochhead 2015). Furthermore, advocates claimed that banning off-leash regulation in the GGNRA would be "a precedent setting judgment, it can (and will) be used against off-leash activity [in] other areas throughout the country" (Kawczynska 2016). Statements from the National Park Service that "non-compliance may lead to tightening of restrictions" likely support this fear (Brooks 2011). In contrast, former Park Superintendent, Frank Dean, stated "We aren't banning dogs. We are creating a special regulation to allow dogs off-leash" (Kwong 2014). During this long period of contention, many reports have publicised perspectives on both sides of the issue.

Methods

Similar to Toohey and Rock's (2015) article, this study reviewed media discourse to understand the conflict over dogs' recreational access to public space. In order to further identify what the arguments were on both sides of dog recreation in this unit managed by the National Park Service, newspaper articles and other online sources of popular media and journal articles were identified, reviewed, coded by argument type and collated. The internet and local news sources were searched using the search terms, "dogs" and "parks", "Golden Gate National Recreation Area", or "GGNRA". Moreover, for half of 2015 and all of 2016, the first author reviewed articles from daily Google news alerts using the terms "dogs" and "park". Scholarly sources were identified initially through Google Scholar using the terms "dog" or "dogs" and "park" or "public lands". Further searches of EBSCO and other databases were conducted to search for potentially relevant sources cited in previously identified scholarly articles and articles that had cited relevant research.

The search yielded 36 popular media articles and five government sources that directly addressed the GGNRA off-leash controversy. An additional 36 popular media sources focussed on other San Francisco Bay area dog issues, and 93 peer-reviewed journal articles addressing issues related to dogs were reviewed for this study. Each popular and scholarly source was initially outlined with a focus on the different aspects of the arguments made for and against restricting on- and off-leash dog recreation. A set of emergent codes about the different arguments made by both sides were developed by reading and re-reading the article outlines. The original articles were then reviewed to further develop the outlines based on the emergent codes. Subsequently, the codes were grouped thematically based on the National Park Service's stated four goals for the policy change. The coding of the article outlines was further developed based on this thematic coding. The goal of the chapter is to provide a rich description of the positions rather than calculating the frequency of each argument in the media. Therefore, when the final outline used to develop this article was constructed using the themes and associated codes, the focus was to include data that represented the diversity of perspectives in the popular media and associated scholarly research.

Arguments

The National Park Service offered four primary goals for the proposed restrictions to canine recreation in the GGNRA: provide a variety of user experiences, reduce user conflict, promote visitor and employee safety and promote preservation and protection of natural and cultural resources (National Park Service 2016b). Arguments held by both sides were organised based on these goals.

Provide a variety of user experiences

The former general superintendent of the GGNRA, Christine Lehnertz, described the intent behind the change in dog recreation rules, "We're trying to be pro-dog, but have a balanced approach" (Colliver 2016). The challenge is finding a balance between multiple parties wanting different, and sometimes conflicting, recreation experiences. There is a related set of questions pertaining to what is the intent of the public land designation and how the perspectives of the local population should be considered versus the directives of the national agency managing the area.

Multiple recreation experiences

Some have claimed the new regulations are necessary to provide experiences to multiple groups of users and avoid conflicts such as, "unregulated dogs are jumping on (picnickers) and eating their food" (Lochhead 2015) and hang gliders, cyclists and joggers being harassed by off-leash dogs (Lochhead 2015). A San Francisco elected official characterised the issue, "(t)here has to be this balance, and we have to just not look at the happiness of dogs and dog owners" (Green 2016).

Dog advocates posit that the attempts to reduce conflict are at the expense of reducing dog recreation opportunities which is based on the experience of the

National Park Service managing rural or wilderness parks, like Yellowstone or Yosemite, rather than the GGNRA which is a natural area adjacent to a major metropolitan area (Jones 2014; Lochhead 2015; Michels 2016; Rubenstein 2016). A San Francisco elected official stated, "The GGNRA properties are not backwoods national parks. These are urban national park areas that San Francisco residents have relied on for decades to walk their dogs and for other recreations" (Bajko 2015). This argument by dog activists implies that the GGNRA should have different rules to accommodate the many urban residents adjacent to the park lands.

Secondly, dog advocates argue that the GGNRA's designation as a National Recreation Area and not a National Park means that recreation opportunities, such as dog walking, should be maximised (Camhi 2014; Lochhead 2015; Stephens 2016).

> From its inception in 1972, (the National Park Service) has been charged with balancing habitat protection with recreational activities that predated (the) creation (of the GGNRA): 'To provide for the maintenance of needed recreational open space.' Foremost among those activities was (and is) off-leash dog-walking.
>
> (Kawczynska 2016)

This is an important argument because dog activists suggest that recreation opportunities for domestic dogs should differ by the area's designation, even though the National Park Service argues that all units, regardless of their designation, need to be managed based on the agency's primary goal of conservation.

The National Park Service rarely directly addresses these arguments except to argue that the GGNRA will continue to have the most dog-friendly policy of any area managed by the organisation (Michels 2016). Moreover, it must abide by national standards of management (Meyer and Shepard 2015; Stupi 2015), which requires that conservation must be favoured if recreation and conservation conflict (Industrial Economics Inc. 2016).

Recreation for whom? The clash between local urban users wanting to recreate with their dogs and the mandate of a national park system is not unique to this case (Sterl, Brandenberg and Arnberger 2008). On the one side, the National Park System posits it needs to not just serve the needs of locals, but all current and future Americans (Brooks 2011).

> The NPS has a responsibility to provide these places for all Americans, not just for the local communities. . . . We are a part of a national system that I can't manage Yellowstone just for the people who live in Cody, nor can we manage Golden Gate just for the people who live in San Francisco.
> (Jonathan Jarvis, National Park Service Director; Stupi 2015)

In contrast to the National Park Service position, dog advocates charge that the National Park Service is not adequately valuing input from locals (Stupi 2015). After a San Francisco resolution was passed against the proposed restrictions, an elected public official asked, "What does it take for the National Park Service to actually listen to the elected officials of the 2 million residents of these three counties?" (Green 2016).

Dog advocacy organisations often take a narrower view of whose interests are not being considered. The leader of a dog advocacy organisation stated, "The GGNRA is pushing ahead with a plan it wants, regardless of what we, who use the recreation area, want or need" (Stephens 2014). Rather than listening to locals that want to recreate with their dogs, dog advocacy organisations claimed the "Sierra Club and Audubon Society and prominent donors held greater sway than national users they represent" (Kawczynska 2016).

Off-leash recreation is part of the San Francisco Bay Area culture

Part of the counter-argument to the position that the GGNRA needs to be managed for a larger group of users is that, given its peri-urban location, the dog-centric values of San Francisco need to be accounted for (Stupi 2011; Codd 2015). A San Francisco elected official summarised this tension, "The National Park Service is trying to import its philosophy, which is pretty oppositional to dog access, and import that into our urban recreation (areas)" (Green 2016).

San Francisco has been described as being at the front of a social movement supporting the rights of domestic dogs (Davidson 2006; Della Cava 2015; Mason 2008). The Bay Area had the first no-kill animal shelter in the USA (Mason 2008), the first official off-leash dog park and continues to have some of the best dog parks in the nation (Bleiberg 2015; Codd 2015). Dogs are part of local politics (May 2007) and dog *owners* are legally "pet guardians" (Nolen 2003). It is often claimed that there are more dogs than children in San Francisco (e.g. Buchanan 2003; Lyman 2013; May 2007), which may be associated with an international trend to relate to dogs as family members rather than as more socially distant owned animals (e.g. Bowes et al. 2015; Fox 2006; Franklin 2006; O'Farrell 1997).

Reduce user conflict and promote visitor and employee safety

The National Park Service has stated that dogs are associated with the majority of the incidents of conflict reported to the National Park Service in the GGNRA (Jones 2014); an average of 300 per year (Johnson 2016). Conflicts include minor negative impacts on others' recreation experiences as well as violence; such as dogs biting people, horses and other dogs (Lyman 2013; Mar and Meyer 2016).

User conflict

The head of the National Parks Conservation described the issue as "wildlife enthusiasts trying to look at birds and seeing roving dogs harassing them . . . people on horses being bitten and attacked" (Lochhead 2015). In other cases the conflict is more subtle, such as a desire by some folks to not have to associate with dogs in public spaces (Rubenstein 2016).

Having a dog bounding along with you on the trail can be one of the most rewarding moments possible in the outdoors. Unless it's not your dog. In that case – for someone afraid of dogs – that moment can become a nightmare (Stienstra 2016).

International visitors, families with small children and people with disabilities are all groups that have been identified as having members that would like to recreate in the GGNRA without the threat of off-leash dogs (Stupi 2011; Palmer 2015; Rubenstein 2016). A review of dog walking studies found that women, older adults and ethnic minorities were the most likely to identify other people's dogs as impediments to their own physical activity (Toohey and Rock 2011). In this and other ways, dogs may have an asymmetrical impact on the recreational experience of other users (Graham, Glover and Grimwood 2015), although increasing leash requirements may decrease interaction of dogs with other dogs and humans (Westgarth et al. 2010).

Is off-leash recreation essential for the health of dogs? A key part of the argument for off-leash recreation is that it is necessary to keep dogs healthy, mentally stimulated and socialised (Burns 2006). "Neither (enclosed dog runs nor on-leash walks) could fully provide the physical and mental stimulation he needs to remain a healthy dog" (Stupi 2011). In contrast, some dogs may not benefit from large off-leash recreation areas due to disability, size or an inability to positively interact with other dogs and people.

Off-leash dog recreation areas may negatively impact dogs' health due to the transmission of disease. A primary method of potential disease transmission is dog faeces. Increasing the use of leashes may increase the recovery of dog droppings. Previous studies have found that dog owners that have their dogs on-leash are more likely to pick up their dog's faeces compared to owners that did not have the dog on leash when it defecated (Wells 2006; Westgarth et al. 2010). A Canadian study on parasites in dogs parks concluded, "reducing the burden of dog faeces in parks could have a positive health impact for dogs and humans by reducing infection risk, but cleaner parks may also offer an indirect health benefit by providing greater incentive to engage in physical and social activity" (Smith et al. 2014, 9).

Off-leash recreation and human's recreation, health, and socialisation

A critical argument against the regulation changes is that it amounts to barring a group of current users from recreating on public land. "For many of us, especially women and seniors, off-leash recreation with our dogs is our only form of exercise. We don't kayak, bike, run or cross-train" (Kawczynska 2016).

Beyond the opportunity to recreate, dog advocates have also charged that the new regulations will have deleterious impacts on their health. The head of a dog advocacy organisation claimed, "I also am a healthier and saner(!) person because of the availability to enjoy these areas with my dog" (Stupi 2011).

This is the claim with the greatest amount of related research; however, the empirical research on the health impacts of pets is inconclusive (Allen 2003;

Bauman Russell, Furber and Dobson 2000; Cline 2010; Evenson et al. 2016; Herzog 2011; Koivusilta and Ojanlatva 2006; O'Farrell 1997; Serpell 1991; Toohey and Rock 2011). Wells's (2007, 2009) review of research on domestic dogs and human health found that "dogs can have prophylactic and therapeutic value for people", but that they also "pose an enormous risk to human health" (2007, 151), and the current research is limited by a lack of longitudinal designs and standardised measures.

Violence

Sometimes the health of both dogs and their human companions can be threatened due to off-leash recreation. Some dog owners claim that "there's never any problems" at area parks (Rubenstein 2016); however, an observational study of dogs in Boulder, Colorado found that about one-fifth of interactions between dogs were aggressive (Bekoff and Meaney 1997) and dogs have been known to kill one another in off-leash parks (CTV News Windsor 2016). Fights between dogs can also promote conflicts between people. In an incident in a San Francisco park, two men who were asked to put their dogs on leash "threatened to stab and shoot the other owners and kick the other dogs" (NextDoor.com 2016). In a different San Francisco dog park, a fight broke out between dog guardians after their dogs got into a tussle (Pratt 2016).

Sometimes it is the dogs that are the victims of violent off-leash encounters with people. In a San Francisco park, a dog chasing a jogger ended in the death of the dog (CBS San Francisco 2015). The man, who had previously been bitten by a dog when jogging, claimed that he shoved, but the dog guardian countered he kicked, the dog away from him. This incident could have been avoided if the dog was truly under voice control, something that is required when dogs are off-leash, but some dog guardians charge is often not the case (Stupi 2011). On the other side of the San Francisco Bay in Oakland, a man killed two dogs and wounded their human companion after the victim's off-leash dogs approached the assailant's dog (Fox News 2016).

Guard dogs

In opposition to the discourse that dogs are the sources of conflict, is the argument noted in previous studies (e.g. Holmberg 2013; Knight and Edwards 2008; Tissot 2011; Urbanik and Morgan 2013) that off-leash dogs increase park security by discouraging undesirable activity. "With the off-leash dogs, the risk of violence is virtually non-existent. It would take a very stupid mugger to attempt anything there. In my daily visits since retiring several years ago, I have never witnessed any problems like that" (Stupi 2011). An Australian study found that dog owners were significantly more likely to feel safe while walking and at home than non-dog owners (Wood et al. 2007). A Canadian study found that female dog walkers were most likely to express that the presence of dogs increased their perceived safety in a wooded park (Graham, Glover and Grimwood 2015).

On-leash dogs are more dangerous

Another argument in favour of the notion that off-leash recreation promotes safety is that off-leash dogs are less dangerous than on-leash dogs. The leader of a dog advocacy group claimed, "dogs are a lot more aggressive on leash than they are off leash" (Camhi 2014). A related strain of this argument is that leashes limit dogs' ability to move based on their owner's mobility, and if dogs do not get their energy out through off-leash recreation then they will be more problematic. "A well-exercised dog is a well-behaved dog. It's better for everybody" (Camhi 2014).

Lack of public space

Dog advocates reframe the issue of conflict as the National Park Service creating conflict by further crowding off-leash recreation into smaller spaces (e.g. Camhi 2014; Colliver 2016; Kwong 2014; Michels 2016; Stephens 2014). Dog advocacy groups claim that the new rules will "lead to the largest loss of public access to the GGNRA since its inception" (Rubenstein 2016). The National Park Service states that the new rules are necessary due to an increase in the number of people and dogs recreating in the GGNRA (Bay City News 2015; Jones 2014). The number of GGNRA users has doubled in the last 20 years (Kwong 2014). The GGNRA is currently the most visited of the more than 400 units managed by the National Park Service in the USA and territories (Jones 2014; Lochhead 2015) with an estimated 14.5 million annual visitors between 2012 and 2014 (Industrial Economics Inc. 2016).

Part of this growth is from the San Francisco Bay Area population. From 1970 (just before the 1972 creation of the GGNRA) to 2016, the population of the San Francisco Bay Area increased 65 percent from 4.6 million to 7.7 million (Bay Area Census 2016; U.S. Census Bureau 2016). The relative density of residents in San Francisco and the high cost of residential space (Wallace 2016) equates to a dearth of private outdoor spaces (e.g. backyards) for off-leash recreation (Stephens 2014). Previous studies have linked a lack of private outdoor space with more reliance on public outdoor space for dog recreation (e.g. Gómez 2013).

Lack of adequate enforcement of existing rules

Some dog guardians suggest that poor dog behaviour is, at least partially, the fault of the National Park Service for failing to guide guardians and properly enforce the rules (Johnson 2016; Stephens 2014).

> I do see many owners who allow dogs on vegetation. I think some education and perhaps a few citations would rein this in quickly. . . . Many dog owners and dog walkers need some stern guidance on appropriate behavior, (picking up feces, keeping dogs within sight and under voice control, abiding by park restrictions) but it is a relationship that can work.
>
> (Stupi 2011)

While the previous quote discussed "many owners", some dog activists characterise the situation as the National Park Service permitting poor behaviour by a few rogue dogs and people. This argument then suggests that the behaviour of this limited element is used to justify collective punishment for all dogs. "Responsible dog owners should not be punished.... If a few people litter on the beach, do they talk about banning people from the beach?" (Jones 2014).

The National Park Service partially disputes the claim that the existing rules just need to be better enforced by arguing that the new policy offers greater clarity, which will make it easier to enforce the rules. A former GGNRA general superintendent stated, "The purpose of this action is to provide a clear, enforceable policy to determine the manner and extent of dog use in appropriate areas of the park" (Brooks 2011).

One of the challenges to effectively managing the dog regulations may be cost. The National Park Service estimated that it would cost about US$2.5 million for the informational materials and personnel needed to implement the new rules (Prado 2016). Without this additional funding, the National Park Service might be forced to follow the lead of other parks in the area, such as the East Bay Regional Park District, that decided to not enforce leash regulations due to the relative cost (Esper 2016).

Enforcement of the dog recreation related rules are much easier if the majority of people understand the rules and voluntarily comply. While some online resources inform guardians about the rules that they should follow e.g. "(d)ogs must be on a leash in the Bank Swallow habitat areas" (Bring Fido 2016); other sites normalise rule-breaking "(t)he rules are that dogs must be on-leash between from Sloat Blvd. and Stairwell 21.... Do people always follow this rule? Nope!" (Pershan 2015). Some dog walking information sites list an area as an off-leash recreation area even though it states that it is "not an official 'off-leash' area" (Bring Fido 2016). Given previous findings that social norms promote an obligation to abide by leash regulations (Williams et al. 2009), online resources and other resources supporting a norm of rule-breaking may make it more challenging to enforce leash laws.

As has been found in other studies (Bowes et al. 2015; Degeling and Rock 2012; Holmberg 2013), some owners disregard the right of law enforcement to ticket them for illegal off-leash recreation and argue it is an opportunity for civil disobedience. When the National Park Service attempted to enforce leash laws on part of the GGNRA, Crissy Fields, it led to a public meeting where 1 500 people showed up; people actively fought the tickets in the court and had the citations dismissed (Mason 2008). A man walking a dog in a different part of the GGNRA, Fort Funston, stated, "If they write me a ticket, I'm just going to tear it up.... Topper and I have some rights, too, don't we?" (Rubenstein 2016).

This lack of recognition of the rights of law enforcements to enforce leash regulations has led to violence. In a well-publicised incident in the GGNRA, a ranger requesting a man to leash his dogs escalated into a conflict ending with the man being stunned by the officer (Ho 2013). The man who was electrocuted sued the

National Park Service, was awarded US$50,000, and the ranger was assigned to a park in a different state (Emslie 2014; Williams 2014).

The rebellion against leash law enforcement is also an issue in area parks. An article noted numerous off-leash dogs at one San Francisco park, even though there were signs banning off-leash recreation at each of the park's five entrances (King 2013). At a different San Francisco park, an observer described the situation when a ranger notified people about the leash law, "We had a park ranger try to advise people of leash rule; he said, 'I've never taken more abuse from anyone on anything I've done in the park system'" (Koeppel 2015).

Similar to what has been found in previous studies (Bowes et al. 2015), part of the resistance to leash enforcement may be that some dog guardians see the leash rules as a secondary offence that should only be enforced if there is some larger issue with the dog, such as if the dog harms other people or animals. After receiving a ticket for over US$100, a San Francisco resident stated, "I think it's ridiculous for well-behaved dogs to get ticketed" (Winegarner 2012).

Promote preservation and protection of natural and cultural resources

Meyer and Shepard (2015) claimed that the GGNRA has more endangered species than two of the most iconic national parks in the area, Yosemite and Sequoia. The head of the local Audubon society expressed concern that "in this process [of debating changes to dog recreation access], you haven't seen the same level of compassion extended to wildlife as to dogs. . . . Everyone who cares about animals should understand that wildlife needs protection, too" (Jones 2014).

The impact of dogs on birds is a frequently mentioned concern. The Western Snowy Plover is one species that is often touted as needing additional protection. Signs warn recreationists about the tiny endangered birds that overwinter in the area. There is estimated to only be about 2 100 individual birds in existence (Johnson 2016). The primary concern is that the birds often "waste valuable metabolic energy" to fly away from people and dogs rather than hunt for food or rest (Johnson 2016).

A study of a Southern California beach found that dogs were about four times as likely to disturb birds compared to humans alone (Lafferty 2001). "Dogs disturbed birds disproportionate to their numbers due to the tendency for some dogs to chase birds and the possibility that some birds, such as snowy plovers are more sensitive to dogs than humans" (Lafferty 2001, 1960). A study set in Australian woodlands determined that human's walking without dogs had about half the negative impact on birds compared to humans walking with dogs (Banks and Bryant 2007). The presence of dogs led to a 35 percent reduction in bird diversity and 41 percent decrease in abundance (Banks and Bryant 2007). A study of an Australia coastal park concluded that "dogs exert a greater effect on shorebird abundance than people as they not only reduce the probability of birds occupying a planning unit, they also reduce the count of birds within a planning unit to a greater extent than people alone" (Stigner et al. 2016, 1210). These findings may be complicated by findings that dog walkers perceive the impact of dogs on wildlife as being significantly lower than people not walking with dogs (Sterl, Brandenberg and Arnberger 2008).

Although there have been negative interactions between dogs and other animals, including horses, the wild mammal that has received the most attention for interacting with dogs in the San Francisco Bay Area are coyotes. Authorities started receiving reports of coyotes in San Francisco in 2007 (Fox Television 2016). Most of the reported incidents between dogs and coyotes have been in the city parks (Fimrite 2015); however, given that the city is estimated to have more than 100 coyotes (Stienstra 2014), and that they will occupy the most marginal of natural spaces, it is likely that reports of interactions between dogs and coyotes in the GGNRA will increase in the future. Furthermore, a regional drought has forced coyotes to travel further for food and thus have more interactions with local residents and their pets (Fimrite 2015).

Beyond animals, there is also concern that dogs may negatively impact vegetation. Although most dogs and their people recreate in highly frequented regions, such as beaches, some people take their dogs to less travelled areas of the GGNRA, including beachside cliffs (Bay City News 2015). Moving off trails and beaches may increase the impact of dogs and their people on sensitive vegetation. In response to vegetation damage in a San Francisco park, a park supporter observed, "You can see large patches of the turf that are torn up and completely worn down to the ground where the dog owners stand around and throw their balls" (Koeppel 2015). Similarly, a different San Francisco park was closed down five months after it was renovated due to erosion caused by dogs and their guardians (Ho 2015).

There is push back against claims that dog walking, and, in particular, off-leash dog recreation, is actually impacting the environment. Dog advocacy organisations have claimed that "there is no scientific basis for this radical change" (Fimrite 2013) and the plan "proposes too many restrictions with too little analysis and factual basis" (Kwong 2014). This raises the question of what evidence is valid to support changes to the rules regulating dogs' movement in the GGNRA. Is it enough to have studies in similar areas that show negative impacts associated with off-leash dog recreation or is it essential to have data of actual impact in the GGNRA? The leader of a dog advocacy organisation supports the latter argument when she states, "the agency lists many impacts from dogs that 'could' or 'might' happen, yet offer no specific evidence that any are occurring in the GGNRA – or ever have" (Stephens 2014).

Conclusion

The disagreement over proposed dog regulations at the GGNRA has lasted for 14 years and will likely continue into the future. The National Park Service claims that reduction in on- and off-leash dog recreation opportunities will support a variety of user experiences, reduce user conflict, promote visitor and employee safety and promote preservation and protection of natural and cultural resources. In contrast, dog advocates charge that the changes will displace many of the current dog walkers. They claim the process implicitly assumes rural guidelines to manage a natural area adjacent to a very dog-friendly city, off-leash recreation is necessary to keep all users healthy and safe, and that the current body of research is not strong enough to justify such drastic changes.

The media reports are often limited and fail to address fundamental aspects of the positions held by both sides. For example, a key point of difference is what value should be placed on the needs of domestic dogs when regulating public space (Carr 2015a; Wolch 2002). Firstly, should dogs be considered beings who have leisure rights that should be acknowledged and respected by the government or are they objects that merely facilitate or detract from the experience of humans (Carr 2015b; Fox 2006; Hultsman 2015)? Assuming that dogs do have justifiable needs, then who has the privilege of defining what those rights should be? Given the inability of dogs to speak for themselves, it has most often been the advocates for increased dog recreation opportunity that have defined what the needs of dogs are, but it is unclear at times whether the people are voicing the dogs' needs or claiming the desire for something, such as space for off-leash recreation, based on their own desire to not have to be personally active or travel further to a different space. Secondly, just as the norms of dogs accessing private spaces have often changed (Franklin 2006), should a similar shift be carried out on public land? If such a shift does occur, is it enough to allow dogs access if they are on a leash, but does the emancipation of dogs in public spaces require off-leash access? Thirdly, when there are asymmetrical conflicts between users, whose rights are privileged and how should this be enforced to minimise public space that is "accessible to everybody in principle but not necessarily in practice" (Tissot 2011, 268). Fourthly, if dogs act poorly, should they be allowed to "act like a dog" or should they be treated as vermin and excluded from public space (Graham, Glover and Grimwood 2015; Holmberg 2013; Wolch, West and Gaines 1995)? To what extent should the needs and preferences of other human visitors be compromised to accommodate access for dogs on public lands? The format of popular media may obliquely reference some of these important issues, but rarely provides a direct analysis of these important issues.

Dogs are the domestic animal that are most likely to be brought out into shared public space; therefore, questions about whether dogs have rights to public space may promote larger questions about the trans-species sharing of urban public space (Degeling and Rock 2012). If the place of dogs, as nonhuman animals, is elevated to be deserving of dedicated public space, what implications does that have for wild animals, such as coyotes, raccoons and skunks (Wolch 2002)? What if the presence of one species in public outdoor spaces threatens the existence of another species (e.g. dogs chasing birds or coyotes eating dogs)?

The current debate has culminated in the restriction of the free movement of dogs in public space. Much of the debate between the parties is waged through popular media reports that often address just a few of the arguments with little analysis of the position. If more complete reviews, such as this one, can help both sides better understand the assumptions and implications of the positions held by parties on both sides of the issue, then perhaps future debates over public space may evolve to more fully acknowledge the views of all parties, including non-humans.

References

Allen, K. 2003. "Are Pets a Healthy Pleasure? The Influence of Pets on Blood Pressure." *Current Directions in Psychological Science* 12(6): 236–239.

Bajko, M. 2015. "Lesbian Named Chief of SF National Park." *The Bay Area Reporter*, March 26. Accessed April 21, 2015. www.ebar.com/news/article.php?sec=newsandarticle=70468.

Banks, P., and J. Bryant. 2007. "Four-Legged Friend or Foe? Dog Walking Displaces Native Birds from Natural Areas." *Biology Letters* 3(6): 611–613. doi:10.1098/rsbl.2007.0374

Bauman, A., S. Russell, S. Furber, and A. Dobson. 2000. "The Epidemiology of Dog Walking: An Unmet Need for Human and Canine Health." *The Medical Journal of Australia* 175(11–12): 632–634.

Bay Area Census. 2016. "San Francisco Bay Area population." www.bayareacensus.ca.gov/counties/counties.htm.

Bay City News. 2015. "Pet Owners Protest Plan That Could Prohibit off-Leash Dogs in Parts of Golden Gate National Recreation Area." *CBS SF Bay Area*, March 4. Accessed April 15, 2015. http://sanfrancisco.cbslocal.com/2015/03/04/pet-owners-protest-plan-that-could-prohibit-off-leash-dogs-in-parts-of-golden-gate-national-recreational-area/.

Bay City News. 2015. "2 Adults, Dog Rescued from Cliff at Fort Funston." *San Francisco Examiner*, March 22. Accessed April 14, 2015. www.sfexaminer.com/sanfrancisco/2-adults-dog-rescued-from-cliff-at-fort-funston/Content?oid=2924314.

Bekoff, M., and C. Meaney. 1997. "Interactions Among Dogs, People, and the Environment in Boulder, Colorado: A Case Study." *Anthrozoös* 10(1): 23–31.

Bleiberg, L. 2015. "10 Best: Amazing Dog Parks Across the USA." *USA Today*, March 27. Accessed April 14, 2015. www.usatoday.com/story/travel/destinations/10greatplaces/2015/03/27/dog-parks/70481392/.

Bowes, M., P. Keller, R. Rollins, and R. Gifford. 2015. "Parks, Dogs, and Beaches: Human-Wildlife Conflict and the Politics of Place." In *Domestic Animals and Leisure*, edited by Neil Carr, 146–173. London: Palgrave Macmillan.

Bring Fido. 2016. Off-Leash Dog Parks in San Francisco, CA. August 20. www.bringfido.com/attraction/parks/city/san_francisco_ca_us/.

Brooks, J. 2011. "GGNRA Dog-Walking Proposal: View Maps and Public Hearing Schedule, Send a Comment." *KQED*, January 14. Accessed April 22, 2015. ww2.kqed.org/news/2011/01/14/ggnra-dog-walking-plan-commence-commenting.

Brooks, J. 2011. "Wide Differences Between GGNRA, Dogwalkers on Leash Plan." *KQED*, March 11. Accessed April 22, 2015. ww2.kqed.org/news/2011/03/03/ggnra-dog.

Buchanan, W. 2003. "S.F. to Put Some Teeth in Its Dog Leash Laws: Police to Start Issuing $27 Tickets to Scofflaws." *SF Gate*, February 28. Accessed April 22, 2015. www.sfgate.com/bayarea/article/S-F-to-put-some-teeth-in-its-dog-leash-laws-2631572.php.

Burns, K. 2006. "Advising Clients About Dog Parks." *Journal of the American Veterinary Medical Association* 229(6): 902–902.

Camhi, T. 2014. "Why Some Bay Area Dogs Are Tied Up in Controversy." *KALW Local Public Radio*, July 31. Accessed April 21, 2015. http://kalw.org/post/why-some-bay-area-dogs-are-tied-controversy.

Carr, N. 2015a. "Defining Domesticated Animals and Exploring Their Uses by and Relationships with Humans Within the Leisure Experience." In *Domestic Animals and Leisure*, edited by Neil Carr, 1–16. London: Palgrave Macmillan.

Carr, N. 2015b. "The Greyhound: A Story of Fashion, Finances, and Animal Rights." In *Domestic Animals and Leisure*, edited by Neil Carr, 109–126. London: Palgrave Macmillan.

CBS San Francisco. 2015. "Jogger Kicks, Kills Dog That Ran Up to Him on East Bay Trail." March 25. Accessed April 15, 2015. http://sanfrancisco.cbslocal.com/2015/03/25/jogger-reportedly-kicks-kills-dog-that-ran-up-to-him-on-east-bay-trail/.

Cline, K. 2010. "Psychological Effects of Dog Ownership: Role Strain, Role Enhancement, and Depression." *The Journal of Social Psychology* 150(2): 117–131.

Codd, L. 2015. "San Francisco's Duboce Park Has Gone to the Dogs." *KALW Local Public Radio*, January 12. Accessed April 14, 2015. http://kalw.org/post/san-franciscos-duboce-park-has-gone-dogs.

Colliver, V. 2016. "San Mateo County Dog Lovers Howl at Federal Lands' Off-Leash Plan." *SF Gate*, March 22. Accessed June 3, 2016. www.sfgate.com/bayarea/article/San-Mateo-County-dog-lovers-howl-at-federal-6975592.php.

CTV News Windsor. 2016. "Windsor Woman Speaks Out After Shih Tzu Killed in Dog Park." September 27. http://windsor.ctvnews.ca/windsor-woman-speaks-out-after-shih-tzu-killed-in-dog-park-1.3091259.

Davidson, K. 2006. "San Francisco: A Doggy-Centric Day in the Park." *SF Gate*, August 27. Accessed April 22, 2015. www.sfgate.com/bayarea/article/SAN-FRANCISCO-A-doggy-centric-day-in-the-park-2554379.php.

Degeling, C., and M. Rock. 2012. 'It Was Not Just a Walking Experience': Reflections on the Role of Care in Dog-Walking." *Health Promotion International* 28(3): 397–406. doi:10.1093/heapro/das024.

Della Cava, M. 2015. "It's Official: E-Commerces Is Going to the Dogs." *USA Today*, March 20. Accessed April 15, 2015. http://americasmarkets.usatoday.com/2015/03/20/its-official-e-commerce-is-going-to-the-dogs/.

Emslie, A. 2014. "Judge: Park Ranger's Tasering of Dog Walker Was Unlawful." *KQED*, October 12. Accessed April 22, 2015. ww2.kqed.org/news/2014/10/12/federal-judge-rules-park-rangers-taser-use-on-dog-walker-was-unlawful/.

Esper, D. 2016. "Albany: Suit Refiled Over Off-Leash Dogs at Beach." *Bay Area News*, April 20. Accessed June 3, 2016. www.mercurynews.com/bay-area-news/ci_29792508/albany-suit-refiled-over-off-leash-dogs-at.

Evenson, K., E. Shay, S. Williamson, and D. Cohen. 2016. "Use of Dog Parks and the Contribution to Physical Activity for Their Owners." *Research Quarterly for Exercise and Sport* 87(2): 165–173.

Fimrite, P. 2013. "GGNRA Managers Unleash Dog-Walking Rules." *SF Gate*, September 6. Accessed April 21, 2015. www.sfgate.com/bayarea/article/GGNRA-managers-unleash-dog-walking-rules-4793377.php.

Fimrite, P. 2015. "S.F. Neighborhood on Edge After Coyote Pack Moves in, Kills Cats." *SF Chronicle*, September 17. Accessed June 3, 2016. www.sfchronicle.com/bayarea/article/S-F-neighborhood-on-edge-after-coyote-pack-moves-6512264.php.

Fox, R. 2006. "Animal Behaviours, Post-Human Lives: Everyday Negotiations of the Animal – Human Divide in Pet-Keeping." *Social and Cultural Geography* 7(4): 525–537.

Fox News. 2016. "California Police Search for Suspect Accused of Stabbing 2 Dogs at Park." July 18. www.foxnews.com/us/2016/07/18/california-police-search-for-suspect-accused-stabbing-2-dogs-at-park.html.

Fox Television. 2016. "Coyotes in San Francisco Are Here to Stay: Dog Owners on Alert." March 24. Accessed June 3, 2016. www.ktvu.com/news/113329590-story.

Franklin, A. 2006. "'Be[a]ware of the Dog': A Post-Humanist Approach to Housing." *Housing, Theory and Society* 23(3): 137–156.

Gómez, E. 2013. "Dog Parks: Benefits, Conflicts, and Suggestions." *Journal of Park and Recreation Administration* 31(4): 79–91.

Graham, T., T. Glover, and B. Grimwood. 2015. "The Potential of Place Meanings for Negotiating Differences Among Birdwatchers and Dog-Walkers at a Multiple-Use Urban Forest." In *Domestic Animals and Leisure*, edited by Neil Carr, 127–145. London: Palgrave Macmillan.

Green, E. 2016. "SF Supervisors Oppose Federal Off-Leash Rules at GGNRA." *SF Gate*, March 15. Accessed June 3, 2016. www.sfgate.com/politics/article/Supervisors-oppose-federal-off-leash-rules-at-6892296.php.

Herzog, H. 2011. "The Impact of Pets on Human Health and Psychological Well-Being: Fact, Fiction, or Hypothesis?" *Current Directions in Psychological Science* 20(4): 236–239.

Ho, V. 2013. "Off-Leash Dog Runner Sues Over Tasing." *SF Gate*, March 21. Accessed April 22, 2015. www.sfgate.com/crime/article/Off-leash-dog-runner-sues-over-tasing-4374463.php.

Ho, V. 2015. "Chronical Watch: San Francisco Dog Park Hounded by Problems." *SF Gate*, January 9. Accessed April 14, 2015. www.sfgate.com/bayarea/article/Chronicle-Watch-San-Francisco-dog-park-hounded-6004934.php.

Holmberg, T. 2013. "Trans-Species Urban Politics Stories from a Beach." *Space and Culture* 16(1): 28–42.

Hultsman, W. 2015. "Dogs and Companion/Performance Sport: Unique Social Worlds, Serious Leisure Enthusiasts, and Solid Human-Canine Partnerships." In *Domestic Animals and Leisure*, edited by Neil Carr, 35–66. London: Palgrave Macmillan.

Industrial Economics Inc. January 22, 2016. *Economic Analysis of the Proposed Rule for Dog Management in the Golden Gate National Recreation Area*. Industrial Economics Incorporated: Cambridge, MA.

Johnson, L. 2016. "Final Dog-Management Plan for GGNRA Has Owners Growling." *SF Gate*, December 8. Accessed December 9, 2016. www.sfgate.com/bayarea/article/Final-dog-plan-for-GGNRA-sure-not-to-please-10781839.php.

Johnson, L. 2016. "Threatened Snowy Plovers Spotted in Record Numbers on Ocean Beach." *San Francisco Chronicle*, March 4. Accessed www.sfchronicle.com/bayarea/article/Threatened-snowy-plovers-spotted-in-record-6871428.php.

Jones, C. 2014. "Dog Owners Unleash Their Opinions About GGNRA Restrictions." *SF Gate*, January 30. Accessed April 14, 2015. www.sfgate.com/pets/article/Dog-owners-unleash-their-opinions-about-GGNRA-5190871.php.

Kawczynska, C. 2016. "Off-Leash Recreation Is Being Threatened." *The Bark*, May 19. http://thebark.com/content/leash-recreation-being-threatened.

King, J. 2013. "Holly Park symbolizes S.F. Dog Situation." *SF Gate*, June 19. Accessed April 22, 2015. www.sfgate.com/bayarea/place/article/Holly-Park-symbolizes-S-F-dog-situation-4608693.php.

Kinney, A. 2014. "Off-Leash Dog Plan in GGNRA Decried by San Mateo County Dog Owners, Rep. Speier." *San Jose Mercury News*, January 31. Accessed April 21, 2015. www.mercurynews.com/pacifica/ci_25037935/speier-dog-owners-decry-ggnras-dog-policy-san.

Knight, S., and V. Edwards. 2008. "In the Company of Wolves: The Physical, Social, and Psychological Benefits of Dog Ownership." *Journal of Aging and Health* 20(4): 437–455.

Koeppel, G. 2015. "New Master Plan for Washington Square to Be Discussed April 8th." *Hoodline*, April 3. Accessed April 15, 2015. http://hoodline.com/2015/04/new-master-plan-for-washington-square-to-be-discussed-april-8th.

Koivusilta, L., and A. Ojanlatva. 2006. "To Have or Not to Have a Pet for Better Health?" *PloS one* 1(1): e109. doi:10.1371/journal.pone.0000109.

Kwong, J. 2014. "Some Residents Continue to Bark at Off-Leash Dog Restrictions." *San Francisco Examiner*, January 31. Accessed April 21, 2015. www.sfexaminer.com/sanfrancisco/some-residents-continue-to-bark-at-off-leash-dog-restrictions/Content?oid=2692765.

Lafferty, K. 2001. "Birds at a Southern California Beach: Seasonality, Habitat Use and Disturbance by Human Activity." *Biodiversity and Conservation* 10(11): 1949–1962.

Lochhead, C. 2015. "New U.S. Parkland Limits Feed Dog Lovers' Outrage." *SF Gate*, March 25. Accessed April 14, 2015. www.sfgate.com/bayarea/article/Let-dogs-run-free-pooch-lovers-tell-Washington-6159080.php.

Lyman, R. 2013. "San Francisco Debates a Proposal to Limit Where Dogs Can Roam." *New York Times*, September 24. Accessed April 22, 2015. www.nytimes.com/2013/09/25/us/san-francisco-debates-a-proposal-to-limit-where-dogs-can-roam.html?_r=2.

Mar, E., and A. Meyer. 2016. "Dog Owners Aren't Only Ones to Consider." *San Francisco Examiner*, April 12. Accessed December 9, 2016. www.sfexaminer.com/dog-owners-arent-ones-consider/.

Mason, M. 2008. "San Francisco, CA 94123: Where Dogs Have Their Day." *National Geographic*, April 12. Accessed April 15, 2015. http://ngm.nationalgeographic.com/ngm/0604/feature7/.

Matisoff, D., and D. Noonan. 2012. "Managing Contested Greenspace: Neighborhood Commons and the Rise of Dog Parks." *International Journal of the Commons* 6(1): 28–51.

May, M. 2007. "S.F.'s Best Friend: Where Pooches Outnumber Kids, Impassioned, Doting Owners and Hounds Dressed to the Canines Treat All Days Like Dog Days." *SF Gate*, June 17. Accessed April 15, 2015. www.sfgate.com/news/article/S-F-S-BEST-FRIEND-Where-pooches-outnumber-2555688.php.

Meyer, A., and W. Shepard. 2015. "Regulate Dogs on the Golden Gate National Recreation Area Lands." *San Francisco Chronicle*, November 8. www.sfchronicle.com/opinion/openforum/article/Regulate-dogs-on-the-Golden-Gate-National-6618414.php.

Michels, S. 2016. "Critics Send Up a Howl Over Proposed GGNRA Rules." *KQUED News*, February 25. Accessed June 3, 2016. ww2.kqed.org/news/2016/02/25/golden-gate-national-recreation-area-dog-rules.

National Park Service. 2016a. "Pets." *Yellowstone National Park*. Accessed January 12, 2017. www.nps.gov/yell/planyourvisit/pets.htm.

National Park Service. 2016b. "Dog Management." *Golden Gate National Recreation Area, California*. Accessed January 8, 2016. www.nps.gov/goga/learn/management/dog-management.htm.

National Park Service. 2016. "GGNRA Dog Management: Final Environmental Impact Statement Released." (email communication), December 8.

National Park Service. 2016. "Dog Management Planning Update- Fall 2016." (email communication), November 15.

National Parks Traveler. 2017. "Congresswoman Calls for Investigation into Handling of Dog Regulations at Golden Gate National Recreation Area." January 12. Accessed January 12, 2017. www.nationalparkstraveler.com/2017/01/congresswoman-calls-investigation-handling-dog-regulations-golden-gate-national-recreation.

NextDoor.com. 2016. "NextDoor" Accessed September 16, 2016. https://sfstateca.nextdoor.com/news_feed/?post=32607436.

Nolen, R. 2003. "Pet Owners in San Francisco Become 'Pet Guardians'." *JAVMA News*, February 15. www.avma.org/News/JAVMANews/Pages/030301d.aspx.

O'Farrell, V. 1997. "Owner Attitudes and Dog Behavior Problems." *Applied Animal Behavior Science* 52(3–4): 205–213. doi:http://dx.doi.org/10.1016/S0168-1591(96)01123-9.

Olson, R., and L. Hulser. 2003. "Petropolis: A Social History of Urban Animal Companions." *Visual Studies* 18(2): 133–143. doi:10.1080/14725860310001632001.

Palmer, T. 2015. "Bay Area Dog Owners Fight Impending Off-Leash Laws for U.S. Parks." *NBC Bay Area*, April 1. Accessed April 14, 2015. www.nbcbayarea.com/news/local/Dog-Owners-Try-to-Save-Fetch-in-San-Francisco-298229881.html.

Pershan, C. 2015. "The 11 Best Dog Parks in San Francisco." *sfist*, January 15. http://sfist.com/2015/01/15/the_best_dog_parks_in_san_francisco.php.

Pershan, C. 2017. "National Park Service Places Controversial New Dog Management Rules on Hold." January 10. Accessed January 12, 2017. http://sfist.com/2017/01/10/new_dog_rules_for_golden_gate_natio.php.

Prado, M. 2016. "Huffman: Keep Muir Beach Off-Leash Dog Area." *marinji.com*, September 28. www.marinij.com/article/NO/20160928/NEWS/160929789.

Pratt, E. 2016. "Man Kicks Black Lab After Scuffle in San Francisco Park, Fellow Dog Owners Attempt to Restrain Him." *Inquisitr*, September 3. www.inquisitr.com/3480487/man-kicks-black-lab-after-scuffle-in-san-francisco-park-fellow-dog-owners-attempt-to-restrain-him-before-he-assaults-other-dogs-video/.

Rubenstein, S. 2016. "Proposal Issued to Further Limit Dogs in GGNRA." *SF Gate*, February 22. www.sfgate.com/news/article/Proposal-issued-to-further-limit-dogs-in-GGNRA-6848065.php.

Rubenstein, S. 2016. "Recreation Area's Off-Leash Rules Bring Praise, Protest." *San Francisco Chronicle*, February 23. www.sfchronicle.com/bayarea/article/Some-dog-lovers-have-bone-to-pick-with-new-6850093.php#photo-9446309.

Serpell, J. 1991. "Beneficial Effects of Pet Ownership on Some Aspects of Human Health and Behaviour." *Journal of the Royal Society of Medicine* 84(12): 717–720.

Smith, A., C. Semeniuk, S. Kutz, and A. Massolo. 2014. "Dog-Walking Behaviors Affect Gastrointestinal Parasitism in Park-Attending Dogs." *Parasites and Vectors* 7(1): 1–10.

Stephens, S. 2014. "Opinion: Off-Leash Areas Should Not Be Closed." *SF Gate*, January 27. Accessed April 14, 2015. www.sfgate.com/opinion/openforum/article/Off-leash-dog-areas-should-not-be-closed-5179985.php.

Stephens, S. 2016. "Stop Calling It 'Golden Gate National Parks'." *San Francisco Examiner*, March 27. Accessed December 8, 2016. www.sfexaminer.com/stop-calling-golden-gate-national-parks-2/.

Stephens, S. 2016. "The Reason So Many Hate Government." *San Francisco Examiner*, December 18. Accessed January 12, 2017. www.sfexaminer.com/reason-many-hate-government/.

Sterl, P., C. Brandenburg, and A. Arnberger. 2008. "Visitors' Awareness and Assessment of Recreation Disturbances of Wildlife in the Donau-Auen National Park." *Journal for Nature Conservation* 16: 135–145.

Stienstra, T. 2014. "Coyotes Seemingly Thrive in San Francisco." March 27. Accessed June 3, 2016. www.sfgate.com/outdoors/article/Coyotes-seemingly-thrive-in-San-Francisco-5045034.php.

Stienstra, T. 2016. "Dog-Friendly Parks Throw Pet Owners a Bone." April 21. Accessed June 3, 2016. www.sfgate.com/outdoors/article/Dog-friendly-parks-throw-pet-owners-a-bone-7278318.php#item-44548.

Stigner, M., H. Beyer, C. Klein, and A. Fuller. 2016. "Reconciling Recreational Use and Conservation Values in a Coastal Protected Area." *Journal of Applied Ecology* 53(4): 1206–1214. doi:10.1111/1365–2664.12662.

Stupi, A. 2011. "Bay Area Responds to GGNRA Dog-Leash Proposal." *KQED News*, January 17. Accessed April 22, 2015. ww2.kqed.org/news/2011/01/17/bay-area-responds-to-ggnra-dog-leash-proposal.

Stupi, A. 2015. "Head of National Parks Responds to Criticisms of GGNRA Dog Management Plan." *KQED*, March 27. Accessed April 15, 2015. ww2.kqed.org/news/2015/03/27/head-of-nationa-parks-responds-to-criticisms-of-ggnra-dog-management-plan/.

Tissot, S. 2011. "Of Dogs and Men: The Making of Spatial Boundaries in a Gentrifying Neighborhood." *City and Community* 10(3): 265–284. doi:10.1111/j.1540–6040.2011.01377.x.

Toohey, A., and M. Rock. 2011. "Unleashing Their Potential: A Critical Realist Scoping Review of the Influence of Dogs on Physical Activity for Dog-Owners and Non-Owners." *International Journal of Behavioral Nutrition Physical Activity* 8(1): 46.

Toohey, A., and M. Rock. 2015. "Newspaper Portrayals, Local Policies, and Dog-Supportive Public Space: Who's Wagging Whom?" *Anthrozoös* 28(4): 549–567.

U.S. Census Bureau. 2016. "California Population by Country." www.census.gov/.

Urbanik, J., and M. Morgan. 2013. "A Tale of Tails: The Place of Dog parks in the Urban Imaginary." *Geoforum* 44: 292–302.

Wallace, N. 2016. "What Is the True Cost of Living in San Francisco." *SmartAsset*, August 15. https://smartasset.com/mortgage/what-is-the-cost-of-living-in-san-francisco.

Wells, D. 2006. "Factors Influencing Owners' Reactions to Their Dogs' Fouling." *Environment and Behavior* 38(5): 707–714. doi:10.1177/0013916505284794.

Wells, D. 2007. "Domestic Dogs and Human Wealth: An Overview." *British Journal of Health Psychology* 12(1): 145–156.

Wells, D. 2009. "The Effects of Animals on Human Health and Well-Being." *Journal of Social Issues* 65(3): 523–543. doi:10.1111/j.1540–4560.2009.01612.x.

Westgarth, C., R. Christley, G. Pinchbeck, R. Gaskell, S. Dawson, and J. Bradshaw. 2010. "Dog behavior on Walks and the Effect of Use of the Leash." *Applied Animal Behavior Science* 125(1): 38–46.

Williams, K. 2014. "Judge Rules Against Park Ranger Who Used Stun Gun on Dog Walker." *SF Gate*, October 10. Accessed April 22, 2015. www.sfgate.com/bayarea/article/Judge-rules-against-park-ranger-who-used-stun-gun-5813401.php.

Williams, K., M. Weston, S. Henry, and G. Maguire. 2009. "Birds and Beaches, Dogs and Leashes: Dog Owners' Sense of Obligation to Leash Dogs on Beaches in Victoria, Australia." *Human Dimensions of Wildlife* 14(2): 89–101.

Winegarner, B. 2012. "Off-Leash Dogs: Owners Fight Increased Ticketing at Glen Canyon Park." *SF Weekly*, August 1. Accessed April 22, 2015. www.sfweekly.com/sanfrancisco/off-leash-dogs-owners-fight-increased-ticketing-at-glen-canyon-park/Content?oid=2185863.

Wolch, J. 2002. "Anima Urbis." *Progress in Human Geography* 26(6): 721–742.

Wolch, J., K. West, and T. Gaines. 1995. "Trans-Species Urban Theory." *Environment and Planning D: Society and Space* 13(6): 735–760.

Wood, L., B. Giles-Corti, M. Bulsara, and D. Bosch. 2007. "More Than a Furry Companion: The Ripple Effect of Companion Animals on Neighborhood Interactions and Sense of Community." *Society and Animals* 15(1): 43–56. doi:10.1163/156853007x169333.

6 Walking the dog – chore or leisure?

Lisel O'Dwyer

Introduction

Given the prevalence of dog ownership in countries like Australia, the USA and Great Britain, we may well assume that most people enjoy spending time with them and that they take pleasure in seeing their dogs happy. Anyone who has a dog knows that going for walks is one of the highlights of a dog's day, (the other highlights being dinner time and the return of their people). In contemporary culture, people have dogs as companions primarily for the pleasure of their company, although some may also have them for a range of other reasons (Serpell 1995).

The physical health and fitness aspects of certain leisure activities – in this case walking the dog – have recently attracted the attention of health promotion and exercise psychology researchers. Providing for dogs' needs for exercise is identified as a prime motivation for humans to exercise, given the central role of physical exercise in health promotion and obesity prevention (see for example Bauman et al. 2001; Brown and Rhodes 2006; Cutt et al. 2007; Cutt, Giles-Corti and Knuiman 2008; Epping 2011; Higgins et al. 2013; Johnson and Meadows 2010; Schofield, Mummery and Steele 2005; Thorpe et al. 2006; Westgarth, Christley and Christian 2014). The literature has concluded that dog owners tend to exercise more than non-dog owners and therefore that dogs provide an important motivation for physical activity in the form of walking. In lay terms, we may well ask whether people walk their dogs because they know it is their duty or responsibility as a dog owner – akin to a chore – or whether they do it because they enjoy it – a leisure activity. There may well be some occasions where walking the dog is indeed a chore, such as during very hot or cold weather, and there may be other times when it is fun, when the person or dog (or both) meet new friends or experience interesting new sights and sounds (and in the dog's case, smells).

The role of dogs in motivating people to walk is not often identified in studies investigating motivation or determinants of physical activity – that is, those *not* specifically examining the role of dog ownership in human physical activity. Michael et al.'s (2010) survey of physical activity resources and changes in walking in a cohort of older men includes a question mentioning dogs in passing: "Over the past 7 days, how often did you walk outside your home or yard for any reason. For example for fun or exercise, walking to work, walking the dog, etc.?"

The role of dogs is not explicitly examined nor mentioned in their results. Biddle and Mutrie (2007) jokingly refer to "walking your dog even if you do not have one" and comment that "we wouldn't dream of depriving our dogs of their walk!" in their book on the determinants and interventions in the psychology of exercise, but fail to take this link any further. Even authors who have specifically published on dog walking as motivating physical exercise have not mentioned it in more general papers on determinants or correlates of physical activity (e.g. Bauman et al. 2011). Van Stralen et al.'s (2009) review of the determinants of physical activity amongst older adults does, however, recognise Thorpe et al.'s (2006) work on dogs as motivators for walking. Van Stralen et al.'s review includes a study (Sallis et al. 2007) reporting that unattended dogs in the neighbourhood are a barrier discouraging older women from walking.

Even though people may be strongly attached to their dogs, most dog trainers and canine behaviourists dealing with problem behaviours in dogs will attest that a great many people simply do not walk them enough or even at all (Kobelt et al. 2003; Linday 2013; Rooney, Gaines and Hiby 2009), even though they know they should, and may well have good intentions to do so. The dog walking and human physical activity literature acknowledges this unfortunate fact (see Bauman et al. 2001 and Schofield et al. 2005). Current and increasing rates of obesity amongst dogs is further evidence that not all dog owners walk their dogs enough (German 2006; Bland et al. 2010; Warren et al. 2011; Degeling et al. 2012; Downes et al. 2014).

Whether dog owners see dog walking as leisure or a chore may determine how often they walk their dogs, which in turn has implications for their dogs' health and wellbeing, as well as their own. Do people fail to walk their dogs because they do not enjoy the experience, or are there other reasons? How many dog owners feel that dog walking is really a leisure activity, and how many do it as a chore, because they know they should? How often is it enjoyable? What makes it a chore at some times and not others? Can we predict which dog owners are more or less likely to enjoy walking their dogs? What do these patterns imply for dogs' quality of life?

Definitions of chore and leisure

As the focus of this chapter is on dog walking amongst the general population, "chore" and "leisure" are defined as popularly understood. "Chore" can mean nothing more than a minor routine duty or obligation, but its common usage is consistent with formal dictionary definitions – a dull, unpleasant or boring task that one is obliged to do. This is not to say that dog owners may not see walking their dog as an "agreeable obligation" (Stebbins 2000, 154) but the focus here is on the extent to which dog owners distinguish between dog walking as a generally positive, neutral or negative experience.

"Leisure" is the time free from work, duties (and chores) used for ease, relaxation, entertainment and enjoyment. Opinions of what counts as a leisure activity may, of course, vary between individuals. Leisure activities are important for personal wellbeing or quality of life not only because they provide opportunities to form and develop social relationships and experience positive emotions, but they can also maintain physical health and fitness (Brajsa-Zganec, Merkas and Sverko 2011; Mannell 2007). Work on the role of dog walking in human physical activity has engendered a new interest in the other meanings attached to dog walking, specific to this chapter and book's focus, the implications for dogs depending on their owners' views of dog walking as chore or leisure.

Respondent profile

An online cross-sectional survey of the general adult population was conducted in August 2016. It was introduced as a survey investigating favourite leisure activities without mentioning its underlying aim – to ascertain if dog owners would spontaneously nominate dog walking as a leisure activity, and to explore relationships between leisure activities and attachment to their dogs. The introduction to the survey read as follows:

> What counts as leisure these days? How do we enjoy our free time and do we spend enough time doing what we enjoy? What factors (such as work or family status, having a dog, or personal motivations) influence our leisure time?

Targeting the general population rather than dog owners only was done to avoid potential bias toward more attached dog owners who are more likely to fill out a survey about dogs and more likely to walk their dogs. The survey was promoted primarily via Facebook, Twitter and other mailing lists (unrelated to dog ownership), attracting 172 responses. Approximately three quarters (73 percent) of respondents were located in South Australia, reflecting the location of the researcher's social and professional networks. The remainder was located in other States within Australia (25 percent) and the USA (2 percent) and were included in the analysis on the basis that they did not otherwise differ demographically from the target population.

As is common in both online and paper-based postal surveys (Kanuk and Berenson 1975; Groves 2006; Smith 2008), the gender balance was biased toward females (79 percent). The age distribution was biased toward the 40–59 age group, with the youngest and oldest age groups (18–29 years and 70 or more years) both under-represented (ABS 2011 Census).[1] The occupational profile was also biased toward professional occupations (64 percent of the sample compared with 35 percent for the total Australian population) and a correspondingly much lower proportion were employed in clerical, sales, administration, machinery operation, driving and labouring occupations (15 percent vs 41 percent for the Australian population) (ABS 2011 Census). The geographic distribution of respondents between urban and rural areas at 70 percent in urban areas was similar to the distribution for Australia, where 66 percent cent of the population lives in the capital cities (ABS 2016).

The auxiliary variables of age, gender and occupation are likely to be correlated with dog ownership and walking. The sample was thus weighted by age, gender and occupation (Kanuk and Berenson 1975; Yansaneh 2003) to better reflect the profile of the Australian population (ABS 2011 Census), which itself has a similar distribution to other developed countries such as the USA and the UK.

Based on their dog ownership status, dog owners were asked a series of questions about their walking patterns and attitudes toward their dogs and walking them while non-dog owners were directed to the standard "end of survey" message.

After weighting, the dog ownership rate amongst the survey respondents was 56 percent. This rate is considerably higher than the 38 percent ($n = 16,000$) for Australia reported by Roy Morgan Research (2015) and the 39 percent ($n = 2000$) for Australia reported by Animal Medicines Australia (2016). The ownership rate amongst respondents was higher for females (61 percent vs. 38 percent for males). Dog owners were more likely to be sole parents (14 percent of dog owners vs. 3 percent of non-dog owners) but less likely to be a single person household (18 percent vs. 26 percent). Dog owners were much more likely to live in a detached or semi-detached house with a big backyard (68 percent) and on acreage (12 percent) than non-dog owners (44 percent and 3percent respectively). They were also less likely to be full-time workers (51 percent vs. 74 percent of non-dog owners) and much more likely to work part-time (33 percent vs. 12 percent). Both groups were equally likely to be retired or not in the labour force (15 percent and 14 percent).

The results reported below focus exclusively on the dog owner subset of the total respondent group, given that respondents without dogs are unlikely to be walking a dog as either a leisure activity or a chore.

Results

Is dog walking a popular leisure activity?

Eighteen percent of dog owners specifically nominated dog walking and 6 percent nominated other dog-related activities such as showing, training or dog sports as one of their three favourite leisure activities. A further 21 percent who nominated "walking", "hiking" or "bushwalking" may be likely to take their dogs with them as a secondary part of the activity (Coby, Seli and Erickson 2003). When asked about how often they walked their dog (or participated in other dog-related activities) *as a favourite activity* (as distinct from walking the dog for other reasons), 41 percent of respondent dog owners did so at least once per day (with most of these reporting daily walks). About half of the remaining 59 percent walked their dogs once per week, and the rest did so once per month. Most (73 percent) dog owners who reported walking their dog as a favourite leisure activity reported that they would like to walk their dogs (or walk in general) more often. Lack of time was the main reason why respondents did not walk their dog as often as they would prefer, affecting 88 percent of respondents who walked their dogs as a leisure activity. The only other major barrier reported was their own health or injuries, accounting for 10 percent of these respondents.

Of the 28 percent of dog owners ($n = 27$) who reported that they were involved in at least one leisure activity they do not particularly enjoy, one specified walking their dog and eight cited walking, running or exercise (whether this exercise was structured, such as formal classes or unstructured, such as walking, was not specified). Structured forms of exercise (usually going to the gym) were the most commonly cited forms of disliked leisure activity (somewhat of an oxymoron given popular and formal definitions of leisure – see Kelly 2009 or Stebbins 2007), accounting for about a third of respondents involved in leisure activities they do not really enjoy, followed by socialising (22 percent).

While dog walking may not rate as a favourite leisure activity for most respondents, when directly asked if they view dog walking as a leisure activity, 77 percent agreed that it was (20 percent neither agreed nor disagreed and 3 percent disagreed). In sum, although most dog owners viewed dog walking as a leisure activity, only 18 percent nominated it as one of their top three favourite leisure activities. Including the 6 percent of respondents involved in other dog-related leisure activities, this brings the percentage to 24, but there is a notable distinction between dog walking as a "casual" leisure activity, and organised dog-based activities, which are more closely aligned with "serious" leisure (Stebbins 1997, 2007). Adding the 21 percent of dog owners who walk, run or hike as a favourite activity to the percentage of dog owners who specifically name dog walking as a favourite leisure activity, suggests that dog walking may be a favourite leisure activity for possibly 25 percent or more of dog owners.

Most respondents (76 percent) agreed that walking their dog is fun and 93 percent agreed that dog walking is a great way to spend time with their dog, but only 47 percent saw walking their dog as one of the best aspects of having a dog (presumably there are other aspects outweighing walking). Fortunately for dogs, only 3 percent ($n = 2$) of respondents thought walking the dog was one of the worst aspects of having a dog (both of these respondents also reported that having to pick up dog faeces when walking in public was one of the worst aspects of owning an dog, which might have something to do with this attitude).

Even respondents who did not report walking their dog as a favourite leisure activity categorised dog walking amongst a list of other activities as leisure or chore (60 percent), but 38 percent of this subgroup also felt that it could be either leisure or a chore. Only 2 percent saw dog walking as solely a chore or duty rather than as leisure. When asked if they view dog walking as a household chore, 18 percent agreed, consistent with the response to the direct question about whether they viewed dog walking as leisure. Just under a third (31 percent) were neutral about whether dog walking is a chore.

Who sees it as leisure? Who sees it as a chore?

When asked to rate their enjoyment of dog walking on a scale of 1 to 10 (with low scores indicating less enjoyment and 5 as neutral), 84 percent of respondents rated it as 6 or more, with 58 percent rating it 8, 9 or 10. Who finds walking the dog to be a less than enjoyable experience?

A comparison of respondents rating their enjoyment of dog walking at 5 or less with those rating it 6 or more shows no difference in gender – men and women are equally likely to be unenthusiastic about walking their dog. Employment status does not seem to affect enjoyment of dog walking, nor does urban or rural location. Not unexpectedly, respondents who did not enjoy walking their dog were twice as likely to have behavioural difficulties with their dog while walking, than those who did enjoy it (26 percent vs 13 percent respectively). A two-sample Kolmogorov-Smirnov test found the difference in the rates of dog behavioural problems between these two groups to be statistically significant (K-S $Z = 1.41$, $p = 0.04$).

People who do not enjoy walking their dogs tended to:

- Be older than those who do enjoy it – 62 percent were aged 50 or more, compared to 53 percent of the group who do enjoy it;
- Be more likely to be sole parents (29 percent of household types, compared with 10 percent who do enjoy it);
- Be less likely to be in couple households (there were more than twice as many couple households without children in the group enjoying dog walking; 21 percent vs. 47 percent);
- Have a large backyard (74 percent vs 64 percent) or live on acreage (14 percent vs 5 percent who do enjoy it);
- Avoid ownership of high energy dog breeds (10 percent vs. 37 percent who do enjoy it) although the sizes of dogs was the same for both groups;
- Experience circumstances preventing them from walking the dog (15 percent were prevented all or most of the time compared with 6 percent of those who enjoy it);
- Have a lower score for emotional attachment to their dog ($\bar{X} = 60$ vs $\bar{X} = 75$) ($t(83) = -2.18$, $p = 0.03$). However, the correlation between enjoyment rating and attachment score (see further details in the next section) was low at $r = 0.3$, $p = .006$, $n = 85$. Half of the group who did not enjoy walking with their dog reported attachment scores matching or exceeding the mean attachment score.

How often do people walk their dog in general?

Most dog owners do not list walking their dog as a favourite leisure activity, but some dog owners do not walk their dogs at all (Bauman et al. 2001; Cutt et al. 2008; Schofield et al. 2005), although they may well spend time with their dogs doing other activities such as swimming and playing, or have dogs that get enough exercise playing with each other. Even amongst subscribers to a dog interest magazine (presumably representing the more conscientious and emotionally invested people within the dog owning population), the daily dog walking rate was only 60 percent (Marcus 2012). The present study found that 46 percent of dog owners walked their dogs daily. An additional 32 percent reported walking their dogs between twice and 5 times per week. Sixteen percent walked their dogs weekly, leaving 8 percent of dog owners never or rarely walking their dogs.[2] This dog walking rate is much lower than the 37 percent for daily walking reported

88 Lisel O'Dwyer

by Bauman et al. (2001), the 23 percent reported by Cutt et al. (2008) and the 31 percent reported by Schofield et al. (2005). The survey may have a bias toward more diligent and active dog owners; the social network sampling frame allowed for dog owning respondents who completed the survey to forward the survey link to their own contacts with a known interest in dogs, possibly resulting in under coverage of the less diligent or active dog owners.

Respondents' age was not associated with frequency of walking (r_s = –0.14, p = 0.28, n = 63) but type of dwelling was – fortunately for the dogs, respondents with little or no outdoor space were more likely to walk their dog at least once per day) ($x^2(4, n = 58) = 15.09, p = 0.005$) (Figure 6.1). Figure 6.1 also shows respondents living on acreage may possibly have interpreted their usual daily movements around their property with their dogs as "daily walking".

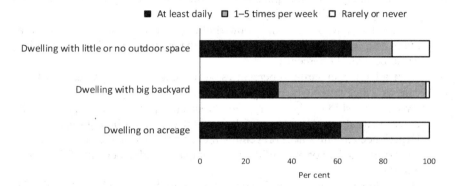

Figure 6.1 Frequency of dog walking by dwelling type

The frequency of dog walking might reasonably be expected to be a function of the dog's age, size (Schofield et al. 2005) and energy level (generally a function of breed), but there was no relationship between frequency of walking and dog's age (r_s = 0.2 p = 0.14, n = 65) or size (r_s = 0.09, p = 0.49, n = 65). In fact, in contrast to Cutt et al.'s (2008) findings, small dogs were more likely to be walked daily and medium-sized dogs most likely to be walked rarely or never. Large dogs were most likely to be walked between once and 5 times per week.

While recognising that the energy level of individual dogs may not necessarily conform to the typical energy level for their breed, energy level for each respondent's dog was estimated based on typical profiles for their breed. For example, fox terriers and pugs are both small but poles apart in their energy levels; border collies are medium size and high energy while basset hounds, also a medium-sized dog, are generally lethargic; and the large breed Rottweilers and Dobermans are also quite different in their energy levels (Coile 2005; Libby 2009). No relationship between walking frequency and dog's energy level was found (r_s = –0.04, p = 0.73, n = 65).

Eighty-four percent of respondents reported that there can be circumstances that prevent them from walking their dog. The most common of these circumstances were being too tired, usually from working all day (79 percent), the weather (77 percent of respondents), and then a variety of other less common reasons including difficulty managing the dog's behaviour while walking (21 percent), concerns for own or dog's safety (15 percent) and the official requirement to pick up one's dog's faeces (10 percent). Six percent of respondents found dog walking so tedious that they would occasionally forgo the walk. For 34 percent of respondents, one of these circumstances occurred twice or more per week; 32 percent experienced them about once per month; and 22 percent experienced them about once per week.

Most respondents who did not enjoy walking their dog did not walk them daily – only 9 percent did so, compared with 52 percent of dog owners who did enjoy walking their dog ($X^2(2, n=59) = 7.97, p = 0.019$). However, those who did not enjoy dog walking generally walked their dog between 2–5 times per week (64 percent) rather than weekly or less (27 percent).

Is level of attachment associated with whether respondents see dog walking as a chore or leisure?

Attachment was measured using the well-validated and widely used Lexington Attachment to Pets Scale (Johnson et al. 1992; Anderson 2007), consisting of 23 items rated from 1–4 on a Likert scale with two of the items reverse scored. The range of possible scores is 23–92 with higher scores indicating stronger attachment. The reliability in the current sample was excellent (Cronbach's alpha = 0.96), comparing favourably with Johnson et al.'s (1992) Cronbach's alpha of 0.93. The mean score was 73 (st.dev. = 11.8, $n = 92$), with the median at 76. The distribution of scores is shown in Figure 6.2, showing a skew toward the higher scores, indicating generally high levels of attachment amongst the sampled dog owners (Johnson et al. 1992 acknowledge that the LAPS may not measure low levels of attachment well due to social desirability response bias).

LAPS scores were grouped below and above one standard deviation below the mean (i.e. so that the cut-off score is 61) to account for the skew and the tendency

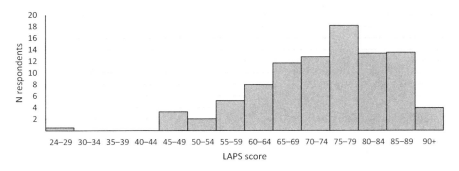

Figure 6.2 Distribution of dog owners' attachment to their dogs (Johnson et al. 1992)

for the LAPS to underestimate low attachment. Note that the small number of cases in the low attachment group ($n = 20$) means that statistically significant differences could not be detected for some items; cell sizes were less than 5 for some survey items when disaggregated by lower or higher LAPS scores, so some of the results should be interpreted as likely or indicative only.

Cutt et al. (2008) reported that people who did not walk their dogs were less attached than those dog owners who did, but the current study found no difference in walking frequency between high and low attached dog owners ($\chi^2(2, n = 62) = 0.32, p = 0.85$). People who walk their dogs daily or more (excluding those who do so 2–5 times per week) had a slightly higher average LAPS score ($\bar{X} = 74, n = 28$) than those who walk them weekly or less ($\bar{X} = 73, n = 13$) but an independent samples t-test showed that the difference is not significant ($t(41) = 0.48, p = 0.64$). A closer examination of dog walkers with lower attachment but who nonetheless walked their dogs either daily or 2–5 times per week (32 percent of the sample, $n = 36$), showed that 82 percent were female, more likely to view dog walking as a duty (55 percent vs 41 percent of the rest of the sample) and more likely to agree that dog walking is mainly for the dog's health or wellbeing (63 percent vs 45 percent).

Although not reflected in frequency of walking, there were notable differences in attitudes toward dog walking associated with attachment level. Statistically significant differences are highlighted with an asterisk after the reported test statistics.

Respondents with lower attachment levels were much more likely to forgo walking their dog in the following circumstances:

- when they were tired (77 percent compared with 51 percent of more highly attached respondents) ($\chi^2(1, n = 86) = 9.25$, Fishers exact $p = 0.007$)*
- when they had other things they preferred to do (20 percent vs. 6 percent) ($\chi^2(1, n = 86) = 3.53$, Fisher's exact $p = 0.08$)
- because they found dog walking tedious (14 percent vs 2 percent) ($\chi^2(1, n = 86) = 6.29$, Fisher's exact $p = 0.04$)*
- if the weather was unsuitable (68 percent vs 52 percent) ($\chi^2(1, n = 86) = 1.71, p = 0.19$)

They were more likely to agree that:

- sometimes it's a pain to walk their dog (67 percent vs 39 percent) ($z = 2.14, p = 0.03$)*
- they walk their dog only when they feel like it (63 percent vs. 28 percent) ($z = 2.69, p = .007$)*

They were less likely to agree that:

- walking their dog is fun (24 percent vs 86 percent) ($z = -5.16, p = .0002$)*
- taking the dog for a walk was one of the best aspects of having a dog (14 percent vs. 50 percent) (assumptions of z-test not met as $n(p)$ and $n(1 - p)$ were not equal to or greater than 5)

- dog walking is important for the dog's health or wellbeing (35 percent vs. 55 percent) ($z = -1.53, p = 0.12$)
- dog walking is a responsibility rather than an optional leisure activity (35 percent vs. 65 percent) ($z = -2.65, p = .008$)*

They were more likely to disagree that:

- dog walking should be compulsory for dog owners (46 percent vs. 17 percent) ($z = 2.63, p = .009$)*
- walking the dog was a top priority for them (39 percent vs. 23 percent) ($z = 1.53, p = 0.13$)

These results are consistent with those of Cutt et al. (2008) who reported that a positive subjective norm about dog walking was less likely in dog owners who did not walk with their dog while the rate of perceived dog-specific barriers was higher than for other dog owners.

Access to places to walk dogs

One key factor influencing the propensity to walk a dog (and walking at all) is access to suitable places in which to do it (Giles-Corti and Donovan 2002; Cutt et al. 2008; Coutts et al. 2013). The vast majority (92 percent) of respondents had access to a park, reserve, oval or other large open space allowing dogs (excluding dog parks) but 26 percent of this group did not take their dog(s) there. The most common reason for not taking their dogs was the dog's poor behaviour, including the dog's poor recalls (coming when called), anxiety and possible aggression to other dogs. The aggressive behaviour of other people's dogs, especially those off-lead, was another common reason.

Just over two-thirds (68 percent) had access to a dog park, but 57 percent of this group did not use it, for the same reasons as those listed above. The smaller confines of a dog park compared to other open spaces were also a concern for several respondents.

Discussion

While dog walking does not rate highly or even at all amongst favourite leisure activities for most dog owners, it is still generally regarded as an enjoyable leisure activity. This public perception does not mean we can expect people who both enjoy walking their dogs and are strongly attached to them to walk them every day, or at least a few times per week, as generally recommended by animal health professionals and welfare organisations (PetPM 2017; RSPCA 2017). In fact, over half of dog owners did not walk their dogs daily. Why not? Cutt et al. (2008) identified a range of factors – owners not believing that their dog provided motivation or social support, owners who did not possess a positive subjective norm for walking with the dog daily and perceptions of dog-related barriers and level of attachment. The present study also suggests that the constructs of rationalisation and cognitive dissonance come into play (Tsang 2002; Shalvi et al. 2015) – respondents who walked their dogs infrequently reported being too tired, agreeing that it would not hurt the dog to miss a walk occasionally, that walks are not really that important for the dog's health and wellbeing, that dog walking is an optional occasional activity rather than a regular daily one and that other things are more important and take priority. Future research on physical activity, dogs and leisure should address the animal welfare aspects of dog walking and seek ways to overcome cognitive dissonance in dog walking rather than intentions to exercise in general or walk the dog in particular (see Chatzisarantis and Hagger (2009) study on cognitive dissonance-related attitude change in the domain of exercise and Sniehotta, Presseau and Araujo-Soares' (2014) criticisms of the Theory of Planned Behaviour).

Another factor requiring more attention in research on dog walking and animals in leisure is the impact of the animal's uncooperative or difficult behaviour on the leisure experience and the likelihood that the experience will be repeated as a form of leisure. Canine behavioural problems were found to be associated with lack of enjoyment of dog walking. Unlike the weather, they are amenable to change but require the commitment of owners. A well-trained dog able to walk on lead without pulling or being distracted by surroundings or aggressive to other dogs and reliably coming when called if off lead, makes dog walking more enjoyable and of benefit for both parties (Dunbar 1999; Miller 2008). Walking with a well-behaved dog begins to match the definition of "leisure" rather than "chore". Often these behavioural difficulties can be easily resolved (depending on how often the behaviour has been practised), although some dog owners may require help from a professional dog behaviourist or suitably qualified trainer. Enjoyable dog walking is then more likely to be undertaken more frequently. Given that half of the group who did not enjoy walking with their dog reported attachment scores matching or exceeding the mean attachment score, such owners may have the motivation to improve their dog's behaviour when walking for their dog's sake – if they could work out how. This process might require some form of targeted promotion and assistance.

Other research has found that unstructured exercise (also known as lifestyle-based activity) is more likely to be maintained over the long term than structured exercise programmes, such as going to the gym and attending formal classes (Sevick et al. 2000; Opdenacker et al. 2008; Opdenacker et al. 2011). Walking the dog is clearly a form of unstructured or lifestyle-based activity, whether it is casual leisure or a duty – 68 percent of respondents reported that they fitted dog walking in around their other commitments. In this light, we might expect that the unstructured nature of dog walking promotes long-term adherence and maintenance, which is certainly to both parties' benefit. Some people prefer structured activities for their social support and motivation to commit (Beauchamp et al. 2007; Wilson et al. 2004) and ways to structure dog walking have been developed (see Johnson et al. 2011). Even arranging regular times to walk with other dog owners may be a sufficient structure for some people to participate in dog walking.

Most previous studies do not account for whether dog walking represents an intrinsic motivation (personally interesting and enjoyable) or an extrinsic motivation (to obtain outcomes separate from the behaviour itself) (Vallerand and Ratelle 2002) for dog owners. This distinction is important because research in health psychology suggests that while people are initially motivated by extrinsic factors when they begin regular exercise, intrinsic motives maintain it (Aaltonen et al. 2012). People with low levels of enjoyment and attachment and who do not walk their dogs daily could be seen as not intrinsically motivated to walk their dogs. Thus not only might they exercise less than they need to, but their dogs' wellbeing may also be compromised.

Proponents of dog walking as a motivation for exercise are not necessarily advocating that people should *acquire* a dog to motivate them to exercise – in other words, viewing a dog as a means to an end, a tool like a piece of gym equipment – but note that it is the group of existing dog owners who never or rarely walk their dogs which needs to be encouraged (Bauman et al. 2001; Schofield et al. 2005; Cutt et al. 2008). In the interest of the dogs' experience within human leisure, we must be careful not to encourage people who have little interest in dogs as companions to acquire a dog on the pretext of improving their own fitness. Focussing on the benefits of dogs for human exercise runs the risk of overlooking the other requirements of dog care, such as housing, socialising (with family members and other dogs), playing, grooming and feeding. People generally want dogs as companions because they have some affinity with these animals in general or want a relationship with them; this must be the motivation for having a dog in the first place, not the potential of the dog to motivate human owners to walk more. Even if the dog-human dyad is initially formed on the basis of the human party wanting a dog as a companion, this does not necessarily ensure the development of attachment (Westgarth, Christley and Christian 2014; also see Platt and Fletcher 2017).

Based on the results presented here, there appear to be four main groups of dog owners – those who are highly attached and walk their dogs frequently (i.e. daily or at least twice per week); those who are not as attached but nevertheless walk their dogs frequently; those who are highly attached but do not walk their dogs very often (or at all) and those who have low attachment and do not walk their dogs very often (or ever). The existence of the second of these groups suggests that some people do walk their dogs out of duty, not as leisure. While many dogs are happy to go for walks regardless of who the handler is and what their motivations and attitudes are, the existence of a bond or relationship (attachment) between the two can be the difference between a leisure experience or a chore for the human. Although some of the current literature accounts for the role of attachment, future research must consider both attachment and the role of dog behaviour in enhancing dog walking as a leisure experience.

Notes

1 Data from the 2016 Census were not available at the time of writing.
2 The number of cases in the "never" category was only 1 and so was collapsed into the low walking frequency category of walking weekly or less (total $n = 14$).

References

Aaltonen, S., T. Leskinen, T. Morris, M. Alen, J. Kaprio, J. Liukkonen, and U. Kujala. 2012. "Motives for and Barriers to Physical Activity in Twin Pairs Discordant for Leisure Time Physical Activity for 30 Years." *International Journal of Sports Medicine* 33(2): 157–163.

Anderson, D.C. 2007. *Assessing the Human-Animal Bond: A Compendium of Actual Measures*. West Lafayette, IN: Purdue University Press.

Animal Medicines Australia. 2016. "Pet Ownership in Australia: 2016 Report." Accessed May 15, 2017. http://animalmedicinesaustralia.org.au/pet-report/.

Australian Bureau of Statistics. 2011. "2011 Census of Population and Housing, Usual Residence." www.abs.gov.au.

Australian Bureau of Statistics. 2016. "3218.0 – Regional Population Growth, Australia, 2015–16: Estimated Resident Population – Greater Capital City Statistical Areas." Accessed March 31, 2017. www.abs.gov.au/ausstats/abs@.nsf/0/797F86DBD192B8F8 CA2568A9001393CD?Opendocument.

Bauman, A.E., H. Christian, R. Thorpe, R. Macniven, R. Johnson, A. Beck, and S. McCune. 2011. "International Perspectives on the Epidemiology of Dog Walking." In *The Health Benefits of Dog Walking for People and Pets: Evidence and Case Studies*, edited by R. A. Johnson, A.M. Beck, and S. McCune, 25–50. West Lafayette, IN: Indiana Purdue University Press.

Bauman, A.E., S.J. Russell, S.E. Furber, and A.J. Dobson. 2001. "The Epidemiology of Dog Walking: An Unmet Need for Human and Canine Health." *Medical Journal of Australia* 175(11–12): 632–634.

Biddle, S.J., and N. Mutrie. 2007 *Psychology of Physical Activity: Determinants, Wellbeing and Interventions*. Abingdon: Routledge.

Bland, I., A. Guthrie-Jones, R. Taylor, and J. Hill. 2010. "Dog Obesity: Veterinary Practices' and Owners' Opinions On Cause and Management." *Preventive Veterinary Medicine* 94(3): 310–315.

Brajša-Žganec, A., M. Merkaš, and I. Šverko. 2011. "Quality of Life and Leisure Activities: How Do Leisure Activities Contribute to Subjective Wellbeing?" *Social Indicators Research* 102(1): 81–91.

Brown, S.G., and R.E. Rhodes. 2006. "Relationship Among Dog Ownership and Leisure-Time Walking in Western Canadian Adults." *American Journal of Preventive Medicine* 30(2): 131–136.

Chatzisarantis, N.L.D., and M.S. Hagger. 2009. "Effects of an Intervention Based on Self-Determination Theory on Self-Reported Leisure-Time Physical Activity Participation." *Psychology & Health* 24(1): 29–48.

Coble, T.G., S.W. Selin, and B.B. Erickson. 2003. "Hiking Alone: Understanding Fear, Negotiation Strategies and Leisure Experience." *Journal of Leisure Research* 35(1): 1.

Coile, C. 2005. *Encyclopedia of Dog Breeds*. New York, NY: Barron' Educational Series.

Coutts, C., T. Chapin, M. Horner, and C. Taylor. 2013. "County-Level Effects of Green Space Access on Physical Activity." *Journal of Physical Activity and Health* 10(2): 232–240.

Cutt, H.E., B. Giles-Corti, M. Knuiman, and V. Burke. 2007. "Dog Ownership, Health and Physical Activity: A Critical Review of the Literature." *Health and Place* 13(1): 261–272.

Cutt, H.E., B. Giles-Corti, L.J. Wood, M.W. Knuiman, and V. Burke. 2008. "Barriers and Motivators for Owners Walking Their Dog: Results from Qualitative Research." *Health Promotion Journal of Australia* 19(2): 118–124.

Degeling, C., L. Burton, and G.R. McCormack. 2012. "An Investigation of the Association Between Socio-Demographic Factors, Dog-Exercise Requirements, and the Amount of Walking Dogs Receive." *Canadian Journal of Veterinary Research* 76(3): 235–240.

Downes, M.J., C. Devitt, M. Downes, and S. J. More. 2014. "Understanding the Context for Pet Obesity: Self-Reported Beliefs and Factors Influencing Pet Feeding and Exercise Behavior Among Pet Owners." *PeerJ PrePrints* 2: e715v711. https://peerj.com/preprints/715v1.pdf. Accessed February 10, 2017.

Dunbar, I. 1999. *Dog Behavior: An Owners Guide to a Happy Healthy Pet*. New York, NY: Howell.

Epping, J.N. 2011. "Dog Ownership and Dog Walking to Promote Physical Activity and Health in Patients." *Current Sports Medicine Reports* 10(4): 224–227.

German, A.J. 2006. "The Growing Problem of Obesity in Dogs and Cats." *The Journal of Nutrition* 136(7): 1940S–1946S.

Giles-Corti, B., and R.J. Donovan. 2002. "The Relative Influence of Individual, Social and Physical Environment Determinants of Physical Activity." *Social Science and Medicine* 54(12): 1793–812.

Gillison, F.B., M. Standage, and S.M. Skevington. 2006. "Relationships Among Adolescents' Weight Perceptions, Exercise Goals, Exercise Motivation, Quality of Life and Leisure-Time Exercise Behavior: A Self-Determination Theory Approach." *Health Education Research* 21(6): 836–847.

Groves, R.M. 2006. "Nonresponse Rates and Nonresponse Bias in Household Surveys." *Public Opinion Quarterly* 70(5): 646–675.

Higgins, J.W., V. Temple, H. Murray, E. Kumm, and R. Rhodes. 2013. "Walking Sole Mates: Dogs Motivating, Enabling and Supporting Guardians' Physical Activity." *Anthrozoös* 26(2): 237–252.

Johnson, R.A., C.A. McKenney, R. Johnson, A. Beck, and S. McCune. 2011. "'Walk a Hound, Lose a Pound': A Community Dog Walking Program for Families." In *The Health Benefits of Dog Walking for People and Pets: Evidence and Case Studies*, edited by R. A. Johnson, A.M. Beck, and S. McCune, 89–104. West Lafayette, IN: Purdue University Press.

Johnson, R.A., and R.L. Meadows. 2010. "Dog-Walking: Motivation for Adherence to a Walking Program." *Clinical Nursing Research* 19(4): 387–402.

Johnson, T.P., T.F. Garrity, and L. Stallones. 1992. "Psychometric Evaluation of the Lexington Attachment to Pets Scale (LAPS)." *Anthrozoös* 5(3): 160–175.

Kanuk, L., and C. Berenson. 1975. "Mail Surveys and Response Rates: A Literature Review." *Journal of Marketing Research* 12(4): 440–453.

Kelly, J.R. 2009. "Work and Leisure: A Simplified Paradigm." *Journal of Leisure Research* 3: 439.

Kobelt, A.J., P.H. Hemsworth, J.L. Barnett, and G.J. Coleman. 2003. "A Survey of Dog Ownership in Suburban Australia – Conditions and Behavior Problems." *Applied Animal Behavior Science* 82(2): 137–148.

Libby, T. 2009. *High Energy Dogs*. Neptune City, NJ: TFH Publications.

Lindsay, S.R. 2013. *Handbook of Applied Dog Behavior and Training, Adaptation and Learning*. Blackwell Publishing, Ames, Iowa.

Mannell, R.C. 2007. "Leisure, Health and Wellbeing." *World Leisure Journal* 49(3): 114–128.

Marcus, D. A. 2012. "Why Walking Your Dog Is Great Exercise." Accessed January 12, 2017. http://thebark.com/content/why-walking-your-dog-great-exercise.

Michael, Y.L., L.A. Perdue, E.S. Orwoll, M.L. Stefanick, and L. M. Marshall. 2010. "Physical Activity Resources and Changes in Walking in a Cohort of Older Men." *American Journal of Public Health* 100(4): 654–660.

Miller, P. 2008. *The Power of Positive Dog Training*, Hoboken: Wiley-Blackwell.

Opdenacker, J., F. Boen, N. Coorevits, and C. Delecluse. 2008. "Effectiveness of a Lifestyle Intervention and a Structured Exercise Intervention in Older Adults." *Preventive Medicine* 46(6): 518–524.

Opdenacker, J., C. Delecluse, and F. Boen. 2011. "A 2-Year Follow-Up of a Lifestyle Physical Activity Versus a Structured Exercise Intervention in Older Adults." *Journal of the American Geriatrics Society* 59(9): 1602–1611.

PetMD. 2017. "Exercising with your dog 101." Accessed May 15, 2017. www.petmd.com/dog/wellness/evr_dg_exercising_with_your_dog101.

Platt, L., and T. Fletcher 2017. "What 'Walkies' Says About Your Relationship With Your Dog." Accessed April 11, 2017. http://theconversation.com/what-walkies-says-about-your-relationship-with-your-dog-71245.

Rooney, N., S. Gaines, and E. Hiby. 2009. "A Practitioner's Guide to Working Dog Welfare." *Journal of Veterinary Behavior: Clinical Applications and Research* 4(3): 127–134.

Roy Morgan Research. 2015. "Doggone It: Pet Ownership in Australia." *Finding No. 6272*, Accessed March 28, 2017. www.roymorgan.com/findings/6272-pet-ownership-in-australia-201506032349.

RSPCA. 2017. "Can You Give Me Some Basic Advice On Caring For My New Dog?" *RSPCA Australia Knowledge Base*. Accessed May 15, 2017. http://kb.rspca.org.au/Can-you-give-me-some-basic-advice-on-caring-for-my-new-dog_20.html.

Sallis, J., King, A., Sirard, J., and Albright, C. 2007. "Perceived Environmental Predictors of Physical Activity Over 6 Months in Adults: Activity Counseling Trial." *Health Psychology* 26(6): 701–709.

Schofield, G., K. Mummery, and R. Steele. 2005. "Dog Ownership and Human Health-Related Physical Activity: An Epidemiological Study." *Health Promotion Journal of Australia* 16(1): 15–19.

Serpell, J. 1995. *The Domestic Dog: Its Evolution, Behavior and Interactions with People*. Cambridge: Cambridge University Press.

Sevick, M.A., A.L. Dunn, M.S. Morrow, B.H. Marcus, G.J. Chen, and S.N. Blair. 2000. "Cost-Effectiveness of Lifestyle and Structured Exercise Interventions in Sedentary Adults. Results of Project ACTIVE." *American Journal of Preventive Medicine* 19(1): 1–8.

Shalvi, S., F. Gino, R. Barkan, and S. Ayal. 2015. "Self-Serving Justifications Doing Wrong and Feeling Moral." *Current Directions in Psychological Science* 24(2): 125–130.

Smith, G. 2008. "Does Gender Influence Online Survey Participation? A Record-Linkage Analysis of University Faculty Online Survey Response Behavior." http://files.eric.ed.gov/fulltext/ED501717.pdf.

Sniehotta, F.F., J. Presseau, and V. Araújo-Soares. 2014. "Time to Retire the Theory of Planned Behavior." *Health Psychology Review* 8(1): 1–7.

Stebbins, R. A. (1997). "Casual leisure: a conceptual statement." *Leisure Studies* 16(1): 17-25.

Stebbins, R. A. (2000). "Obligation as an aspect of leisure experience." *Journal of Leisure Research* 32(1): 152.

Stebbins, R.A. 2007. *Serious Leisure: A Perspective for Our Time*. New Brunswick: Transaction Publishers.

Thorpe, R.J., E.M. Simonsick, J.S. Brach, H. Ayonayon, S. Satterfield, T.B. Harris, M. Garcia, and S.B. Kritchevsky. 2006. "Dog Ownership, Walking Behavior, and Maintained Mobility in Late Life." *Journal of the American Geriatrics Society* 54(9): 1419–1424.

Tsang, J-A. 2002. "Moral Rationalization and the Integration of Situational Factors and Psychological Processes in Immoral Behavior." *Review of General Psychology* 6(1): 25–50.

Vallerand, R.J., and C.F. Ratelle. 2002. "Intrinsic and Extrinsic Motivation: A Hierarchical Model." Chap.2 In *Handbook of Self-Determination Research*, edited by E.L. Deci and R.M. Ryan, 37–63. Rochester: University of Rochester Press.

Van Stralen, M.M., H. de Vries, A.N. Mudde, C. Bolman, and L. Lechner. 2009. "Determinants of Initiation and Maintenance of Physical Activity Among Older Adults: A Literature Review." *Health Psychology Review* 3(2): 147–207.

Warren, B.S., J.J. Wakshlag, M. Maley, T.J. Farrell, A.M. Struble, M.R. Panasevich, and M.T. Wells. 2011. "Use of Pedometers to Measure the Relationship of Dog Walking to Body Condition Score in Obese and Non-Obese Dogs." *The British Journal of Nutrition* 106(S1): S85–S89.

Westgarth, C., R.M. Christley, and H.E. Christian. 2014. "How Might We Increase Physical Activity Through Dog Walking? A Comprehensive Review of Dog Walking Correlates." *International Journal of Behavioral Nutrition and Physical Activity* 11(1): 83.

Wilson, P.M., W.M. Rodgers, P.J. Carpenter, C. Hall, J. Hardy, and S.N. Fraser. 2004. "The Relationship Between Commitment and Exercise Behavior." *Psychology of Sport and Exercise* 5(4): 405–421.

Yansaneh, I.S. 2003. "Construction and Use of Sample Weights." *Designing Household Surveys Samples: Practical Guidelines*. Accessed October 21, 2016. https://millenniumindicators.un.org/unsd/demographic/meetings/egm/sampling_1203/docs/no_5.pdf.

7 Recentring companion species wellbeing in the leisure experience

Towards multispecies flourishing through dog walking

Katrina Myrvang Brown and Petra Lackova

Introduction: dog walking and wellbeing

> Regular dog walking is likely a symbiotic relationship between the needs of the dog and its owner. This relationship has seen limited attention.
>
> (Lim and Rhodes 2016, 65)

For many people, outdoor activity is often done together with dogs. In Scotland, for example, a 2012–2013 survey of adults found not only that almost half of visits to the outdoors (48 percent) were accompanied by a dog, but also that in the previous 10 years the overall proportion of outdoor visits accompanied by a dog had increased from 41 percent to 48 percent (SNH 2014). For such people, dogs are central to their (typically daily) outdoor leisure experience, and in turn to their wellbeing (Johnson, Beck and McCune 2011), which dog walking is found to enhance physically (Cutt et al. 2007), mentally (Clark Cline 2010), socially (Antonacopoulos, Duvall and Pychyl 2014) and even spiritually (Boisvert and Harrell 2014).

Some of these studies also identify key motivations and barriers to dog walking and thus some of the contingencies of the associated wellbeing benefits. Yet arguably more is understood about the positive correlation between dog walking and human wellbeing than the processes through which the generation of such wellbeing depends. Westgarth and colleagues (2014, 11) highlight that "there has been little explicit research as to what dog walking actually is, to both the owner and the dog; what actually happens on a 'dog walk' and what functions it performs". One intriguing area requiring further exploration is how the wellbeing needs of humans intertwine with the wellbeing needs of dogs in the spaces of a dog walk. The positive associations between dog ownership and physical activity are found to "hinge on human – animal bonds, and thus on people's commitment to meet the physical and emotional needs of dogs" (Rock et al. 2014, 980). Moreover, Cutt et al. (2008) found that people were *more* motivated to walk their dog for the dog's health and wellbeing than their own.

Yet little is understood about how notions of what dogs want and need from a dog walk, as perceived by guardians, actually infuse and shape dog walking practices and related management. The literature conveys a general appreciation that dogs require regular exercise in alignment with their size, age, breed and energy levels (Lim and Rhodes 2016) and that dog walkers will usually be motivated to seek out opportunities for their dogs to be off-leash (Cutt et al. 2007; Westgarth et al. 2014). However, this work tends not to deal so much with the details of what guardians think qualitatively matters in making a dog walk enhancing to the dog's wellbeing. As Rock et al. (2014, 980) state, "[f]uture research could delve deeper into how caring for pet dogs influences physical activity for owners and other people . . . [and] . . . consider the extent to which meeting a pet's emotional and physical needs may contribute positively to a sense of self-efficacy", since self-efficacy is positively associated with dog-walking (Richards et al. 2013). Neither does it deal with how humans come to 'know' their dog's needs and preferences (Brown and Dilley 2012; Brown 2015). Nor do they tend to ponder the implications for how dog walking co-generates human and canine – and indeed broader social and ecological – wellbeing. Such knowledge could be useful in addressing issues of inadequate dog walking, given that many dogs are thought to be given insufficient exercise and training (British Veterinary Association 2017) and that many dog owners are still not getting the physical activity recommended in official health guidelines (Christian et al. 2013).

This chapter helps to address this gap by expanding on how perceived canine wellbeing matters in the leisure experience surrounding dog walking. Drawing upon an ethnographic study of outdoor recreation (including with dogs) in the Cairngorms National Park in Scotland which took place between 2008–2016 using mainly mobile and video methods, the chapter explores how dogs' needs and desires come to be "known" and experienced by their guardians in relation to dog walking (and indeed running, biking, skiing and swimming), and how this matters for dog walking practices, as well as how this intersects with human wellbeing. The findings prompt broader questions of whether dogs have leisure rights, and, moreover, if they do what form these should take (e.g. to what kind of outings ought dogs be entitled?), and the possible implications for multispecies wellbeing if canine wellbeing was taken more seriously in (more-than-) human leisure, management and health promotion.

What a dog wants from a dog walk, how we 'know', and why it matters

The wellbeing dogs are thought to get from a walk has been identified as a factor shaping the motivation for, incidence and duration of, dog walking (e.g. Oka and Shibata 2012; Richards et al. 2013; Westgarth et al. 2014). Furthermore, the intervention studies of Rhodes et al. (2012) suggest that targeting dog rather than human needs from dog walking may be a good approach to health promotion. However, more needs to be known about the particular aspects of canine health that are most persuasive and effective in this regard (Westgarth et al. 2014)

Many researchers frame a guardian's concern for canine wellbeing through dog walking as a sense of duty, obligation or responsibility, often coupled with perceived exercise needs (e.g. Brown and Rhodes 2006; Oka and Shibata 2012). Some identify this concern as a function of attachment and social interaction (Westgarth, Christley and Christian 2014; Lim and Rhodes 2016) where the stronger the dog-human relationship the more motivating the sense of obligation is to walk the dog more often and for longer. Others have expanded notions of guardian wellbeing concern even further to conceive of dog walking as a practice of care (Degeling and Rock 2012; Degeling et al. 2016; Fletcher and Platt 2016). Here more conceptual space is made for the dog walk as wanted, needed and co-performed by *both* dog and human; not something that is simply done *by* the human *for* the dog.

Yet, beyond this, there is still relatively little understanding of the relationships interlinking the perceived canine wellbeing associated with dog walks – whether anticipated or interpreted – to actual dog walking practices and their co-generation of human wellbeing, including the many possible factors, processes, nuances and circumstances of importance. We still need deeper knowledge of from what exactly it is about dog walks that guardians think or feel their dog will gain wellbeing, how this is negotiated in relation to the experience they themselves desire, and how that shapes their dog walking practices. In particular we need to know more about the nature and distribution of agency guardians ascribed to particular environments, features of environments, objects and technologies, as well as the guardians themselves and other humans, in making the dog walk conducive to canine wellbeing, and how this influences the spatialities, duration, experience and interactivity of the dog walk. This would help build a more relational understanding of the "many dynamic aspects of the networks of care that surround a dog" that Degeling and Rock (2012, 405) assert are central to making sense of dog walking practices and how they produce health.

Post-humanist theory would conceive of the dog walk as inextricably embedded within continually becoming, multiplicitous, human-nonhuman relations of articulation and response. For example, Haraway (2003) emphasises human and canine co-agency as she describes in depth the process of person and dog 'training-together', in which both partners increasingly attune to and care about how they articulate to, and respond to, each other through repeated practices of attuning and becoming significant to one another. Similarly, Despret (2004) conceives of animal and human as partners actively making and transforming each other through their mutual availability and affect.

Such more-than-human relating can also involve broader ecologies and highlight the agency of the environment in activating dog wellbeing. Brown (2015), for example, found that some dog walkers purposely sought 'wild' landscapes through which to let their dog 'run wild' as they felt a 'wild' or 'wolf-like' dimension of their dog needed to be fulfilled, or that they had to walk somewhere 'interesting' to fully realise the 'dogness' of the dog (see also Fletcher and Platt 2016). Jenkinson (2017) identifies one of the key "Specifications for Dog Walking Friendly Sites" as "[b]ushes, trees, long grass and smells of wildlife to provide stimulation for [the] dog" (1) and the desirability of activity trails for dogs, dog training areas, and adequate areas for dogs to run off-leash. Jenkinson also stated that

> [p]eople who took their dogs to urban woodlands and other green spaces described how much their dogs enjoyed exercising off-lead, running freely,

stimulated by a natural environment. Seeing their dogs enjoy themselves in this way gave the owners a great sense of wellbeing and enjoyment for the owners.

(3)

Thus, there are questions of how concerns of canine stimulation interweave with a guardian's priorities for gaining their own restorative effects from the dog walk, whether it be physical exertion, being in nature, social interaction with other humans, sense of community or interaction with the dog (Cutt et al. 2007). Ultimately, if human wellbeing from dog walking, and indeed canine wellbeing from dog walking, is contingent upon perceptions of the latter, as studies suggest, then we need to investigate further how such more-than-human relations are co-performed and their ethical implications.

Methodology

The chapter is based on an ethnographic study of outdoor access and recreation conducted in the Cairngorms National Park from 2006 to 2016, employing a range of qualitative methods, including interviews, videos and observation. Dog walking practices were explored mainly through "walk along" interview techniques and minicam video-recorded outings with 30 individual dog walkers, as well as 14 land, conservation and recreation managers (see Brown and Banks 2014, for a more detailed elaboration of the method). Dog walkers participating in the study encompassed both residents and visitors to the Park, but the focus in this chapter is on residents. The visual and discursive material was subject to thematic and performative analysis, and was especially attentive to the relationship between the bodily practices and experiences of people and dogs, and the discursive practices surrounding them.

Employing video allowed human–nonhuman engagements (including their more fleeting, non-verbal and taken-for-granted dimensions, see Lorimer 2010; Laurier, Maze and Lundin 2006) to be made visible, as well as how they unfolded in relation to specific ecologies and materialities. Such interactions were then made available for contextualisation and the development of further layers of meaning-making in post-outing interviews where the footage was used as a prompt to discussion. It was then possible to examine how notions of canine and human wellbeing became interwoven with the agencies of environments, objects, humans and animals to work materially and semiotically to enable and sustain particular practices of dog walking.

How perceptions of a dog's needs and desires influence dog walking practices

It was found that the needs and desires of dogs – as articulated and perceived by their significant human others, and always negotiated in relation to the latter's human needs and desires – played a key role in motivating dog walking practices and shaping how they unfolded in terms of: the nature and degree of handler-dog interaction; the type of environments sought; the socialities sought in terms of proximity to or interaction with other dogs and people and; how a leash or other objects (e.g. toys or a muzzle) were enrolled. Each will be discussed in turn.

The agency of the dog

Virtually all human participants in the study said or implied that they controlled and dictated the terms of the dog walk. For example, Penny[1] emphasised that "we're the ones that take them for the walk and tell them where they're going to go". Laura went further to suggest that one of her dogs had no particular preferences, "You don't care Bailey do you". Yet each human-dog partnership also indicated a plethora of ways in which the dog, by actively expressing its requirements and predilections, shaped both the instigation of the dog walk, and how, where, when and with whom the walk unfolded. In numerous ways dogs showed their guardians not only that "they *need* walking" (Megan) but also the *kind* of walking they need (e.g. "you get used to your own dog and what your own dog likes and doesn't like sort of thing" (Penny)).

Haraway (2003) notes that dogs have preferences, many of which will be expressed through their behaviour and body language, but which are not necessarily 'heard' or responded to by their 'significant other' humans. Crucially, in this study, the characteristics of the dog walk depended on how humans understood and responded to these articulations of the dog. Degeling and Rock (2012) found that guardians tried to tailor their walks to their assessment of dogs' interests, preferences and needs, but did not expand on how participants thought they 'knew' their dog's needs and preferences. Thus, the dog's 'voice' was rather silent, despite their alignment with post-humanist thought.

This study found that dogs were felt by their guardians to 'speak' in myriad ways central to the dog walk, before, travelling to, during and after the outing. Through their bodily movements, gestures, facial expressions, sounds, tactility, enrolment of objects in particular ways (e.g. toys, leads, sticks), leaving of traces (e.g. poo, door scratches, chewed objects) and the sheer intensity or reiteration of these activities (or indeed through their absence), dogs invited their humans to sense and respond to the articulations of their dog walking desires, and in influential ways. Effective ways of dogs getting their human out of the house included waiting at the door, sustained eye contact, making 'big eyes', licking, putting their head in the human's lap, following, jumping up, barking. For some humans there was a promise of fun and a deep joy in witnessing the dog's joyful anticipation. For Megan the enthusiasm is infectious, "I like looking at the dog, I like watching him bounce-bounce about, be all waggy and stuff".

During outings dogs often seemed to make humans take notice by using movement and body language to express what they like to sniff, look at, immerse themselves in, follow and chase, and by seeking out particular activities. For example, Olivia notices that her dog becomes particularly absorbed in the scents close to the car park and responds to the dog's reluctance to be rushed through this part of the walk, "[as dog sniffs fervently] I think the entrance of the woods is the *most* exciting spot for dogs. Checking in and checking out!". The sought activities included: swimming and paddling (in a pond, river or puddles):

"the water always makes him hyper!" (Cara)
"Come on Rosie! *Every* puddle!" (Patrick)

finding, digging up, carrying items such as sticks and even stones:

"Usually it's like, 'mum there's a huge stone here!' We can just see this like proud look on his face and a kind of wag wag wag wag! 'It's here! It's here! It's so big it can't even fit in my mouth!'"

(Megan)

rolling (on particular textures, such as heather, in particular smells, especially wildlife scat, livestock poo or fish guttings):

"he goes a wee bit crazy for deer scat . . . and then he's [big smile]"

(Lindsey)

which is an example of dog happiness with which Lindsey is less happy, and will change her route to avoid whilst there is a particularly bad favourite 'smelly' spot; and, chasing. Dogs often show that they love to chase other creatures but different guardians took different tacks regarding how chasing might affect canine wellbeing. Some turned a blind eye to, or actively facilitated, their dog having a little chase. Penny assured me Molly would never catch anything and "the fun is in the chase . . . it's a strong instinct", and Fiona similarly felt the dogs enjoyed a good rabbit chase, conveyed with a glee echoing the perceived canine glee and the disclaimer that "they [rabbits] are just vermin anyway". However, others (such as Megan, Lindsey) worked hard to anticipate and intervene before any chasing desire was activated, worried about the dog's wellbeing in the more fundamental sense of not being run over by a car or shot by a farmer.

Dogs could be skilled in conveying the practices for which they had most passion and endurance. Cara translated what her dog was trying to tell me about his sustained appetite for retrieving sticks from the river through his pricked ear, stare and one-leg-up poise, "That's a 'please more throw', that . . . he can do it for ages". Conversely, dogs sometimes indicated when they wanted the walk to slow or stop. Patrick noted his ageing dog increasingly wanted the walk to be over as he now tended to speed up in a homeward direction. Cara's dog had a joint condition to which she was particularly alive and often changed her route accordingly: "Yeah there you go you squeaked! [with pain] . . . Come on then you let's keep you on the flat". Dogs also exerted agency in route choice directly at times. When I asked Penny if she usually walks a planned route, she replied "No I improvise as I go along" and explained how the dog sometimes decides which track to take at a junction. More than anything dogs were thought to signal adequate dog walking by being 'settled', 'mellow', 'tired' or 'sleepy' afterwards: "I always try and take her out first thing, that's one of the things we've always done and it just settles her down for the day" (Penny).

However, such dog articulations were responded to variously depending on the human in question, with wellbeing implications for both partners.

Human agency

For some of the human participants, an enjoyable walk was contingent upon having a minimum degree of influence or 'control' over the dog. Some felt they got a sufficient sense of control from using a lead (e.g. Andrew, Laura, Patrick, Hannah, Jacob). Others wanted more. For them, an enjoyable walk was an interactive walk, with dog and human actively enjoying each other, and building and affirming a relationship with one another (e.g. Megan, Penny, Lindsey). In contrast, others still saw the human's role as little more than taking the dog to a sufficiently interesting environment and/or facilitating its physical exercise through their physical proximity and pace-making (e.g. Cara, Kirsty, Greg). One reason for this disparity could be that the more interactive approach echoes what Haraway (2003) calls 'training-together', which takes huge amounts of time and effort; an ongoing investment in weaving in with the dog continuous layers of human attending – tendering invitation and responding – before and during each dog walk for months and years.

Some (most notably Lindsey and Megan) relished the opportunity dog walking presented for such dog-human relationship-building and emphasised how much it added to the wellbeing and satisfaction they got from walking with dogs: "I totally enjoy him enjoying it [the interaction]". Lindsey feels strongly that Buddy has a mode of enjoyment beyond free play:

> I think he *enjoys* it as well, he likes the *challenge* and if we can um . . . take him out, you can see him sort of *learning*, and he's like *what's next, what's next?* Right okay we're *doing something* rather than . . . I think when he's out walking and he's like on you go, out and free walking and he's just like dah-de-dah-de-dah, follow my nose, what's that over there? And then as soon as you give him a command he's like oh right okay we're going to do something here. So it's nice just to switch him back on and keep him alert and attentive. And it might be a ball gets thrown or I might have already thrown a ball, told him to wait . . . it's just he uses . . . it gets his brain working really. It's nice to have a wee bit of a play both [of us].

Buddy's continued rapt engagement is taken as a sign that Lindsey is not the only one experiencing a kind of joy at two-way mutual attending. She is aligned here with Hearne (cited in Haraway 2003, 52) for whom the happiness of companion animals is "the capacity for satisfaction that comes from striving, from work, from fulfilment of possibility . . . bringing out what is within". This frames wellbeing in terms of satisfaction-through-achievement more than happiness.

There were also echoes of Haraway's (2003) discussion of how dogs and humans come to be important to, and care about, one another through the power of their mutual affect. Megan saw a core part of her role in dog walking to be more interesting and 'attractive' than all the various distractions that could threaten the coherence of their more-than-human 'conversation' and the related safety and joy that came from it. She explained that once, when an out-of-control dog (Bruno) was trying to tempt Rocky away by teasing him with a ball, "I picked up a stick, I had to be more exciting than Bruno with a ball with this stick, you know". Being deserving of the dog's attention was something humans talked of gaining through 'hard work' and a 'learning curve', involving games, drills and rewards. Lindsey described how Buddy came to increasingly care where she was: "we played a lot of hide 'n' seek as well so . . . he didn't want to go too far away because he never knew where we were going to be". For Lindsey and Buddy it was clear that dog freedom and wellbeing hinged upon effective training-together, and that 'work' with dogs was too rewarding to be the sole domain of 'working dogs', challenging notions of dog-based leisure as necessarily involving certain kinds of freedom. These humans felt that their playing with boundaries gave a mutual trust and security that allowed dogs and humans enjoy more freedoms when out walking together.

Alternately, other guardians did not relish the relationship-building elements of dog walking. Megan saw such guardians as having more of a human-oriented agenda, prioritising their own physical or mental health, rather than the experience of the dog:

> say you've had a tough day and you're going out and you need to switch off . . . because if you're going to stomp out in the forest, right I'm going out for a walk, oh I'll take the dog because I'm going out because I need to go out. I need to go out because I need to focus on getting my head back to where it needs to be in order to come back in and carry on with whatever I was dealing with. And then you know some people are just like dragging the dog out with them because that's what they do and so they're not going to be thinking about um . . . concentrating on what's going to be happening with the dog you know, the dog is secondary to the person's purpose of being out and about.
> (Megan)

Going out with some participants backed up the idea that some people were more into making the dog 'fit in' to their own outdoor ambitions (e.g. when they described the list of places they wanted to see, exercise they needed to take to get/ stay fit and friends they needed to catch up with almost to the exclusion of any dog-based outing requirements) or were sometimes just ticking the box of 'taking the dog out'. Interestingly too, the material suggested that guardians foregrounding their own health needs in terms of physical fitness tended also to frame their dog's needs as primarily physical, rather than mental or social. This begs the question of dog walking as an act of care for whom, and in which ways?

Agency of the environment

It was clear that guardians sought particular kinds of environments and routes to enhance the wellbeing gained from the dog walk, with a far more sophisticated geography than merely seeking somewhere 'off-lead', and it was very difficult to disentangle human and canine wellbeing. Specific places were often described as particularly interesting to the dog, in terms of its general character (e.g. rugged, natural or wild, somewhere to 'get a good run') and/or specific features (e.g. water, good smells, vegetation, things to chase, secure fencing). But if the human did not want the dog to engage with interesting features, the fact both were familiar with a particular route and its canine 'crux points' meant the human could anticipate circumstances that could rupture the coherence of their relationship (see also Brown and Dilley 2012) and keep the outing 'lower stress' (David). Nevertheless, virtually all participants wanted some variety and did a range of 'favourite' routes within the week.

Some environments were thus felt more conducive to human-dog play or coherence. For example, there were participants who preferred the moorland to the forest, or the birchwood to the pinewood, in each case because of the better sightlines and finding greater security, and therefore relaxation in being able to "see them [the dogs] most of the time" (Hannah), "know when she might try to run away" (Penny), and therefore be able to anticipate unwanted encounters with wildlife or other people and dogs, "can't just attack my dog by surprise" (Julie). For others, such as Laura, taking away these stimulations would make it 'more boring' too. Like others, she felt the woods were most exciting for dogs, though wavered in her explanation between facets of human and canine wellbeing:

> I could stick to the moor and I wouldn't necessarily need to come into the woods at all but it's not such a great walk for them . . . I suppose another option for me but we like coming into the woods. We like . . . it's a walk and it's a longer walk, and so from a health perspective I suppose I know it's better for me to do an hour and a half walking in the woods in the morning than do three-quarters of an hour over the moor . . . [but] I suppose they get more smells in the wood than they would do so they get a change of smell . . . there is something nice about walking through the woods and there is always the prospect of seeing something [wildlife], that you certainly aren't going to see on the moor because the moor is so open . . . it'll see you before you're anywhere . . . near it.

Here the human feels the need for exercise and the chance of seeing some wildlife and is grappling with how this supports or diverges from possible dog-needs. Laura goes on to add that she wants to go somewhere more secluded for 'thinking time' (see next section). In this and other instances, the environment (mainly the pinewoods) was mobilised as a relative release from dog-human interaction. Here the dog could be easily exercised and stimulated as they "find their own entertainment" (Dave) – commonly taking the form of following scents and tracking wildlife (mainly rabbits and squirrels) – which freed up the human to be able to "unwind and relax" (Sal) and be "busy with my own thoughts" (Alec).

Agency of socialities of other dogs and humans

Dog walking practices in the study were clearly driven by the social needs of both dog and guardian. Penny exemplified well what Antonacopoulos, Duvall and Pychyl (2014) found about dog walking serving the human desire to make and meet up regularly with friends – "it's good to meet people now I'm not working" – and what Degeling and Rock (2012) found about adapting the walk purposely to the socialisation needs of the dog: "we take her to things, and walk her around places where there are other dogs". Though I would go further here to suggest that one was inextricably linked to the other. In Penny's case, her dog had been rescued and had issues with aggression towards other dogs. Penny's response was to purposely orchestrate walks to seek out other dog walkers and work on training-together to make their encounter less fraught, sometimes enrolling the help of particular objects, notably ball, lead and muzzle: "I had to put a bit of work in certainly but uh . . . you know she's very good now, if she's a see dog she'll sit down which is great because that means I can catch hold of her and put her on the lead". She (Penny) and a good friend started working on their dog walking together as "a sort of social activity". But why so much effort? From our sessions together it became clear that interaction with other humans was a crucial facet of dog walking for Penny and in many ways she could not 'afford' (in terms of her human social wellbeing needs) a dog who could not mingle with others, especially as she was now retired, so the priority was to "socialise *with* her [the dog]".

Penny's behaviour contrasted markedly with the majority of other participants in a similar position with 'difficult' dogs who took the opposite tactic of avoidance, and said they preferred to meet no-one. Ascribing reasons for such avoidance to enhancing wellbeing in the human versus the dog was rarely clear-cut. Some participants articulated clearly how their mental health needs involved some "alone time" (Sal), usually in the further, denser part of the woodland. Patrick too was emphatic that "I walk the dogs and don't want to meet people, . . . I just get some head space really". Like Patrick, Laura has a full-time job and hectic routine, and says the principal factor dictating her dog walking route is "just purely *not* to meet people, and I suppose it's a feel good thing because I like being out on a walk, it's my thinking time". It turns out that her young dog is "not so good with other people and dogs" so it is "much more relaxing" to go somewhere "you don't have to worry about others" with "interesting tracks and smells" where the dogs "leave you alone" and "get a good run". Here the quality of the dog walking becomes more reliant on the agency of the environment to provide social seclusion for humans and stimulation and exercise for dogs.

Agency of the leash

As in previous studies, the pursuit of off-leash dog walking opportunities was central to most guardians' daily or weekly outing strategy. Most participants felt that their dog's wellbeing hinged on the experience of 'freedom' and having sufficient opportunity to 'run free' or "run with the pack" (Lindsey). Penny emphasised that "they [dogs] need to run. They need the exercise", which was always associated with being off-leash, as illustrated by Laura who said "I don't feel that the dogs are getting a proper walk if they're on a lead". However, there were different and sometimes complex ways of (dis)enrolling a leash in dog walking in order to generate or maintain human and canine wellbeing. For some humans, they needed some off-leash time to experience freedom at least as much as their dog did: "if he's on the lead I have to concentrate all the time and we're getting all tangled in the trees. And sometimes I need to get a good run in myself" (Rob) and "especially after work I just need to clear my head, decompress" (Alice).

But for others, they could not really switch off *unless* their dog was on a lead, indicating that they, like Olivia, "like to be in control". Patrick keeps his dog on a long lead all the time unless on a beach or other 'safe' area:

> it just reduces any stress on me to be honest and I think also I think it would probably reduce the stress on the dogs because if they got themselves into a situation they'd either injure themselves or injure something else and then . . . the repercussions from that could be quite bad. . . . It's about controlling the things you can control and getting rid of the things you can't control.

His partner added, "I feel bad for them, it would be nice to see them run around but they . . . they are either badly trained or uncontrollable! [Laughter]". Likewise, Andrew feels his dogs get most freedom on a long lead as they can go a little bit off the path without him having to worry: "If they were off the lead in here then I would be wondering where they were. . . . They would tear off". He is also aware that his concentration is often on other human concerns: "[I'm usually] plotting . . . everyone has issues in their life somewhere. . . . You find yourself rehearsing your arguments . . . you do a lot of thinking".

It is interesting how both camps enrol similar narratives of human stress yet different prevailing narratives of dog wellbeing – as maximised by being 'free' versus being kept out of harm's way – which produced divergent dog walking practices. Often those finding on-leash most relaxing had previously had a bad experience off-leash, in some cases fatal. Another factor affecting both on/off-leash practices was the co-agency of dog-lead-human in terms of whether and how much the dog 'pulled', which in turn depended on training-together. Megan was unusual in being relaxed whether her dog was on or off lead, since he did not pull and his recall was 'solid' Penny conversely explained how pulling affected her route choice: "we always try to make it possible that she goes off [leash] fairly quickly yeah, yeah. So . . . she's not that bad on the lead, she doesn't pull that much, but you do get dogs that do". The riverside route being promoted to take people away from the sensitive wildlife zone was therefore less pleasant for Penny because of the agency of her dog pulling: "it means that you've got to start off walking up the road and I personally like her to run when she first goes out".

Towards multispecies wellbeing: whose agency is it anyway?

This study illustrates the importance of considering not only what companion animals get out of human-animal leisure practices, but also how their significant other humans come to 'know' this, and how such knowledges become negotiated with the pursuit of human wellbeing needs, desires and priorities to shape those leisure practices. Only by considering dog walking as an activity in which notions and experiences of human and canine wellbeing are inextricably linked can we have the deeper understanding of the motivations for dog walking called for by Westgarth and colleagues (2015). Given that humans and dogs have coexisted and co-evolved with each other for thousands of years, as Haraway (2003) underlines, it perhaps should come as no surprise that their ability to thrive is so intertwined with each other.

The findings illustrate some important contingencies regarding how the wellbeing of dog and human are co-generated through dog walking, particularly about how the burden of agency in producing wellbeing can be distributed between humans, dogs, environment and technology (e.g. a leash), and how this varies from one partnership to another. Much depends on how the dog is able to express its preferences in relation to dog walking and, moreover, how their human 'hears' and is affected by these articulations, especially when at the same time they are being affected by their own human wellbeing needs and desires. Sometimes it was challenging to discern whether a dog's wellbeing needs were being 'heard' or whether they were reframed human wellbeing desires (e.g. no dog aims to have 'exercise' per se). In other cases it was clearer that decisions had been taken over how much to enrol the agency of human versus environment, or human versus leash, in enhancing the dog's wellbeing. Notions of a dog's 'freedom' or 'protection' (through 'control') were mobilised differently (sometimes, but not always at odds with each other, depending on the human's commitment to training-together with the dog and the nature and intensity of their own wellbeing needs) and thus led to differences in where and how dog walking was done. Building on Degeling and Rock (2012), future work could fruitfully explore the management implications stemming from the range of ways in which dog walking can be *co*-constituted as a practice of care.

Thinking about how to take these insights forward, we must be aware that, at present, most of the debate surrounding dog walking and wellbeing is framed almost wholly in terms of what dogs (and their need for walks) can do for humans, reflecting the humanist orientation of health promotion noted by Rock and Degeling (2013). Certainly the findings presented in this chapter allow us to argue for a recentring of companion animal agency in understanding leisure experiences and management. But do we also need to use these insights to help think through the kind of dog walking experiences to which a dog may be entitled (e.g. which places, with whom, which kinds of human, canine and ecological interactions)? If we are taking animal agency seriously – as individuals as well as species – then being prescriptive may be neither possible nor desirable. As Haraway (2003) states, "[t]his kind of happiness is about yearning for excellence and having the chance to reach it in terms recognisable to concrete beings, not to categorical abstractions. . . . The specificity of their happiness matters" (Haraway 2003, 52).

A question underpinning this book is whether domestic species such as dogs have leisure rights? I would qualify this question further by asking whether domestic species have the right to *particular ways of doing* leisure, perhaps to the enrolment of particular more-than-human agencies? In one sense this invokes the question raised by Carr (2014) of: does a dog have a right to unstructured, free play? But we could equally ask does a dog have a right to the "disciplined spontaneity" (Haraway 2003, 62) of play generated through training-together? If we subscribe to the view that leisure has the notion of freedom at its heart, it is interesting to note that the dog-human partnerships that seemed to enjoy the most freedom and restoration from their dog walking were also those that had *worked* the hardest at it, thus troubling any easy work-leisure binary. Indeed, I would argue that we need to take care when asserting that domestic animals need *leisure* as if in opposition to *work*, since any experience they have of freedom may come from something more like work, more like training, intra-action and human and animal learning to attend better to one another.

We could give more serious consideration to dog walking as one of many forms of cross-species acts of 'getting along together' discussed by Haraway. For Haraway (2003), following Hearne, the rights of dogs cannot be served by any simple extension of human rights; "the origin of rights is in committed relationship, not in separate and pre-existing category identities. Therefore, in training, dogs obtain 'rights' in specific humans. In relationship, dogs and humans construct 'rights' in each other, such as the right to demand respect, attention and response" (53–54). In this she emphasises how dogs obtain from their human something akin to an expectation and entitlement to particular forms of human attention and response as part of a reciprocal exchange of their own attention and response to the human. More than a bestowal of rights upon dogs to standardise adequate dog walking, dogs need us to consider more deeply the role of a human on a dog walk, and people might do better in constructing rights together with dogs by building a more genuinely reciprocal communication. If "(d)ogs' survival . . . depends on their reading humans well" (Haraway 2003, 50) then mutual wellbeing from dog walking could involve humans taking a greater burden of agency insofar as learning to better 'hear' and respond to what dogs are telling us.

Note

1 All dog and human names have been changed to preserve anonymity.

References

Antonacopoulos, Nikolina, M. Duvall, and Timothy A. Pychyl. 2014. "An Examination of the Possible Benefits for Well-Being Arising from the Social Interactions That Occur While Dog Walking." *Society & Animals* 22(5): 459–480.

Boisvert, Jennifer A., and W. Andrew Harrell. 2014. "Dog Walking: A Leisurely Solution to Pediatric and Adult Obesity?" *World Leisure Journal* 56(2): 168–171.

British Veterinary Association. 2017. "Dog health and welfare." Accessed April 11, 2017. www.bva.co.uk/News-campaigns-and-policy/Policy/Companion-animals/Dog-health-and-welfare.

Brown, Katrina M. 2015. "The Role of Landscape in Regulating (Ir)Responsible Conduct: Moral Geographies of the 'Proper Control' of Dogs." *Landscape Research* 40(1): 39–56.

Brown, Katrina M., and Esther Banks. 2014. "Close Encounters: Using Mobile Video Ethnography to Understand Human-Animal Relations." In *Video Methods: Social Science Research in Motion*, edited by Charlotte Bates, 95–120. London: Routledge.

Brown, K.M., and R. Dilley. 2012. "Ways of Knowing for 'Response-Ability' in More-Than-Human Encounters: The Role of Anticipatory Knowledges in Outdoor Access with Dogs." *Area* 44(1): 37–45.

Brown, Shane G., and Ryan E. Rhodes. 2006. "Relationships Among Dog Ownership and Leisure-Time Walking in Western Canadian Adults." *American Journal of Preventive Medicine* 30(2): 131–136.

Carr, N. 2014. *Dogs in the Leisure Experience*. Oxfordshire: CABI.

Christian, Hayley E., Carri Westgarth, Adrian Bauman, Elizabeth A. Richards, Ryan E. Rhodes, Kelly R. Evenson, Joni A. Mayer, and Roland J. Thorpe Jr. 2013. "Dog Ownership and Physical Activity: A Review of the Evidence." *Journal of Physical Activity and Health* 10(5): 750–759.

Clark Cline, Krista Marie. 2010. "Psychological Effects of Dog Ownership: Role Strain, Role Enhancement, and Depression." *The Journal of Social Psychology* 150(2): 117–131.

Cutt, Hayley, Billie Giles-Corti, Matthew Knuiman, and Valerie Burke. 2007. "Dog Ownership, Health and Physical Activity: A Critical Review of the Literature." *Health & Place* 13(1): 261–272.

Cutt, Hayley E., Billie Giles-Corti, Lisa J. Wood, Matthew W. Knuiman, and Valerie Burke. 2008. "Barriers and Motivators for Owners Walking Their Dog: Results from Qualitative Research." *Health Promotion Journal of Australia: Official Journal of Australian Association of Health Promotion Professionals* 19(2s): 118.

Degeling, Chris, and Melanie Rock. 2012. "'It Was Not Just a Walking Experience': Reflections on the Role of Care in Dog-Walking." *Health Promotion International* 28(30): 397–406.

Degeling, Chris, Melanie Rock, Wendy Rogers, and Therese Riley. 2016. "Habitus and Responsible Dog-Ownership: Reconsidering the Health Promotion Implications of 'Dog-Shaped' Holes in People's Lives." *Critical Public Health* 26(2): 191–206.

Despret, Vinciane. 2004. "The Body We Care for: Figures of Anthropo-Zoo-Genesis." *Body & Society* 10(2–3): 111–134.

Fletcher, Thomas, and Louise Platt. 2016. "(Just) a Walk With the Dog? Animal Geographies and Negotiating Walking Spaces." *Social & Cultural Geography* published online: http://dx.doi.org/10.1080/14649365.2016.1274047 1–19.

Haraway, Donna Jeanne. 2003. *The Companion Species Manifesto: Dogs, People, and Significant Otherness*. 1. Chicago: Prickly Paradigm Press.

Jenkinson, Steven. 2017. "Getting Dog Owners. (and Their Dogs) More Active in Woodlands: Let's Go Walkies!" Dog Walking Insight Research Report, Paths for All, Forestry Commission Scotland and The Kennel Club. Accessed May 4, 2017. www.pathsforall.org.uk/component/option,com_docman/Itemid,69/gid,2135/task,doc_details/.

Johnson, Rebecca A., Alan M. Beck, and Sandra McCune. 2011. *The Health Benefits of Dog Walking for Pets and People: Evidence and Case Studies*. West Lafayette, IN: Purdue University Press.

Laurier, Eric, Ramia Maze, and Johan Lundin. 2006. "Putting the Dog Back in the Park: Animal and Human Mind-in-Action." *Mind, Culture, and Activity* 13(1): 2–24.

Lim, Clarise, and Ryan E. Rhodes. 2016. "Sizing Up Physical Activity: The Relationships Between Dog Characteristics, Dog Owners' Motivations, and Dog Walking." *Psychology of Sport and Exercise* 24: 65–71.

Lorimer, Jamie. 2010. "Moving Image Methodologies for More-Than-Human Geographies." *Cultural Geographies* 17(2): 237–258.

Oka, Koichiro, and Ai Shibata. 2012. "Factors Associated with the Stages of Change for Dog Walking Among Japanese Dog Owners." *Journal of Physical Activity and Health* 10(1): 124–133.

Rhodes, Ryan E., Holly Murray, Viviene A. Temple, Holly Tuokko, and Joan Wharf Higgins. 2012. "Pilot Study of a Dog Walking Randomized Intervention: Effects of a Focus on Canine Exercise." *Preventive Medicine* 54(5): 309–312.

Richards, Elizabeth A., Meghan H. McDonough, Nancy E. Edwards, Roseann M. Lyle, and Philip J. Troped. 2013. "Psychosocial and Environmental Factors Associated with Dog-Walking." *International Journal of Health Promotion and Education* 51(4): 198–211.

Rock, Melanie, and Chris Degeling. 2013. "Public Health Ethics and a Status for Pets as Person-Things." *Journal of Bioethical Inquiry* 10(4): 485–495.

Rock, Melanie J., Chris Degeling, and Gwendolyn Blue. 2014. "Toward Stronger Theory in Critical Public Health: Insights from Debates Surrounding Posthumanism." *Critical Public Health* 24(3): 337–348.

SNH. 2014. "Scotland's People and Nature Survey 2013/14 Special Interest Report No.7: Visits To The Outdoors With Dogs, Scottish Natural Heritage." Accessed April 4, 2017. www.snh.gov.uk/docs/A1522938.pdf.

Westgarth, Carri, Hayley E. Christian, and Robert M. Christley. 2015. "Factors Associated with Daily Walking of Dogs." *BMC Veterinary Research* 11(1): 116.

Westgarth, Carri, Robert M. Christley, and Hayley E. Christian. 2014. "How Might We Increase Physical Activity Through Dog Walking? A Comprehensive Review of Dog Walking Correlates." *International Journal of Behavioral Nutrition and Physical Activity* 11(1): 83.

8 Domesticated dogs and 'doings' during the holidays

*Bodil Stilling Blichfeldt and
Katarína Leci Sakáčová*

Introduction

Sanders and Hirschman (1996) point to companion animals being friends and family members, Voith (1986) reported that 99 percent of pet owners define pets as family members and 80 percent of Hirschman's (1994) interviewees spontaneously described their pets as a member of the family. Defining dogs as fully fledged family members has vast implications for how families 'do' leisure and particularly holidays as the holiday environment and context changes families' habits, routines and practices. Although families may choose to leave the dog behind during the holidays, dogs sometimes go on holiday together with the rest of the family. There is still, though, a research gap when it comes to dogs as fully fledged family members taking active part in the family holiday.

Using caravanning as an example, this chapter discusses how some families-including-dogs 'do' holidays and how considerations about dogs as sentient beings with leisure needs (that are not necessarily identical to those of other family members) effects the 'doings' of these families during the holidays. Furthermore, the chapter points to how family 'doings' and practices when including dogs in a holiday context differ from including dogs in more mundane, everyday life leisure activities. Empirically, the chapter draws on observations and 210 qualitative interviews with families spending the holidays at Danish caravan sites. At Danish caravan sites, roughly one out of five travel groups bring along their dog(s) during these holidays. At caravan sites tourists and their dwelling units are physically very close to each other and families-without-dogs share space with families-with-dogs and therefore, the opinions of families-without-dogs are also included in the chapter. The chapter investigates how dogs are not only full-fledged members of many travel units, but also influence what activities families do (and do not) engage in while caravanning in Denmark. Accordingly, the chapter digs into family-holidays-including-dogs and what more there is to a 'dog-friendly' holiday than simply 'dog tolerant'.

Dogs as nonhuman family members

Cohen (2002, 261) argues that "the family is a cornerstone of human society and a resource for its members". Nonetheless, understanding what family 'is' is rather complex because society constantly changes, leading to new understandings and conceptualisations of families. For example, the traditional understanding of 'family' as nuclear families has been challenged and complemented by, amongst others, notions of binuclear families, extended families, rainbow families, single parent families and families as bricolage. Still, notions of family emphasise human family members. Contemporary definitions of family should, however, take nonhuman family members into account as "the household pet has worked its way up the family tree" (Hill, Gaines and Wilson 2008, 553). This is corroborated by Holbrook and Woodside (2008, 377), who argue that "our animal companions emerge as beloved friends and, indeed, as full-fledged members of the family" and by Hill, Gaines and Wilson's (2008, 561) argument that "permanent friendships and loving intimacy . . . give way to integration of beloved pets into their human families". Likewise, Cohen (2002, 632) elucidates that "at least for some urban dwellers, pets are firmly inside the family circle. Like human family members, pets provide comfort and companionship." In line with these arguments, this chapter is based on an understanding of family where both human and nonhuman family members are resources that bring each other permanent friendship, loving intimacy and companionship.

Twenty years ago, Hirschman pointed to pet ownership having received little academic attention although the human desire for companionship with other species is strong and manifests itself in the widespread practice of keeping companion animals. Hirschman (1994, 630) also pointed to dogs as particularly relevant animal companions and she concluded that consumers incorporate animals into their lives "in the role of *companions*, rather than possessions", hereby pointing to the problem of simply defining families with dogs as "dog owners". Holbrook (2008, 546) follows up on this issue and argues:

> Despite what misguided property laws might say, we do not own them [pets]. Rather than regarding them as possessions, we think of them as animal companions, with whom we share consumption experiences – walking, running, watching television, listening to music, talking, travelling, eating, sleeping – in ways that resemble those shared with other humans.

Ellson (2008, 565) continues this line of reasoning by arguing that "ownership implies dominion, mastery or title of the dog: companionship suggests a more convivial camaraderie or comradeship; relationship invokes possibilities of affinity, dependency, and possibly, complementary reciprocity". Furthermore, Kropp et al. (1992) found that values and lifestyles of pet owners differ from those of non-owners and Gillespie, Leffler and Lerner (1996) showed how raising a particular dog-breed fundamentally changes people's practices as well as interactions with other people in various situations. The difference between 'ownership' and 'companionship' is therefore more than simply a matter of semantics as it points to fundamental differences in how 'family' should be defined – the first pointing to dogs as objects with little bearing on family structures, the second to dogs as family members in their own right.

Although dogs may act as objects (e.g. ornaments, status symbols, avocation or equipment) to be 'owned', they also play many other roles in consumers' lives.

Holbrook et al. (2001) argue that the relationship between humans and companion animals is an experience that transcends the ordinary consumer domain of possessions. Hirschman's (1994, 628) study points to companionship as the key reason why people have dogs. She argues that people who grow up in households with pets view the 'people-plus-animals' family as normal and right and that they, later in life, will form families that include both human and nonhuman members. She further argues that "almost always . . ., the type of animal they wish to include is a dog or a cat – the most anthropomorphized of the animal species commonly kept as companions". In regard to this issue, two of Hirschman's (1994, 628) interviewees opinioned: "[pets] sort of complete the family picture in my mind. You have your spouse, your kids and your pets", and "we just have always had pets. I couldn't image a house without them". In the same vein, Holbrook and Woodside (2008) point to animal companions taking on different roles in the family (e.g. as surrogate children or grandchildren) and Dotson and Hyatt (2008, 465) go as far as to recommend that marketers "should reformulate the life-cycle conceptualization to include dogs in the definition of family". Sanders and Hirschman (1996) point to the same issues by arguing that companion animals "alternatively or at the same time, are anthropomorphized and defined as friends and family members" and that living together with "nonhuman others shape our emotional experiences and understandings of who we are". Accordingly, dogs are seen as beings in their own rights, with whom humans develop mutual understanding, experiences and relationships that define their lives together as they 'grow into' one another's lives through daily rituals and habits. Beck and Katcher (1983) reported that 70 percent of pet owners defined their animals as family members, Voith (1986) reported that 99 percent of owners did so, and 80 percent of Hirschman's (1994) interviewees spontaneously described their pets as a member of the family. The familial role of pets might be that of a sibling such as for younger people who have grown up with the pet; or a child or grandchild for childless couples as well as empty nesters (Savishinsky 1986). Savishinsky (1986) further points to families having animal companions in order to teach children to be responsible/nurturing and Hirschman (1994) to people who from childhood have been socialised to care for, for example, dogs, seeking out the same type of pet throughout their lives.

Domesticated dogs and holidays

That dogs may qualify as fully fledged family members has vast implications for not only family research, but also for family *tourism* research. As an example of how dogs influence family life, Hill, Gaines and Wilson (2008, 553) follow up on their statement "dogs are not our whole life, but they make our lives whole" by arguing that "from birthdays to holiday events to other celebrations, beloved pets fully engage in traditional activities and come to personify the essence of what makes these times truly extraordinary" (558). Hill, Gaines and Wilson (2008, 560) thus point to family-as-structure as well as everyday family life being grounded in "the many ways animal companions and their owners co-consume each other as well as the larger world around them". If dogs as nonhuman family members fully engage in family rituals and activities as well as personify truly extraordinary family times, does this mean that dogs go on holiday together with the rest of the family, or might families even go on holiday because of their beloved dogs? Are dogs fully fledged family members in everyday family life contexts only, but excluded from the family holidays?

Dotson and Hyatt (2008, 462) argue that whether dogs go on holiday with the family depends on how families define both themselves and their dog(s), as people who see themselves as 'dog people' will allow their dogs to play a more central role in their lives and that "dog-related consumer behavior goes far beyond the mere purchase of dog-related products". Subsequently they argue that the introduction of a dog into a household causes significant changes in lifestyle, which may also change holiday preferences and behaviours. But are dogs decisive for not only whether families go on holiday or stay at home, but also for the types of holidays families take? Dotson and Hyatt (2008, 458) argue that "with the increasingly mobile American lifestyle, dog owners have to deal with taking their pets along on trips and vacations or leaving them behind". Dorsey (2003) estimates that over one third of dog owners take their animal companions along on vacation. As pointed to by both of these references, families with dogs can choose between taking their dogs on holiday and leaving them behind. However, the decision whether to go holidaying with dogs may be rather complex. Carr and Cohen (2009, 301) found "that although the desire to take holidays with their pets may be high among dog owners in Australia, the actualization of this desire is comparatively low", because of "a lack of dog-friendly accommodation." Hence "dog owners have to compromise their holiday desires in order to take their pets on vacation with them" (Carr and Cohen 2009, 301). Such compromises might mean that families with dogs vacation somewhere more 'dog-friendly' instead of going holidaying without their dogs. At the same time, if they choose to go holidaying without their dogs, they need to consider where the dog should be whilst the human family members are away from home.

Mosteller (2008) found that human-pet relationships depend not only on more general issues such as emotional attachment, pet experience and traits or childhood socialisation, but also on practical issues such as housing and home spaces, indicating that dog-friendly indoor and outdoor spaces are important in order to develop and maintain human/nonhuman companionships. Leaving the dog behind during the holidays might ensure that it remains in a comfortable, anxiety-reducing, dog-friendly setting compared to taking it to new and potentially anxiety evoking and unfriendly places. Ellson (2008) points to the complexities of these decisions and lists the options available to dog owners as kenneling, house-sitting and leaving the dog with friends. On top of this comes the opportunity to take a dog-friendly holiday; bearing in mind and dealing with the fact that some resorts, hotels, holiday homes, hostels and camping/caravan sites do not accommodate dogs; and that travelling overseas with dogs can be very problematic. Ellson points to options being limited and adjustments having to be made and he ends up pointing to the solution chosen by him and his family, who, after some disappointing experiences in kennels, settled for using trusted house/dog sitters. Carr (2014) discusses boarding kennels, dog day-care centres and other elements of the 'professional pet-sitting industry' and how the changing nature of human-dog relations (from dogs as possessions to dogs as companions and family members) has led to traditional kennels being a less favourable solution than in the past. As preparation for our study, we used Facebook to ask dog owners what arrangements they make for their dogs during the holidays and home/dog-sitting, leaving the dog with trusted friends or taking the dog along on dog-friendly holidays were the preferred solutions (in that order).

Although many families choose to leave the dog behind during the holidays, dogs are the pet that most often accompanies families when travelling. Dotson, Hyatt and Clark (2010) point to an American survey that suggests that dogs account for 78 percent of the situations where people travel with pets. The increased visibility and mobility of families-with-pets has led marketers to develop a series of new products and services including not only dog-daycare centres and dog walking services, but also hotels and motels allowing pets and various pet travel products (Gardyn 2002). According to Sapsford (2005), Honda Motor Company even designed a concept car meant to cater to the needs of Japanese dog owners, along with a new line of 'Travel Dog' car accessories (including cargo liners, seat covers, dog beds, harnesses, bowls, feeders, ramps and steps). Between 20 and 25 percent of guests at Danish caravan sites bring their dogs along (oral conversation with the Danish association of Camping sites (Campingraadet) in December 2015) and between 30 and 40 percent of the tourists renting Danish holiday houses bring their dogs along on holiday (information provided directly by the holiday house owners' organisation in Denmark). Furthermore, dogs are not only part of many travel units, but also have a major impact on what activities these families do (and do not do) while holidaying in Denmark. Unfortunately, apart from Carr's seminal work, tourism researchers do not address this issue. Hirschman's (1994) research participants reported that dogs are taken on recreational excursions such as car rides and one of her interviewees, who boards dogs for owners during the holidays, notes that: "(e)ach of these animals is somebody's beloved pet. These are people who are in a total panic about leaving their dogs. They'll cry. They'll carry on. It's terrible". Holbrook (2008) argues that marketers should remind people that they are not really pet owners and that pets are not possessions; but that pets deserve to be treated as animal companions with needs, wants and rights comparable to those of other family members. Unfortunately, we do not know much about how the needs, wants and rights of dogs are dealt with by families who take the dog along on holiday and the purpose of this chapter is to contribute to the knowledge base on this issue.

Methodology

Caravanning has a long tradition in Denmark. With increased car ownership it developed as a popular type of vacationing and soon became the 'epitome of freedom' (Mikkelsen and Blichfeldt 2015). Danish caravan sites come in many forms; ranging from very primitive campgrounds to five-star 'resort-like' sites and whereas the term 'camping' relates to the more primitive sites, 'caravanning' is a more correct term for most Danish sites as they offer a wide range of activities and facilities for tourists than a campground would. The research this chapter presents was done at caravan sites with more activities and facilities; such as swimming pools, mini-golf, grocery stores, restaurants and entertainment for children. Most guests at Danish caravan sites are either families with young children or empty nesters and around 20 percent of visitors bring with them one or more dogs. Most families have one dog, but it is not unusual to see families with two dogs and a few families bring along as many as five, six or seven dogs (findings from our research corroborated by Campingraadet's statistics).

The paper draws on 210 qualitative interviews with 437 people spending their holidays at five different Danish caravan sites. Generally, guests were very willing to participate in interviews; probably due to the sociability and 'vacability' (i.e. the wish and ability to 'do nothing' during the holidays) that characterises caravanning (Blichfeldt and Mikkelsen 2013). Empty nester couples (163) and traditional nuclear families (177) with one to three younger children are highly over-represented in the study, and although some blended families participated in the study we met very few single parents and no rainbow families at the caravan sites. Around half of the interviewees (200) were domestic (Danish) tourists whereas the rest of the interviewees were from Germany (155), Norway (44), Holland (19), Sweden (12) and other nations (7). Most interviewees stay in caravans (236), tents (31) or mobile-homes (RVs, 79) but a few stay in rental cottages or bring with them camplets (a trailer product including tent, hard floors and a 'kitchen section' to be unfolded before use), camper vans (half a van, half a RV) etc. As we wanted to keep interviews informal, we did not ask explicitly for household income or occupational status and therefore, we only obtained such facts insofar as they naturally arose during interviews. That said, participants seemed to represent a broad sweep of income and social groups.

The average length of interview was around 30 minutes. Some interviews were very short (often when family members were on their way to 'do something' or when interviewees felt uncomfortable about being interviewed) whereas other interviews were well over an hour in length. Consequently, the quality of interviews varies from very short interviews where interviewees mostly offered very factual information, to in-depth conversations covering both this type of holidaying and contrasts to other types of holidays as well as everyday life. Out of the 210 interviews, the forthcoming analysis predominantly draws on around 40 interviews undertaken with families accompanied by dogs. However, other interviews (including some with families who were caravanning without their family dog, and families without dogs who sometimes felt strongly about dogs being part of the caravanning experience) are incorporated in the analysis where the opinions and experiences of these interviewees are relevant.

Findings: accommodating, making sacrifices and value adding – dogs on holidays

Dotson and Hyatt's (2008) survey of 749 dog owners showed that willingness to adapt (including choices of home and vehicle) was an important element of dog companionship. However, to the interviewees that bring along their dogs when caravanning, willingness to adapt also includes what kind of holidays these families take. In regard to this issue many interviewees pointed to not going to other countries, not staying in hotels and not taking a plane as being caused by their dog not being welcome, or it being too problematic to bring their dog along. Hence, many interviewees pointed to caravanning being 'better', 'more of a holiday' or 'a real holiday' for dogs. Or, as a woman in her fifties, travelling with her husband and two dogs, stated:

> Of course, I would rather stay in hotel. But as I said before: When you have a dog, you have to make sacrifices.

Making sacrifices in terms of taking a holiday that fits not only the needs and wants of human family members, but also nonhuman members was widespread across interviewees. Choosing a caravan site with 'room' and 'space' for dogs was as important to interviewees with dogs as, for example, choosing a caravan site with a swimming pool (for the children's sake) or a site close to the beach. This is in line with Carr and Cohen's (2009) finding that families with dogs have to compromise when going on a holiday. Furthermore, caravanning enables families to bring along their own 'housing' (caravan or mobile home) as well as material objects such as the dog's bed, favourite toys, bowls and feeders, hereby allowing them room for domesticity.

Getting out and going for a walk

Dotson and Hyatt's (2008) survey pointed to dog companionship positively influencing other family members' levels of activity and playfulness. Elsewhere, we have argued that caravanning is a rather 'lazy' type of holiday, pointing to 'vacability' (i.e. the wish and ability to 'vacare', 'be vacant' and 'do nothing') as something that characterises caravanning holidays (Blichfeldt and Mikkelsen 2013). A favourite physical activity mentioned by almost all interviewees was to go for a walk – whether it was going down to the beach, taking a stroll around the caravan site in the evening or nature walks lasting hours. But families with dogs generally 'get out more' than families without dogs. Especially in regard to walking, families with dogs differ from families without dogs as walking is often a more fundamental part of the holidays for families with dogs. As two guests (one being the mother in a nuclear family with small children and the other being an empty nester in her sixties) with dogs explained:

> You know what? The weather can never be too bad and the good thing is that we have to get out because of the dog.

> I really like caravanning and it's so nice that our little dog comes along, so that we can go for a walk.

As exemplified by these two interviewees, when caravanning with the family dog, the dog takes on what Hirschman (1994) defined as an intermediating role between nature and culture. Having a dog with them makes humans 'have to get out' and becomes a reason to "go for a walk". This intermediating role between nature and culture is institutionalised by families with dogs to such an extent that 'going/walking with the dog' is 'habitualised' (Berger and Luckmann 1966) and repeated so frequently that it is cast into a pattern that becomes a deeply rooted habit. Such institutionalisation and habitualisation were especially evident when families accounted for their daily habits, practices, routines and 'doings' during these holidays; as demonstrated by the following accounts offered by women in their thirties travelling with spouses, children and one dog each):

> We stay in bed longer than at home, we take longer time eating breakfast than at home, he [her husband] fetches bread rolls and somebody walks the dog. Then we decide what to do. Yesterday we went to the beach and sometimes we go to the harbor.

> Our daughter wakes up at seven or half past seven when my husband and son are still asleep. But when they get up, they walk with the dog and they bring back bread rolls and then we have breakfast. Then we play with the kids or something.

> We usually go down to the beach with the dogs very early in the morning.

Four of the five caravan sites are located close to the beach and for guests at these four caravan sites the beach was used more by families with dogs than by other guests, as exemplified by the following four families' (two empty nester couples and two younger families with children) habits:

> I hardly ever use the beach – but my husband walks there with the dog – but otherwise we stay at the caravan site, reading, having a cozy time.

> WIFE: "I'm mostly here [at the caravan].
> HUSBAND: "I go to the beach every day – I always walk the dog there several times a day."

> When we go caravanning, we want to go to the ocean – we bring the dog and he loves the ocean.

> I think the best thing ever is to take a walk on the beach, in the morning, with the dog, enjoying the morning sun. We don't have to do anything, so we spend half an hour, just running around on the beach.

Although interviewees point to 'doing nothing' and 'lazing around' as key elements of their holidays, they also exhibit what Dotson and Hyatt (2008) labelled activity/youth in the form of increased levels of activity and play as part of 'dog companionship' during the holidays. It may mean walking with the dog on the beach several times a day, combining the walk with the dog with bringing bread rolls for breakfast or running around on the beach in the morning.

Inclusion and exclusion of dogs in different activities

Institutionalisation and habitualisation of being with the dog(s) during the holidays not only manifests itself in certain 'doings' (such as walking with the dog), but also in *not* doing certain things, and *not* engaging in certain activities. This may include not visiting amusement parks or dining out due to the dog being a member of the family unit that one either *cannot* take along (e.g. when restaurants or museums do not allow dogs) or when one *should not* take the dog along (e.g. when a visit to an amusement park or a city centre would be "too stressful" for the dog). Some interviewees did take the dog along to amusement parks such as Legoland ("because there's a family area that's not as crowded as the rest of the park") or going shopping in the nearby town ("because we only do that if it's not too hot for him to sit and wait in the car"). Other families with dogs mentioned that some guests at the caravan site would "take the dog with them everywhere", but made it very clear that they themselves "would never do that" because it would be "too stressful" for the dog". Companion dogs often restrain their families from engaging in a variety of 'doings' during the holidays. For example, one family with a large German Shepherd felt "restricted a lot in where to go" and does not barbeque while caravanning because they "don't like open fires as our large dog might knock over the barbeque, risking to start a fire". These tourists' drive to indulge in 'vacability' during the holidays is reinforced by bringing along their dog companions. Or, as some interviewees put it, the dog qualifies as a reason "not to 'go and do things'".

Some interviewees engage in activities without their dog(s) during the holidays. Often this is done by splitting up the travel unit so that some family members, including the dog, stay at the caravan site while others undertake activities such as grocery shopping or visiting nearby attractions. In some instances, all human family members do things without their dog. In a few families this is made possible through 'dog-sitting', resembling the kind of dog-sitting that takes place at home. This was exemplified by the Danish woman whose father-in-law has a holiday house nearby, where they can leave the dog if the-father-in-law is staying there. If this dog-sitting option is not available, the family chooses not to go elsewhere because "the dog shouldn't be dragged along to all kind of places". Another example is a family who stays at the caravan site while the father's parents stay close-by in a holiday house. Occasionally they leave the dog with his parents because it is "a pity to drag the dog along" because that "would be too much and too hot for him". Other interviewees sometimes leave their dog(s) behind in the caravan or mobile home when they go somewhere but this may cause problems. In the words of a couple in their sixties that sometimes caravan with their children and/or grandchildren, but mostly caravan as a family unit including them and their two poodles:

WIFE: "We're never gone for more than three hours and then the dogs can easily stay here in the caravan. As long as it is not too hot, they get some air [open windows] and have fresh water."

HUSBAND: "They usually get some treats and then they both sleep [in the caravan] – we roll down the curtains, so it's dark in here."

WIFE: "But of course we ask the neighbors to tell us if they bark; we'd like to know that, because you can't put the other guests through that."

Limited space and sociability

Miller and Howell (2008) pointed to the problems dog owners encounter when bringing their dogs into nature and/or public spaces. Hirschman (1994) argued that animal companions reside in an intermediate position between nature and culture that calls for different rites of transition that mark the differences between 'outside' and domestic space. These problems seemed to be bigger for interviewees when caravanning than when being at home because many people share a limited space at a caravan site. At a caravan site 'neighbours' are truly close by, making both formal and unwritten rules imperative. All interviewees talked about the unwritten rules that allow guests with different values, norms, habits and behavioural patterns to co-inhabit the limited space at a caravan site. However, as all interviewees pointed to 'freedom' being a major reason to go caravanning, the overarching theme is that everyone can behave as they want to . . . as long as they are not a nuisance to others and the general discourse is that there "should be room for everyone", including "kids playing, a dog barking or people having an argument". Interviewees pointed to a wide variety of both written and unwritten rules such as not being too loud during the day and being quiet at night, respecting the privacy of others, not leaving trash around, being polite and saying 'hello', and not driving too fast around the site. However, a recurring theme was how dogs, and their families, should (not) behave. Examples of this (that covers a variety of family forms) include:

> Your dog shouldn't run around freely and disturb other people.

> You clean up everything that the dog leaves.

> A dog shouldn't run freely around at the site. . . . Some people are afraid of dogs, and therefore, they shouldn't run freely around. And when a dog does what he has to do, you clean it up afterwards. You shouldn't leave it there.

> The only thing that can really get under our skin is if a dog is left alone and it barks and barks until its family gets back home. Apart from that, we never have any problems with the other guests.

The problems with dogs being 'a nuisance' to other guests were also evident when interviewees told about the (few) bad experiences they have had while caravanning, exemplified by the following two accounts:

> In Greece, there was a German couple with adult children next to us. The children had 2 small dogs; Cindy and Sunny. And Cindy and Sunny loved to bark every night till 2 o'clock. And their favorite toilet was our plot. That is the worst that has happened to us. It sometimes happens that the neighbors have parties that last longer than we'd prefer, but that is okay.

> Some other guests told us that there were two Danish couples that were a problem. They were having a party every night and they had a dog that stayed

on the plot the entire time because they didn't go out with him, so the plot was really dirty. And there was rubbish all over the place. So somebody from the reception came and they had to clean. But this is not our own experience. We just heard about it.

Although stories of 'misbehaving' guests were few, the stories that were told almost always included stories about dogs (and oftentimes their droppings and barking). In regard to this issue, some interviewees pointed to it being a problem that guests at caravan sites bring along more dogs than previously, thereby pointing not to dogs being the problem, but the increasing *number* of dogs within a limited space being the problem, or as three of our interviewees opinioned:

> Some people have too many dogs. We'd like if there was a rule that you can have maximum 2 dogs per caravan.

> One thing I don't like about this caravan site is that there are unbelievably many dogs here. I have never been to a caravan site where there were so many dogs. I think it is too much.

> Some people take along many dogs. In the past people brought along one dog, but now some people bring along two, three, or more dogs. It's escalating.

The stories presented paint a somewhat one-sided picture of dogs being a problem when caravanning. However, the general discourse across the interviewees was that there should be "room for everyone". Interviewees also pointed to bringing the dog along as something that facilitates positive encounters with other guests. The sociability in caravanning was noted by Blichfeldt and Mikkelsen (2013); a sociability often mediated by companion dogs, or as a woman in her twenties travelling with her partner and two children and a man in his fifties travelling with his wife said:

> When caravanning, you just talk to your neighbors, you ask something about their caravan or tent or you talk through the dogs and then you continue talking.

> We certainly do [talk to the other guests] – the dog she attracts lots of people [laughing].

As exemplified by these two interviewees, dogs often facilitate "chance encounters" with other guests, which makes the caravan experience more pleasant and satisfies people's needs to socialise. Wood, Giles-Corti and Bulsara (2005) and Wood et. al. (2007) found that pet ownership is positively associated with neighbourhood friendliness and that pets can act as 'ice-breakers'. Our study suggests that this is also the case when it comes to the temporary neighbourhoods people inhabit while caravanning.

Protective and punitive restrictions

Hirschman (1994) argued that dog owners may see a fence as a mediating structure that enables the dog to have the best of both the natural and the cultural world. In an everyday setting (i.e. home), special arrangements such as fences, pet entrances, cleaning the animal, location barriers and behavioural norms permit for transition from outside (nature) to inside (culture). These kinds of arrangements were also found at the caravan sites in a variety of forms. This included families with dogs avoiding the most crowded part of the beach to seek the loneliness and tranquillity away from the other tourists because "it is better for the dog". Some families put a portable fence around their entire caravan plot because "it is cozy and it is less stressful for our dog". Finally, at one of the caravan sites, guests with dogs appreciate the dog bath that is available and often use it after dogs have been swimming or playing in the ocean. At a caravan site that does not offer such dog bathing facilities, one of the interviewees remarked:

> There's nowhere to clean him [a German Shepherd] when he's been in the salt water. There's only cold water, but he doesn't like that. We've used the fire hose, but he's really not keen on that.

As exemplified by this quote provision of facilities such as a dog bath enhances the quality of holidaying for both human and nonhuman family members. Close to one of the caravan sites there is both a 'dog forest' and 'dog yard at the beach' (areas where dogs are permitted to run free if the companion human is in control and can call the dog back if necessary). Off-season and also on some parts of the beaches during peak season dogs are allowed to be off the leash. Many families with dogs use the dog forest and dog yard and argue that the use of these facilities compensates for the dog being subjected to more restrictions at the caravan site than at home.

Sanders and Hirschman (1996, 114) argue that families sometimes experience normally safe situations as problematised by the presence of their dogs. Ellson (2008, 73) argues that dogs "succumb to the prohibitions and demands of the host family throughout life. These restrictions are protective and punitive, underpinning the values and beliefs of the human." Two protective and punitive restrictions that dogs succumb to are the dog collar and the dog leash. A number of interviewees pointed to restrictions in terms of dog leashes being different when they take the dog caravanning. For example, when outside in front of the caravan (a place where families spend lots of time barbequing, chatting, eating, reading, playing games and relaxing) dogs are often on a leash even though this is mostly not the case when people are in their gardens back home. As a couple who lives in the countryside explained:

> It's annoying that she has to be on a leash when we are here, and we get tangled into her leash and stuff like that, and we can't leave her here when we go to do the dishes and things like that. We use the dog yard at the beach every day so that she has a chance to really run and get stretched out.

Another couple, with two dogs, had them on long leashes at the plot when they began camping with them; but that "was a nightmare, because the leashes would be around the table and all the chairs" so now, when they go caravanning, they fence in the plot so that the dogs can be freed from the leashes allowing the dogs the same extent of freedom that they have at home in the family garden.

Holbrook (2008, 547) reminds us that pet owners are "sitting ducks for the marketing effort of firms catering to the needs and wants of our animal companions. The pets themselves are the end users or ultimate consumers, of course, but we cheerfully serve as the ever-vigilant and always-generous purchasing agents". Given the wide range of opportunities caravan sites have for catering to the needs of animal companions, and particularly dogs, it seems rather surprising that in a Danish context, where one out of every four to five families bring along their beloved dogs, it is far from unproblematic to bring the dog. Belk (1988, 155) boldly stated: "(l)ove me, love my dog", a statement that not only implies a fusion of human and nonhuman identities, but also points to a potential for caravan sites to offer more (e.g. dog-sitting) for families that bring their beloved dogs with them when caravanning in Denmark and elsewhere. When caravanning the sharing of consumer experiences with animal companions becomes the sharing of holiday experiences with dog-family members. It requires adaption and careful consideration on the part of human family members. Yet as these families want to share their holiday experiences with their dogs they willingly adapt, positioning themselves as "dog people" who see their dogs as fully fledged members of the family with both similar and different needs, wants and restrictions than human family members.

Conclusion

This chapter points to seeing dogs as fully fledged family members with needs (including leisure needs) having vast implications for families' holidaying. It influences many decisions connected to holidays: e.g. where to go, what kind of activities to do and what kind of activities to avoid for the sake of the dog. Many interviewees stressed that they do not travel to other countries, do not stay in hotels or take a plane because it is too challenging or "too much" for the dog. Caravanning is easier and the dog enjoys it more. When choosing a holiday, these families are willing to make sacrifices and compromises to satisfy needs and wants of all family members (human and nonhuman). Furthermore, leisure needs of nonhuman family members seem to be as important as those of human family members.

'Having' a dog brings restrictions in terms of choices of both mundane and touristic activities while caravanning. The interviewees often mentioned that they do not go to crowded places or amusement parks because it would be too stressful for the dog. However, some families do engage in some activities, leaving the dog behind. This is facilitated in two different ways. The first option is that one or a few human family members stay with the dog at caravan site while other family members engage in activities not suitable for the dog. The second option is that all human family members do some activities together but without their dog. This option is enabled through 'dog sitting'.

Taking a dog on a family holiday is not only about restrictions and compromises. It also has positive aspects which seem essential to the interviewees' caravanning experiences. Dogs influence human family members to be more active as they need to walk with the dog every day no matter the weather. Therefore, walking and playing with the dog is for them a very important part of the holidays, which makes these families more active in comparison with caravanning families without a dog.

Another positive aspect of bringing a dog on a caravanning holiday is connected to socialisation. The inter families pointed out multiple times that dogs make it easier to talk to the other guests at a caravan site and that they help 'break the ice'. Therefore, it could be argued that dogs play an important role in satisfying peoples' needs to socialise while caravanning and make the whole caravanning experience more enjoyable and fulfilling for the human members of the family.

References

Beck, A., and A. Katcher. 1983. *Between Pets and People: The Importance of Animal Companionship*. New York, NY: Putman.

Belk, R.W. 1988. "Possessions and the Extended Self." *Journal of Consumer Research* 15(2): 139–168.

Berger, P. L., and T. Luckmann. 1966. *The Social Construction of Reality*. New York, NY: Anchor Books.

Blichfeldt, B.S., and M.V. Mikkelsen. 2013. "Vacability and Sociability as Touristic Attraction." *Tourist Studies* 13(3): 235–250.

Carr, N. 2014. "The Boarding Kennel and Dog Day-Care Centre: Dog Holidays." In *Dogs in the Leisure Experience*, edited by N. Carr, 107–116. Wallingford, UK: CABI.

Carr, N., and S. Cohen. 2009. "Holidaying with the Family Pet: No Dogs Allowed!" *Tourism and Hospitality Research* 9(4): 290–304.

Cohen, S.P. 2002. "Can Pets Function as Family Members?" *Western Journal of Nursing Research* 24(6): 621–638.

Dorsey, C. 2003. "Cuddling up to Rover." *Brandweek* 44(8): 14–15.

Dotson, M.J., and E.M. Hyatt. 2008. "Understanding Dog-Human Companionship." *Journal of Business Research* 61(5): 457–466.

Dotson, M.J., E.M. Hyatt, and D. Clark. 2010. "Traveling with the Family Dog: Targeting an Emerging Segment." *Journal of Hospitality Marketing and Management* 20(1): 1–23.

Ellson, T. 2008. "Can We Live Without a Dog? Consumption Life Cycles in Dog-Owner Relationships." *Journal of Business Research* 61(5): 565–573.

Gardyn, R. 2002. "Animal Magnetism." *American Demography* 30–37(May).

Gillespie, D.L., A. Leffler, and E. Lerner. 1996. "Safe in Unsafe Places: Leisure, Passionate Avocations, and the Problematizing of Everyday Public Life." *Society and Animals* 4(2): 169–188.

Hill, R.P., J. Gaines, and R.M. Wilson. 2008. "Consumer Behavior, Extended-Self, and Sacred Consumption: An Alternative Perspective from Our Animal Companions." *Journal of Business Research* 61(5): 553–562.

Hirschman, E.C. 1994. "Consumers and Their Animal Companions." *Journal of Consumer Research* 20(4): 616–632.

Holbrook, M.B. 2008. "Pets and People: Companions in Commerce?" *Journal of Business Research* 61(5): 546–552.

Holbrook, M.B., D.L. Stephens, E. Day, S.M. Holbrook, and G. Strazar. 2001. "A Collective Stereographic Photo Essay on Key Aspects of Animal Companionship: The Truth About Dogs and Cats." *Academy of Marketing Science Review* 2001(1): 1–20.

Holbrook, M.B., and A.G. Woodside. 2008. "Animal Companions, Consumption Experiences, and the Marketing of Pets: Transcending Boundaries in the Animal-human Distinction." *Journal of Business Research* 61(5): 377–381.

Kropp, F., G. Malcolm, C. Smith, G.M. Rose, and L.R. Kahle. 1992. "Values and Lifestyles of Pet Owners." In *Proceedings of the Society for Consumer Psychology*, edited by M. Lynn, and J. M. Jackson, 46–49. Clemson, SC: CtC Press.

Mikkelsen, M., and B.S. Blichfeldt. 2015. "We Have Not Seen the Kids for Hours': The Case of Family Holidays and Free-Range Children." *Annals of Tourism Research* 18(2): 252–271.

Miller, R., and G. Howell. 2008. "Regulating Consumption with a Bite: Building a Contemporary Framework for Urban Dog Management." *Journal of Business Research* 61(5): 525–531.

Mosteller, J. 2008. "Animal-Companion Extremes and Underlying Consumer Themes." *Journal of Business Research* 61(5): 512–521.

Sanders, C.R., and E. Hirschman. 1996. "Involvement with Animals as Consumer Experience." *Society and Animals* 4(2): 111–119.

Sapsford, J. 2005. "Honda Caters to Japan's Pet Population Boom." *Wall Street Journal*, October 5. Accessed April 17, 2017. www.wsj.com/articles/SB112847257508160163.

Savishinsky, J.S. 1986. "Pet Ideas: The Domestication of Animals, Human Behavior and Human Emotions." In *New Perspectives in Our Lives with Companion Animals*, edited by A. Katcher and A. M. Beck, 112–131. Philadelphia: University of Pennsylvania Press.

Voith, V. 1986. "Animal Behavior Problems: An Overview." In *New Perspectives in Our Lives with Companion Animals*, edited by A. Katcher and A. M. Beck, 181–186. Philadelphia: University of Pennsylvania Press.

Wood, L., B. Giles-Corti, and M. Bulsara. 2005. "The pet Connection: Pets as a Conduit for Social Capital?" *Social Science & Medicine* 61(6): 1159–1173.

Wood, L.J., B. Giles-Corti, M.K. Bulsara, and D.A. Bosch. 2007. "More Than a Furry Companion: The Ripple Effect of Companion Animals on Neighborhood Interactions and Sense of Community." *Society and Animals* 15(1): 43–56.

9 From labour to leisure

The relocation of animals in modern Western society

Janette Young and Amy Baker

Introduction

Even just 100 years ago cities such as our hometown of Adelaide, Australia were filled with not only cars and people as they are now, but also horses and the vehicles they powered, and other animals such as cattle and sheep (Sumerling 2011). The pivotal role that animals played in international human politics at that time is reflected in the estimated 1.2 million horses and mules used by the British forces alone in World War I where close to half a million of these animals died on the battlefield (BVA 2011). Other animals 'served' as well, including dogs, pigeons, donkeys and camels (Cook and Iarocci 2013; IWM 2017). 'Served' being a questionable word to use as the animals transported to war had no choice as to their involvement, and no recognition as worthy citizens of the countries for which they were being forced to suffer high rates of death, disease and trauma (Johnston 2012). World War I is sometimes recognised as a pivotal point in time for the transition from cavalry or horse-based military might, to military strength based in machinery and technology (Carver 1998). By the end of World War I, tanks and machine guns had revealed the vulnerability of horses in military attacks, even if horses were still needed to pull men and supplies through places where newly invented trucks were incapacitated (Schafer 1996).

Though a sombre introduction to the focus of this chapter, it is timely given that the centenary of World War I is occurring as we write, locating us neatly in time with the human:animal societal transition that is our focus. Through the early decades of the twentieth century, most of the labour roles that animals played in Western societies disappeared as they were replaced by machinery. Cars, trucks, electric trams, semi-trailers and other vehicles took up the labour that had once been powered by nonhuman beings. The shared labour environment of human and nonhuman animals has largely been erased. Few of us now labour with nonhuman beings. Rather, for most people living in Western societies, our contact with animals has become predominately a leisure experience. Sitting with the dog or cat on the couch in the evening, having a horse that we can ride on the weekend, or visiting nature parks, zoos and aquariums as part of our leisure activities are all examples. Animals are rarely co-participants in our work and non-leisure spaces now.

From labour to leisure 129

The aim of this chapter is to unpack the multiple implications of this shift from animals being key participants (whether willingly or not) in human non-leisure spaces to predominately leisure companions for humans. What may have been lost and gained in this shift – for animals, humans and for our cross-species understandings and experiences? Our approach to this topic is to provide a snapshot of the presence of animals, then and now, in Adelaide. This is followed by a description of the research and theoretical frameworks used, followed by an exploration of the gains and losses for humans and animals in the demise of labouring roles for animals. We conclude by considering where these thoughts might take us into the shared future we have with domesticated animals.

Animals in a city: then and now

Urban historians are revealing that the animal-free cities that characterise contemporary Western societies are surprisingly different from past times. Authors such as Velten (2013) in her history of "Beastly London" and Atkins's (2016) edited collection, entitled "Animal Cities", reveal that cities such as Paris, London, Edinburgh and Australian suburbia were places where animals were historically far more present than now. Livestock animals jostled with working/labouring animals, entertaining animals, stray animals, sporting animals and pets (Velten 2013). Within these cities facilities that addressed the needs of animals (water troughs, stables, pens) and the reasons they were in the city (butchering yards, carriage barns) were present. Adelaide was no different.

Figure 9.1 provides a snapshot of the animal accommodation facilities that existed in the city of Adelaide prior to the uptake of the motor car and other motorised transport such as electric trams, trolley buses and trucks (the horse and cattle symbols), and those that exist now (see circled). What this visual shows is that prior to the take-over of the motor car, there were nine stables across the city. In the northern corner, there was also a cattle yard where cattle were transported to the city for sale. None of these stables or the cattle yard exist anymore. The only remaining animal facilities in the city are the Adelaide Zoo (established in 1883), which sits on the northern edge of the city (circled), and the Victoria Park racecourse (first race meet held in 1846) (circled) on the south-eastern corner, where animals are accommodated periodically in line with the racing calendar. Both of these facilities exist primarily to serve human leisure.

The arrow identifies the War Horse Memorial Trough, which originally functioned as a horse water trough in the city and is now a memorial to the horses of World War I. The horse memorial actually predates the obelisk it now sits beside by two years. According to contemporary news reports the horse memorial was desired by the men who had ridden these horses (Register Jan 30 1925). It was two years later that the obelisk memorial to the Light Horsemen was unveiled (Register Apr 15 1925). In addition to what is shown in Figure 9.1, sheep and cattle were allowed to graze in the park lands around the city until the end of the 1960s (Sumerling 2011).

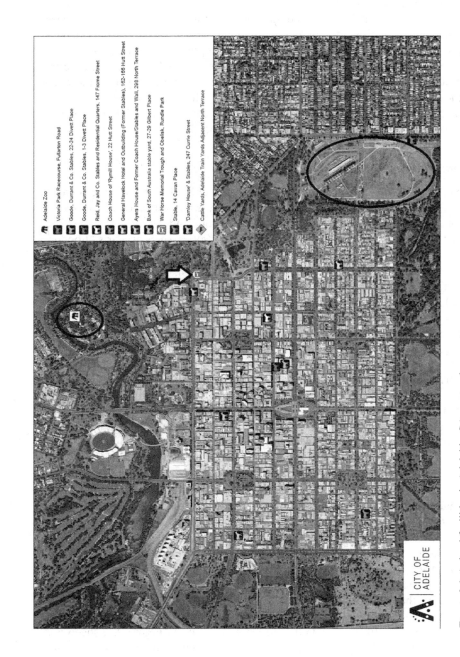

Figure 9.1 Animal facilities in Adelaide, SA, past and present
Courtesy of City of Adelaide, used with permission

Figure 9.2 "A day out" sculpture by Marguerite Derricourt
Photograph provided by sculptor, used with permission

What this snapshot presents is a striking change from a time when domesticated animals were embedded in the life of a city, to now, where human interaction with animals is positioned as novelty. Larger, living creatures are now safely contained in a corner of the city (aka the zoo) or deceased, stuffed and arranged for presentation (the museum). Four bronze pigs in the city mall can also be found, which according to their collective title, 'A day out' (Figure 9.2), do not live in the city. Photos of tourists and children sitting on or with them can be found on the internet. They are safe, clean . . . and non-living. Adelaide is no longer a city where humans and domesticated animals cohabitate, it has become a single-species, human, city.

Theoretical and research framework

The theoretical and methodological framework that underpins this research is historical sociology and ethnography. History is a tool for understanding. Historical sociology is sociological analysis with a keen awareness of the longitudinal nature of social phenomena (Skocpol 1984). Historical sociology seeks to make connections between the past and the present, tracking changes and the impacts of these on predominately human society. This speciesism of historical research has been critiqued (Hribal 2007; Johnston 2012) and it is this critique that this chapter hinges on: seeking to explore the inter-species impacts of social change.

Historical ethnography (Mead and Metraux 1953) is a useful methodological approach for historical sociology. Historical ethnography uses the multi-source approach that characterises ethnography (Tedlock 2003) and applies it to cultures and societies that may be inaccessible due to barriers such as time and politics. The technological revolution of the internet, and the wealth of online access to historical data, newspapers, books and photographs is making the process of seeking past connections much less onerous. This access to historical documents offers the opportunity to "observe" past generations, and get a sense of their lived experiences and perspectives about topics that are still pertinent today. In the case of this chapter, it allows us to see some of the intersections between human and nonhuman lives in leisure and non-leisure/labour, and to speculate on the implications of changes.

A simple history-based definition of leisure is that it is those activities that occur outside of paid employment (Bailey 1978). It is acknowledged that this definition has been superseded by some leisure theorists (Rojek 1995; Roberts 2006). However, for the purpose of this chapter and the focus of the research on which it is based, this old theoretical understanding is useful. The industrial revolution regulated the distinction between leisure and non-leisure time as (debatably) industrial workers were freer outside the factory walls than they had been in previous eras. Outside of the factory, employees had no obligations to their employer, as distinct from pre-industrial times and society when the divide between employer obligated time and personal leisure was not clear-cut (Bailey 1978).

Marx critiqued the industrial revolution as oppressing humans, positioning them as animals (Perlo 2002), arguing that humans had a right to non-labour time (leisure). From a human labour/leisure perspective, early activists argued that giving workers leisure time enhanced their opportunities to participate in civic and democratic activity (Henderson and Presley 2003). From an anti-speciest approach, as Perlo (2002) identifies, nonhuman workers were not included in Marx and his theoretical descendants' anti-oppressive framework. However, this does not mean that ideas from Marxist theory cannot be used and applied to the situation of animals. Recently, Young (2015) has argued that animal rights/welfare have progressed at the interface between leisure and non-leisure, as leisure-time civic engagement (volunteer-based animal welfare organisations) partnered with non-leisure activities within the political sphere (e.g. key politicians).

As a twist on the species hierarchy that exists now, animal and child rights were homogenised in early civic rights/welfare movements. Many of the first animal welfare organisations focussed on both child and animal welfare, in "humane" (Pearson 2011, 21) societies. In the USA between 1866 and 1908 (based on McCrea 1910 in Pearson 2011), there were 185 dual focus societies: 104 animal only ones and 45 focussed on child welfare. As indicated by this imbalance, at times animals were valued more highly than children. Animals provided commercial benefits and legislation was enacted to protect them as economic commodities before substantive laws regarding children were enacted. Indeed, the first child welfare rescue in the USA was on the basis of animal welfare legislation that made animal cruelty illegal (Pearson 2011). Pearson (2011) argues that the philosophical development and integration of sentimentalism with liberalism lead to a separation and re-ordering of the valuing of children and animals. Children came to be viewed as citizens, of equal democratic value to adult humans, with rights. Animals remained in the subservient position of not being considered potential citizens. Their wellbeing remained in the conceptual space of welfare; concern for their wellbeing could be requested/chosen but there was no demand for consideration of them as equals to humans (Pearson 2011). Children's labour was increasingly regulated (Anderson 2011), while legislation focussed on preventing cruelty to animals was less of a specific focus.

Animals at work and animal labour

While Marx may not have considered animals in his writing and thinking, as the photo in Figure 9.3 shows, animals provided literally horse-power much of the time, inhabiting the labour space with humans. Horses are the most visible to us now via photographs often taken in cities. Bullocks were another common transporting animal in South Australia and Afghan cameleers transported goods and supplies on camel-back (Bull 1884) providing the origin of the feral camels now in the Australian Outback. Dogs, like horses, were bred for specific tasks and the diversity of breeds of each species reflects histories of multiple labour roles. With regard to dogs we have the legacy of guarding, hunting and companioning (Serpell 1995); horses, the powerful farming and industry workers of draught breeds (Angus and Morris 2008) and the hardy Australian "Waler", many of whom were taken overseas in World War I (Khanshour, Duras and Cothran 2013).

Figure 9.3 shows humans and animals labouring to build tram tracks through the centre of Adelaide. Labour was risky and potentially harmful for animals. For example, the following newspaper article appeared in the *Evening Journal*, Friday 14 January 1910:

> EXCITEMENT IN WAYMOUTH STREET [Adelaide].
> Horse and Dray Fall Over Embankment.
>
> At about 2 o'clock on Friday afternoon an unusual accident occurred in the excavation at the side of Waymouth Chambers, Waymouth street, where the

Figure 9.3 Preparation for tram tracks, King William Street, Adelaide, SA (1909)
City of Adelaide Archives ACC HP0938 (used with permission)

foundation to a new building is being laid. A horse attached to a dray was being backed down an incline which ended abruptly with a drop of a few feet at the bottom, when the horse became restless and slipped over the embankment at the side. For some time the animal rested on the brink of the excavation, with the prospect of a drop of about 12 ft., and despite the efforts of the men it eventually dropped over the embankment upon a partition some distance below. Luckily the dray remained poised upon the incline, otherwise the horse's back must have been broken. The combined efforts of the men at last succeeded in freeing the animal from the dray, and it came out of the ordeal with nothing but slight injuries to the mouth. After some trouble the dray was dragged back out of harms way. But it was necessary to cut much of the incline.

This sounds like a terrifying ordeal for the horse, but the animal did survive this scenario. However, it is not uncommon to read of horses being killed in accidents. For example the *Advertiser* newspaper reported this incident on March 19, 1912 (*Advertiser*, March 19, 1912):

HORSE KILLED IN A COLLISION
Kapunda. March 19

On St Patrick's Eve a collision occurred on McCarthy's-bridge, over the River Light, a few miles from Kapunda. Two vehicles came into contact, and a valuable colt was killed through the shaft penetrating its chest.

This regular section in the newspaper, entitled "Fatalities and Accidents", reported a range of mishaps and calamities, including and impacting both humans and animals. Yet another article shows the, at times, dangerous intersection between human and animal lives in an era where animal labour was crucial to human daily lives:

A LITTLE BOY KILLED.
Launceston. March 19.

Whilst Elsie Stephens, aged 13, was driving a light vehicle near Scottsdale, having with her a boy named Sweeney, aged 5 years, a dog ran out and frightened the horse which bolted. The vehicle upset, falling across the boy's back, injuring his spine, and he died shortly afterwards.

What these newspaper reports demonstrate is that the intersection of human and animal lives, and deaths, was far more visible in the past than it is now. Both human and animal lives were vulnerable at times from the use of animal labour. Morris (2007) provides a graphic picture of the manner in which this intersection of human and animal lives made living in American cities (and others which were highly horse dependent) an unpleasant, smelly and unhealthy experience in the nineteenth century. "American cities were drowning in horse manure as well as other unpleasant by-products of the era's predominant mode of transportation: urine, flies, congestion, carcasses, and traffic accidents" (Morris 2007, 2). Horses were literally driven to death, with the average lifespan of a streetcar horse being just two years. Animal welfare groups had highly visible evidence to argue for responses to animal cruelty and neglect as horse deaths in the street whilst undertaking labour were common. The overcrowding of streets meant it was not uncommon for horse carcasses to be left in the streets until they had rotted and were easier to remove in parts (Morris 2007).

Horse manure was a major sanitation and urban space problem. A "horse manure crisis" lead to the first international urban planning conference held in New York in 1898 (Morris 2007) – a forum that having been planned to last for 10 days was called off after just three as the problem of horse manure was seen to be intractable. In fact, the advent of motor transport provided the unanticipated alleviation to what was a public health crisis. It also led to a dramatic reduction in levels of public systemic animal abuse. While such changes can be seen as positive for both humans and animals, Hribal (2007), using a Marxist analysis and historical examples of animal responses to human mistreatment, argues that the changes also had a sting as animal resistance to labour and the harsh conditions imposed on them was overcome by the non-negotiated imposition of mechanisation. Perhaps to some extent, horses may be seen to have had the last laugh, remaining as farm (and some urban) labour into the 1950s, and having a micro-resurgence post-World War II in the era of petrol rationing (Angus and Morris 2008). But as shown in Figure 9.4, by the 1930s the streets of Adelaide were dominated by automobiles with just a few horse-drawn vehicles remaining.

Figure 9.4 Rundle Street, Adelaide, SA (c1930s)
City of Adelaide Archives ACC HP1620 (used with permission)

Inter- and intra-species gains and losses for animals and human animals

It seems reasonable to state that there have been gains for some groups of animals as their labouring roles have largely disappeared. They are no longer the common victims of vehicular accidents, public abuse is less possible (there are fewer animals in public) and they are not overworked pulling massive loads or forced to labour in all conditions. Where public animal labour does occur, there is often protest. For example, the carriage horses in New York, now a tourist novelty (Kumar 2013), the responses to circus animals (Cornish 2017) and concerns for zoo animals (Carr and Cohen 2011).

For humans, the gains can be seen to include major urban hygiene improvements (Morris 2007), and we do not see animals abused publicly in a systemic fashion as in the past. For example, imagining the horses in Figure 9.5 pulling that laden horse trolley in the 40 degree Celsius days that Adelaide routinely experiences in summer is distressing. Removal of this burden is a positive step for both species – horse and human.

Reduction in abuse – or hiding of it?

There are now fewer large animals to be abused in cities and it is possible to suggest that some past animal welfare concerns, such as the abuse of animals, has been reduced. But it is far more complicated than simply 'cars rectified overt animal cruelty'. Institutionalised animal abuse and use is now largely hidden. Farming has been moved to the outskirts of urban locales. Factory farming, the mass production of animals for slaughter in particular, is hidden – commonly

Figure 9.5 Horses pulling dual level trams, Grenfell Street, Adelaide (1896)
City of Adelaide Archives LS0/LS0642 (used with permission)

undertaken in enormous sheds, distant from towns and cities where the lives of animals and conditions in which they exist are hidden from everyday view (Taylor, Butt and Amanti 2016). The numbers of these animals also works to 'hide' their plight as individuals, akin to the manner in which mass human starvations and crises can become overwhelming to psyches (Singer 1993). We would save a child we saw in danger, but for many people, knowing that thousands or tens of thousands of children die each year from simple, easily preventable conditions does not mobilise individuals leading to mass action.

For example, in the Pinery fire that occurred in South Australia in November 2015, it was estimated that 51,000 chickens and 500 pigs died when several sheds were engulfed in a fast-moving fire front (Rose 2015). There was little information about these large numbers of animal deaths and an official published comment illustrates the de-individualising impact that mass farming of animals engenders: "(w)hen you think that some of these poultry farms have 500,000 or 1 million birds on them, then 50,000 pales into insignificance to be frank" (Rose 2015, np). Pictures of injured pets and native animals made the response to individual animals much more public and graspable (Williamson 2015).

Selectively bred to labour?

There are animals which have been evolved over time via selective breeding to be labouring animals; and now these animals are 'freed of labour'. But is this a 'freedom' that they would choose (Hribal 2007) and for animals 'bred to labour' or selectively bred over generations to be best suited to human identified tasks, might this be akin to the experiences of unemployment and lack of occupation experienced by humans?

Unemployment can have detrimental effects on human health and wellbeing, particularly with regard to mental health, but also physical wellness (Drydakis 2015; Gathergood 2013). These patterns of reduced health can be tracked longitudinally; that is, unemployment at one stage in life is statistically linked to poorer health in later life (Strandh et al. 2014, Kaspersen et al. 2016). Hence, would a loss of engagement in activities that animals had been specifically bred for generations to undertake not impact on the wellbeing of animals? While horses, once driven to death pulling heavy loads of buses and trams in city streets and denied adequate rest and recreation when not undertaking such labour, are spared some significant negatives; might the loss of possibly meaningful engagement, reduced everyday contact with other horses and non-horses not create sub-optimal wellbeing in some, if not all of these creatures? Today's individuals are descendants of animals bred selectively, from friendlier, stronger, less fearful ancestors who were allowed to breed to create genetic strengths that enhanced their labouring abilities. Might these animals not actually suffer some losses from "forced non-obligated time" (Stebbins 1992, 131)? This is akin to the gilded cage concerns that helped to drive feminist agendas of extending the labour market to married women in the 1960s (Strachan 2010), and concerns that people with significant disabilities should be able to engage in meaningful labour (Murphy 2013). Do (some) animals want to labour?

138 *Janette Young and Amy Baker*

Do animals need meaningful labour?

Exploring the notion that there has been a loss of cross-species labour in modern societies prompts considerations as to possible animal perspectives of this shift, including the potential for boredom, depression and anxiety when they are only able to engage in 'leisure'.

Animals can be seen to engage in productive activity or occupation. Productivity as a human concept has been defined as "contributing to the economic and social fabric of [a] . . . community" (CAOT 1997, 34). If we look at animals in their 'natural state or environment', there is a need to engage in productive occupations to survive individually and collectively. For example, ants and bees create and maintain their nests and hives (Visscher 2007), their collective homes. Animals need to search for food, whether carnivores, herbivores or omnivores – a life-sustaining requirement and another example of productivity. Indeed, competition for food or productivity resources with humans can be a reason why domesticated-gone-wild (feral) animals can be regarded with anathema. Examples include feral dogs killing sheep (Treves and Karanth 2003), cats killing wildlife, especially in native environments (Loss, Will and Marra 2013), and animals such as pigs, goats and horses competing for resources with farmed, contained animals (DEWR 2007).

'Working dogs'

The canine literature has an understanding of animal needs to labour and experience more than the freedom of leisure (Carr 2015). For example 'working dog' breeds – descendants of lineages bred for specific tasks such as hunting, guarding and herding need to be kept occupied (Coppinger and Coppinger 2002). These breeds often fill rescue shelters (as shown by this analysis of petfinder data: https://mom.me/pets/19900-dog-breeds-commonly-found-animal-shelters/item/rottweiler/). Having perhaps arrived as a cute, sleepy (much of the time), puppy, they may become destructive, noisy co-habitants in human spaces if not exercised (mentally and physically) regularly. The selective breeding that lead to them being the animal of choice by humans for a particular task may become the characteristics and behaviours that can lead to them losing their homes, or being surgically adapted to changed human requirements and environments. One of us (Janette) lives with a small pomeranian dog (Sooks) who is an exemplar of such a mismatch. These feisty, pint-sized fur balls, with a sharp bark and a blindness to their own relative size and capacity, are the descendants of larger spitz guard dogs in Northern Europe (Vanderlip 2007). However, over the last 150 years they have become predominately a domestic non-labouring breed. Now the characteristics that made them such good guard dogs (the bark and self-confidence) can be the cause of significant neighbourhood tensions in modern suburbia. Sooks was debarked as the outcome of such conflict prior to coming to live with her current guardians. According to her previous caretaker, it was this or being 'put to sleep' aka euthanized. For her part, Sooks seems oblivious to the lack of volume that she produces, and maintains her feisty guarding approach to her property and people. Her need to labour, to be active in undertaking a task that she identifies as important, seems clear when one spends a day at home with her. Simply leisurely snoozing at her humans' feet is not enough. She has a mission and an occupation to fulfil.

Loss of chances for meaningful cross-species time and engagement

This moves us to the next question: do (some) animals want to labour with humans? Having evolved alongside each other as species for so long that the human need for occupation and labour may be paralleled in some domesticated animals, might there even be an inherited 'need' to work together? For perhaps both humans and animals there has been a loss of the opportunity to labour, and experience (meaningful) occupation and endeavour, not to mention simply time, together.

Angus and Morris's edited book (2008) is a collection of highly personal stories of what life was/has been like to labour with working horses, often in farming endeavours but also more broadly as people recalled driving horse-drawn milk carts, brewery wagons and holiday caravans. People speak of the shared rituals that humans and animals undertook in these activities. For example, the "cup of tea time" (66) when workmen would ensure that the horses had a feedbag and drink before their humans had their meal break. There is also talk of the cross-species 'respect' needed to ensure that both human and animal were able to undertake the required work as safely and efficiently as possible, linking to the concept of animal welfare, but within a shared human and animal labour environment that is far less common now. At times human workers risked their lives to save horses they knew in a similar manner to that of people who lose their lives seeking to save their nonhuman (including equine) companions in natural disasters now (Thompson 2013).

In contemporary Western societies, there has been a loss of human:animal interactions/interface across the working day. Interests in canine performance sports (Hultsman 2015) and the evidence that the vast majority of dogs in Australia (85 percent see AMA 2016) go places outside of the home with their owners indicates a desire to spend more time with non-humans on the part of some humans. While there are some initiatives such as 'pets at work days' and animal petting setups especially focussed on human mental wellbeing, this is focussed on human needs and animal instrumentality. It is also a therapeutic framework rather than a shared labour/occupation approach. There is not a concern to give animals any rights or recognition as equals, or as 'workers' in these processes (Cochrane 2016).

Suggestions that support the possibility that some animals may actually want to labour with humans exist. For example, there are arguments that rather than humans domesticating some animals, the animals actually made the decision to stay with humans (Beck and Katcher 1996). These animals benefitted from having more ready access to food when they spent time near or in human settlements. The differences we see between domestic dogs and wolves, for example, may be the outcome of tamer, less fearful wolves breeding with similarly natured wolves in or on the outskirts of human settlements (Serpell 1995). The physiological changes that are linked to domestication (Trut, Oskina and Kharlamova 2009) may be at least partially agentic outcomes of self-selected interbreeding by these human-seeking/co-habiting canines. There is evidence that some dogs are now more attached to humans than to other dogs (Tuber et al. 1996). We would argue that there is space to theorise that while operating with an element of reproductive agency there may be some populations of domesticated animals, the descendants of those who desired to associate closely with humans, who may have self-selected over time and generations who desire engagement and activity with humans; the engagement is desired hence it is meaningful. Given the evolutionary breeding history of other domesticated animals, it is not unreasonable to think that this trait is not unique to canines. Yet from our searching of the literature, there does not seem to be a field of research exploring animals' needs for meaningful engagement, aka non-leisure with humans.

New roles? Pets as family?

There is a belief that pets, the animals with which we live, are increasingly anthropomorphised (Franklin 1999). But while they lack democratic rights (see Donaldson and Kymlicka 2011), our positioning of pets (and also larger domesticated animals that some people feel a similar pet-like sense of attachment to such as horses – see chapters by Danby and Henderson), embeds these animals in a welfare, subservient-to-humans position. Pets are recipients of our emotional benevolence not co-species with rights. 'Working animals' tend to be conceptually situated with pets (commonly dogs). For example, Shane the retired police dog (Sarkauskas 2014) has become his handler's family pet, despite having a distinguished career finding narcotics, cadavers and other things that his unique species-based abilities have provided to the human public for many years. The idea that this nonhuman retired worker might feel the same sense of loss of meaningful occupation that human workers can experience (Nuttman-Shwartz 2004) does not seem to be given any validity. Shane is either a resource assisting humans, or a leisure-bound, reborn 'pet'. Not a retiree with rights to a pension and care from the state that he has spent his healthiest years providing services to as Cochrane (2016) has recently been arguing could be the case.

Humans on the animal spectrum

Perhaps one reason for the failure to consider the breadth of meaningful occupation possible to animals, domesticated ones in particular, is that as modern humans, we tend to not recognise, ignore or forget our inherent animality. In his book "Dependent Rational Animals" (2009), Alasadair MacIntyre reminds us of the chief importance of acknowledging our animal nature. MacIntyre suggests that it is our animality – humans' underlying state of being as first and foremost an animal one – that has been forgotten in recent times, putting our understanding: "at odds both with older Aristotelian modes of thought and with modern post Darwinian evolutionary naturalism" (2009, 11). According to MacIntyre, we conceive of ourselves as "exempt from the hazardous condition of 'mere' animality" (2009, 4).

One reason for this separation, between humans and nonhuman animals, has been a tendency to award humans 'non-animal' status because of our language skills. Yet it is crucial to consider the skills and abilities we share with other animals, which often form a basis for our action: "we still rely in very large part on just the same kind of recognitions, discriminations, and exercises of perceptual attention that we did before we were able to make use of our linguistic powers.... Much that is intelligent animal in us is not specifically human" (MacIntyre 2009, 40). Although the language ability of humans, and specifically our "ability to put language to certain kinds of reflective use" sets us apart from other animals in important ways (MacIntyre 2009, 58), MacIntyre suggests it is more apt to talk of many animals as 'prelinguistic' rather than 'nonlinguistic', illustrating this with examples of more intelligent species of animal such as dolphins and chimpanzees. In addition, what this belies is that there are humans who are not able to use language (for example those with significant intellectual disability, or some stroke victims, or those who are experiencing late stage dementia). A lack or loss of language does not mean that nonlinguistic humans or animal viewpoints should not be taken into consideration.

The animal studies field argues strongly that the distinction between animal and human is far more blurred than generally accepted. In recent times Donaldson and Kymlicka (2011) have constructed an argument for animal citizenship on the basis of this diversity of human language and high level intellectual skills using severe intellectual disability as their pivot point for the citizenship of domestic and domesticated animals. Their argument is that animals are akin to these humans in that they may be unable to vote, require support to obtain their basic needs and may be inarticulate, but we afford them rights as citizens to have their interests, desires and needs addressed and considered. Hence, we should provide the same kind of response to domestic animals, in particular, who share our human environments. Our argument would be that animal needs for meaningful non-leisure, or purposeful engagements should be part of frameworks that seek to pursue justice for animals, particularly domestic and domesticated ones.

Conclusion

We have argued that non-leisure and meaningful occupation is important for humans to achieve a balanced and fulfilling lifestyle; and that given our shared animality, there is scope to consider that nonhuman animals, in particular domesticated animals, may well share these needs. Radical historical changes have created a scenario for pets and some of our previously co-labouring animal companions that may mean that they are now destined to live a life of unfulfilling 'leisure'. With the demise of many co-labourer roles, are some domesticated animals now deprived of important occupations which bring meaning to their life? From a human-animal perspective at least, there is a strong argument that a lack of meaningful occupation can lead to boredom and depression, not to mention loneliness, as many occupations are social in nature. What of domesticated animals?

We would argue that there is scope for thinking that some animals need labour, and perhaps even need and desire to labour with us as cross-species companions. Furthermore, that for some species or maybe just some individual members of a variety of previously labouring species, a lack of meaningful engagement and occupation with (and maybe without) humans is a loss and a detriment to thriving for them. Into the future these are ideas, possibilities and potentials that research can and, we would argue needs, to explore.

There are capacities and skills that humans are yet to master, and these are often the skills recognised in the animal co-labour roles that exist. These are predominately opportunities for dogs to use their superior olfactory abilities – sniffing out drugs (Dunn and Degenhardt 2009), bombs (Gazit and Terkel 2003) and people (Stitt 1991). There are also increasing roles that we entitle 'on the verge'. These are the service/assistance and therapy animals (Fine 2010) where the human-animal intersection and bond is being recognised as inherently beneficial – to humans; but we wonder about its need by some animals as well. Maybe in the future, there will be new, currently un-thought of roles for animals; perhaps these roles will grow out of the skills and capacities that some animals have that humans lack. While the concern is often that we are usurping animals' capacities simply in the aid of humans, considering the potential animal needs for meaningful activity and engagement suggests that we may add to the quality of some animals lives by re-integrating them back into human non-leisure.

Stebbins, the doyen of serious leisure, has stated "I remain convinced that serious leisure is an important antidote to the dreary state of being unemployed" (1992, 133). Is this the potential for domestic animals who have been 'relieved' of labour as well? Are some now condemned to endless 'leisure' and pampered slavery? As Hribal states: "(s)lavery is not just a human condition" (2007, 107); in this scenario, what losses are we accruing to ourselves as a co-species? Considering the leisure and non-leisure needs of our fellow animals suggests hidden losses and gains across species that merit further investigation that could enable cross-species flourishing.

References

Anderson, J.L. 2011. "Protection for the Powerless: Political Economy History Lessons for the Animal Welfare Movement." *Stanford Journal of Animal Law and Policy* 4(1): 1–63.

Angus, D., and S. Morris, eds. 2008. *Clydesdale and Working Horses: A Pictorial History*. Stepney, S. Australia: Axiom.

Animal Medicines Australia. 2016. "Pet Ownership in Australia/2016." Animal Medicines Australia Pty Ltd, Barton, ACT: Australia. Accessed April 24, 2017. http://animalmedicinesaustralia.org.au/wp-content/uploads/2016/11/AMA_Pet-Ownership-in-Australia-2016-Report_sml.pdf.

Atkins, P., ed. 2016. *Animal Cities: Beastly Urban Histories*. New York, NY: Routledge.

Bailey, P. 1978. *Leisure and Class in Victorian England: Rational Recreation and the Contest for Control, 1830–1885*. London: Routledge & Kegan Paul.
Beck, A., and A. Katcher. 1996. *Between Pets and People: The Importance of Animal Companionship*. West Lafayette, IN: Purdue University Press.
British Veterinary Association. 2011. "Remembering the Real War Horses." *The Veterinary Record* 169(21): 543. doi:http://dx.doi.org/10.1136/vr.d7342.
Bull, J.W. 1884. *Early Experiences of Life in South Australia and an Extended Colonial History Adelaide*. Australia: E.S. Wigg & Son.
Canadian Association of Occupational Therapists (CAOT). 1997. *Enabling Occupation: An Occupational Therapy Perspective*. Ottawa: CAOT Publications ACE.
Carr, N. 2015. *Dogs in the Leisure Experience*. Wallingford, UK: CABI.
Carr, N., and S. Cohen. 2011. "The Public Face of Zoos: Images of Entertainment, Education and Conservation." *Anthrozoös* 24(2): 175–189.
Carver, M. 1998. *Britain's Army in the 20th Century*. London: Palgrave Macmillan.
Cochrane, A. 2016. "Labour Rights for Animals." In *The Political Turn in Animal Ethics*, edited by R. Garner and S. O'Sullivan, 15–32. London: Rowman and Littlefield.
Cook, T., and A. Iarocci. 2013. "Animal Soldiers." *Canada's History* 93(5): 20–27.
Coppinger, R. and L. Coppinger. 2002. *Dogs: A Startling New Understanding of Canine Origin, Behavior & Evolution*. Chicago: University of Chicago Press.
Cornish, R. 2017. "Circus Featuring Performing Animals Met with Protest in Coffs Harbour." *ABC News*, March 9. www.abc.net.au/news/2017-03-09/circus-with-performing-animals-sparks-protests-in-coffs-harbour/8339994.
Department of the Environment and Water Resources. 2007. *A National Strategy for the Management of Vertebrate Pest Animals in Australia*. Canberra:Commonwealth of Australia, Department of the Environment and Water Resources.
Donaldson, S., and W. Kymlicka. 2011. *Zoopolis: A Political Theory of Animal Rights*. Oxford: Oxford University Press.
Drydakis, N. 2015. "The Effect of Unemployment on Self-Reported Health and Mental Health in Greece from 2008 to 2013: A Longitudinal Study Before and During the Financial Crisis." *Social Science & Medicine* 128(March): 43–51. doi:https://doi.org/10.1016/j.socscimed.2014.12.025.
Dunn, M., and L. Degenhardt. 2009. "The Use of Drug Detection Dogs in Sydney, Australia." *Drug and Alcohol Review* 28(6): 658–662. doi:10.1111/j.1465–3362.2009.00065.x.
Fine, A. 2010. *Handbook on Animal-Assisted Therapy: Theoretical Foundations and Guidelines for Practice*. London: Academic Press.
Franklin, A. 1999. *Animals and Modern Cultures*. London: Sage.
Gathergood, J. 2013. "An Instrumental Variable Approach to Unemployment, Psychological Health and Social Norm Effects." *Health Economics* 22(6): 643–654. doi:10.1002/hec.2831.
Gazit, I., and J. Terkel. 2003. "Domination of Olfaction Over Vision in Explosives Detection Dogs." *Applied Animal Behavior Science* 82(1): 65–73. doi:10.1016/S0168–1591(03)00051–0.
Henderson, K., and J. Presley. 2003. "Globalization and the Values of Volunteering as Leisure." *World Leisure Journal* 45(2): 33–37. doi:10.1080/04419057.2003.9674314.
Hribal, J. 2007. "Animals Agency and Class: Writing the History of Animals from Below." *Human Ecology Review* 14(1): 101–112.
Hultsman, W. 2015. "Dogs and Companion/Performance Sport: Unique Social Worlds, Serious Leisure Enthusiasts, and Solid Human-Canine Partnerships." In *Domestic Animals and Leisure*, edited by N. Carr, 35–66. Hampshire- Palgrave Macmillan.

International War Museums. 2017. "15 Animals That Went To War." Accessed April 24, 2017. www.iwm.org.uk/history/15-animals-that-went-to-war.

Johnston, S. 2012. "Animals in War: Commemoration, Patriotism, Death." *Political Research Quarterly* 65(2): 359–371. doi:10.1177/1065912910391982.

Kaspersen, S., K. Pape, G.Å. Vie, S. Ose, S. Krokstad, D. Gunnell, and J. Bjørngaard. 2016. "Health and Unemployment: 14 Years of Follow-Up on Job Loss in the Norwegian HUNT Study." *European Journal of Public Health* 26 (2): 312–317. doi:10.1093/eurpub/ckv224.

Khanshour, A., R. Juras, and E.G. Cothran. 2013. "Microsatellite Analysis of Genetic Variability in Waler Horses from Australia." *Australian Journal of Zoology* 61(5): 357–365. doi:10.1071/ZO13062.

Kumar, N. 2013. "New York Mayor Vows to Put City's Horses Out to Pasture." *Independent*, December 31. www.independent.co.uk/news/world/americas/new-york-mayor-vows-to-put-citys-horses-out-to-pasture-9032079.html.

Loss, S., T. Will, and P. Marra. 2013. "The Impact of Free-Ranging Domestic Cats on Wildlife of the United States." *Nature Communications* 4. doi:10.1038/ncomms2380.

MacIntyre, A. 2009. *Dependent Rational Animals: Why Human Beings Need the Virtues*. London: Duckworth.

Mead, M., and R. Metraux, eds. 1953. *The Study of Culture at a Distance*. Chicago: University of Chicago Press.

Morris, E. 2007. "From Horse Power to Horsepower." *Access* 30(Spring): 2–9.

Murphy, K.P. 2013. "Encouragement Toward Employment for Those with Disabilities." *Developmental Medicine & Child Neurology* 55(8): 683–684. doi:10.1111/dmcn.12177.

Nuttman-Shwartz, O. 2004. "Like a High Wave: Adjustment to Retirement." *The Gerontologist* 44(2): 229–236. doi:10.1093/geront/44.2.229.

Pearson, S. 2011. *The Rights of the Defenseless: Protecting Animals and Children in Gilded Age America*. Chicago: University of Chicago Press.

Perlo, K. 2002. "Marxism and the Underdog." *Society & Animals* 10(3): 303–318.

Roberts, K. 2006. *Leisure in Contemporary Society*. Cambridge: CABI.

Rojek, C. 1995. *Decentring Leisure: Rethinking Leisure Theory*. London: Sage.

Rose, J. 2015. "Pinery Fire: 51,000 Chickens, 500 Pigs Perish in Blaze." *Stock Journal* November 26. www.stockjournal.com.au/story/3521547/pinery-fire-animal-casualties-increase/.

Sarkauskas, S. 2014. "From Working Dog to Family Pet: Police Dogs in Retirement." *Daily Herald*, August 31. www.dailyherald.com/article/20140831/news/140839813/.

Schafer, E. 1996. "Animals, Use of." In *The European Powers in the First World War: An Encyclopedia*, edited by S. Tucker, 52–54. New York, NY: Taylor & Francis. ISBN 0–8153-3351-X.

Serpell, J. 1995. *The Domestic Dog: Its Evolution, Behavior and Interactions with People*. New York: Cambridge University Press.

Singer, P. 1993. *Practical Ethics*. New York, NY: Cambridge University Press.

Skocpol, T. 1984. *Vision and Method in Historical Sociology*. Cambridge: Cambridge University Press.

Stebbins, R.A. 1992. *Amateurs, Professionals, and Serious Leisure*. Ottawa: McGill-Queen's Press.

Stitt, B. 1991. "Practical, Ethical and Political Aspects of Engaging 'Man's Best Friend' in the War on Crime." *Criminal Justice Policy Review* 5(1): 53–65. doi:10.1177/088740349100500105.

Strachan, G. 2010. "Still Working for the Man? Women's Employment Experiences in Australia Since 1950." *Australian Journal of Social Issues* 45(1): 117–130.

Strandh, M., A. Winefield, K. Nilsson, and A. Hammarström. 2014. "Unemployment and Mental Health Scarring During the Life Course." *European Journal of Public Health* 24(3): 440–445. doi:10.1093/eurpub/cku005.

Sumerling, P. 2011. *The Adelaide Parklands: A Social History*. Kent Town, South Australia: Wakefield Press.

Taylor, E., A. Butt, and M. Amanti. 2016. "Done Like a Chicken Dinner: City Fringes Locked in Battles Over Broiler Farms." *The Conversation*, March 7. https://theconversation.com/done-like-a-chicken-dinner-city-fringes-locked-in-battles-over-broiler-farms-54886.

Tedlock, B. 2003. "Ethnography and Ethnographic Representation." In *Strategies of Qualitative Inquiry*, edited by Norman K. Denzin and Yvonna S. Lincoln, 165–213. Thousand Oaks, CA: Sage.

Thompson, K. 2013. "Save Me, Save My Dog: Increasing Natural Disaster Preparedness and Survival by Addressing the Human-Animal Relationship." *Australian Journal of Communication* 40(1): 123–136.

Treves, A., and K. Karanth. 2003. "Human-Carnivore Conflict and Perspectives on Carnivore Management Worldwide." *Conservation Biology* 17(6): 1491–1499.

Trut, L., I. Oskina, and A. Kharlamova. 2009. "Animal Evolution During Domestication: The Domesticated Fox as a Model." *Bioessays* 31(3): 349–360.

Tuber, D., M. Hennessy, S. Sanders, and J. Miller. 1996. Behavioral and Glucocorticoid Responses of Adult Domestic Dogs (Canis Familiaris) to Companionship and Social Separation." *Journal of Comparative Psychology* 110(1): 103.

Vanderlip, S. 2007. *The Pomeranian Handbook*. New York, NY: Barrons' Educational Series, Inc.

Velten, H. 2013. *Beastly London: A History of Animals in the City*. London: Reaktion Books.

Visscher, P.K. 2007. "Group Decision Making in Nest-Site Selection Among Social Insects." *Annual Review of Entomology* 52: 255–275.

Williamson, B. 2015. "SAVEM Vets and Nurses Rescue Animals Affected by the Pinery Bushfires in South Australia." *ABC Radio Adelaide*, November 30. www.abc.net.au/news/2015-11-30/rescuing-animals-affected-by-the-pinery-bushfires/6985820.

Young, J. 2015. "At the Nexus: Serious Leisure, Civic Engagement and Animal Welfare and Wellbeing." In *Domestic Animals and Leisure*, edited by N. Carr, 67–88. Hampshire: Palgrave Macmillan.

10 Post-humanistic insight into human-equine interactions and wellbeing within leisure and tourism

Paula Danby

Introduction

Over time humans and animals have had varied relationships within a multitude of spaces for diverse reasons. In the last century human attitudes towards animals in Western societies have changed considerably from an anthropocentric ontology where humans were regarded as central to the universe in that realities were interpreted from human experiences (Franklin 1999). Humans used animals for their own benefit and exploited their superiority with regards treatment (Franklin 1999). Recently, the post-modern period has witnessed a prominent shift from such philosophical thought, whereby human society has begun to adopt a bio-centric ontology, which considers all forms of life to have intrinsic value, acknowledging nonhuman life as a fundamental element of the universe (Franklin 1999). Thus encouraging the formation of more sentient and empathetic human-animal relations, through a sense of partnership worthy of moral consideration.

Increased leisure time, technological advances, education and the values associated with wellbeing in post-modern society have encouraged animals to be incorporated into a range of leisure landscapes that encourage humans to interact with animals in close proximity within diverse environments (Franklin 1999; Carr 2015; Dashper 2015; Markwell 2015). Markwell (2015, 1) argues that

> (a)nimals are so much a part of our day-to-day lives that we often fail to register their presence, or when we do, they are frequently relegated to the background. Regardless of whether we live in highly urbanised cities or rural villages, non-human animals co-habit these spaces with us.

In this sense, animals can be viewed superficially in that humans coexist with animals daily without recognition, through food and associated products and other interactions. In addition Markwell refers to the fact that some animals are regarded as companions to be loved and cared for, with whom we share resources and spaces, whereas others are regarded as pests which we try to exclude from our lives (Markwell 2015).

Post-humanistic theory is drawn upon within this chapter as an attempt to develop the argument towards innovative ways of understanding human-non-human relations where boundaries between the two become blurred through shared, lived leisure spaces. In this case, regarding humans and horses, it can be seen that the human-equine divide is reconceptualised as a result of interrelations, where networks of interdependencies are demonstrated within the realm of leisure, arguably through which wellbeing is encountered through a multitude of interactions between both actors. Equestrianism provides leisure opportunities for humans to interact and gain myriad close encounters, relations and experiences with horses in diverse landscapes, contributing toward the mutual wellbeing of horses and humans. In this sense, horses are viewed as key actors within the human-equine relationship, playing active roles (Danby and Hannam 2016) and providing humans with companionship.

Previously, human-animal relations have focussed around human consumption and utilisation of animals for peoples' individual benefit whereas the post-human approach towards human-equine interactions displays an appreciation of the horse for its intrinsic value in post-modern society. In turn, this reflects the empathetic and sentimentalised attitudes where horses have been introduced into the leisure landscape as a form of 'pet culture'. As a result, humans look beyond human agency and form strong bonded relationships and emotional attachments with horses as well as contributing huge commitments towards securing the individual needs of horses and humans.

Empirically, this chapter exemplifies how horses have been incorporated into the 'leisure landscape' where interactions with humans are now common. Such spaces have a profound impact on the way human-equine interactions take place, relations formed and the experiences encountered. All of these play a fundamental role in mutual wellbeing and secure the welfare of the equine industry. Humans invest considerable finances and time in equine leisure and tourism pursuits securing horse welfare, yet despite this it remains under-researched. Helgadóttir and SigurÐardóttir (2008) acknowledged that despite horse-based tourism becoming a growing sector and an important niche of the tourism industry, it has not been extensively researched. However, recently authors have begun to explore the human-horse relationship in complex ways within the context of leisure, tourism and sport (Daniels and Norman 2005; Ollenburg 2005; Helgadóttir 2006; Oliveria 2009; Birke, Hockenhull and Creighton 2010; Dashper 2012, 2015, 2017; Gilbert and Gillett 2014; Goodrum 2015; Kline et al. 2015; Siguroadóttir and Helgadóttir 2015; Danby and Hannam 2016). This chapter demonstrates how humans and horses have developed sentimentalised relations through leisure that enhance reciprocal physical, emotional and social wellbeing.

I begin the chapter by developing the post-humanistic concept towards human-equine relations. Secondly, an empirical qualitative methodology is formulated to interpret ethnographic accounts relating to human-equine relations. Thirdly, the analysis of the themes derived from the human-equine leisure encounters and associated wellbeing are presented. I conclude by elaborating upon the post-humanist stance towards human-equine relations within the leisure context as an approach to enhance mutual wellbeing.

A post-humanistic approach towards human-equine relations and leisure

Human relations with non-humans have become a focus of attention in many ways, particularly in discourse surrounding human-animal interactions and associated encounters through time and space. A new 'animal' geography explores relations focussing on the complex entanglements of human-animal relations within place and landscape (Philo and Wilbert 2000).

Various theoretical approaches rethinking human-centredness focus on the complexities surrounding interactions between humans and animals. Wilbert (2009) articulates this perspective in alliance with post-humanism along with non-representational theory and actor network theory. Such theories seek to further develop the spatialities, politics and ethics of human-non-human associations. Hybrid animal geographies seek to discover how animals have been socially defined, used as food (Philo and Wilbert 2000) or indeed, as this chapter demonstrates, identified as pets. Urbanik and Morgan (2013) allude to the fact that pet keeping transcends the boundaries of human-animal relationships to include a 'more-than-human' 'other'. A post-modern world blurs boundaries between nature, society, humans and animals (Instone 1998). Bowes et al. (2015) argue that such trans-species social bonds are driven by a variety of factors, including a desire for power, control, affection, kinship and companionship that promote wide-ranging benefits.

A post-humanist approach towards human-animal relations within the leisure landscape thus aims to explore innovative ways of being within post-modern society, with emphasis being placed on what Wilbert (2009) refers to as the human-animal divide from one of oppositional dualism into networks of intricate dependencies focussed around kinship. Post-humanistic theory challenges the singular focus around human subjects, blurring boundaries between the human and nonhuman. Actor Network Theory has been influential to more-than-human theories, as it refuses to see animals (and humans) as centred pre-existing beings, and does not acknowledge a distinction of separate worlds surrounding humans and animals as well as nature and culture (Lorimer 2009).

Crouch (2010) examines ways through which lives and spaces interact over time where individuals' lives may be changed or influenced by various encounters. In a similar vein, reflecting from a post-humanist stance, Thrift (2004) relates to emotion, arguing that feeling is not entirely individual. Instead it is something that emerges between bodies, whether human or otherwise. In light of these notions, Game and Metcalfe (2011) similarly acknowledge that emotions may not only come from the subject but from the living space, through an understanding of experiences of interconnectedness. The work of Game (2001) explores the interconnectedness between humans and animals, with specific focus on horses. Game (2001) questions humanist assumptions and alludes to this blurring of human-non-human boundaries. She articulates ways of being involved in experiences of such connections and the spatial and temporal qualities of lived spaces with non-humans, proposing that through such interconnections we are already part-horse, and horses, part-human.

Game (2001) manifests the notion of interconnectedness between two species, demonstrating the need to respect and understand each other's difference to effectively communicate with each other. To work effectively with horses, humans need to respect difference and to understand the culture of the horse. Once humans adopt this perspective they are able to interact with and relate to the horse more successfully (Game 2001). What Game refers to is an 'in-between' stage where the human becomes part-horse and the horse becomes part-human through interaction, particularly through riding. Subsequently, respecting difference is important in acquiring effective human-equine relations (Game 2001) and indeed mutual understanding and wellbeing.

Pet owners see cross-species communication as possible, allowing reciprocal relationships to be formed (DeMello 2012). Opening up to cross-species communication and animal inclusion (especially horses), emergent through leisure landscapes, enables a sharing of mutual reality between humans and horses. As a result of social exchanges and embodiment both humans and non-humans play an equal role in the encounters and are able to anticipate and acknowledge each other's needs and interests, hence the human-animal relationship is based upon mutual respect and equality (DeMello 2012). Through positive cross-species communication and interaction between humans and companion animals such as horses, mutual, affectionate responses are encountered.

Animal welfare literature illuminates the notion that animals are as important as humans in the world; thus they should obtain the same level of appreciation, respect and welfare as humans (Philo and Wilbert 2000). According to Hemsworth, Jongman and Coleman (2015) the welfare of recreational horses has become an increasingly important issue in recent years, where the primary responsibility rests with the horse owner. In this context industry reports suggest the welfare of recreational horses is determined by the horse owner's performance of husbandry and management (Hemsworth, Jongman and Coleman 2015).

Methodology

Post-humanist insights through an interpretative, experiential approach towards human-equine relational wellbeing was considered appropriate, enabling an empirical and innovative focus, in that the world associated with human-animal relations is constituted of multiple realities. Data was collected using a variety of qualitative methods including participant observation, in-depth interviews and participant diaries between April 2009 and September 2010. The interview sample consisted of 21 respondents and the diary sample consisted of 15 completed diaries. Participants were encouraged to talk or write about their interactions, associated emotions and experiences with horses within leisure spaces. All participants interacted on a regular basis with horses and participated in a range of equine leisure pursuits including riding, caring for horses, learning about horsemanship and equine culture, competing or engaging in equestrian tourism. Some respondents owned their horses and others loaned or interacted with various horses. Personal diaries were completed by respondents who kept a log of individual interactions, experiences and emotions as a result of horse riding activities and associated human-equine relations. Once transcribed data from the interviews and diaries was prepared, coding assisted with identifying and exploring fundamental themes encompassing human-equine motivations, relational encounters and associated wellbeing through engagement within equine leisure landscapes. Diary respondents remained anonymous to encourage them to speak more freely about their emotions and experiences with horses. Names of interview respondents and horses' were changed to ensure anonymity throughout.

Human-equine reciprocal wellbeing

Over the last two decades researchers have begun to assess the possibility that animals could have positive effects on humans (Friedmann, Thomas and Eddy 2005). Research into human-animal bonds acknowledges the emotional, psychological and physical benefits that living with animals can give humans (DeMello 2012). However, my curiosity about human-animal relations stems from the mutual benefit of the relationship and moral consideration for both actors, which is an underlying argument throughout this chapter. Moreover, if we identify the benefit of the relationship to humans why should we diminish the benefits to non-humans? Surely non-humans deserve the same moral consideration and welfare as humans in order to effectively coexist? Research is beginning to acknowledge the importance of pet keeping not only to human wellbeing, but also animal wellbeing (Hausberger et al. 2008; Danby 2013; Hemsworth, Jongman and Coleman 2015).

Horses are large herbivores that require space and intense management, exercise, feeding and grooming (Birke, Hockenhull and Creighton 2010). Hemsworth, Jongman and Coleman (2015) argue that providing optimum conditions to ensure animals' needs are met depends on factors such as the work that the horse is required to do, the keeper's budget and circumstances, as well as the expense of riding horses. Such diversity has raised a wide range of welfare issues faced by horses and owners alike (Hemsworth, Jongman and Coleman 2015). In an ideal post-modern context, the relationship is structured not only by human need but animal need as well (DeMello 2012). This reinforces the human-animal relationship from a post- humanistic stance as Beth, a horse owner in her early thirties, notes:

> They [horses] completely control my life. I can't go to work until I've seen to them. If I'm coming home late, I've got to make arrangements. If I go on holiday I have to put arrangements in place. You do your weekly shop, monthly purchase of horse food. You prepare for the winter in advance . . . umm . . . you buy them clothes, shoes, it's no different to having another member of the family.

The social nature surrounding horses enables them to emotionally attach and seek companionship from humans in the absence of other horses (Game 2001). Horses enjoy human company and through positive interactions they gain benefit through security, comfort and overall welfare. Although horses cannot verbally communicate, Toth (2000) explains that horses are highly sensitive to sensory stimulation and communicate through means of sight, touch, smell, sound, rhythm and kinaesthetic cues. Communication with a horse is both mental and intensely physical. The absence of verbal communication allows deep connections and bonds to develop between the two actors through embodiment. Kinaesthesia provides intense feelings between the human and the horse that allows harmonious connections. Such multi-sensual and emotional bodily experiences are fundamental to human-equine interpretations of interactions and the overall human-equine leisure experience. Both horse and human rely heavily upon embodiment in order to interconnect, allowing for haptic (sensory, tactile) encounters to occur. It is this connection that enables humans and horses to encounter what Hallberg (2008) refers to as 'entrainment', which respondents such as Charlotte, a non-horse owner, in her late forties, senses when riding:

> With Beauty, I feel I have a real connection. I feel he likes me, he likes me riding him and I like riding him. I feel I get a lot out of him sometimes you watch other people struggle riding him but I don't feel I have that.

Toth (2000, 35) asserts "(t)he joy of the ride is not only in the perfect toe position or completion of a pattern or a test but also in successful communication with the horse leading to paired harmonious movement". Irwin (1998) believes that horses need to respect their riders in order to feel safe. Human-equine interactions are intimate and embedded in powerful emotions, which instil a sense of togetherness, rhythm and harmony (Evans and Franklin 2010). Human-equine engagement through leisure forces boundaries to become blurred. Entering into such 'human-equine zones' enables human and horse bodies to experience the world through physically and spiritually interacting with their minds, personalities, sensations and emotions whilst in motion (Danby and Hannam 2016). This interface allows humans to sense the part human-part horse way of being to which Game (2001) refers. The sense of otherness is erased where human and nonhuman boundaries become blurred, allowing a sense of partnership, respect and equality within the relationship. Humans and horses learn how to be together, how to interact and move together through the bodies of each partner (Dashper 2017) and by observing bodily postures. Hallberg (2008) refers to this interconnectedness in that horses can interpret humans through the smallest of actions, body posture, smells, voice tone, sensing the human's emotional and physical cues. In addition, the horse translates subtle cues and is responsive to every single movement that the human has within its presence. Every emotion is assessed and utilised by the horse whereby a social exchange is created (Dashper 2017). Likewise, humans who know their horses well are able to pick up bodily cues and get a sense of what Brandt (2006) refers to as 'feel'; whether the horse is listening, responding and communicating effectively with the rider in partnership. As Penelope, a horse owner aged in her late fifties describes:

> I know when he needs assurance and I know when he needs to be left alone as well. Mostly I know when he needs to be left alone and I let him get on with his job [whether that's jumping or hacking out] he'll look to me for assurance as if to say 'Did I do that ok?' I say yes we did that really well [with a nice pat on this neck] so it's a two way street.

Human-equine relations within the leisure landscape

In late modernity and early post-modernity, animals have been incorporated into what is known today as 'pet culture'. This is illustrative of how human-animal interactions have been introduced and are commonplace within leisure spaces, signifying how some animals have become identified as companions to humans and live close by providing kinship roles (Franklin 1999). DeMello (2012) indicates that a pet or companion animal is defined by its close relationship with humans. Pet keeping is a widespread and accepted phenomenon within today's society, emphasising the enormous role that companion animals play in their owner's lives by providing a source of companionship, support and entertainment (Wells 2009). Consequently, companion animals now have a 'social place' within family households and daily routines (DeMello 2012).

Haraway (2003) relates the pet-human relationship to negotiating understanding between two different species. Bowes et al. (2015) refer to the transcendence of animals such as dogs that are embedded into our daily lives, living in close proximity to humans where they hold a significant place in our hearts. Subsequently, "(l)iving intimately with animals on a day-to-day basis means that pets and owners come to know each other's individual personality quirks and traits, viewing their animals as subjective beings and attributing them with human-like characteristics" (Fox 2006, 531). Furthermore, research into human-animal bonds acknowledges the emotional, psychological and physical benefits that living with animals can provide (DeMello 2012).

The human-horse relationship has a long and varied history according to Hausberger et al. (2008), who explain that in the early stages of the relationship, meat may have been the primary motivation, then through domestication horses became progressively important 'tools' for transportation. Fundamentally, this articulates the humanist approach towards human-equine relations, predominantly for human consumption, where horses were utilised for their instrumental value. Through globalisation and the increased development and consumption of leisure, increasingly animals have been incorporated into leisure and tourism processes through recreational activities. Dashper (2012) similarly acknowledges that once the horse was considered a vital partner to humans with regards to agriculture, warfare and transport, whereas nowadays it is predominantly a partner in sport and leisure. In today's post-modern society, horses are used increasingly as companion animals just like other domestic animals (Digard 1999 cited in Hausberger et al. 2008) and are now acknowledged for their intrinsic value. Horses have been associated with kinship through recognition of their individual identity and as a result, sentimentalised and close-bonded emotional attachments have been formed with humans through leisure and tourism engagement, which becomes a reoccurring argument throughout this chapter.

Within the leisure landscape, humans interact with horses in many ways. These range from occasional rides at weekends or whilst on holiday, to keeping a horse for many years and riding regularly (Robinson 1999). Robinson acknowledges the complex associations humans have with horses, in that some people own and ride their horses but are not responsible for their day-to-day care, whilst some care for horses on a daily basis but never own the animals. Others own, ride and care for their own animals. Keeping horses is labour intensive, besides riding, horses requires daily care and devotion. Dashper (2015, 7–8) identifies that "horses need substantial amounts of space and grass, a constant clean water supply as well as shelter and bedding". "Caring and training of horses must be done daily regardless of weather, human health or inclination. Daily manual labour is required to 'muck out' stables, carry hay, straw and heavy buckets" (Dashper 2015, 9). Horses need to be groomed and feet picked, rugged up and put away at night (during the winter) and let out in the morning. Horses require exercise and physical stimulation, potentially gained through riding, along with substantial amounts of financial resources towards their upkeep. Additional costs associated with horses can include livery, vets, farriers, the purchase of equine equipment and specialised clothing for both humans and horses, along with riding lessons and competition affiliation.

Encounters with horses are a means to avocation, which introduces the notion that human-equine experiences can be associated with what Stebbins (1992, 1997, 2001, 2007) refers to as a 'serious form of leisure'. Humans invest considerable amounts of emotional and physical energy, time and financial commitment in caring for and exercising their horses. In return, they gain pleasure through engagement in equine pursuits, as well as the development of close-bonded partnerships.

The concept of leisure is described by Edington et al. (1995, 33): "Leisure whether viewed as activity, free time or state of mind, provides opportunities not only for relaxation, self-improvement, cultural and family stability and interaction, but also for escape, novelty, complexity, excitement and fantasy."

Dashper (2015) specifies that horse riding is an important part of the leisure world, particularly in rural communities, within the UK, where horses form an integral part of the countryside. Motivations towards human-equine leisure interactions vary and are determined by a combination of humans' as well as horses' lifestyles, interests, needs and characteristics (Danby 2013). Belinda, a horse owner aged sixty refers to her leisure involvement with horses:

> Totally leisure related . . . it's been purely as a hobby for all those years. It involved hacks, long distance riding. I did quite a bit of hunting, pleasure rides, schooling . . . the whole general sphere of the horse world.

Within this chapter, human-equine interactions are mostly referred to within leisure landscapes, including recreational riding, grooming and sustenance of the horse. Furthermore, respondents within this study revealed that they purposefully travelled to unfamiliar destinations both within the UK (with or without their horses) and overseas to primarily engage in equestrian tourism including equine holidays, competitions or training workshops to experience, learn and appreciate cultural factors surrounding human-equine relations for the wellbeing of their horses as well as themselves.

Adventure leisure tourism as Buckley (2012) refers to, is a trillion-dollar global industry, which has emerged and grown through commercialisation of outdoor recreation (Buckley 2000, 2004; Hackbert and Lin 2009). Equestrianism incorporates elements of adventure and risk through riding as well as offering horse enthusiasts an opportunity to travel to unique destinations to engage in equestrian tourism to experience different cultures and indeed unfamiliar landscapes (Danby 2013).

Oliveria's (2009) work is illustrative of the concept of equestrianism, where she argues it can be referred to as a tourist activity because it involves leisure time, recreation, travel, supply, demand, planning, promotion and infrastructure. Olivieria considers the type of tourism associated with horses which she refers to as *of* the horse '*horse tourism*' and *on* the horse '*riding tourism*' which she argues are important considerations when creating and promoting different types of horse-related products. Torkkola (2013) depicts equestrian tourism as being represented as nature tourism, adventure tourism, rural tourism and activity tourism. Horse-based tourism ranges from shows where the tourist is passive to active recreation where the tourist is a rider travelling by horse involving adventurous or sedentary activities (Ollenburg 2005).

"Equiscapes"

Human-equine leisure pursuits and associated experiences provide an essentially hedonistic activity, allowing interaction and the opportunity to develop relationships between humans and non-humans. 'Equiscapes' as I coin the term, provide temporal, natural spaces where humans can escape from mundane routines by crossing boundaries and emerging into the horse environment, to interconnect and develop relations within the leisure landscape through various activities. 'Equiscapes' and associated human-equine experiences involve 'emotional' recreation as humans and horses are able to gain intellectual, physical and spiritual stimulation from their interactive experiences (Danby 2013).

Respondents referred to their experiences with horses as hedonistic, instilling a sense of human-equine euphoria. Such experiences are illustrative of their continuous dedication and commitment, indicating that their encounters with horses are a means to avocation or what Stebbins (2007) refers to as a 'serious form of leisure'. In this study, respondents recognised the contribution that human-equine experiences make towards wellbeing, in that human-equine encounters make the respondents as well as their horses happy, whether it's caring for or interacting with horses as a recreational activity or engaging in equestrian tourism.

Due to the social nature of horses, as Keaveney (2008) highlights, they socialise differently to humans; being herd animals their primary attachment is to the herd. However through time and a sense of trust horses will develop attachment to their humans as they form partnerships and enjoy positive interaction and being cared for, which instils them with a sense of comfort and security (Keaveney 2008). In this context, Dashper (2015) argues that horses have physical, emotional and social requirements that need to be catered for too.

Research participants' emerge as having a post-humanistic approach toward their relations with horses. They enjoy spending quality leisure time with horses, recognising them as individual sentient beings. Research respondents recognised the contribution that horses make towards their (human) emotional wellbeing and value horse companionship and the enjoyment of developing human-equine relations through coexistence. As a result of such pleasurable human-equine experiences, respondents recognised the reciprocal benefits of horses living closely with humans, in that they have both become dependent upon one another for their welfare. DeMello (2012) similarly acknowledges the spatial arrangements of animals living in close proximity with 'others' makes them amenable to living with humans in exchange for feeding and care. Whitney, a horse owner aged in her late forties, acknowledges the time spent with her horse and the reciprocal benefits:

> Oh I see him more than my children, I love him more I think than I love my children [laughs] and I think my children would say yeah you do [laughs]. No . . . umm . . . after this interview when you see me with him you'll realise the love . . . do you know what I mean? I absolutely adore him but what you put into him you get back just as much if not more. So you'll see the relationship we have when you see us both together.

Lilly a horse owner, aged early thirties, highlighted the reciprocal communication that she has with her horse when she first sees him:

> He recognises me when I go. He has a little whistle that he answers to [by whinnying] he's just lovely, I love him to bits.

Penelope, a horse owner in her late fifties revealed the pleasure of getting to know horses through social contact adds value to the relationship:

> If I'm riding another horse, I like to groom that horse. I don't like to just get on the horse and ride, I like to spend time you know having a bit of time before hand just talking to that horse and getting it to know a little bit about me so that when we ride it's not just me sitting on top of the horse and off we go. I really value that.

Penelope appreciates the importance of spending her leisure time with horses, getting to know one another through grooming. Toth (2000) similarly outlines the rapport that can be developed with horses through providing quality leisurely grooming time, explaining that the tactile and pressure sensations are calming to the horse and communicate caring intentions.

Respondents frequently spoke of the physicality associated with human-equine interactions in that horse riding as a leisure pursuit, provides a very physically intense and challenging activity where the interconnectedness between humans and horses evokes intimacy and a powerful emotional attachment which intensifies the relationship. In this sense, Keaveney (2008) argues that the human-horse intimacy is unique from anything experienced with household animals. Riding provides an exhilarating and enjoyable activity (Toth 2000) both to humans and to horses as Whitney, a horse owner, in her late forties, relates the importance of riding and general welfare responsibilities for the wellbeing of her horse as well as herself:

> Well it's my own fitness it's his fitness you know. If you had a dog and you were taking a dog on board and you were gonna look after it to the best of your ability, you would exercise it and you know I get up on a morning, first thing I do before I feed myself is feed my animals and I make sure they're alright then I come in and feed myself and get myself ready to go out to work and then when I come in on a night that's the same thing that I do again you know . . . umm . . . a bit like a neurotic mother I suppose but in ten years it's never changed.

For Whitney, the welfare of her horse and other non-humans is of utmost importance. Interestingly, her priority is the wellbeing of her animals within her daily routine. Consequently, she relates to them as kinship, regarding herself as a neurotic mother, signifying the emotional attachment and responsible attitude she has towards them.

The following section describes the experiential themes derived from interspecies (human-equine) encounters within the leisure landscape, or 'equiscape'. It becomes apparent from the testimonies of the respondents that a combination of physical and emotional benefits is obtained by horses and humans.

Escapism

Consumers of horse experiences dedicate time away from everyday life to participate and go to a special place to engage in the activity such as a riding facility (Keaveney 2008). Keaveney (2008) highlights that significant psycho-temporal sacrifices are required, as the following diary extract indicates; human spatial and temporal awareness and self-transformation surrounding the transcendence into the equiscape:

> The minute I drive through the gates I change, I love everything about the stables, smell, horses, dogs, ponies and people. Its somewhere I enjoy being.

Horse owners tend to feel totally focussed and completely in the moment when they are with their horses (Keaveney 2008), and indeed all the respondents reflected upon this. Riders encounter interconnectedness through a sense of being 'one with the horse' both in heart and spirit (Keaveney 2008). Horses have the ability to take you away from whatever you wish to escape (Toth 2000). Respondents revealed a distancing of themselves from their everyday lives when encountering equiscapes. Humans became aware of these spatial separations from their hectic schedules and family commitments. Once in close confinement with horses their self-awareness and life perceptions suddenly altered where the horse became solely the focus. Equiscapes allow humans an insight into the lives of horses, by interacting and acknowledging the world from the horses' perspective, which enhances the notion of post-humanism whereby humans are able to view the world through the nonhuman lens. These equiscapes encourage interconnectedness and cross-species communication to occur that can result in positive mutual understanding and the development of trusting partnerships which Jane, an instructor and horse owner aged in her mid-fifties, relays the consciousness of the partnership between herself and her horse:

> They're so big and strong and gentle and when you have a relationship with a horse they're so trusting. You just feel you're in a different world. It is escape . . . you escape into this sort of world . . . you just have a feeling of contentment and partnership. You know you're away from everything and you've just got this big strong trusting animal.
> (Danby and Hannam 2016)

Jane reflects upon the transition of entering into an "equiscape" where there becomes a blurring of spatial boundaries and bodies through inter-species communication and the formation of human-equine relations.

Nature-based, adventurous encounters

The benefits of being outdoors in the countryside and natural spaces were frequently acknowledged by respondents, which they described as contributors towards mutual pleasurable experiences, tranquillity and associated wellbeing, through human-equine leisure engagement. Consequently, it can be argued that the environment or space that the human-equine interaction or activity takes place in complements the human-equine experience. Respondents spoke of themselves and their horses being immersed and connected with nature as a result of equine leisure pursuits that contribute towards mutual wellbeing, which becomes evident in the following diary extract response:

> A hack is a totally different experience than going around the arena. The horses enjoy themselves out in the open they are always ready to trot and canter when they can. Riding in the woods is so scenic and peaceful.

When riding a horse, people see nature differently, their human consciousness alters, by having a different psychological perspective they become a part of nature

(Toth 2000). Sharpley and Jepson (2011) signify a connection between the natural environment and a sense of belonging, a connection with the world and harmonious feelings. An appreciation of the landscape and the tranquillity of nature were commonly referred to by respondents when relating to their human-equine experiences. Enjoying the natural scenery, the sounds and smells of nature, and horses, getting away from the usual demands of life and experiencing tranquillity and solitude were important factors that contributed towards human-equine wellbeing. Experiencing 'equiscapes', provides an opportunity for recreationists or tourists to engage with the environment not only on a physical level but at a deeper emotional level which Sharpley and Jepson (2011) suggest can enhance enjoyment of participant's activities.

Respondents spoke of the importance of visual consumption, their 'aesthetic' judgement of the countryside as Jane, an instructor and horse owner, aged mid-fifties, comments on the benefit of this to horses as well as for her:

> It's lovely to sort of see new areas and ride different paths and things . . . umm . . . it can be a little bit you know, you've got to be a bit more careful cos the horse is in a new place, a new environment. Going out on the hack it's a little bit more exciting for the horse and you but I think it does the horse good to have a little change.

Numerous respondents revealed the motive of travelling to other destinations in their leisure time to engage in equine tourism activities for the welfare of the horses and to spend quality time with them within a new landscape. Although their experiences relate to recreation, the following respondents specifically travelled away from their home to consume commercial horse riding adventure products. The riding experiences discussed are evident of both domestic and international travel, where Belinda, a horse owner in her sixties, commented:

> The one that springs to mind is the Lake District where we went with neighbours and we did a shuttle service three journeys up and down in the horse box with an absolute load of horses and we stayed in accommodation in the Lake District and rode our horses there . . . umm . . . I have done Hamsterley Forest, that's another place and Kielder. It was a mixture of the two we took our horses it was quite a few years ago and went for about four nights, stabled them up there and hacked [a leisurely ride] around both Kielder and Hamsterley Forest. I absolutely adored it. The horses loved it. It's great for them to have a change.

Katie, a horse owner in her early forties, discussed one of the international horse charity challenge rides that she was involved with to raise funds towards equine welfare. Her experience here relates to Kenya:

> I did two of the Charity Challenges . . . umm . . . the first one well actually they were both horse charities, the first one was called The Brook and we

did . . . umm . . . a ride through the Rift Valley . . . umm . . . through Kenya. I think we had to raise £3,000 each so Stephen [husband] and I did that.

When asked if she could describe her equestrian charity challenge adventure, Katie replied:

> We stayed in different places, well campsites every night. We basically rode to a different campsite, but the people who were organising it basically took your campsite down and we would be riding and we would see them coming past with all of our tents and . . . umm . . . and they would set up camp on the night so when we got to the campsite it was all set up and what have you but that was a real experience. The whole experience was absolutely fabulous. We got so close to some of the animals, a little bit dangerous on occasions as well but . . . umm . . . we got a bit close to some elephants in fact we had to be diverted away because the elephants were heading our way. We could see them but it was that fine line of being able to watch them but not get too close.

What respondents frequently enjoyed about their equine travel related experiences was the opportunity to visit new destinations to experience natural landscapes and to learn about other cultures and their interactions with horses.

Close-bonds and cultural understanding

Companion animals living in close contact with humans benefit from having their physical needs met and from the emotional bonds they experience (DeMello 2012). Animals that have close relations with humans are likely to have better physical, emotional and mental health and more social interaction than those living in isolation (DeMello 2012). Social interaction is fundamental for horses; studies by Hama, Yogo and Matsyyama (1996) revealed that human-animal interaction is good for horses as stress levels decrease while being petted as well as other benefits associated with wellbeing. The following respondents commented on the close-bonded relations they had developed with horses through leisure and the benefits associated with human-equine relations.

Tiffany, an instructor and horse owner in her early forties, stated:

> There are quite a lot of benefits really . . . umm . . . part of it is just bonding with your horse and being out on your horse. . . . Hacking out might not be as strenuous as being in the school but it's a way to see the countryside it's nice, pleasurable and relaxing, but the main thing is just to be with your horse.

Sharon a horse owner in her early forties commented on the reciprocal affection that a horse provides and the unconditional love associated with the relationship:

> If you've got a horse to look after or you've got an animal to look after the love and affection that you get back from them it's unconditional you know

and it's just lovely that something with a mind of its own loves you as much as you love it and I think that's just amazing, absolutely amazing.

Cultural understanding was frequently referred to when discussing wellbeing associated with leisure-related interactions with horses. Keaveney (2008) asserts that horse experiences teach their owners a lot about themselves as well as their relationships with others, including trust, empathy, respect, confidence and responsibility. Equine workshops and training events portray animal friendly messages to humans, enabling humans and animals to connect more effectively through greater understanding. Many workshops and leisure events offer post-humanist insights into relationships by promoting 'Natural Horsemanship' techniques for the welfare of humans and horses through mutual understanding and an appreciation of horse culture as Laura, an instructor and horse owner in her early thirties, discussed:

Well the benefits are the improvement of my own riding and my understanding of them [horses] and their needs and what works and what doesn't. Just my understanding of the horse in general really is always evolving.

Conclusion

The post-humanist approach serves as a framework in this chapter, by providing an innovative way to understand the lives and relations of humans and animals within today's post-modern world (MacCormack 2012). This approach towards human-animal relations has enabled us to explore human-equine relations, providing us with a new mode of enquiry and an innovative lens through which to contextualise human-equine interactions and experiential encounters within the leisure landscape. Due to the growing influence of pet culture and greater opportunities for leisure engagement, the post-humanist approach towards human-non-human relations demonstrates the blurring of cross-cultural boundaries between humans and horses through coexistence. In leisure encounters intimate close-bonded relationships have become an underlying expectation on the part of humans. But often there is a lack of descriptive reflection on the part of humans meaning that it is difficult to assess how the horses for their part are perceiving these relationships.

Empirically, we witnessed how humans hold post-humanistic views in that human and nonhuman lives' and spaces entangle through time as a result of leisure pursuits. Furthermore, this chapter revealed how 'equiscapes' provide temporal spaces where humans can escape from mundane routines by crossing boundaries and entering into the horse's landscape to interact and develop relations. Equiscapes and associated human-equine experiences incorporate 'emotional' recreation as humans and (we hope) horses are able to gain intellectual, physical and spiritual stimulation from their interactive experiences (Danby 2013).

This chapter shows how some humans and horses contribute to and influence the lives of each other daily. Moreover, horses have increasingly become dependent upon humans both physically and emotionally as a result of leisure processes and humans may serve as an important source of companionship to horses. Positive human-equine relations may be instrumental in securing the welfare and enjoyment of both species through the engagement and development of leisure and tourism pursuits. Within a similar vein, DeMello (2012) argues that non-humans ideally should enjoy a life of love and attention as well as humans. It became evident that the shift in human attitudes towards animals incorporates greater equality within the partnership. Valuing animals for what they are individually, enabling them to have a core focus, improves their quality of life and overall welfare. Evidently leisure processes and equine adventure travel enhances cultural understanding towards mutual wellbeing and assists in developing close-bonded inter-species relations.

The post-humanistic approach towards human-equine relations provides theoretical insight into the sharing of human-equine lifestyles and leisure related activities. The leisure landscape provides a platform that can facilitate successful partnerships between humans and non-humans. Valuing the horse as a sentient being within today's post-modern world encourages us to better understand the cultural dimensions surrounding humans and horses and assists humans to think about promoting mutual wellbeing and the fundamental welfare issues regarding human-equine relations within the leisure landscape.

References

Birke, L., J. Hockenhull, and E. Creighton. 2010. "The Horse's Tale: Narratives of Caring for/about Horses." *Society and Animals* 18: 331–347.

Bowes, M., P. Keller, R. Rollins, and R. Gifford. 2015. "Parks, Dogs, and Beaches: Human-Wildlife Conflict and the Politics of Place." In *Domestic Animals and Leisure*, edited by N. Carr, 146–174. Hampshire: Palgrave Macmillan.

Brandt, K. 2006. "Intelligent Bodies: Embodied Subjectivity Human-Horse Communication." In *Body Embodiment Symbolic Interaction and the Sociology of the Body*, edited by D.V. Waskul, 141–152. Hampshire: Ashgate Publishing Ltd.

Buckley, R. C. 2000. "NEAT Trends: Current Issues in Nature, Eco and Adventure Tourism." *International Journal of Tourism Research* 2(6): 437–444.

Buckley, R.C. 2004. "Skilled Commercial Adventure: The Edge of Tourism." In *Environmental Horizons in Tourism*, edited by T.V. Singh, 37–48. Wallingford, UK: CAB International.

Buckley, R. C. 2012. "Rush as a Key Motivation in Skilled Adventure Tourism: Resolving the Risk Recreation Paradox." *Tourism Management* 33: 961–970.

Carr, N. 2015. "Defining Domesticated Animals and Exploring Their Uses by and Relationships with Humans Within the Leisure Landscape." In *Domestic Animals and Leisure*, edited by N. Carr, 1–16. Hampshire: Palgrave Macmillan.

Crouch, D. 2010. "Flirting with Space: Thinking Landscape Relationally." *Cultural Geographies* 17(1): 5–18.

Danby, P. 2013. "A Critical Investigation into Human-Equine Interactions and Associated Experiences as a Leisure and Tourist Activity in the North East of England." Unpublished Ph.D. Thesis.

Danby, P., and K. Hannam. 2016. "Entrainment: Human-Equine Leisure Mobilities." In *Tourism and Leisure Mobilities: Politics, Work and Play*, edited by J. Rickly, K. Hannam, and M. Mostafanezhad, 27–38. Oxon: Routledge.

Daniels, M.J., and W. Norman. 2005. "Motivations of Equestrian Tourists: An Analysis of the Colonial Cup Races." *Journal of Sport Tourism* 10(3): 201–210.

Dashper, K. 2012. "Together, Yet Still Not Equal? Sex Integration in Equestrian Sport." *Asia-Pacific Journal of Health, Sport and Physical Recreation* 3(3): 213–225.

Dashper, K. 2015. "Strong, Active Women: (Re)Doing Rural Femininity Through Equestrian Sport and Leisure." *Ethnography* 17(3): 350–368.

Dashper, K. 2017. "Human-Animal Relationships in Equestrian Sport and Leisure." In *Human-Animal Relationships in Equestrian Sport and Leisure*, edited by K. Daspher, 159–177. Oxon: Routledge.

DeMello, M. 2012. *Animals and Society: An Introduction to Human-Animal Studies*. New York, NY: Columbia University Press.

Digard, J.P. 1999. "Research into the Social Science of Horses: Why? and How?" *Equine Veterinary Journal* 28: 56–57.

Edington, C.R., D. Jordan, D. DeGraaf, and S. Edington. 1995. *Leisure and Life Satisfaction: Foundational Perspectives*. Dubuque, IA: Benchmark and Brown.

Evans, R., and A. Franklin. 2010. "Equine Beats: Unique Rhythms (and floating harmony) of Horses and Riders." In *Geographies of Rhythm: Nature, Place, Mobilities and Bodies*, edited by T. Edensor, 173–188. Farnham: Ashgate Publishing Ltd.

Fox, R. 2006. "Animal Behaviors, Post-Human Lives: Everyday Negotiations of the Animal-Human Divide in Pet Keeping." *Social and Cultural Geography* 7(4): 525–537.

Franklin, A. 1999. *Animals and Modern Cultures: A Sociology of Human-Animal Relations in Modernity*. London: Sage.

Friedmann, E., S. Thomas, and T. Eddy. 2005. "Companion Animals and Human Health: Physical and Cardiovascular Influences." In *Companion Animals and Us, Exploring the Relationships Between People and Pets*, edited by A.L. Podersbeck, E.S. Paul, and J.A. Serpell, 129–142. Cambridge: Cambridge University Press.

Game, A. 2001. "Riding: Embodying the Centaur." *Body and Society* 7(4): 1–12.

Game, A., and A. Metcalfe. 2011. "'My Corner of the World': Bachelard and Bondi Beach." *Emotion, Space and Society* 4: 42–50.

Gilbert, M., and J. Gillett 2014. "Into the Mountains and Across the Country: Emergent Forms of Equine Adventure Leisure in Canada." *Society and Leisure* 37(2): 313–325.

Goodrum, A.L. 2015. "Riding Dress History, with a Twist: The Side-Saddle Habit and the Horse during the Early Twentieth Century." In *Domestic Animals and Leisure*, edited by N. Carr, 175–200. Hampshire: Palgrave Macmillan.

Hackbert, P.H., and X. Lin. 2009. "Equestrian Trail Riding: An Emerging Economic Contributor to the Local Rural Appalachian Economy." *Journal of Business Case Studies* 5(6): 47–58.

Hallberg, L. 2008 *Walking the Way of the Horse: Exploring the Power of the Horse-Human Relationship*. New York, NY: iUniverse.

Hama, H., M. Yogo, and Y. Matsyyama. 1996. "Effects of Stroking Horses on Both Humans' and Horses' Heart Rate Responses." *Japanese Psychology Research* 38(2): 66–73.

Haraway, D.J. 2003. *Companion Specifies Manifesto*. Cambridge: Prickly Paradigm Press.

Hausberger, M., H. Roche, S. Henry, and E. Visser. 2008. "A Review of the Human-Horse Relationship." *Applied Animal Behavior Science* 109(1): 1–24.

Helgadóttir, G. 2006. "The Culture of Horsemanship and Horse-Based Tourism in Iceland." *Current Issues in Tourism* 9(6): 535–548.

Helgadóttir, G., and I. SigurÐóttir. 2008. "Horse-Based Tourism: Community, Quality and Disinterest in Economic Value." *Scandinavian Journal of Hospitality and Tourism* 8(2): 105–121.

Hemsworth, L.M., E. Jongman, and G. Coleman. 2015. "Recreational Horse Welfare: The Relationships Between Recreational Horse Owner Attributes and Recreational Horse Welfare." *Applied Animal Behavior Science* 165: 1–16.

Instone, L. 1998. "The Coyote's at the Door: Re-Visioning Human-Environment Relations in the Australian Context." *Ecumene* 5(4): 452–467.

Irwin, C. 1998. *Horses Don't Lie*. New York: Marlowe and Company.

Keaveney, S.M. 2008. "Equines and Their Human Companions." *Journal of Business Research* 61(5): 444–454.

Kline, C.S., D. Cardenas, P. Viren, and J. Swanson. 2015. "Using a Community Tourism Development Model to Explore Equestrian Trail Tourism Potential in Virginia." *Journal of Destination Marketing and Management* 4(2): 79–87.

Lorimer, J. 2009. "Posthumanism/Posthumanistic Geographies." In *International Encyclopedia of Human Geography*, edited by R. Kitchin and N. Thrift, Oxford, Elsevier, 344–354.

MacCormack, P. 2012. *Posthuman Ethics*. Surrey: Ashgate Publishing Ltd.

Markwell, K. 2015. "Birds, Beasts and Tourists: Human-Animal Relationships in Tourism." In *Animals and Tourism: Understanding Diverse Relationships*, edited by K. Markwell, 1–23. Bristol: Channel View Publications.

Oliveria, C. 2009. *Turismo de Tradição – Estudo do caso do turismo equestre em Portugal -Tese de Doutoramento.* Perpignan, França: Université de Perpignan.

Ollenburg, C. 2005. "Worldwide Structure of the Equestrian Tourism Sector." *Journal of Ecotourism* 4(1): 47–55.

Philo, C., and C. Wilbert 2000. "Animal Spaces, Beastly Places: An Introduction." In *Animal Spaces, Beastly Places, New Geographies of Human-Animal Relations*, edited by C. Philo and C. Wilbert, 1–34. Oxon: Routledge.

Robinson, I.H. 1999. "The Human-Horse Relationship: How Much Do We Know?" *Equine Veterinary Journal* 31(S28): 42–45.

Sharpley, R., and D. Jepson. 2011. "Rural Tourism: A Spiritual Experience?" *Annals of Tourism Research* 38(1): 52–71.

Sigurðardóttir, I., and G. Helgadóttir. 2015. "Riding High: Quality and Customer Satisfaction in Equestrian Tourism in Iceland." *Scandinavian Journal of Hospitality and Tourism* 5(1–2): 105–121.

Stebbins, R. 1992. *Amateurs, Professionals and Serious Leisure*. Montreal: McGill-Queen's University Press.

Stebbins, R. 1997. "Casual Leisure: A Conceptual Statement." *Leisure Studies* 16(1): 17–25.

Stebbins, R. 2001. "The Costs and Benefits of Hedonism: Some Consequences of Taking Casual Leisure Seriously." *Leisure Studies* 20(4): 305–309.

Stebbins, R. 2007. *Serious Leisure: A Perspective for Our Time*. London: Transaction Publishers.

Thrift, N. 2004. "Intensities of Feeling: Towards a Geography of Effect." *Geografiska Annater B* 86(1): 57–78.

Torkkola, J. 2013. *Seeing the World From Horseback: An Overview of Hungarian and Finnish Equestrian Tourism with Special Focus on Akác-tanya Farm*. Saarbrücken: Lambert Academic Publishing.

Toth, D.M. 2000. "The Psychology of Women and Horses." In *Of Women and Horses*, edited by R. Berman, 31–41. Irvine, CA: Bow Tie Press.

Urbanik, J., and M. Morgan. 2013. "A Tale of Tails: The Place of Dog Parks in the Urban Imaginary." *Geoforum* 44: 292–302.

Wells, D.L. 2009. "The Effects of Animals on Human Health and Well Being." *Journal of Social Issues* 65(3): 523–543.

Wilbert, C. 2009. "Animal Geographies." *International Encyclopedia of Human Geography* edited by R. Kitchin and N. Thrift, Oxford, Elsevier 122–126.

11 Pampered prisoners

Meeting the ethological needs of the modern sport horse to enhanced equine welfare

Antonia J. Z. Henderson

Introduction

Not quite a pet, yet certainly a more intimate companion than agricultural livestock, the modern sport horse holds a unique position in the human-animal dynamic. The term "sport horse" (sometimes referred to as "performance horse" or "show horse") refers to those horses that are bred for and perform at the higher echelons of equestrian sport in the traditional Olympic disciplines of show jumping, three-day eventing, combined driving and dressage, and are generally of European bloodlines. It is these equine elite that I am referring to in this chapter.

In spite of over 6000 years of domestication (Budiansky 1997) that has selected for a myriad of highly specialised physiological and psychological attributes designed for demanding disciplines, the horse's ethological needs for continual foraging, movement and social interaction have changed little from those of their ancestors (e.g. Christensen et al. 2002). Yet today's current sport horse husbandry practices too often fall short in meeting those needs.

Feral[1] horses typically live in bands or harems consisting of one dominant stallion, several adult mares and their young offspring. Herd stability is paramount for survival and bands form cohesive units, with members often remaining together for life (Araba and Crowell-Davis 1994). To make the best use of the available food resources, bands graze almost continuously over large territories, varying in size from 1 to 48 square kilometres (Kieper 1986). The feral horse's life of liberty comes with a price; horses are vulnerable to the perils of predators, parasites, harsh climatic changes and scarce resources, making survival a precarious business.

Domestication over the millennium has necessitated more intensive management practices to arrive at the extreme end of the continuum evidenced in the housing of the modern sport horse. These horses, in contrast to their ancestors, are safely housed in luxurious multi-million dollar facilities, exercised and groomed regularly and see a plethora of healthcare professionals (farriers, veterinarians, grooms, chiropractors, massage therapists etc.). These horses can usually see their equine neighbours but not touch them. Some are afforded "turn-out" (time spent outside of the stall in small paddock enclosures for a few hours per day). Contact with other horses is discouraged with electric wire or double fencing separating enclosures. The dietary norm for today's North American sport horse, emphasising quality and necessarily limited in quantity, consists of highly palatable concentrates and rich timothy or alfalfa hay all of which is consumed quickly, leaving the horse for many hours in the stall with an empty stomach and nothing to do. When domestic horses are given the opportunity to live in natural conditions, their social organisation and time budgets are similar to those of their feral counterparts – forming lifelong, stable, social groups and foraging 16–20 hours per day over vast home ranges (Cooper and Albentosa 2005; Feh 2002).

Undoubtedly, as many equine scientists have suggested, today's sport horses' psychological wellbeing would be immeasurably enhanced from living with their herd mates on the open range, grazing at liberty on medium quality roughage (e.g. Luescher, McKeown and Halip 1991; Sarrafchi and Blokhuis 2013). However, this is not a solution that is generally palatable and/or feasible for owners or equine facilities managers, who assume responsibility for 15 to over 100 sport horses at a boarding facility, where horses are housed, fed, turned out for exercise and maintained, and owners come regularly to ride and receive coaching. Not only are owners protective of their costly investment, most develop a strong bond with their horses. Competing and working intensely with an animal over a number of years toward specific competition goals enhances this bond. Most riders describe their horses as they would a best friend and care intensely about their wellbeing. They fear their horses will injure themselves if provided greater liberty, let alone liberty with other horses. In an increasingly litigious society, stakeholders are reluctant to take what they believe to be unnecessary risks. Owners who sustain extravagant costs at a training facility expect their performance horses to feed on the best quality hay and grain, and to look the part of a sleek sport horse. Even if owners were willing to allow their horses a more "natural" existence, prohibitively costly real estate makes pasture acreage a luxury many facilities cannot provide. Thus, most sport horses live a life far removed from their ancestors – where the evidence presented in this chapter will suggest that their well-intentioned owners have subjected them to a life of significant suffering.

My focus is to illustrate how we might bridge the divide between the disparate lifestyles of sport horses and their free-ranging ancestors. A walk down the aisle of a typical sport horse training facility, with horses housed in spacious, deeply bedded stalls, or enjoying an appointment with their massage therapist does not bring images of animal cruelty to mind. Certainly few owners would knowingly consent to their animals being abused. However, as I will outline in this chapter, the psychological and physiological wellbeing of today's sport horse is compromised; their suffering is immense, invisible and thankfully reversible. Relatively minimal management changes can enhance sport horses' wellbeing without compromising the goals of industry professionals and owners.

Fraser et al.'s "integrative model"

In a theoretical paper discussing the assessment of animal welfare, Fraser and colleagues have proposed an "integrative model" to assess all animal welfare (Fraser et al. 1997). In the accompanying figure (see Figure 11.1) I have modified their model to fit specifically the dilemma of the modern sport horse (entitled "The Equine Prisoner's Model"). Circle A depicts the "*evolved adaptations*" that horses bring to their present environment, and Circle B depicts the "*environmental challenges*" that these horses must currently meet. When horses live in the environment for which they were evolutionarily designed, adaptations and challenges correspond, and the overlap between the circles is large; when they are moved out of their natural environment, as is the case with sport horses, the circles no longer overlap entirely. It is this imperfect correspondence between adaptations and challenges that becomes critical for sport horse welfare.

In the area to the left of the overlap, we have the horse's evolved adaptations that no longer serve a useful purpose. Here, we can place the feral horse's hair trigger flight response, the aptitude to form stable and lasting pair bonds with conspecifics, or the capacity to live on poor forage spread over large territories. We compromise the sport horse's welfare because the adaptation includes a motivational need to perform behaviours that now have no outlet for expression (e.g. a motivational need to graze is frustrated when the horse has no access to pasture), while simultaneously blocking the positive benefits associated with that behaviour (e.g. grazing promotes healthy gut functioning, exercise, opportunities for socialisation etc.)

In the area to the right of the overlap we have challenges in the environment for which the horse does not possess the corresponding adaptations. Here we can situate equine welfare problems discussed in this chapter such as the failure to cope with confinement, social isolation and a concentrated, high quality, low quantity diet.

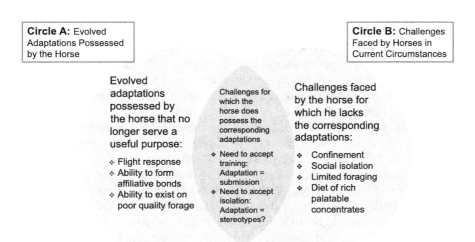

Figure 11.1 Equine Prisoners Model; based on Fraser et al. (1997) and Henderson (2007)

In the centre overlap we have challenges faced by horses for which they *do* possess the corresponding adaptations. This would include qualities such as the horse's strength, athleticism and an evolved social structure, based on dominance hierarchies, that predisposes horses to willingly acquiesce to the one in charge. These characteristics are what have allowed us to domesticate the horse so successfully through the centuries as a beast of burden, method of transport and now primarily for sport (Budiansky 1997).

A perfect correspondence of adaptations and challenges does not necessarily ensure optimal welfare; a starving pregnant mustang *is* living in the environment for which she was evolutionarily designed. When we have orchestrated the horse's transfer into an environment of our choosing, however, this places a moral responsibility on industry professionals and owners to present these horses with challenges that are within reach of their adapted behavioural and psychological limits – that is, to increase the overlap of Fraser's circles (see Figure 11.1).

Circle A and equine stereotypies: when adaptations no longer serve a useful purpose

Since horses make difficult research subjects due to obvious language barriers, and consistently perform well in spite of immense physiological and psychological suffering (injuries, lameness, ulcers, depression, anxiety etc.), measuring equine wellbeing has been an imprecise science. When adaptations have no outlet for expression, but where the motivation to perform them remains high, the expression of these behaviours may surface in the form of stereotypies. Albeit a crude measurement, the presence of stereotypies provides a starting point for exploring equine wellbeing.

Stereotypies, observed in a wide variety of species living in captivity, have been defined as repetitive behaviours that follow a ritualised, invariant sequence and appear to serve no obvious purpose (Houpt and McDonnell 1993; Luescher, Mc Keown and Halip 1991). The stereotypy is thought to derive from a normal behaviour to satisfy a goal which cannot be satisfied in the current environment. The resulting behaviour becomes an abbreviated version of what was once a purposeful and normal activity, and, as the stress is prolonged, the behaviour becomes repetitive, invariant and chronic.

Examples of stereotypies include *Weaving*, where the horse remains stationary, but shifts weight between the front legs, or among all four legs. This may originate as an impeded walking sequence where a stall-bound horse is highly motivated to reach an intended goal – most likely, food, companions or freedom – but is prevented from doing so. *Cribbing* – where the horse grasps the edge of a horizontal surface with the front incisors, and extends and draws the neck backwards to produce a burp-like sound, or *windsucking* which is accomplished without holding onto any surface – both appear to be associated with frustrated feeding behaviour. Stall-bound horses generally consume their typically rich and highly palatable feeds quickly, and thus satisfy their biological needs while the motivational drive to forage remains acute (Henderson 2007; Sarrafchi and Blokhuis 2013; Wickens and Heleski 2010).

Evidence for stereotypies being indicative of compromised welfare is apparent when considering the context in which they develop. They are greater in single-housed than group-housed animals, associated with restricted diet and impoverished environments, are greater in intensely managed systems for horses in demanding disciplines and may result in self-damage (e.g. as in self-mutilation) (Mason and Latham 2004; McDonnell 2008; Sarrafchi and Blokhuis 2013). Although appearing relatively benign, less extreme stereotypies (e.g. mild stall walking, head nodding, or tongue playing) may still indicate welfare issues, and have been associated with the later development of more serious stereotypic behaviour (Nicol 1999; Waters, Nicol and French 2002).

Indeed, since stereotypies have never been observed in free-ranging feral horses, yet are seen at rates of 2.5 percent to 67 percent in domesticated horses (McGreevy, French and Nicol 1995b; Waters, Nicol and French 2002, Visser, Ellis and Van Reenen 2008), stereotypies have more aptly been named the "*disease of domestication*" (Marsden 2002).

Circle B: environmental challenges for which the horse does not possess the corresponding adaptations

From a human perspective, modern day equestrian facilities are designed with the horse's best interest, health and safety at heart, yet confront horses with environmental challenges that stretch their ability to adapt. Confinement, solitary confinement, high quality/low quantity diets and the extra toll of competition all place extraordinary demands on today's sport horses, which they often endure so invisibly that their suffering is not readily apparent.

Confinement and solitary confinement

Horses have been evolutionarily designed to forage over large territories, and periodically explode with sudden bursts of speed to flee actual or perceived threats. Sport horse stables that afford little or no turn-out, or turn-out in tiny enclosures compromise wellbeing by thwarting this innate desire to move. Studies across the globe overwhelmingly come to the same robust finding that as the time outside of the stable increases, rates of stereotypic behaviour decrease (e.g. Lesimple, Poissonnet and Hausberger 2016). Although confinement is stressful, it is the solitary nature of that confinement that exerts the heavier toll on these highly social animals. The fact that stereotypies are almost never seen in cavalry mounts (Houpt and Ogilvie-Graham 2002) and mares used for urine collection to make estrogen supplements (Houpt, Houpt and Johnson 2001; Flannigan and Stookey 2002) who live in highly restricted tie-stalls, but can touch and interact with neighbours, speaks to fact that tactile companionship may be even more important than freedom (Houpt, Houpt and Johnson 2001).

Recent research is providing convincing *causal* evidence about the link between impoverished environments and the development of stereotypies. For example, Yarnell and colleagues found when horses were group-housed with full visual and tactile contact with conspecifics, they showed the lowest physiological indicators of stress (heart rate, eye temperature, cortisol levels etc.) and were also the easiest to handle. When housed singly, with no social contact, they experienced the highest stress responses and were also much more difficult to manage (Yarnell et al. 2015). The repeated measures design (i.e. the *same horses* participated in each of the housing conditions) demonstrates that the restrictive housing was the contributing factor to the horses' increasing stress and decreasing compliance.

In an elegant prospective study, Visser, Ellis and Van Reenen (2008) examined the impact of first time stabling on 36 two-year-old, non-stereotypic, Warmblood colts and fillies. For 12 weeks half the horses were housed in individual stalls while the other half pair-shared a larger stall. Strikingly, by the study's end, 67 percent of the individually stalled horses developed serious stereotypies such as cribbing and weaving, whereas none of the pair-housed horses did so. Since none of the horses exhibited stereotypies at the study's onset, this longitudinal study provides a convincing causal link between social isolation and development of stereotypies.

In short, housing horses in individual stalls may be a great idea for humans, but is a poor idea for horses. As Davidson comments, "Stabling our horses usually benefits only one half of the horse-human relationship – the human" (1999, 9).

Isolation of stereotypic horses

Since many sport horse trainers and facilities managers mistakenly believe that horses learn stereotypies from one another, "offenders" are commonly isolated, further compromising their welfare (e.g. McBride and Long 2001). However, there has been no evidence for this "copycat" hypothesis (Nicol 1999; Wickens and Heleski 2010), nor that horses learn any behaviours by modelling conspecifics (Houpt 1998; Murphy and Arkins 2007). One explanation for purported stereotypy mimicry, is that the environment that precipitated the development of a stereotypy in one horse will do so in another (Houpt and McDonnell 1993). Ninomiya (2007) proposes that stereotypies may appear to be "copied" only if the non-stereotypical horse is motivated to learn the behaviour – in other words, both the "demonstrator" (the stereotypic horse) and the "observer" (the non-stereotypic horse) are living in a stressful environment. Observers pick up olfactory and visual stress cues from the demonstrator, which intensifies the stressful environment, the observer tries out the stereotypy, the behaviour is rewarded through the dopamine neural pathway, and stress is reduced. Consequently, the reinforced behaviour will continue to be performed in the future.

Current feeding practices: the best is not the best

The typical sport horse diet of high quality, and necessarily limited quantity, concentrates and forage is problematic for horses designed to spend the majority of their time budgets grazing. Their psychological drive to forage remains long after their meal has disappeared, making them vulnerable to the development of stereotypies. Long periods with an empty stomach also makes horses vulnerable to equine gastric ulcer syndrome (EGUS), the result of an imbalance between the protective and acid producing functions of the stomach. Designed to have a consistently full gut, horses produce gastric juices constantly, and when there is no food to buffer them the protective stomach tissue is eroded. Indeed, the association between an empty stomach and the formation of ulcers is so reliable that food deprivation is used as a mechanism for creating ulceration in research animals (Murray and Eichorn 1996; Murray, Eichorn and Jeffrey 2001). Clinical signs of ulcers include weight loss, poor appetite, listless performance, depression and gastrointestinal discomfort. However, symptoms can be sufficiently subtle as to go undetected. A definitive confirmation of EGUS is only possible through endoscopy (Murray, Eichorn and Jeffrey 2001; Murray 2004). Endoscopically proven prevalence rates have been reported in 58 percent – 66 percent of hunter, jumper and dressage horses (Luthersson et al. 2009; Marqués et al. 2011), and a surprising 53 percent of pleasure horses (Luthersson et al. 2009).

The prevention and cure of ulcers is straightforward; temporarily easing the training regime and pasture turn-out (or, next best, free-choice hay) will cure ulcers in a matter of days. The medication, Omeprazole ®, which suppresses gastric acid secretion and increases gastric juice pH, is a standard, highly effective treatment. However, most researchers concur that medication needs to be accompanied by management changes to promote ulcer healing and prevent reoccurrence (e.g. Sutton 2014).

Challenges of competition

Jones and McGreevy (2010) comment that we set out extraordinary challenges for the horse in competition, because the desire to win goes beyond the notions of fun or even success; it requires that we outperform other competitors. By definition, each successful competition requires increasingly greater challenges. As challenges increase, animal welfare is compromised. And, because competition requires practice, more intense, longer, harder training of increasing difficulty, welfare is again compromised (more travel, more social isolation, changing environments, changing feeding schedules, changing social groups, and more taxing performances). Even at home, competition horses face numerous environmental challenges outside of their evolutionary adaptations, which are further exacerbated when on the road. McClure and colleagues (2005) found that exposing horses to a simulated typical horse show environment (transport to and from the site, and housing without turn-out, in an unfamiliar environment) reliably produced ulceration in horses without pre-existing ulcers, and could do so in less than 5 days.

The overlap

Horses adapting to environmental challenges: the "coping hypothesis"

There is some evidence that stereotypies may serve as an adaptive mechanism, so called do-it-yourself enrichments (Mason and Latham 2004), that may act as a buffer against psychological distress (Cooper and Albentosa 2005; Fejsáková et al. 2013; McGreevy 1997). The complex relationship among stereotypies, palatable grains and the release of beta endorphins supports the notion of the coping mechanism (Dodman et al. 1987; Gillham et al. 1994; Pell and McGreevy 1999). These sweet grains trigger a release of opioid peptides in the central nervous system, which then bind to and activate the parts of the brain associated with stereotypies and intensify the stererotypic behaviour (Gillham et al. 1994). Equine stereotypies are also believed to provide a "mantra effect" similar to that described by individuals on the autism spectrum, who note the calming and focussing properties of "stimming" (repetitive and stylized pacing, rocking, twirling etc.) (Mason and Latham 2004).

Cribbing may also offer relief for ulcers by momentarily extending the stomach and releasing pressure on ulcerated tissue, while increased salivary flow attenuates the acidity of stomach excretions. The erroneous belief that cribbing causes colic is more likely explained by the presence of ulcers, which, when treated, often reduces the occurrence of both.

Convincing support for the "coping hypothesis" has been provided by Briefer Freymond and colleagues (2015) who experimentally induced a physiological stress response with a synthetic adrenocorticotropic hormone (ACTH) injection in a group of cribbers and non-cribbers, and then compared physiological indicators of stress such as heart rate and salivary cortisol levels. Chronic cribbers who cribbed during the ACTH test had salivary cortisol levels similar to non-cribbing controls, whereas chronic cribbers who did not crib had elevated cortisol levels.

Although this research suggests that some stereotypies may be partially successful in coping with environmental deficiencies, we cannot then assume that simply allowing their continued expression ensures good welfare. A weaving horse will not experience improved psychological wellbeing by simply being allowed to weave. To significantly improve welfare, one must also address and satisfy the end goal – in the weaver's case, undoubtedly, contact with other horses.

Returning to the Equine Prisoner's Model, stereotypies may serve as the horse's own attempt to embrace the more desirable overlap area in the model – environmental challenges for which the horse *does* possess the corresponding adaptations. This valiant, albeit not entirely effective, new adaptation to reduce physiological arousal in stressful circumstances is possibly the horse's best bid to gain a modicum of control in an uncontrollable situation.

The horse's adaptations thwarted: the cruelty of prevention

Horses meet yet another roadblock when they are prevented from performing the very behaviours that may alleviate their distress in an adverse environment. This new, compounded, welfare problem may be one of the most egregious, albeit inadvertent, cruelties (Briefer Freymond et al. 2015; Cooper and McGreevy 2002; Hothersall and Casey 2012; McGreevy 1997, Wickens and Heleski 2010). Cribbing, in particular, has precipitated a wealth of "remedies".

Various collars that reduce or eliminate cribbing by applying pressure, electric shocks or spikes into the neck are common industry practice. However, McGreevy (1997) found that collars reduced cribbing while on, but when removed, horses cribbed more aggressively. Consequently, the collars actually result in an *increased* motivation to crib.

"Cribbing rings", inserted through the gums between the upper incisors, cause pain in the gums when the horse attempts to crib. Some veterinarians have suggested using larger rings drilled into the bone, as these are less apt to shift (Campbell Smith 2006; Smith-Thomas 2009).

Surgical intervention, the "Modified Forssell's Myectomy", involves cutting out a section of the ventral branch of the spinal accessory nerve on both sides of the neck along with major neck muscle tissue. Although marketed as a successful procedure, particularly if performed at the first instance of cribbing (Baia et al. 2015), "success" rates are modest – 61 percent (Krisová, Žert and Žuffová 2015), and surgical complications significant – 21 percent (Baia et al. 2015).

Even more benign, so-called, "humane" collars[2] effectively stop the horse from performing the adaptation he has created to cope with his challenging environment, and thus impose ever greater and eventually insurmountable welfare challenges.

Increasing the overlap: human challenges

A further difficulty in increasing the overlap in the Equine Prisoner's Model is recognising when we have succeeded in providing that elusive space where adaptations and challenges correspond. There is a default assumption that horses are happy when there are no obvious indicators to the contrary. However, there is evidence that industry professionals and owners often misinterpret, or miss entirely, many behavioural indicators of equine distress (e.g. Lesimple and Hausberger 2014).

THE INVISIBILITY OF BEHAVIOURAL CUES OF DISTRESS

In a study of 373 horses from 26 riding schools, Lesimple and Hausberger (2014) found large discrepancies between what caretakers reported about the horses in their care (5 percent stereotypy prevalence) and what researchers observed in the stable (37 percent prevalence). The discrepancy was evident for milder stereotypies, and for more maladaptive and obvious stereotypies (researchers observed 23 percent of horses weaving, but only 8 percent were identified by caretakers). Greater exposure to stereotypies exacerbated this effect. In the stable where stereotypies reached 70 percent, the discrepancy between caretaker reports and objective researcher measurements was the greatest. Lesimple and Hausberger (2014) note that caretakers' consistent underestimation of these poor-welfare indicators mirrors that found in nurses and doctors who tend to underestimate the severity of patients' pain (as do Hirsh, Callandar and Robinson 2011; Lidén et al. 2012). Prolonged exposure to large populations of suffering individuals presumably distorts healthcare professionals and horse caretakers' perceptions of "normal" behaviours and expressions.

Horses' propensity to suffer silently (might we call it stoicism?) further complicates the task of ensuring their wellbeing. Yarnell, Hall and Billet (2013) found that horses undergoing an abbreviated, 10-minute "sham"[3] clipping, mimicking an actual clipping procedure but with clipping blades removed, experienced significant physiological stress (higher cortisol levels, elevated heart rate etc.), regardless of whether they had been categorised as "compliant" or "non-compliant" based on their previous clipping history. The authors suggest that compliant horses may suppress flight responses when escape is not possible, leading to adverse physiological health and the development of abnormal behaviours – in short, a state of "learned helplessness".

LEARNED HELPLESSNESS

Learned helplessness occurs when horses (like other animals, including humans) face prolonged inescapable stress, and passively resign themselves to their dire circumstances even when an escape route has been reintroduced (Seligman, Maier and Geer 1968). Hall and colleagues (2008) suggest that learned helplessness is a logical adaptation; when behaviour has no impact on consequences, there ceases to be any motivation to trial novel strategies. This passivity becomes maladaptive because it generalises to other aspects of horses' behavioural repertoire, and results in negative manifestations such as ulcers, weight loss and stereotypic behaviour.

What trainers may mistake as obedience and successful training may more likely represent a horse who has given up trying to escape from inescapable, conflicting pressure. When the equine discipline requires a flat affect such as western pleasure horses, show hunters, or "bomb proof" school horses, a state of learned helplessness is often considered not only normal, but desirable.

Increasing the overlap: human adaptations

Almost all research agrees that preventing stereotypies initially is far more effective than trying to eradicate them once they become established (e.g. Luescher et al. 1991). Over time, stereotypies become emancipated from the original stressor, requiring little cognitive processing or need for sensory feedback. They are said to have moved into "central control" where they are triggered more readily, performed in more diverse situations and are more resistant to modification (Hothersall and Casey 2012; Mason and Latham 2004).

Although these "scars of the past" (Mason and Latham 2004, 563) will likely persist in spite of enrichment modifications, a failure to reduce or eliminate stereotypies should not be interpreted as a failure to improve welfare. Welfare may still be substantially enhanced through a variety of alternative management practices, both for horses with existing stereotypies and their compliant, non-stereotypic, but potentially more compromised, neighbours.

FORAGE: DECREASE QUALITY; INCREASE QUANTITY

Although free pasture access remains the gold standard, alternatives are available to satisfy feeding motivation that may be more realistically provided in sport horse boarding facilities. The industry standard of providing the richest, finest quality hay may not be in the best interests of the horse (Cooper and Albentosa 2005; Mazzola et al. 2016; McGreevy et al. 1995a). For sport horses with higher energy needs, some high quality hay may be necessary, but can be supplemented with higher-fiber (less delicious) hay that will allow horses to eat for longer periods, and satisfy foraging needs without contributing to obesity (Davidson and Harris 2002). Forage consumption can also be slowed with the use of small-holed hay nets, doubling and tripling up small-holed hay nets (Ellis et al. 2015b), mangers with difficult access, spreading hay thinly over a larger area (Davidson and Harris 2002), or placing several hay nets in multiple locations (Ellis et al. 2015a).

Providing a variety of forage choices at multiple feeding stations also slows consumption, more closely mimics natural grazing and thus enriches the environment of stabled horses (Goodwin, Davidson and Harris 2002; Davidson and Harris 2002; Thorne et al. 2005). Goodwin et al. (2002) note that when given a choice of multiple forages, horses always consumed their less preferred forage along with their preferred forage. The authors suggest that the flexibility to selectively graze on a variety of available forages likely evolved as an adaptation that allowed horses to meet their energy requirements from whatever scarce resources were available (see also Thorne et al. 2005).

REDUCE CONCENTRATES

For sport horses competing in demanding disciplines, forage generally needs to be supplemented with high protein concentrates (oats, corn, pelleted grains etc.). However, palatable grains seem to be involved in the complex relationship between stereotypies and endogenous opiates, both of which promote dopamine production and seem to exacerbate stereotypies, particularly cribbing (Wickens and Heleski 2010).

As with forage, making horses work harder to access their grain (e.g. adding chaff to concentrates, placing smooth large stones in the bottom of the feeding tub, or using foraging devices that allow small amounts of food to fall out of a rolling ball or barrel) increase feeding time and encourage foraging behaviour (Malpass and Weigler 1994; Winskill, Waran and Young 1996). Mazzola and colleagues trained cribbers and matched controls to use a food dispenser (Quaryka ®) where horses activated a wheel to deliver small amounts of concentrates. Quaryka ® increased the time spent feeding for both cribbers and non-cribbers, and cribbers showed a significant reduction of their cribbing behaviour. Although cribbing "rebounded" to pre-intervention levels when Quaryka® was removed, the authors note that the 15-day intervention may have been insufficient to impact cribbing behaviour over the long term (Mazzola et al. 2016).

Interestingly, simply increasing meal frequency of concentrates does not necessarily reduce stereotypic behaviour, and in some cases exacerbates it. From survey data from 622 Swiss performance horse stables and 2341 horses, Bachmann, Audige and Stauffacher (2003) found that feeding four times per day *increased* the likelihood of stereotypic activity, compared with horses fed *less* or *more* often (see also McGreevy et al. 1995a). Horses fed less often may have experienced less emotional stress, having had fewer opportunities to anticipate food, whereas horses fed more often were presumably more satiated and less likely to perform anticipatory behaviours. Cooper et al. (2005) also found that increasing meal frequency *increased* locomotor stereotypic behaviour (weaving and head nodding), but *decreased* oral stereotypies (such as cribbing). As horses learned the new schedule, anticipatory weaving and head nodding peaked around feeding, and these behaviours were subsequently reinforced with food. Not surprisingly, horses not being fed while other horses were, or while feeding cues were present, also increased stereotypic behaviour.

Cooper's group discussed the advantages of feeding free-choice forage, as satiated horses are less easily aroused when grain concentrates are being fed. Forage may also reduce cribbing duration and intensity by reducing gastric pain and making the horse's need to crib less urgent (2005). Clearly, there is value in exploring the motivation behind stereotypical behaviour. Differing underlying motivations will not be universally ameliorated by a one-size-fits-all solution. Additionally, overall stereotypic activity may increase unless feeding schedule modifications are universally applied.

LET THEM HAVE FRIENDS

Group or paired turn-out reduces stereotypies, improves welfare, reduces housing costs and may not be as radical as it is currently perceived (van Dierendonck 2009; Keeling et al. 2016; Ladewig 2013). Contrary to popular wisdom, in stable herds aggression is rare, and almost never results in injury (Hartmann, Christensen and Keeling 2009; Hartmann, Keeling and Rundgren 2011; Heitor, Oom and Vicente 2006; Keeling et al. 2016; Ladewig 2013). Horses living in a natural herd form clear dominance hierarchies that serve to minimise aggression rather than exacerbate it. In an established herd of Sorraia horses, Heitor's (2006) group found that dominance relationships were clear, linear and seldom contested. Even after the introduction of a breeding stallion, dominance ranks remained stable and served to keep aggression to a minimum. As Heitor and collegues explain, once ranks have been established, a dominant horse who wants access to a resource need only threaten a subordinate, who in turn avoids or acquiesces. Similarly, in 46 tests of introducing new horses to residents in various conditions of pre-exposure, Hartman and colleagues observed only one incidence of actual body contact, and the resulting injury was minor (2009).

Cozzi et al. (2010) demonstrated that horses are also unlikely to stay angry after aggressive encounters. In horses living in a stable social group, 86 percent of conflicts were followed by a friendly reunion between the opponents within 10 minutes after conflict. Reconciliations involving a third horse were even more likely. Third horses acted both as *appeasers* (initiating friendly contact with the aggressor), or *consolers* (initiating friendly contact with the victim). Cozzi proposes that these triadic interactions may provide a critical social mechanism for conflict resolution and the maintenance of social cohesion.

Recommended strategies for successful and peaceable group or paired turn-out include:

- *Pre-exposure to potential herd mates*. Pre-exposure reduces conflict. How much pre-exposure is still up for debate, but Hartman et al. (2009) reported that as little as 5 minutes of tactile contact (i.e. letting horses smell, touch and interact) in adjacent stalls or paddocks before being turned out together all but eliminated aggressive encounters.

    In herd living, horses choose their friends (Ladewig 2013), and since we cannot ask them who they would choose, we may well be wrong. Some stall neighbours or turn-out partners may be less compatible than others, and caretakers should be prepared for some trial and error pairings during the pre-exposure phase.
- *Keep groups consistent*. New additions, and even new subtractions, to stable herds force horses to reestablish dominance hierarchies and create greater potential for positions to be challenged (Jørgensen, Liestøl and Bøe 2011). If groups must be changed, or when setting up groups initially, removing hind shoes can reduce injury while ranks are being established (Briefer Freymond, et al. 2013). Once challenges have been reconciled, the shoes can be replaced.
- *Keep resources plentiful*. The concern that group-housed horses will injure one another before or during feeding is only true when resources are scarce. The provision of widely dispersed multiple watering sources, several shelter alternatives (from snow, rain, *and sun*), straw bedding (which affords another foraging opportunity as horses seek out oat grains in the straw), numerous scratching stations or trees, and (in an ideal world) plentiful pasture, makes arguments over resources superfluous.

    Burla et al. (2016) in a sample of 390 horses (50 groups of four to 21 horses), featuring a variety of forage feeding options (ground, hay racks, hay nets etc.), and duration (from 1.5 hours to 24-hour access), found that threatening behaviours diminished when feeding stations were individually separated by partitions or sufficiently distant from one another. Aggressive and threatening behaviours disappeared altogether when horses had 24-hour access to hay. Horses bedded on straw also showed reduced aggressive behaviours suggesting that aggressiveness disappears when there is nothing to fight about.

    An intriguing study by Benhajali and colleagues (2008) that took scientific advantage of an extreme equine housing situation, demonstrated that horses are still reluctant to resort to violence even when their circumstances are dire. Forty-four Arabian brood mares were housed at a meagre breeding facility with high-density housing, minimum vegetation and virtually no shelter from the 45 C temperature (the authors note that these conditions were the facility's norm and clearly not designed for their study). The mares were continually moving, and ordinary behaviours such as rolling, lying down, resting and elimination were almost never observed. Although the most commonly observed behaviours were antagonistic interactions, real aggression was rare even in this sub-standard housing. Rather, the difficult environment jeopardised positive social interaction; mares had few preferred partners and mutual grooming was never seen.

- *Yes, you can turn stallions out together.* Even the widely held belief that stallions are too aggressive for group turn-out has been refuted. Granquist et al. (2012) introduced a new stallion and his nine-horse harem into a pre-existing, large, semi-feral herd of four distinct stallion/harem groups, and found that direct interactions among stallions were rare and always non-violent. Stallions were more likely to communicate indirectly through dung and urine markings, and maintained their sovereignty with timely harem herding to prevent interactions between their mares and other harems.

  Successful group stallion turn-out has also been demonstrated with elite, fit, sport horses living in intensive management systems for a portion of the year. At the Swiss National Stud, Briefer Freymond and colleagues (2013) successfully pastured five to eight elite breeding stallions together during their non-breeding season. Stallions were housed in large pastures away from mares, had multiple feeding stations, met in adjacent stalls before group turn-out, hind shoes were removed before the initial encounter and groups remained stable throughout the season. Briefer Freymond noted that stallions engaged in ritualistic behaviours (abbreviated, non-contact behaviours that substitute for actual aggression) to establish social hierarchies, and that in each subsequent year even these ritualistic behaviours subsided. There were no injuries, welfare was greatly enhanced and management costs significantly reduced. The study was so successful that the Swiss National Stud continues to pasture this "bachelor band" every year.

- *Create heterogenous groups.* Contrary to popular wisdom, mixed groups of mares and geldings are no more aggressive, nor more likely to inflict or sustain injury than segregated gender groups (e.g. Jørgensen et al. 2009). Interestingly, Jørgensen did find that boys appear to have more fun, with mixed groups and all gelding groups showing significantly more play behaviour than all female groups. Ladewig (2013) notes that in heterogeneous groups, horses learn multiple aspects of social communication, can more readily find a compatible partner and more easily avoid those who are not, all of which serve to diminish aggression. Giles and colleagues (2015) also found that aggression *increased* as herd variability (in size, age, body condition etc.) *decreased*.

- *Aggression is rare because it is evolutionarily costly.* According to the theory of "evolutionary stable strategies", aggression is always weighed in a cost/benefit "is it worth it?" scenario (Aureli, Cords and Van Schaik 2002). It does not pay to make a bid for a higher rank unless the desired resources are highly prized, the risk of injury is low and the chances of winning are in your favour. For animals living in stable social organisations, behaviours that mitigate conflict rather than escalate it are adaptive, and thus become evolutionarily selected. An aggressor expends energy resources, risks serious injury and potentially forfeits the benefits of group membership should he or she lose. Aggression may have equally grim consequences for the winner by threatening group cohesiveness and jeopardising future cooperation (Aureli, Cords and Van Schaik 2002). In the grand scheme of herd living, serious aggression seldom reaps a benefit that outweighs its cost.

LET THEM TOUCH

Where owners are still not convinced about group or paired turn-out, singly housed horses may still benefit from stable designs that allow tactile contact (e.g. grilled windows between stalls, half walls, or half wood/half grill walls). Cooper and colleagues (2000) eliminated weaving in a group of chronic weavers when the horses were housed in stalls that were open on all sides, allowing them to interact with compatible neighbours (see also Hothersall and Casey 2012; Dezfouli et al. 2014). In modern stable designs where stalls are separated with floor to ceiling wooden planks, gradually removing the upper planks so that eventually horses can put their heads into their neighbours stall is a cost effective way to increase interaction (see Figure 11.2).

MIRRORS

Mirrors have demonstrated a moderating effect on some stereotypies (McAffee, Mills and Cooper 2002; Mills and Davenport 2002). In a group of six chronic weavers and head shakers, McAffee and colleagues found that the installation of an acrylic mirror eliminated these stereotypies entirely, along with other undesirable behaviours such as head nodding and aggressive head threats. The effect lasted over the study's 5-week duration, even when the horses transitioned to a winter

Figure 11.2 Allowing horses to interact between stalls

Photograph: Antonia Henderson

schedule of very limited turn-out. There appeared to be no "rebound effect" (i.e. an increase in motivation to perform the stereotypy once the intervention had ceased). Horses may interpret the mirror image as a new friend, enjoy the increased visual horizons or stimulation that the mirror provides or a combination of these factors. Arguably, the low cost, easy installation and portability make mirrors an environmental enrichment worth pursuing for horses that have limited equine contact.

WITH WEANLINGS, LESS IS MORE

Weaning places youngsters at high risk of developing stereotypies (see Figure 11.3). Good management for youngsters means "less management" – less weaning interference, less confinement and less grain (Wickens and Heleski 2010). In a study of breeding farms in North America, Europe and Australia "natural weaning," where mares weaned the foals themselves, was associated with a decreased incidence of stereotypies in the foals (Parker et al. 2008). Confinement, even part-time, makes weanlings much more likely to develop stereotypies than those living in paddocks or pasture (Heleski et al. 2002; Waters et al. 2002; Parker et al. 2008). Feeding concentrates to weanlings is also problematic. Foals fed concentrates after weaning have been reported to be four times more likely to become cribbers than those who are not (Waters et al. 2002).

Figure 11.3 Weanling practising cribbing

Photograph: Antonia Henderson

Provide a safe 'injection site'

A plethora of research evidence points to the futility and cruelty of attempting to prevent stereotypic horses from engaging in their abnormal behaviours (e.g. Briefer Freymond et al. 2015; Mason and Latham 2004). For confirmed, chronic cribbers a practical, humane and realistic solution is to provide them with a place where they can crib safely without destroying their surroundings (Henderson 2007; Marsden 2002). A metal u-shaped bar, fitted with PVC piping, that reduces tooth wear and stall damage, provides a very satisfactory cribbing station for a committed cribber. It can be permanently mounted around an automatic water bowl (often a preferred, and disastrous, cribbing site – see Figure 11.4).

Alternatively, or additionally, a cribbing station mounted solidly on a plywood board that can be removed, transported and reinstalled in a horse show stall provides a welcome security blanket for a showing cribber on the road (Henderson 2007) (see Figure 11.5).

WHEN THERE IS NOTHING ELSE, A HUMAN WILL DO

Horses are hard-wired to form social bonds. When other horses are not available, they will make do with other species, including donkeys, goats, dogs, cats and humans. As Budiansky (1997, 84–85) comments,

> our horses' affection for us, their owners, is unquestionably real, grounded in a basic instinct to form friendship bonds; it is slightly bruising to our egos, though, to realize that they bond with us only for lack of better company.

Figure 11.4 Cribbing station installed around water bowl
Photograph: Antonia Henderson

182 *Antonia J. Z. Henderson*

In herd living, allogrooming, the mutual, synchronous, nibbling around the withers and neck observed between pairs of horses, plays an integral role in establishing, maintaining and strengthening pair bonds, and herd mates generally have one or two preferred and enduring allogrooming conspecifics (Budiansky 1997; see Figure 11.6). Allogrooming has been associated with physiological effects of stress reduction, including lowered heart rate, blood pressure and cortisol levels;

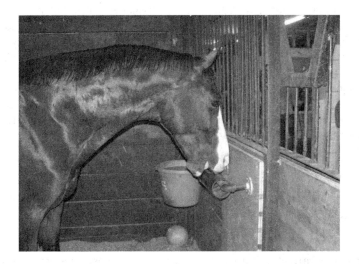

Figure 11.5 Cribbing on a portable cribbing station
Photograph: Antonia Henderson

Figure 11.6 Horses engaged in allogrooming
Photograph: Antonia Henderson

increased immunity; and a rise in beta endorphins (Feh and de Mazières 1993; Normando et al. 2003). Vigorous wither grooming by humans appears to have similar stress reduction effects for horses (Feh and de Mazières 1993), and may have similar bonding properties (McLean et al. 2013). Although it has not been tested, I would argue that it may also have similar calming and bonding properties for the human groomer!

Letting the nice guys finish first

Given the disparity between sport horses as they have evolved (Circle A) and the environmental challenges that we have asked of them (Circle B), it is remarkable that there is *any* overlap between these two circles. Arguably, this correspondence exists because the horse, for the most part, is the quintessential "nice-guy". Unless we have done something to shatter their trust, most horses are affable, imminently social and extraordinarily adaptable (dare I say generous) in their efforts to cope with the taxing environments we have created for them. As Budiansky comments:

> What we are exploiting in our relationship with horses is a well-developed set of equine behaviors, developed within the context of the equine social structure. . . . It is the [horse's] innate social behavior that provides the raw material we of necessity must work with: this is the basis for the bonding and subordination that makes learning even possible.
>
> (1997, 81)

Horses' intensely social nature is both the quality that defines them and that which we have exploited to use for our sport and pleasure. It is such a travesty then, that we take these social beings, whose survival for millennium has depended upon the stability and cohesion of their social structures, and destine them to a life of solitary confinement.

Competitive riders face the unpleasant reality that they will always make greater demands on their horses than their horses would ever make on themselves. There is some comfort in knowing that in return we offer them a lifestyle of rich resources that would never be afforded to them toughing it out on the range. Yet, given the choice of an hour in the dressage or jumping arena, or eating grass with their equine friends, our horses would not choose us. Horses do extraordinary things for us, often against their inherent nature, but it is unlikely that they do so out of a competitive spirit or a desire to work in partnership toward a common goal. The horse has come a *long* way into our world. They are forced to use their athleticism and their intellect to configure themselves into whatever version of a horse we have invented for them in each equine discipline.

Perhaps it is time that we embrace their needs – needs not so very different from their ancestors. In the Equine Prisoner's Model we can expand the overlap by modifying the environmental challenges we have set out for our horses and thus create a better fit with their evolutionary adaptations. As Budiansky (1997, 2) comments, "we have all too often confused the horse's willing nature in the company of man with its inherent nature". By recognising the challenges horses face in the environment we have created and making minimal modifications, we can begin to give back to the horse a modest fraction of what the horse has provided for us.

Notes

1 "Feral" refers to animals that were once domesticated and have returned to living in the wild. There are in fact no truly "wild" horses remaining outside of captivity. In private parks and zoos there exist only 1100 Przewalski's horses, the last remaining truly "wild" horses (Budianksy 1997).
2 Current crib collars such as the "Miracle Collar" ® or the "Dare Control Collar" ® are marketed as "humane", presumably because they exert pressure when the horse attempts to crib, rather than electric shock or painful spikes driven into the horse's gullet of the neck. Even if there were only scant evidence of the "coping hypothesis," removing the horse's one avenue to cope with his adverse environment is anything but humane.
3 The sham clipping duration was 10 minutes rather than the customary 2 to 2.5 hours, the clipping sound and motion were real as the clippers were turned on and moved over the horse's body, but no actual clipping took place as clipping blades were removed. Presumably, this was done so as not to be left with an unsightly partially clipped horse.

References

Araba, B.D., and S.L. Crowell-Davis. 1994. "Dominance Relationships and Aggression of Foals (*Equus caballus*)." *Applied Animal Behavior Science* 41(1–2): 1–25.
Aureli, F., M. Cords, and C.P. Van Schaik. 2002. "Conflict Resolution Following Aggression in Gregarious Animals: A Predictive Framework." *Animal Behavior* 64(3): 325–343.
Bachmann, I., L. Audigé, and M. Stauffacher. 2003. "Risk Factors Associated with Behavioral Disorders of Crib-Biting, Weaving and Box-Walking in Swiss Horses." *Equine Veterinary Journal* 35(2): 158–163.
Baia, P., D.J. Burba, L.M. Riggs, and H. Beaufrere. 2015. "Long Term Outcome After Laser Assisted Modified Forssell's in Cribbing Horses." *Veterinary Surgery* 44(2): 156–161.
Benhajali, H., M.A. Richard-Yris, M. Leroux, M. Ezzaouia, F. Charfi, and M. Hausberger. 2008. "A Note on the Time Budget and Social Behavior of Densely Housed Horses: A Case Study in Arab Breeding Mares." *Applied Animal Behavior Science* 112(1–2): 196–200.
Briefer Freymond, S., D. Bardou, E.F. Briefer, R. Bruckmaier, N. Fouché, J. Fleury, A. L. Maigrot, A. Ramseyer, K. Zuberbühler, and I. Bachmann. 2015. "The Physiological Consequences of Crib-Biting in Horses in Response to an ACTH Challenge Test." *Physiology and Behavior* 151 (November): 121–128.
Briefer Freymond S., E.F. Briefer, R. Von Niederhäusern, and I. Bachmann. 2013. "Pattern of Social Interactions After Group Integration: A Possibility to Keep Stallions in Group." *PLoS ONE* 8(1): 1–9. doi:10.1371/journal.pone.0054688.
Budiansky, S. 1997. *The Nature of Horses: Exploring Equine Evolution, Intelligence, and Behavior*. New York, NY: The Free Press.
Burla, J.B., A. Ostertag, A. Patt, I. Bachmann, and E. Hillmann. 2016. "Effects of Feeding Management and Group Composition on Agonistic Behavior of Group-Housed Horses." *Applied Animal Welfare Science* 176(March): 32–42.

Campbell Smith, D. 2006. "Cribbing Rings: Give Stall Walls and Fences a Break." *The Horse*, October. www.thehorse.com/articles/17201/cribbing-rings-give-stall-walls-and-fences-a-break.

Christensen, J.W., T. Zharkikh, J. Ladewig, and N. Yasinestskaya. 2002. "Social Behavior in Stallion Groups (Equus Przewalskii and Equus Caballus) Kept Under Natural and Domestic Conditions." *Applied Animal Behavior Science* 76(1): 11–21.

Cooper, J.J., and M.J. Albentosa. 2005. "Behavioral Adaptation in the Domestic Horse: Potential Role of Apparently Abnormal Responses Including Stereotypic Behavior." *Livestock Production Science* 92(2): 177–182.

Cooper, J.J., N. Mcall, S. Johnson, and H.P.B. Davidson. 2005. "The Short-Term Effects of Increasing Meal Frequency on Stereotypic Behavior of Stabled Horses." *Applied Animal Behavior Science* 90(3–4): 351–364.

Cooper, J. J., L. McDonald, and D. S. Mills. 2000. "The Effect of Increasing Visual Horizons on Stereotypic Weaving: Implications for the Social Housing of Stabled Horses." *Applied Animal Welfare Science* 69(1): 67–83.

Cooper, J.J., and P. McGreevy. 2002. "Stereotypical Behaviour in the Stabled Horse: Causes, Effects and Prevention without Compromising Welfare." In *The Welfare of Horses*, edited by N. Waran, 99–124. New York, NY: Kluwer Academic Publishers.

Cozzi, A., C. Sighieri, A. Gazzanob, C.J. Nicol, and P. Baraglib. 2010. "Post-Conflict Friendly Reunion in a Permanent Group of Horses (Equus Caballus)." *Behavioral Processes* 85(2): 185–190.

Davidson, H.P.B. 1999. "Natural Horse Unnatural Behavior: Why Understanding Natural Horse Behavior Is Important." In *Proceedings of the British Equine Veterinary Association: BEVA Specialist Days on Behavior and Nutrition*, edited by P. A. Harris, G. M. Gomarsall, H. P. Davidson, and R. E. Green, 7–10. Newmarket, Ontario, Canada: Equine Veterinary Journal.

Davidson, N., and P. Harris. 2002. "Nutrition and Welfare." In *The Welfare of Horses*, edited by N. Waran, 45–76. New York, NY: Kluwer Academic Publishers.

Dezfouli, M.M., H. Tavanaeimanesh, B.D. Naghadeh, S. Bokaei, and K. Corley. 2014. "Factors Associated with Stereotypic Behavior in Iranian Stabled Horses." *Comparative Clinical Pathology* 23(5): 1651–1657.

Dodman, N.H., L. Shuster, M.H. Court, and R. Dixon. 1987. "Investigation into the Use of Narcotic Antagonists in the Treatment of a Stereotypic Behavior Pattern (Crib-Biting) in the Horse." *American Journal of Veterinary Research* 48(February): 311–319.

Ellis, A.D., M. Fell, K. Luck, L. Gill, H. Owen, H. Briars, C. Barfoot, and P. Harris. 2015a. "Effect of Forage Presentation on Feed Intake Behavior in Stabled Horses." *Applied Animal Behavior Science* 165(April): 88–94.

Ellis, A.D., S. Redgate, S. Zinchenko, H. Owen, C. Barfoot, C., and P. Harris. 2015b. "The Effect of Presenting Forage in Multi-Layered Haynets and at Multiple Sites on Night Time Budgets of Stabled Horses." *Applied Animal Behavior Science* 171(October): 108–116.

Feh, C. 2002. "Relationships and Communication in Socially Natural Horse Herds: Social Organization of Horses and Other Equids." In *Horse Behavior and Welfare*, edited by S. MacDonnell and D. Mills. Dorothy Russell Havemeyer Foundation Workshop Horse Behavior and Welfare, Holar, Iceland. June. https://research.vet.upenn.edu/Default.aspx?TabId=3119.

Feh, C., and J. de Mazieres. 1993. "Grooming at a Preferred Site Reduces Heart Rate in Horses." *Animal Behavior* 46(6): 1191–1194.

Fejsáková, M., J. Kottferová, Z. Dankulincová, E. Haladová, R. Matos, and I. Miňo. 2013. "Some Possible Factors Affecting Horse Welfare Assessment." *Acta Veterinaria Brno* 82(4): 447–451.

Flannigan, G., and J. M. Stookey. 2002. "Day-Time Budgets of Pregnant Mares Housed in Tie Stalls: A Comparison of Draft versus Light Mares." *Applied Animal Behaviour Science* 78(2–4): 125–143.

Fraser, D., D.M. Weary, E.A. Pajor, and B.N. Milligan. 1997. "A Scientific Conception of Animal Welfare That Reflects Ethical Concerns." *Animal Welfare* 6: 187–205.

Giles, S., C.J. Nicol, P.A. Harris, and S.A. Rands. 2015. "Dominance Rank Is Associated with Body Condition in Outdoor-Living Domestic Horses (Equus Caballus)." *Applied Animal Behavior Science* 166(May): 71–79.

Gillham, S.B., N.H. Dodman, L. Shuster, R. Kream, and W. Rand. 1994. "The Effect of Diet on Cribbing Behavior and Plasma !b – endorphin in Horses." *Applied Animal Behavior Science* 1994(3–4): 147–153.

Goodwin, D., H.P.B. Davidson, and P. Harris. 2002. "Foraging Enrichment for Stabled Horses: Effects on Behaviour and Selection." *Equine Veterinary Journal* 34(7): 686–691.

Granquist, S.M., T.A. Gudrun, and H. Sigurjónsdóttir. 2012. "The Effect of Stallions on Social Interactions in Domestic and Semi-Feral Harems." *Applied Animal Behavior Science* 141(1–2): 49–56.

Hall, C., D. Goodwin, C. Heleski, H. Randle, and N. Waran. 2008. "Is There Evidence of Learned Helplessness in Horses?" *Journal of Applied Animal Welfare Science* 11(3): 249–266.

Hartmann, E., J.W. Christensen, and L.J. Keeling. 2009. "Social Interactions of Unfamiliar Horses During Paired Encounters: Effect of Pre-Exposure on Aggression Level and Risk of Injury." *Applied Animal Behavior Science* 121(3–4): 214–221.

Hartmann, E., L.J. Keeling, and M. Rundgren. 2011. "Comparison of 3 Methods for Mixing Unfamiliar Horses (*Equus Caballus*)." *Journal of Veterinary Behavior* 6(1): 39–49.

Heitor, F., M. Oom, and L. Vicente. 2006. "Social Relationships in a Herd of Sorraia Horses Part I. Correlates of Social Dominance and Contexts of Aggression." *Behavioral Processes* 73(2): 170–177.

Heleski, C.R., A.C. Shelle, B.D. Nielsen, and A.J. Zanella. 2002. "Influence of Housing on Weanling Horse Behavior and Subsequent Welfare." *Applied Animal Behavior Science* 78(2–4): 291–302.

Henderson, A.J.Z. 2007. "Don't Fence Me in: Managing Psychological Well Being in Elite Performance Horses." *Journal of Applied Animal Welfare Science* 10(4): 309–329.

Hirsh, A., S. Callander, and M. Robinson. 2011. "Patient Demographic Characteristics and Facial Expressions Influence Nurses' Assessment of Mood in the Context of Pain: A Virtual Human and Lens Model Investigation." *International Journal of Nursing Studies* 48(11): 1330–1338.

Hothersall, B., and R. Casey. 2012. "Undesired Behaviour in Horses: A Review of Their Development, Prevention, Management and Association, with Welfare." *Equine Veterinary Education* 24(9): 479–485.

Houpt, K. A. 1998. *Domestic Animal Behavior for Veterinarians and Animal Scientists*. 3rd ed. Ames: Iowa State University Press.

Houpt, K.A., T.R. Houpt, and J.L. Johnson. 2001. "The Effect of Exercise Deprivation on the Behavior and Physiology of Straight Stall Confined Mares." *Animal Welfare* 10(3): 257–267.

Houpt, K.A., and S.M. McDonnell. 1993. "Equine Stereotypies." *The Compendium on the Continuing Education for the Practicing Veterinarian* 15(9): 1265–1271.

Houpt, K. A., and T. S. Ogilvie-Graham. 2002. "Comfortable Quarters for Horses at Research Institutions." In *Comfortable Quarters for Laboratory Animals*. 9th ed., edited by V. Reihardt and A. Reinhardt. Washington, DC: Animal Welfare Institute. http://ebooks.lib.ntu.edu.tw/1_file/AWI/96122405/16.htm.

Jones, B., and P. McGreevy. 2010. "Ethical Equitation: Applying a Cost Benefit Approach." *Journal of Veterinary Behavior: Clinical Applications and Research* 5(4): 196–202.

Jørgensen, G.H.M., L. Borsheim, C.M. Mejdell, E. Søndergaard, and K. E. Bøe. 2009. "Grouping Horses According to Gender – Effects on Aggression, Spacing and Injuries." *Applied Animal Behavior Science* 120(1–2): 94–99.

Jørgensen, G.H.M., S.H. Liestøl, and K.E. Bøe. 2011. "Effects of Enrichment Items on Activity and Social Interactions in Domestic Horses (Equus Caballus)." *Applied Animal Behavior Science* 129(2–4): 100–110.

Keeling, L.J., K.E. Bøe, J.W. Christensen, S. Hyyppä, H. Jansson, G.H.M. Jørgensen, J. Ladewig, C.M. Mejdell, S. Särkijärvi, E. Søndergaard, and E. Hartmann. 2016. "Injury Incidence, Reactivity and Ease of Handling of Horses Kept in Groups: A Matched Case Control Study in Four Nordic Countries." *Applied Animal Behavior Science*, 185(December): 59–65.

Keiper, R.R. 1986. "Social Structure." *Veterinary Clinics of North America: Equine Practice* 2(3): 465–483.

Krisová, Š., Z. Žert, and K. Žuffová. 2015. "Assessment of Modifed Forssell's Myectomy Success Rate in the Treatment of Crib Biting in Horses." *Acta Veterinaria Brno* 84(1): 63–69.

Ladewig, J. 2013. "What About the Other 23 Hours of the Day?" Paper presented at the 9th International Society of Equitation Science Conference. Conference Proceedings: Embracing Science to Enhance Equine Welfare and Horse-Human Interaction. University of Delaware, Newark, DE, USA and University of Pennsylvania, New Bolton Center, Kennett Square, PA, USA.

Lesimple, C., and M. Hausberger. 2014. "How Accurate Are We at Assessing Others' Wellbeing: The Example of Welfare Assessment in Horses." *Frontiers in Psychology* 24(January): 1–21.

Lesimple, C., A. Poissonnet, and M. Hausberger. 2016. "How to Keep Your Horse Safe? An Epidemiological Study About Management Practices." *Applied Animal Behavior Science* 181(August): 105–114.

Lidén, Y., N. Olfsson, O. Landgren, and E. Johansson. 2012. "Pain and Anxiety During Bone Marrox Aspiration/Biopsy: Comparison of Ratings among Patients Versus Health-Care Professionals." *European Journal of Oncology Nursing* 16(3): 323–329.

Luescher, U.A., D. B. McKeown, and J. Halip. 1991. "Reviewing the Causes of Obsessive-Compulsive Disorders in Horses." *Veterinary Medicine*, 86(May): 527–530.

Luthersson, N., K.H. Nielsen, P. Harris, and T.D. Parkin. 2009. "Risk Factors Associated with Equine Gastric Ulceration Syndrome." *Equine Veterinary Journal* 41(7): 625–630.

Malpass, J.P., and B.J. Weigler. 1994. "A Simple and Effective Environmental Enrichment Device for Ponies in Long-Term Indoor Confinement." *Contemporary Topics* 33(6): 74–76.

Marqués, F.J., T. Epp, D. Wilson, A.J. Fuiz, N. Tokateloff, and S. Manning. 2011. "The Prevalence and Risk Factors of Oesophageal and Nonglandular Gastric Lesions in Thoroughbred Racehorses in Saskatchewan." *Equine Veterinary Education* 23(5): 249–254.

Marsden, D. 2002. "A New Perspective on Stereotypic Behaviour Problems in Horses." *In Practice* 24 (10): 558–569.

Mason, G.J., and N.R. Latham. 2004. "Can't Stop, Won't Stop: Is Stereotypy a Reliable Animal Welfare Indicator?" *Animal Welfare* 13(February): 557–569.

Mazzola, S., C. Palestrini, S. Cannas, E. Fè, G. L. Bagnato, D. Vigo, D. Frank, and M. Minero. 2016. "Efficacy of a Feed Dispenser for Horses in Decreasing Cribbing Behaviour." *Veterinary Medicine International* 2016(October): 1–6. doi:10.1155/2016/4698602.

McAfee, L.M., D.S. Mills, and J.J. Cooper. 2002. "The Use of Mirrors for the Control of Stereotypic Weaving Behavior in the Stabled Horse." *Applied Animal Behavior Science* 78(2–4): 159–173.

McBride, S.D., and L. Long. 2001. "Management of Horses Showing Stereotypic Behaviour: Owner Perception and the Implications for Welfare." *Veterinary Record* 148(26): 799–802.

McClure, S.R., D.S. Carithers, S.J. Gross, and M.J. Murray. 2005. "Gastric Ulcer Development in Horses in a Simulated Show or Training Environment." *Journal of the American Veterinary Medical Association* 227(5): 775–777.

McDonnell, S. 2008. "Practical Review of Self-Mutilation in Horses." *Animal Reproduction Science* 107(3–4): 219–228.

McGreevy, P.D. 1997. "Do Stabled Horses Cope?" *Journal of Biological Education* 31(3): 207–211.

McGreevy, P.D., P.J. Cripps, N.P. French, L.E. Green, and C.J. Nicol. 1995a. "Management Factors Associated with Stereotypic and Redirected Behavior in the Thoroughbred Horse." *Equine Veterinary Journal* 27(2): 86–91.

McGreevy, P.D., N.P. French, and C.J. Nicol. 1995b. "The Prevalence of Abnormal Behaviors in Dressage, Eventing and Endurance Horses in Relation to Stabling." *Veterinary Record* 137(July): 36–37.

McLean, A., C. Henshall, M. Starling, and P. McGreevy. 2013. "Arousal, Attachment, and Affective State." Paper presented at the 9th International Society of Equitation Science Conference. Conference Proceedings: Embracing Science to Enhance Equine Welfare and Horse-Human Interaction. University of Delaware, Newark, DE, USA and University of Pennsylvania, New Bolton Center, Kennett Square, PA, USA.

Mills, D.S., and K. Davenport. 2002. "The Effect of a Neighbouring Conspecific *Versus* the Use of a Mirror for the Control of Stereotypic Weaving Behavior in the Stabled Horse." *Animal Science* 74(1): 95–101.

Murphy, J., and S. Arkins. 2007. "Equine Learning Behavior." *Behavioral Processes* 76(1): 1–13.

Murray, M.J. 2004. "Equine Gastric Ulcer Syndrome." *DVM: The Newsmagazine of Veterinary Medicine* 35(September): 1–2.

Murray, M.J., and E.S. Eichorn. 1996. "Effects of Intermittent Feed Deprivation, Intermittent Feed Deprivation with Ranitidine Administration, and Stall Confinement with Ad Libitum Access to Hay on Gastric Ulceration in Horses." *American Journal of Veterinary Research* 57(11): 1599–1603.

Murray, M.J., E.S. Eichorn, and S.C. Jeffrey. 2001. "Histological Characteristics of Induced Acute Peptic Injury in Equine Gastric Squamous Epithelium." *Equine Veterinary Journal* 33(6): 544–560.

Nicol, C. 1999. "Understanding Equine Stereotypies." *Equine Veterinary Journal Supplement* 28(April): 20–25.

Ninomiya, S. 2007. "Social Learning and Stereotypy in Horses." *Behavioral Processes* 76(1): 22–23.

Normando, S., A. Haverbeke, L. Meers, F.O. Odberg, M. Ibáñez Talegón, and G. Bono. 2003. "Effect of Imitation of Grooming on Riding Horses' Heart Rate in Different Environmental Situations." *Veterinary Research Communications* 27(1): 615–617.

Parker, M., E.S. Redhead, D. Goodwin, and S.D. McBride. 2008. "Impaired Instrumental Choice in Crib-Biting Horses (Equus Caballus)." *Behavioral Brain Research* 191(1): 137–140.

Pell, S.M., and P.D. McGreevy. 1999. "A Study of Cortisol and Beta-Endorphin Levels in Stereotypic and Normal Thoroughbreds." *Applied Animal Behavior Science* 64(2): 81–90.

Sarrafchi, A., and H.J. Blokhuis. 2013. "Equine Stereotypic Behaviors: Causation, Occurrence, and Prevention." *Journal of Veterinary Behavior* 8(5): 386–394.

Seligman, M., S.F. Maier, and J.H. Geer. 1968. "Alleviation of Learned Helplessness in the Dog." *Journal of Abnormal Psychology* 73(3): 256–262.

Smith-Thomas, H. 2009. "Cribbing Rings: Cruel or effective?" *The Chronicle of the Horse*. www.chronofhorse.com/article/cribbing-rings-cruel-or-effective.

Sutton, D. 2014. "Management and Therapeutic Options for Equine Gastric Ulceration – Looking Beyond Omeprazole." *Livestock* 19(6): 368–376.

Thorne, J.B., D. Goodwin, M.J.K. Kennedy, H.P.B. Davidson, and P. Harris. 2005. "Foraging Enrichment for Individually Housed Horses: Practicality and Effects on Behaviour." *Applied Animal Behaviour Science* 94(1–2): 149–164.

van Dierendonck, M.C., H. de Vries, M.B.H. Schilder, B. Colenbrander, A.G. Þorhallsdóttir and H. Sigurjónsdóttir. 2009. "Interventions in Social Behavior in a Herd of Mares and Geldings." *Applied Animal Behavior Science* 116(1–2): 67–73.

Visser, E.K., A.D. Ellis, and C.G. Van Reenen. 2008. "The Effect of Two Different Housing Conditions on the Welfare of Young Horses Stabled for the First Time." *Applied Animal Behavior Science* 114(3–4): 521–533.

Waters, A.J., C.J. Nicol, and N.P. French. 2002. "Factors Influencing the Development of Stereotypic and Redirected Behaviors in Young Horses: Findings of a Four Year Prospective Epidemiological Study." *Equine Veterinary Journal* 34(6): 572–579.

Wickens, C.L., and C.R. Heleski. 2010. "Crib-Biting Behavior in Horses: A Review." *Applied Animal Behavior Science* 128(1–4): 1–9.

Winskill, L., N.K. Waran, and R.J. Young. 1996. "The Effect of a Foraging Device (a Modified 'Edinburgh Football') on the Behavior of the Stabled Horse." *Applied Animal Behavior Science* 48(1–2): 25–35.

Yarnell, K., C. Hall, and E. Billett. 2013. "An Assessment of the Aversive Nature of an Animal Management Procedure (Clipping) Using Behavioral and Physiological Measures." *Physiology and Behavior* 118(June): 32–39.

Yarnell, K., C. Hall, C. Royle, and S.L. Walker. 2015. "Domesticated Horses Differ in Their Behavioral and Physiological Responses to Isolated and Group Housing." *Physiology and Behavior* 143(May): 51–57.

12 Human-initiated animal fights

Erik Cohen

Introduction

The recent proliferation of publications on human-animal relations and on animals in tourism (e.g. DeMello 2012; Fennell 2012; Franklin 1999; Markwell 2015) does not pay systematic attention to the variety of human-initiated animal fights, though some authors relate to bullfighting or cockfighting. In this chapter, I shall propose a classification of human-initiated fights, and then focus on one particular category, animal-to-animal fights.

Human-initiated fights can be divided into fights with multiple participants and binary fights (a single pair of adversaries). The former are rare and will not concern us here; the latter can be further divided into three basic categories:

1 Human-to-human fights; the most extreme example are gladiatorial fights to death (Köhne and Ewigleben 2000; Meijer 2005), but the category also includes duels (McAleer 1994) and some agonistic sports, such as boxing, wrestling, fencing and chess.
2 Human-to-animal fights; the most well-known example is bullfighting (Brandes 2009; Cohen 2014a; Douglass 1997; Marvin 1994; Shubert 1999), but the category also includes such practices as alligator wrestling (West 2008), crocodile wrestling (James 2012), steer wrestling (Cowboy Lifestyle Network n.d.) and hog wrestling (WBIW 2015).
3 Animal-to-animal fights; these fall into two sub-categories:

   3.1 Intra-species fights, such as fights between domestic animals, such as dogs, camels, buffalos and cocks or rams (Razaq 2015) horses (Horsefund.org 2014; Stygelar 2014) and elephants (Pearson 1984), but also between insects, such as beetles (Wannamontha 2011) crickets (Raffles 2008; Suga 2006) and spiders (Matejowsky 2003).
   3.2 Inter-species fights, such as fights between a tiger and a buffalo, a dog and a boar, or between different species of dogs; multiple combinations between species exist, but detailed information is not available.

I will here focus only on intra-species fights and present case studies of fights between those domestic animal species, on which the best detailed information is available: dogs, camels, buffalos and cocks. The order of presentation reflects the relative popularity of the fights and the degree of their exposure to domestic visitors and foreign tourists. The case studies are followed by a brief comparative analysis and some wider conclusions.

Dog-to-dog fights

The following provides a description of contemporary dogfighting in the USA.

> In a dogfight, two dogs are put into a square pit, which measures twelve, sixteen, or twenty feet on each side. The dogs fight until one is declared a winner. There are two handlers and one referee in the pit with the dogs. Spectators surround the pit, the sides of which are wooden and three to four feet high. The dogfight begins when the referee tells the handlers to pit their dogs, at which time the dogs are released and attack. Once the fight starts, the spectators place bets with one another on which dog will win. The dogs continue fighting until one of them makes a 'turn,' which is defined as turning the head and shoulders away from the opponent.
>
> (Forsyth and Evans 1998, 203)

Dogfighting is at present a disreputable and illegal activity, condemned and stigmatised in most Western countries; but it is still clandestinely practised in some localities in the USA, the UK and Australia. Though prohibited in many non-Western countries, according to various sources it is still found in Eastern Europe (Larson 2014), some Asian countries, such as Afghanistan (Larson 2014), Pakistan (Hafeez 2014), India (Sarkar 2012), China (Wellman 2015) and the Philippines (Daugherty 2012); in South Africa (National Council of SPCAs 2016) and in some Latin American states (Larson 2014).

According to Yilmaz et al. (2015), dogfighting can be traced to the ancient Chinese and Roman civilizations. These authors claim that in the past valuable fighting dogs were exchanged as gifts between royal courts. However, modern dog fighting has its roots in the "baiting sports . . . first introduced to society by [European] royalty and aristocrats" (Evans, Gauthier and Forsyth 1998, 828). Once "bloodsports were officially eliminated in 1835 as Britain began to introduce animal welfare laws . . . bloodsports proponents turned to pitting their dogs against each other" since such fights were easier to conceal than other baiting sports (ESDAW n.d.). During the nineteenth century "attending a dogfight came to be considered a rite of passage into manhood for wealthy young men" (Evans, et al. 1998, 828), not unlike shooting a tiger in colonial India (Cohen 2012). At that time dogfighting was a reputable activity and served "as a means of emulation [of the leisure class], in which the traits of honor and reputability . . . could be aspired to by the lower classes of society" (Evans et al. 1998, 828).

The interest in dogfighting in the British working classes began to rise "as the popularity of bull baiting began to wane" (Ortiz 2010, 7–8). As rural labourers flocked to the cities, they lacked the space for other bloodsports. But dogfights "could be held indoors artificial light allowing evening matches, and workers could still go to work the next day" (Russell 2007, cited in Ortiz 2010, 8). British immigrants brought fighting dogs to the USA where the "American Pit Bull Terrier (the dog of choice for dog fighting)" was eventually bred (Ortiz 2010, 9). In the USA "dogfighting was a lawful sport for a short period," but "states began outlawing this activity in the latter half of the nineteenth century" (ibid., 10). It is now outlawed in all the states of the USA.

Contemporary dogfighting "no longer conveys the reputability it once did" in the Western world (Evans, et al. 1998, 829), but continues to thrive clandestinely among the lower classes and marginalised people. Carr (2014, 139) maintains that dogfighting is likely to be increasingly pushed to the margins and castigated by society. According to Ortiz (2010, 10–11) it constitutes "a half–billion dollar industry in the U.S.," and is apparently "still on the rise." Dogfighting draws support predominantly from the white working- class, and is found mostly in poorer areas of some southern states (Larson 2014), but some participants still come from the middle and upper classes (Evans et al. 1998). It is an "exclusively male sport, in which individual men can earn status within the dogfighting subculture, through the accomplishments of their dogs." (Evans et al. 1998, 827) The "sport" is regulated by "elaborate rules . . . which reflect and reinforce the traditional masculine characteristics of competiveness, aggression, strength, toughness and courage" (Evans et al. 1998, 827) in the fighting dogs that are then by extension ascribed to their owners.

For the attending public, the main attraction of dogfighting is betting. Stakes are often very high. In the USA, "a single [dog]fight may involve bets in excess of $10,000, and total purses for an evening of organised dogfighting activity commonly exceeds $50,000 to $100,000 at a single venue" (Perdue and Lockwood 2014, 54). It was estimated that in the USA "at least 40,000 people engage in high-stakes dogfighting" (Ortiz 2010, 6, see also Larson 2014).

Though dogfighting is publicly condemned as repulsive or disgusting and according to Carr (2014, 139) is "likely to be increasingly pushed to the margins and castigated by society", the large number of dogfighting videos available on the Internet, some of which were viewed 1–3 million times, indicates that there is still a fairly widespread covert interest in dogfighting. Harding ascribes its attractiveness to latent antinomian inclinations: "Dog fighting in the UK and the US can be viewed as largely a transgressive act – one that crashes traditional social norms and boundaries. It is both oppositional and . . . also attractive" (Harding 2014, 158). Harding speculates that

> A darker analysis might suggest that those engaged in dog fighting are taking symbolic revenge on the emblem of family-oriented life, the [pet] dog. By forcing dogs to engage in barbaric acts of gladiatorial combat, they . . . undermine the animal's place in society and in family life (ibid. 158).

Since "the [fighting] dog . . . is used to operate in an excluded world where it is forced to fight for its own survival," (ibid., 158) it seems to represent an anthropomorphised version of excluded young men who feel that they must fight for survival. These men are, like their dogs, "puffed-up, muscular, angry, aggressive, ready to fight to win or survive, using street skills and brute force in a pit not of their own making" (ibid., 158–9). Harding concludes that "A fighting pet embodies anti establishment social norms – the anti-thesis of domesticity and conventional values" (ibid., 159).

In the USA dogfighting constitutes a clandestine subculture, or a number of sub-cultures, whose members are often engaged in other criminal activities, such as "gambling, the illegal possession of weapons or banned substances, and even prostitution" (Ortiz 2010, 6). The audience at dogfights is restricted to invitees, while the intrusion of outsiders is precluded. Most individuals attending dogfights have possessed fighting dogs in the past or will possess them in the future. Participants thus "rotate between the roles of spectator and handler" (Evans et al. 1998, 836).

Ortiz (2010) distinguishes between three types of dogfighters, or dogfighting sub-cultures in the USA, the professionals, the hobbyists and the streetfighters, which differ considerably in the level of their organisation, in the extent to which they take care of their dogs and the gruesomeness of their dogfights. The professionals are both, fighters and breeders and condition and train their dogs for the fight. They "work on a national and, sometimes, international level and fight at the highest stakes. . . . Fights at the professional level are the most secretive and the most lucrative." Professional dogfights are not easily accessible: "(m)eeting a professional dogman or attending a professional's fight usually requires a personal introduction from a current member of that dogfighting circle, and the location of a fight is usually not revealed until hours before the fight" (Ortiz 2010, 14).

In contrast to the professionals, streetfighters often "participate in impromptu fights, with traditional dogfighting rules often ignored" (Ortiz 2010, 16). They instantiate "the brutal twist that urban fights have taken" (ibid., 17). Some streetfighters engage in forms of dogfighting such as "trunking" (in which two dogs are thrown into a car's trunk, but only one will re-emerge alive) in which the "traditional reasons for watching a dogfight – to see the display of gameness" are abandoned. Such fights, at which there are no spectators, "have little resemblance to professional dogfights," except for the gambling (ibid., 17).

Dogfighting is more openly practised in some non-Western countries. In Pakistan, for example, though legally banned, "the enforcement authorities seem to have turned a blind eye to this deeply rooted and sickening mode of entertainment" (Hafeez 2014, np). Hence, in rural Pakistan, dogfight "tournaments are carried out unofficially via scheduled meetings by breeders, who decide dates and the venue" (Hafeez 2014, np). The fights are open to the public: "The fact that [dogfights] are illegal doesn't curtail large numbers of people coming out to witness this appalling entertainment. The fun infused with this outing has its fair share of sadism and utter disregard for animals" (Hafeez 2014, np). Hafeez reports that "there is a high price on the dogs that win accolades for being the most menacing in the country." However,

> if the master of the losing dog [in a fight] calls the fight a quit . . . he will club his hound with hockey sticks, electrocute it, poison it, or simply just drown

it with its legs tied. The master does this because his brittle ego has been punctured.

(Hafeez 2014, np)

Camel-to-camel fights

Description of a contemporary camel fight in Turkey:

> Wrestling matches are held between male camels of a type called *Tülü*, which are bred by mating a single-hump female Arabian dromedary camel ... with a double-hump male Asian Bactrian camel. ... One day before the wrestling contest the camels are decked out in sumptuous manner as prescribed by tradition. They are then walked through the streets accompanied by music played on drums and *zurnas* [a conical oboe] to Zeybek [a historical bandit community] tunes. ... The area where wrestling matches are held is called, as in English, the 'arena' and is on flat soil surrounded by slopes, which act as [a] makeshift amphitheatre for the spectators. [At the start of the event] the *cazgır* [commentator] ... calls out the competitors. The *cazgır* also reads poems praising each camel. ... Within the wrestling organization there is a referee committee,

which includes a match referee, who decides the winners and losers of the contests (Aydin 2011, 56–57).

> In the ring [i.e. arena], camels twist their necks and wrestle for up to 10 minutes. ... Some camels are famed for signature moves, such as pinning their opponent's head with their knees, or sweeping the foe's legs from underneath him. ... Biting ankles and forelocks is also a recognized fighting technique, although contestants are muzzled to limit injuries.

(Parkinson 2011, np)

> Camel wrestling is judged in four categories. A camel can win by making the other camel retreat, by making the other camel scream, by making the other camel fall, [or] when the [other] camel's owner takes his fighter out of the contest in order to prevent him from being hurt.

(Aydin 2011, 57)

"The award of the winner camel in the wrestle is the carpet laid on the camel after the game" (Çalişkan 2009, 127). "But often the game ends in a draw" (Aydin 2011, 57), owing to "precautions [taken] in order for camels not to be injured and worn out" (Çalişkan 2009, 124).

Camel fighting, or more correctly "wrestling," is presently practised mainly in Western Turkey (Çalişkan 2009, 125), but is also found in Afghanistan and Pakistan (ibid., 124). The custom has allegedly a 2400-year history (Robehmed 2014). Its roots are said to be in "nomadic times, [when] camel wrestling developed among competing caravan owners" (Donlon, Donlon and Agrusa 2010, 34). But Çalişkan (2009, 124) maintains that "it is uncertain where and how camel wrestles originated." Camel wrestling in Turkey was first reported 200 years ago, at a festival in the southwestern province of Aydın (Aydin 2011, 55). The English author Parley (1835, 85) wrote in the early nineteenth century that "(a)t particular seasons of the year, Camel fights are common in Smyrna [presently Izmir]," and quotes from the report of a traveller that "(t)he pasha of Smyrna used frequently to regale the people with these spectacles in an enclosed square before his palace" (ibid., 86).

Despite the long tradition of camel wrestling in Turkey,

> the government discouraged the sport after the Turkish Republic was formed in 1923, proclaiming it backward and non-European. It was only after a military coup in 1980 that a new regime revived the art as it promoted Turkey's pre-Islamic heritage.
>
> (Parkinson 2011, np)

The organiser of the annual camel wrestling tournament in Selçuk district in Izmir province, the main contemporary wrestling event, maintains that "the sport is about keeping alive the bond between Turks and the animal that served their nomadic ancestors for centuries, and which he sees as an integral part of Turkish heritage." (Aydin 2011, 55) While in the past "the lives of the camels and humans were in a symbiotic relationship," modern transportation technology "made camels redundant for trading purposes, but camel wrestling is still an important event for the preservation of local culture" (Aydin 2011, 55). The number of camels in Turkey has declined from 118,000 in 1935, to 12,000 in 1980, 1350 in 1999 and 811 in 2005, but rose again to about 1000 in 2006, a rise attributed to "the increase in the interest in camel wrestling" (Çalişkan 2009, 126), in which about 460 camels participate (ibid., 125). Most of the present camel population was imported from neighbouring countries (Yilmaz et al. 2014, 906). With the importation of well-bred camels, the quality of wrestling has increased, but so have the prices of wrestling camels (ibid., 908).

Camel wrestling events are organised in "the winter months when camels begin to go into heat during the mating period" (Çalişkan 2009, 127–8) in about 60–70 locations (Yilmaz et al. 2014, 905). Camel wrestling remains a local affair: "(i)n spite of economic, social and cultural advantages of camel wrestling events, there have been no institutions or organizations, which are interested in or plan camel wrestles at [a] regional or national scale in Turkey" (ibid., 909). However, Donlon et al. (2010) argue that, with the increased coverage of camel wrestling in mainstream media and in travellers' guidebooks, "these cultural performances have become another of the many threads in the tapestry of attractions Turkey offers its visitors" (ibid., 35). These authors believe that "outsider or visitor interest imbues sites [such as camel wrestling] with prestige otherwise unavailable" (ibid., 36). Hence "strong efforts are made to introduce the events to visitors and explain that the livestock are very well cared for" (ibid., 35). The authors point out that "the sites of camel wrestling function as nodes around which a variety of related traditional commercial undertakings revolve," so "viewers may also have the opportunity to shop for local handicrafts, buy regional music, and haggle for costumes and clothing" (ibid., 37). These authors admit that contemporary camel wrestling has been modified and has undergone increased commoditisation (ibid., 37). Advertisements are even pinned on the flanks of the fighting camels, which came to serve "as commercial bill-bordage [like] the outfield fence of a base-ball's pitch" (ibid., 36).

Though camel wrestles are popular events, betting on the camels is not a major motive for attendance. If it exists at all, it is done secretly (Vardar 2014). Çalişkan (2009, 133) calculated that in 2007–2008 more than 170,000 spectators attended wrestling events. The principal event, the Camel Wrestling Festival (Çalişkan 2010), held in the town of Selçuk close to the ruins of Ephesus (which are an important tourist destination), was reorganised by Turkey's Ministry of Culture and Tourism in 1982 (Robehmed 2014). It is annually attended "by about 20,000 domestic and foreign tourists" (Yilmaz and Ertugrul 2014, 2003). The number of foreigners at the Festival in 2008 was estimated at close to 500 (Çalişkan 2009, 133). Though Çalişkan (2009) and other authors stress the touristic potential of the wrestles, they are still a predominantly domestic affair. Events are not yet specifically adapted for foreign visitors, and no tourist-oriented performances are on offer.

Buffalo-to-buffalo fight

Description of a buffalo-to-buffalo fight in Tana Toraja, south Sulawesi, Indonesia:

> [In a buffalo fight] the buffalo[s] almost never hurt each other. They usually just lock horns and push for a few minutes. Sometimes, despite their handlers kicking them in the rear end to try to get them angry, they graze peacefully while thousands of observers sit patiently waiting for something to happen. But occasionally there will be a really good match when the buffalos lock horns, one loses its footing in the mud, and the contest turns into horned wrestling, with the fallen buffalo straining to get back up while the other one pushes down on it with its horns. . . . The match ends when one buffalo runs away. Sometimes the loser just runs a few yards across the field. But sometimes the winner chases the loser . . . the vanquished bull keeps running until it reaches the crowds that line the edge of the field. Then the fleeing buffalo runs right into the crowd, with the pursuing buffalo right behind.
> (Hicken 2012, np)

Water buffalo fights are a popular form of rural entertainment in several Asian countries, particularly China (EasyTourChina n.d.; Emerging Money 2012), Vietnam, Thailand and Indonesia. The historical roots of buffalo fighting are not well known. But they are probably deep, since buffalo fighting in Asia is often related to religious customs and conducted at ceremonies, festivals and fairs. Thus, the annual buffalo fight fair in a village in Shimla district, north India, "is held to honor Hindu gods and deities" (*ANI News* 2013, np); while the Bo Son festival in northern Vietnam is "attached to a Water God worshipping ceremony" (Vietnam Ethnic Cultures 2011, np). Among the Tana Toraja, the buffalo fights constitute "an essential part of a large funeral" (Budiman 2013, 74) and are slaughtered after the fights (together with other buffalos) in the belief that the souls of the sacrificed buffalos will accompany the deceased's soul to *puya* (land of souls or afterlife) (ibid., 71).

The Bo Son Buffalo Fighting Festival in Vietnam and the Ta'na Toraja funerals in Indonesia are the two principal examples of buffalo fighting in Asia, which constitute significant attractions for foreign tourism (though smaller buffalo fighting festivals are staged, mainly for foreign tourists, in some popular destinations, such as Koh Samui in southern Thailand (*Koh Samui News* 2014).

The Do Son festival, which "was recently recognized as intangible national heritage by the Ministry of Culture, Sports and Tourism" (Vietnam National Administration of Tourism 2015, np), is celebrated on the ninth day of the eighth lunar month. It is customarily preceded by a long period of preparations. Each hamlet of Bo Son village collects contributions to purchase a buffalo. Members of the hamlet scour stock markets to find a fighting buffalo with the desired features, such as

> big with a broad chest, big thighs, and a strong, round neck . . . [a] back . . . curved and thick . . . [a] stork-neck [so that it] can bend its head effortlessly. . . . Its horns must be black as ebony or bow-shaped and slanted. . . . A good buffalo must have even teeth . . . big legs with furry knees [and] black, hanging genitals.
>
> (Festivals in Vietnam n.d., np)

The buffalo "is kept alone so that it can never see other buffaloes . . . to restore its wildness . . . [Before the fights, its] nutrition is gradually raised." (Festivals in Vietnam) During the training period "another buffalo is brought in to be its rival. People [are] beating drums or cheering to make the buffalo familiar with the festival atmosphere. The wild animal is trained to understand the best tricks for defeating its rivals" (ibid.).

Customarily, only six buffalos were permitted to fight at the festival: three from Bo Son and three from two other villages; the fights were held on a flat area in Bo Son village. However, the event was recently moved to the Bo Son Stadium in the port city of Hai Phong. The fights are preceded by a Water God worshipping ceremony and a "colorful procession [in which the] buffalos, covered with red cloth and red band around their horns, are taken to the fighting ring by 24 young men . . . dressed in red, [who] dance and wave flags. [Their dance is] mingled with the ebullient sound of drums and gongs, bringing a hectic atmosphere to the festival" (Vietnam-Beauty.com 2008, np).

The festival presently features "competitions among 16 buffaloes selected from qualifying rounds at ward and district levels" (Vietnam National Administration of Tourism 2012), similar to a human sports championship. In 2015, the owner of the winning buffalo won a cash prize of VND 70 million, about US$3,130 (Vietnam National Administration of Tourism 2015). However, all participating buffalos, losers as well as winners, are killed after the fights as an act of worship of the god (Vietnam National Administration of Tourism 2012).

The festival has become a major tourist attraction. In 2012 it "attracted over 30,000 local people and tourists" (ibid., np). It is also "a big-money event with high-priced sponsorships, high stakes gambling and thousands of dollars in prize money" (*Taipei Times* 2009, np).

With increased popularity, buffalo fighting in Vietnam became commercialised. A Buffalo Fighting Stadium, with a capacity of 5000 seats, was established by a private company in a park in Ho Chi Min City (Saigon) where buffalo fights are occasionally staged on Sunday afternoons. An entrance fee is charged. The company acquired 20 strong buffalos and trained them to fight for three to six months. The company "cut the top of their animals' horns to avoid wounds so that the buffalos can fight many times" (Saigon Tourist 2005).

Cock-to-cock fights

Description of a cockfight in Quezon City, the Philippines:

> there are four men in the ring, two of them calmly squatting, each with a cigarette between his lips and a chicken between his legs. The other two are referees. Thousands of spectators, all men, are standing and shouting, making distinctive gestures to one another . . . each gesture part of an intricate system of betting on the birds below. The noise is deafening. Suddenly, the squatting smokers release the birds, and the roosters approach each other at a wary angle, hackles rising . . . from their necks. As they explode forward with the speed and aim of heat seeking missiles, the clamor outside the ring abruptly halts. The only sound is the vibration of pounded air from hard-flapping wings. In less than a minute, it is over. The white-feathered victor sends up a triumphant crow next to the still body of its dead opponent. Losers pay up their bets in a rain of folded peso notes.
>
> (Lawler 2014, np)

Of all the human-induced animal-to-animal fights, cockfighting is the most widespread one, found all over the globe (Forsyth 1996, 15; Lawler 2014). Even though Geertz's (1972) celebrated paper on Bali cockfighting constitutes a landmark of modern anthropology, cockfighting has not been widely studied.

Cockfighting has deep historical roots. According to Forsyth (1996, 15) "anthropologists believe that chickens were domesticated as early as 3000 BC and that fighting them for sport also developed about the same time." In some localities, as in Bali (Stankiewicz 2014), cockfighting still plays a ritual role, but at present it is in most instances practised as an entertainment or a "sport," devoid of express religious significance. However, some contemporary authors, following Geertz, ascribe to cockfighting some deeper symbolic meanings. Thus Donlon (2014, 7) argues that bloodsports, particularly cockfights, "represent the symbolic approximation of humanity's control of unregulated wild nature, and a negotiation of mortality itself, a species of sacrament." Hawley (1993, 163) points out the multiple meanings of the cock to its owner: "the cockfighter views the bird on several levels: bird as totem, emblem of bravery, sexual potency, and perhaps symbolic sacrifice." Donlon (2014, 8) emphasises the identification of the cocker with his cock: "(p)articipants [in cockfights] often see a kind of representative trope or surrogacy, the bird *acting out* a displaced episode of courage or *standing in* for the human being (in the way that the joust was a surrogate for actual war)." Donlon (ibid., 7) also stresses "the passionate connection between cockfighters and their birds." However, the identification of the cockfighter with any *particular* cock seems to be less intensive than that of dog-, buffalo- or camel-owners with their particular fighting animals. Hawley (1993, 163) reports that he has "seen cockers with misty eyes leaving the pit cradling their limp, winged champions;" but he adds that, "however nostalgic the cocker may feel about his birds, I have never noted a theme of bird as friend or companion among mature cockfighters." Stuart (2014) states expressly that, in the Philippines, "there is no bonding between cock and owner." This may well be due to cockfighters handling a big number of cocks, as the fighting life of each one is usually brief.

Like dogfighting, cockfighting is perceived as an affirmation of masculinity (Hawley 1993, 159; see also Marwin 1984) and a means to establish one's identity. Thus, a study in Hawaii concluded that cockfighting served to express a local Hawaiian identity and constituted "a positive cultural assertion that honors perpetrators' family and histories and establishes perpetrators' value as intelligent, trustworthy members of the local community" (Young 2016, 1159).

In the Western world, cockfighting was in the past popular among all social classes (Garcia 2015, 362). However, beginning with the first half of the nineteenth century, cockfighting was gradually outlawed, though exceptions were made for some regions, specifically in France and in Spain, where it has been an uninterrupted local tradition (Sadet 2011). The status of cockfighting varies widely in the rest of the world. It is popular and legal in several countries with a historical link to Spain, such as Mexico and Peru, while it is illegal in others, such as Costa Rica and Brazil. Cockfighting is widespread in Southeast Asia, especially in the Philippines, where it is legal and in Thailand, where it is officially regulated (Na Thalang 2015). I shall here focus on the USA and the Philippines, the two countries on which relatively abundant information is available, and which differ substantially in terms of the context in which cockfighting is practised.

In the USA, cockfighting was in the past popular among all classes, counting among its adherents even such personalities as Washington and Jefferson (Garcia 2015). However, from the 1830s onwards, cockfighting was gradually outlawed by state legislatures (ibid.). With its prohibition in 2007 in Louisiana, where it has been highly popular among the Cajun people (Donlon 2014), cockfighting became illegal in all the 50 states (but not in the US territories, such as Guam, Puerto Rico and the Virgin Islands). A recent federal law even prohibits transfer of cockfighting implements across state borders (Garcia 2015). However, though cockfighting has been outlawed in the USA, owning and breeding fighting cocks is permitted (Zarley 2015). There are in fact thousands of gamefowl breeders in the USA, with their own associations (Herzog 1985; Kilborn 2000; Zarley 2015); some export fighting cocks to the Philippines (Lawler 2014), where cockfighting is a legal "sport" and a "national pastime" (Yacobucci 2012).

In 1985, when cockfighting was still legal in several USA states, the number of participants in the practice has been estimated at about half a million (Herzog 1985). However, even after it had been outlawed, cockfighting continued to be clandestinely practised, furtively in some derelict urban areas, such as the Bronx (Kilborn 2000) and more widely in some rural areas of the southern states. Considering the number of cockfights busted by the police in the last few years, the practice seems to be still quite widespread, though the number of participants cannot be established.

Cockfighting has been widely condemned by American animal welfare and rights organisations, but its supporters argue that "the [urban] opponents of cockfighting did not understand the sport's meaning in many rural areas" (Kilborn 2000, np), and point out that "devotees feel it is a legitimate form of recreation with a long and noble history" (Herzog 1985, 114).

Access to cockfighting events in the USA is restricted to cockers (owners of fighting cocks) and local spectators. The participants are mostly male, though women sometimes attend the fights (Herzog 1985). Outsiders are generally not admitted. Cockfighting's principal attraction is betting, a highly conventionalised, informal activity, based on trust. Though not enforceable by any formal sanctions, betting debts are generally promptly paid (Herzog 1985).

Herzog reports that in the rural south in the early 1980s, "for the majority of cockers the sport [was] a leisure activity rather than a source of income. . . . If he is lucky, a cocker will make enough money to cover expenses during the season" (Herzog 1985, 121–122). However, Forsyth (1996, 15) found a decade later that "the intrusion of large amounts of gambling money in the game is transforming cockfighting and has the potential of shattering the familiar atmosphere of the fights."

In contrast to the USA, in the Philippines, where it has allegedly been practised even before Magellan's visit in 1521 (Lawler 2014), cockfighting is a legal and enormously popular spectator sport of incomparable magnitude. It is practised in thousands of stadiums around the islands, the largest of which has a 20,000 seat capacity (Lawler 2014). Between 7 and 13 million roosters are allegedly killed annually in the fights (Cortez n.d.).

There are several types of cockfights in the Philippines. The simplest is the hack, a contest between two cocks, of which there may be "20 to 30 in an afternoon or evening" (Stuart 2014, np). The derby is more complex: it involves teams, who enter the event

> with a team-name and a fixed 'pot money' amount . . . that becomes the prize-money for the team with the most wins. A 3-cock derby may last deep into the night . . . a 7- or 9-cock derby may last for days (ibid.).

While small-scale cockfighting events are ubiquitous, the hallmarks of the cockfighting calendar are a few international events. One, the semi-annual five-day World Slasher Cup, is "undoubtedly the most prestigious [derby] . . . regarded internationally as the 'Olympics of Cockfighting,' joined by the best cockfighters from here [the Philippines] and abroad." (*Philippine Daily Inquirer* 2009, np) It is held in the "historic Araneta Coliseum [in Queson City] for more than 30 years" (ibid., np) and features "a five-day series of 648 matches" (Lawler 2014). Another major event is the three-day Candelaria Derby, at the Feast of Our Lady of Candles, in the Jaro district of Iloilo City on Panay island (Western Visayas), which is "known worldwide as one of the toughest derbies where the small breeders and cockfighters . . . meet . . . against the best breeders in the world" (Locara 2013, np). The event, held at the Iloilo Coliseum, is attended primarily by "local aficionados, but a large percentage . . . are visitors from all places in the country," and some "foreigners led by American breeders who are out not only to compete but also to enjoy and watch the fights" (ibid., np).

In the Philippines, cockfighting is "not confined to just the poorer sections of society, it also has a huge following among the crème de la crème of Philippine society" (Philippine Travel Guide n.d., np). But the class differences do not blur. Rather, they are reflected in the quality of the classes' respective fighting cocks: "The poorer section of society uses the native breed, low-pedigree *mestizo* cocks, usually for hack fights," while the "moneyed aficionados are usually involved with expensive brood cocks of pedigree lineage bred for 'fastest kill' and trained for big money derby events" (Stuart 2014, np). The rich "normally import their breeds," and "have veterinarians and trainers to build up the muscles of [their] birds" (Philippine Travel Guide n.d., np). For the rich, cockfighting is "the 'sport of kings' – of nerve and verve, macho and ego, and tens-of-thousands of pesos, or even millions, won or lost with a shrug." But for the poor it is "a sport of dreams, pitting their lowly-rural-bred against a *burgis* [pedigree lineage bred] cock . . . on belief that on any day . . . his gamecock can win" (Stuart 2014, np).

In contrast to cockfighting in some other places, the Philippine cockfight is usually a fight to death. Owing to the long slasher, "a curved heel blade known as the *tare*" (Philippine Travel Guide n.d.; see Ill. in Herzog 1985, 117) fitted on the cock's left leg, the duration of the fights is usually brief. The cockfight is said to be "very fast paced and exciting to watch" (Philippine Travel Guide n.d., np). But betting is the main source of tension in the cockfighting arena and also the principal reason for the fights' high popularity. Hence as the Philippine Travel Guide (n.d.) points out, the betting session "is the most anticipated" stage of the match; while Stuart (2014, np) asserts that "betting is the sine qua non of *sabong* [cockfight]. In fact, without betting, *sabong* [would] be transformed into an unrecognizable namby-pamby sport."

In the Philippines, a cockfight involves a variety of functionaries conducting the matches, among whom the "*kristo*" or bet-taker plays a central role (Alabanza, Gonzaga and Obligacion 1979), reflecting the centrality of betting in Filipino cockfighting. But the sheer magnitude of the "sport" has generated, and depends upon, a ramified infrastructure. Thousands of gamefowl breeders, from the Philippines and abroad, supply the cocks for the fights; the local breeders have their own associations, assembled in two national breeders' organisations (*Philippine Daily Inquirer* 2009). Further, "there are more than 20 big companies engaged in the production, marketing and distribution of gamefowl feeds, feed supplement, vitamins, medication, vaccines," and "a lot of small manufacturers producing slashers, boxes, incubators, gloves, carrying cases, folding pens, feeding cups, cords etc" for the cockfighting business (Bantay-Sabong 2008, np). Finally, there are "training schools [for cocks] specializing In fast kills" (Stuart 2014, np).

Filipino cockfighting is a potential, but ambiguous, tourist attraction: though foreign tourists seek occasionally to "catch a cockfight" (Yacobucci 2012), and some tour companies offer cockfighting tours (Smokey Tours n.d.), the "sport" as yet apparently attracts few foreigners, presumably owing to its reputation for gruesomeness (Stuart 2014). But cockfighting generates domestic tourism, while some Filipino aficionados living abroad time their home visits to be able to view major cockfight events, such as the World Slasher Cup (*Philippine Daily Inquirer* 2009).

Comparative analysis

The four kinds of animal-to-animal fights discussed in the preceding paragraphs, differ significantly in their legal standing and the gruesomeness and deadliness of their fights, but they nevertheless share several significant commonalities.

One, all have deep historical roots. Except for dogfights, in the past all played some religious or ritual roles. However, in most instances they have gradually been severed from their roots, became secularised activities, and in some cases underwent commercialisation.

Two, with the exception of buffalo fights, all share a similar socio-historical trajectory. They were in the past introduced or cherished by members of the higher social classes, but have gradually filtered down to the lower classes, even as their popularity in the higher ones declined. Consequently they lost their respectability and became gradually outlawed.

Three, sub-cultures have formed around the various kind of fights, and generated their own codes and criteria of evaluation, by which the personal honour, respectability and even identity of their practitioners is established. The sub-cultural world views served as an underpinning for the justification of illegal animal fighting practices in marginal groups, despite the abhorrence and condemnation of the wider society.

Four, animal fighting practices are heavily gendered, in terms of the composition of their membership, the machismo of their sub-cultural values and even the gender of the fighting animals.

Five, the animals in animal-to-animal fights serve as surrogates for their owners: hence an animal's win or loss reflects upon its owner's social standing, masculine honour and identity. Winning animals are therefore cherished; losers may be destroyed by their owners.

Six, members of the sub-cultures breed, feed, condition and train their animals to increase their fighting ability. In some instances, such as cockfighting in the Philippines, a complex supporting industry underpins the practice.

Seven, while the various animal fights fascinate their aficionados, betting by the public is the principal factor keeping the industry alive or even expanding (except in camel wrestling). Betting is based on the sub-cultures' code of honour, with which bettors generally comply, though it lacks any wider formal or legal support. This is a particular instance of a "paradoxical situation wherein people who compete with each other in an illegal activity must also establish their reputations for honesty and trustworthiness [for their bets to be accepted]" (Darden and Worden 1996, 211).

Eight, the legal prohibition of animal fights in virtually all Western and many non-Western countries clashed with allegedly long-established local animal fighting traditions. In some instances the conflict was resolved by the exemption of such localities from the application of the law, while in others the practice was protected by allotting it the status of a national heritage.

Nine, attendance at animal fights varies from a limited number of involved practitioners or aficionados (as in dogfighting or cockfighting in Western countries) to a huge local and domestic audience. Foreign tourists play, if at all, only a limited role in the attendance at such events or the modification of their practices. Except in very few cases, such as the Cockfighting Centre recently established in northern Thailand (Reddy n.d.), no animal fight demonstrations intended for foreign tourists have come to my attention.

Conclusions

The principal conclusion indicated by our case studies is that, paradoxically, the very traits which the domestication of animals by humans sought to suppress, namely their natural wildness and ferocity, have been re-cultivated for the single purpose of winning of human-induced animal-to-animal fights. While domestic animals may be treated as mere objects by their owners, and induced to fight their opponents against their own inclination, once in the arena they display an agency, expressed in aggressiveness and ferocity, generally denied them in everyday life. But even if victorious, they are rarely rewarded for their prowess, while enabling their owners to gain prestige and monetary rewards.

In contrast to human-animal fights, such as bullfighting, in human-initiated animal-to-animal fights humans compete with other humans by proxy. Animals serve as the means for their success. To increase their chances of winning, humans tend to interfere with nature, by breeding, feeding, conditioning and training their animals to increase their innate ferociousness, in order to overwhelm the animals owned by their human opponents. This tendency is the opposite of the contemporary efforts to breed less aggressive bulls for bullfighting, and to clandestinely weaken their fighting capacity, to facilitate the matador's victory over them (Cohen 2014a, 551).

Human-initiated animal fights are arguably ethically less acceptable than bullfighting or big animal hunting. The latter contain some marks of "equal chances" (Cohen 2014a) or of a "fair play" (Cohen 2014b) in the sense that both human and animal are exposed to a degree of danger, though in both cases the chances of survival are heavily weighted against the animal (Cohen 2014a). In human-initiated animal-to-animal fights, the animals may have equal chances of survival, but their human owners, while enjoying the fruits of their victories (or suffering the shame of their defeat), are not exposed to any mortal danger. Animal-to-animal fights are thus marked by a manipulative trait: humans reviving or enhancing the natural ferociousness of an animal and turning it into an instrument for the achievement of their owners' goals.

The savage or "uncivilised" character of animal-to-animal fights might have led to their gradual prohibition in Western, and in many non-Western countries. However, the prohibition was resisted by their practitioners, fostering the emergence of sub-cultural ideologies, particularly among the disadvantaged, marginal or minority groups of society. For these, the fights figured either as an antinomian manifestation of protest against exclusion from mainstream society (as in dogfighting), or as long-standing local traditions, to be protected from the civilising or sanitising efforts of modern governments (as in cockfighting).

Insiders of animal fighting sub-cultures either rationalise the gruesomeness of their practice, or callously disregard it. For outsiders such animal fights pose a dilemma: while repulsed by the gruesomeness of such illegal or disapproved activities, the fights might have for some an antinomian allure, not unlike a "forbidden fruit": an Otherness at once attractive and repulsive. I suggest that attending a cockfight or a dogfight holds for such individuals a voyeuristic fascination, just as bullfights do for some tourists.

The information culled from the case studies indicates that, in contrast to the considerable (though presently declining) interest tourists have shown in Spanish bullfighting (Cohen 2014a), their attendance at animal fights, even where these are legally and openly practised, does not seem to be remarkably strong. Moreover, the moderate kinds of animal fights, such as those between camels or buffalos, seem to have been more attractive to foreign tourists than the more extreme ones, such as cockfighting (or dogfighting would be, if it were accessible). However, most reports on tourist attendance at such events seem to relate to Western tourists in non-Western settings. As the proportion of Asians and other non-Westerners in international tourism grows, the size of foreign tourist attendance at legal animal fights could substantially increase in the future. The impact of the rapidly changing demography of global tourism on animal fight events could be an interesting topic of future research.

References

Alabanza, M., A. Gonzaga, and F. Obligacion. 1979. "The 'Kristo' of the cockpit: An Unsung Phenomenon." *Philippine Journal of Psychology* 12(2): 36–44.

ANI News. 2013. "Traditional Buffalo Fight Enthralls Spectators in Shimla." November 11.

Aydin, A.F. 2011. "A Brief Introduction to the Camel Wrestling Events in Western Turkey." Paper presented at Camel conference at SOAS, University of London, May 23–25, 2011, 55–59.

Bantay-Sabong. 2008. "Philippine gamefowl industry info." Accessed 1 Dec 2017. http://bantay-sabong.blogspot.com.au/2008/03/philippine-gamefowl-industry-info.html.

Brandes, S. 2009. "Torophiles and Torophobes: The Politics of Bulls and Bullfighting in Contemporary Spain." *Anthropological Quarterly* 82(3): 779–794.

Budiman, M. 2013. *Contemporary Funeral Rites of Sa'dan Toraja: From aluk todolo to "New" Religion*. Prague: Charles University in Prague.

Çalişkan, V. 2009. "Geography of a Hidden Cultural Heritage: Camel Wrestling in Western Anatolia." *Journal of International Social Research* 2(8): 123–137.

Çalişkan, V. 2010. "Examining Cultural Tourism Attractions for Foreign Visitors: The Case of Camel Wrestling in Selçuk (Ephesus)." *Turizam* 14(1): 22–40.

Carr, N. 2014. *Dogs in the Leisure Experience*. Wallingford, UK: CABI.

Cohen, E. 2012. "Tiger Tourism: From Shooting to Petting." *Tourism Recreation Research* 37(3): 193–204.

Cohen, E. 2014a. "Bullfighting and Tourism." *Tourism Analysis* 19(5): 545–556.

Cohen, E. 2014b. "Recreational Hunting: Ethics, Experiences and Commoditization." *Tourism Recreation Research* 39(1): 3–17.

Cortez, C. n.d. "Cockfighting Craze Takes Wing: The Philippine National Betting Pastime Is Going International." Accessed March 1, 2016. http://mangossubic.com/cock_fighting.htm.

Cowboy Lifestyle Network. n.d. "Steer Wrestling." Accessed March 15, 2016. http://cowboylifestylenetwork.com/in-the-arena/rodeo/steer-wrestling/.

Darden, D., and S. Worden. 1996. "Marketing Deviance: The Selling of Cockfighting." *Society and Animals* 4(2): 211–231.

Daugherty, P.M. 2012. "Philippines Police Bust What Could Be World's Largest Pit Bull Fighting Ring." *Opposing Views*, April 16. Accessed March 15, 2016. www.opposingviews.com/i/society/animal-rights /philippines-police-bust....

DeMello, M. 2012. *Animals and Society*. New York, NY: Columbia University Press.

Donlon, J.G. 2014. *Bayou Country Bloodsport: The Culture of Cockfighting in Southern Louisiana*. Jefferson, NC: McFarland & Company.

Donlon, J., J.H. Donlon, and J. Agrusa. 2010. "Cultural Tourism, Camel Wrestling and the Tourism 'bubble' in Turkey." *Anatolia* 21(1): 29–39.

Douglass, C.B. 1997. *Bulls, Bullfighting and Spanish Identities*. Tucson: University of Arizona Press.

EasyTourChina. n.d. "Dong's Buffalo Fighting Festival." Accessed March 10, 2016. www.easytourchina.com/fact-v992-dong-s-buffalo-fighting-festival.

Emerging Money. 2012. "Water Buffalo Fights May Indicate Rise of the Chinese Consumer." *Nasdaq*. April 30. Accessed March 20, 2016. www.nasdaq.com/article/water-buffalo-fights-may-indicate....

ESDAW. n.d. "Dog Fighting – One of the Most Serious Forms of Animal Abuse." Accessed April 1, 2016. www.esdaw.eu/dogfighting1.html.

Evans, R., D. Gauthier, and C. Forsyth. 1998. "Dogfighting: Symbolic Expression and Validation of Masculinity." *Sex Roles* 39(11–12): 825–838.

Fennell, D.A. 2012.*Tourism and Animal Ethics*. London and New York, NY: Routledge.

Festivals in Vietnam. n.d. "Do Son's Festival of Buffalo Fights." Accessed April 20, 2016. http://festivals-in-vietnam.com/sons-festival-buffalo-fights/.

Forsyth, C.J. 1996. "A Pecking Disorder." *International Review of Modern Sociology* 26(1): 15–25.

Forsyth, C., and R. Evans. 1998. "Dogmen: The rationalization of Deviance." *Society and Animals* 3: 203–218.

Franklin, A. 1999. *Animals and Modern Cultures: A Sociology of Human-Animal Relations in Modernity*. London: Sage.

Garcia, J. 2015. "Cockfighting." In *Sports in America from Colonial Times to the Twenty-First Century*, edited by S.T. Riess, 361–363. Oxford: Routledge.

Geertz, C. 1972. "Deep Play: Notes on the Balinese Cockfight." *Deadalus* 101(1): 1–37.

Hafeez, Z. 2014. "The Bloody World of Dog Fighting: Victory or Death, There Is No Mercy!" *The Express Tribune Blogs*, April 28. https://blogs.tribune.com.pk/story/22043/the-bloody-world-of-dog-fighting-victory-or-death-there-is-no-mercy/

Harding, S. *2014. Unleashed: The Phenomena of Status Dogs and Weapon Dogs*. Bristol: Policy Press.

Hawley, F. 1993. "The Moral and Conceptual Universe of Cockfighters: Symbolism and Rationalizations." *Society and Animals* 1(2): 159–168.

Herzog, H.A. 1985. "Hackfights and derbies." *Appalachian Journal* 12(2): 114–126.

Hicken, A. 2012. "Tourists – Have Fun, But Take Care, at Toraja Buffalo Fights." *Jakarta Post*. August 24.

Horsefund.org. 2014. "Horse Fighting Fact Sheet." Accessed March 22, 2016. www.horsefundorg/horse-fighting-fact-sheet.php.

James, C. 2012. "See a Crocodile Wrestling Show in Thailand: Dangerous? Depends." *Examiner.com*. February 27. Accessed April 10, 2016. www.examiner.com/article/see-a-crocodile-wrestling-show-thailand....

Kilborn, P.T. 2000. "In Rural Enclaves of U.S. Cockfighting Is Flourishing." *New York Times*, June 5.

Koh Samui News. 2014. "Buffalo Fighting Festival: Ten Days of Fights." Accessed March 10, 2016. http:/samuidays.com/product/buffalo-fighting-festival-10-dnej-boev-bujvolov-na-samui/.

Köhne, E., and C. Ewigleben. 2000. *Gladiators and Caesars: The Power of Spectacle in Ancient Rome*. Berkeley: University of California Press.

Larson, E. 2014. "'Blood Sports': America's Dog Fighting Industry Is Still as Strong as Ever." *Mashable.com*. December 24. Accessed April 2, 2016. http//mashable.com/2014/12/24/america-dog-fighting-industry/.

Lawler, A. 2014. "Birdmen: Cockfighters Spread the Chicken Across the Globe." Accessed April 2, 2016. www.slate.com/articles/health_and_science/science/2014/12/cockfighting_and_chicken.

Locara, L. 2013. "All Set for Candelaria Derby 2013 Edition." *Iloilo Metropolitan Times*, January 23.

Markwell, K. ed. 2015. *Animals and Tourism: Understanding Diverse Relationships*. Bristol: Channel View Publications.

Marvin, G. 1994. *Bullfight*. Champaign: University of Illinois Press.

Marwin, G. 1984. "The Cockfight in Andalusia: Images of the Truly Male." *Anthropological Quarterly* 57(2): 60–70.

Matejowsky, T. 2003. "Spider Wrestling and Gambling Culture in the Rural Philippines." *Philippine Studies* 51(1): 147–163.

McAleer, K. 1994. *Dueling: The Cult of Honor in fin-de-siécle Germany*. Princeton NJ: Princeton University Press.

Meijer, F. 2005. *The Gladiators*. New York, NY: Thomas Dunne Books.

Na Thalang, J. 2015. "Fighting to Rule the Roost." *Bangkok Post, Spectrum* (November 29): 10–13.

National Council of SPCAs. 2016. "Dog Fighting – A Real and Shocking Reality in South Africa." *NSPCA Webmaster*. June 28. Accessed September 10, 2016. http:// nspca.co.za/dog-fighting-real-shocking-reality-south-africa.

Ortiz, F. 2010. "Making the Dogman Heel: Recommendations for Improving the Effectiveness of Dogfighting Laws." *Stanford Journal of Animal Law and Policy* 3: 1–75.

Parkinson, J. 2011. "What's a Bigger Draw Than a Camel Fight? A Camel Beauty Contest, of Course." *The Wall Street Journal*, January 22.

Parley. P. 1835. *Tales of Animals*. London: Thomas Tegg and Sons.

Pearson, M.N. 1984. "Recreation in Mughal India." *The International Journal of the History of Sports* 1(3): 335–350.

Perdue, A., and R. Lockwood. 2014. *Animal Cruelty and Freedom of Speech*. West Lafayette, IN: Purdue University Press.

Philippine Daily Inquirer. 2009. "Sabong: A Sport and Industry Filipinos Can Be Proud of." Accessed Dec 1, 2017. https://bulang.wordpress.com/2009/03/24/sabong-a-sport-and-industry-filipinos-can-be-proud-of/.

Philippines Travel Guide. n.d. "Philippines Cockfighting *sabong*: Cockfighting in the Philippines." Accessed April 10, 2016. www.philipinnes-travel-guide.com/philippines-cockfighting.html.

Raffles, H. 2008. "Cricket Fighting." In *Best American Essays*, edited by A. Gopnick, 128–144. New York, NY: Houghton-Mifflin.

Razaq, P. 2015. "Ram Fighting Is Here Again . . . and the Rams are Proving Their Mettle." *Daily Times* [Nigeria], September 22.

Reddy, S. n.d. "Cockfighting Centre, Thailand." [video] Accessed April 9, 2016. http://guidemore.com/v/54275584/.

Robehmed, S. 2014. "Do the Participants of Turkey's Annual Camel Wrestling Festival Enjoy It as Much as the Audience?" *The Independent*, January 16.

Sadet, G. 2011. "Les Combats de coqs dans le Nord de la France: au nom de la tradition." *Nature – ailes*, January 21. Accessed April 10, 2016. www.nature-ailes.com/article-les-combats-de-coqs-dans-le-nord-de-la-france....

Saigon Tourist. 2005. "Buffalo Fights – Exciting Weekend Entertainment in HCMC." Accessed April 5, 2016. www.saigontourist.hochimincity.gov.vn/news/detail_en.asp?id=2096.

Sarkar, J. 2012. "Latestmetro 'sport': Dogs in the Ring." *Times of India*, June 14.

Shubert, A. 1999. *Death and Money in the Afternoon: A History of the Spanish Bullfight*. Oxford: Oxford University Press.

Smokey Tours. n.d. "Cockfighting Tour." Accessed April 9, 2016. www.smokeytours.com/cockfighting-tour/.

Stankiewicz, M. 2014. "The Surviving Bali Cockfighting Rituals." *Jakarta Post*, August 15.

Stuart, G.U. 2014. "Sabong: Cockfighting." *Philippines for the Intrepid Traveler*. Accessed April 2, 2016. www.stuartxchange.com/Sabong.

Stygelar, F-A. 2014. "Horse-Fights and Cow-Fights in Norwegian Folk Tradition." *Sport und Spiel bei den Germanen Nordeuropas von der römischen Zeit bis zum Mittelalter* 88: 457–464.

Suga, Y. 2006. "Chinese Cricket Fighting." *International Journal of Asian Studies* 3(1): 77–93.

Taipei Times. 2009. "Trained, Loved, Eaten: Vietnam's Buffalo Fights." October 7.

Vardar, N. 2014. "Animal Rights Activists Urge Banning of Camel Fights." *Bianet*. Accessed March 5, 2016. http://bianet.org/english/animals/161185-animal-rights-activists-urge-banning....

Vietnam Ethnic Cultures. 2011. "Buffalo Fighting Festival." http://vietnam-culture.blogspot.com/2011/10/buffalo-fighting-festival.html.

Vietnam-Beauty.com. 2008. "Do Son Buffalo Fighting Festival – Hai Phong City Festival." September 23. Accessed March 20, 2016. www.vietnam-beauty.com/vietnamese-culture/festivals-and-ceremonies/15-festivals....

Vietnam National Administration of Tourism. 2012. "Buffalo Fighting Festival Attracts Over 30,000 Visitors." September 25.

Vietnam National Administration of Tourism. 2015. "Do Son Buffalo Fighting Festival Attracts Large Audiences." September 23.

Wannamontha, T. 2011. "Brawling Beetles Crawl for It All." *Bangkok Post, Brunch* (October 2): 5–7.

WBIW.com. 2015. "Hog Wrestling Events at Country Fair Target of Animal Advocates." August 4. Accessed April 10, 2016. www.wbiw.com/local/archive/2015/08/hog-wrestling-event-at-country-fair....

Wellman, A. 2015. "Horror Photos Show Bloody Battle as Dogs Fight to Death for Vile Festival 'Entertainment'." *Mirror*, March 4.

West, P. 2008. *The Enduring Seminoles: From Alligator Wrestling to Casino Gambling*. Gainesville, FL: University Press of Florida.

Yacobucci, I. 2012. "Cockfighting in the Philippines: Catching a Cockfight in Valencia." *Borderless Travels*. February 20. Accessed December 1, 2016. http://borderlesstravels.com/gp/asia/republic-of-the-philippines/cockfighting-in-the-philippines.

Yilmaz, O., and M. Ertugrul. 2014. "Camel Wrestling Culture in Turkey." *Turkish Journal of Agriculture and Natural Sciences* Sp. Issue 2: 1998–2005.

Yilmaz, O., Y. Ertürk, F. Cosçun, and M. Ertuğrul. 2014. "Camel Wrestling Economy in Modern Turkey." Fifth International Scientific Agricultural Symposium 'Agrsym 2014.' Jahorina, Bosnia and Hezegovina, October 22–26, 2014, 905–911.

Yilmaz, O., M. Sarikaya, F. Coscun and M. Ertugrul. 2015. History of dog fighting in the world. *Journal of Animal Science Advances* 5(6): 1304–1305.

Young, K.M. 2016. "Criminal Behavior and Local Resistance: The Sociological Significance of the Hawaiian Cockfight." *California Law Review* 104: 1159.

Zarley, B.D. 2015. "On the Edge of the Pit: Cockfighting in America." *VICE Sports*, March 11. Accessed April 15, 2016. http:sports.vice.com/en_us/article/on-the-edge-of-the-pit....

13 Domestic animals' leisure, rights, wellbeing

Nuancing 'domestic', asymmetries and into the future

Janette Young and Neil Carr

Introduction

This book emerged out of a call for papers for the 2015 ANZALS (Australian and New Zealand Association for Leisure Studies) conference. The theme of the conference was leisure as a human right, and our interest was piqued at the opportunity to further explore the intersection of humans and animals, rights and leisure. It was an interest that can be seen to mesh with what has been entitled 'the animal turn' across a range of disciplines, including cultural studies (Andersson Cederholm et al. 2014), human geography (Buller 2014), politics and justice (Garner and O'Sullivan), religious studies (Peterson 2016) and leisure studies (Carr 2014, 2015). Within all of these fields there has been an increasingly sophisticated exploration of the human:animal interface, accompanied by a broad recognition that humans share the Earth with many other nonhuman beings and that human lives are intertwined in myriad ways with nonhuman animal others.

The distance between animals' lives and humans varies dramatically across the spectrum that we humans define as wild to domestic animals. Across this spectrum we see from one extreme to the other sea creatures being 'discovered' by humans (The Telegraph 2017) at astronomical depths below the surface of the ocean with no known direct human contact to date; the animals we think of as 'wild' living independently in environments relatively untouched by humans; those animals living independently in human-engineered environments such as villages, towns and cities (rats, mice, sparrows and foxes, for example); the animals we use for 'products' (food, clothing, garden fertiliser); and finally those we cuddle up with at night and may even think of as 'family'. Animals are part of the global environment that humans occupy. Yet some animal's lives and everyday living are integrally enmeshed with those of humans. It has been these animals, whose everyday lives are intertwined with those of humans' domestic everyday lives and leisure that this book has sought to focus on.

Domestic animals exist predominately within modern Western humans' leisure lives though increasingly they are becoming a feature of the rest of the world (Pregowski 2016). Few of us (our authors, ourselves as editors and we assume you, our readers) get the opportunity to take our companion dog, cat or bird to work with us; or to work with animals in some way. Hence our closest encounters with animals are with domestic animals, in our homes, in our leisure lives, and this of itself makes it important to consider the lives and leisure needs of these animals and our leisured interactions with them.

While some work has begun to examine the benefits of human-domestic animal interaction the focus has been predominately on benefits to humans in these relationships (see for example Martin et al. 2015; Schreiner 2016; Brooks et al. 2016; Wood et al 2007). In Chapter 1 we identified that far more work was needed to conceptually unpack and identify the complexities that might exist in our (human-wellbeing promoting) leisure intersections with domestic animals. Such a need is based on the recognition of animals as sentient beings rather than simply objects of and for human leisure. While the position of wild animals as sentient beings in leisure have been debated for some time (Cohen 2009; Markwell 2015, Carr and Young 2018) there has arguably been a gap in exploring animal rights, welfare and leisure in the everyday worlds of humans and domestic animals, with a few notable exceptions (Carr 2014; Carr 2015).

The chapters presented in this book have progressed understandings of human-domestic animal interactions in the leisure space; how humans understand the leisure needs of these animals; and how they interact with them in the leisure experience. The chapters also provide insights into how in future we can continue to develop our understandings of animal leisure by listening to them. This fits within Broom's (2010) conceptualisation of animal obligations rather than animal welfare and the need for humans to meet these obligations. The notion of obligations is particularly relevant when considering the power difference that exists between humans and domestic animals as these animals 'live' with us in human-engineered environments and may have been 'constructed' by us (through generational breeding), to be highly dependent upon humans. Having created these beings and their environments, it behoves humans to actively consider and respond to their needs, including their needs for leisure.

All of the authors in this book are in agreement that domestic or domesticated animals have rights to experience leisure and to welfare in the human leisure experience. But as with any grand and sweeping ideal, as soon as this topic is approached inherent complexities and contradictions begin to emerge. The discussion presented in this final chapter hinges on understandings that emerge from the chapters in the book. In particular the need to recognise the diversity of domestic animals and to recognise the power imbalance that exists between humans and animals, and also between animals and animals.

Wild: domestic, domestic/ated, domestic/wild – nuancing 'domestic'

As readers' may have picked up in the introductory chapter and elsewhere in the book the terms "domestic" and "domesticated" are frequently used interchangeably. As Hart (2003) and Carr (2015a) have discussed, categorisation of animals into blunt boxes is a human endeavour and it may be more useful to think of animals as existing across a spectrum that relates to their positioning in human lives and societies. Focussing on the term 'pet' as an example, the discussion presented in Anthrozoos in 2003 (republished online in 2015; see Eddy 2003; Hart 2003; Sanders 2003 as a start) can offer readers a sense of the reality that trying to pin down categorisations of animals can lead to more confusion than clarity.

This said, it is important to maintain a sense of differentiation across a spectrum from 'wild' to 'domestic' conceptions of the animal kingdom, including considering nuances across concepts of domestic and domesticated. This is because the impacts of human choices on the lives of animals identified as domestic or domesticated is more direct than that usually experienced by wild animals. The non-wild animals focussed on in this book are in a paradoxical position of having opportunities to experience both high quality human-enabled leisure (exercise in natural places with human protection for many dogs and horses; parading at dog shows for animals who have an individual passion for this activity; free-range domesticity for treasured rabbits) and savage destruction by humans or their own kind in human-contrived leisure environments (the deaths of animals generationally bred to fight). The vulnerability of these animals living in close proximity to humans to experience category change (from loved pet to abandoned and homeless overnight) is amplified in comparison to that experienced by their wild, more-distant-from-humans compatriots who are not as reliant upon human care and benevolence.

The chapters in this book suggest a teasing out and fluidity of understandings of 'domestic' and 'domesticated' animals. These distinctions have implications when considering the leisure needs, interests and opportunities of various species. These are not concrete unchangeable categories; rather, individuals and groups of animals can be seen to slip from one definition or category to another, with implications for their wellbeing and right to leisure. All of the definitions explored here hinge on the relationship of these groups of animals to humans. Humans create and contest categories of animals (Hart 2003; Sanders 2003) and humans (think ethnic and religious identities) and may then proceed to act and engage in discussions as though these categories were 'real'. Our position is akin to Sanders (2003) who notes the sociological maxim – that "what people define as real is real in its consequence" (114). How we define or recognise animals as falling into categories will make a difference to how their leisure needs will be defined by the humans who have the power to enable these animals to access animal-defined 'leisure'. Hence the categorisation we suggest aims not to create inflexible boxes, but to prompt considerations as to the differing needs and desires of a spectrum of domestic animals to leisure.

Domestic/ated animals

The lives and experiences of 'domesticated' animals are intensely diverse. Most readers will be familiar with the vast difference in life and leisure opportunities experienced by, for example, domesticated pet dogs compared to pigs or chickens raised in factory farms. Both are 'domesticated' as per Clutton-Brock's (1989) definition. But their leisure lives are extremely different. Pet dogs may be integral to the leisure lives of the humans they live with, walking, sitting on the couch watching TV together, or attending dog agility or other human-constructed animal leisure activities. Animals living in intensive farming scenarios are commonly physically contained in small spaces where they may be highly restricted in their movements or live in highly crowded sheds with vast numbers of their peers (Imhoff 2010). These animals are however also 'domesticated'. This book is not about domesticated, factory-farmed animals; but it does include description of domesticated animal lives that are distinctly different from either beloved pets, or factory- farmed animals.

The lives of factory-farmed and pet animals are both in contrast to the dogs bred to fight presented by Cohen in his chapter on animal to animal fighting by cocks, dogs, camels and buffalo. All these animals are domesticated. We suggest that the term domestic/ated may be useful to distinguish animals who are generally presumed to live in close contact with humans. Domestic/ated animals share some of the features that are commonly used to define 'pets' as they are domesticated (generationally bred by humans), and are known individually – otherwise how could you distinguish your best fighting camel/buffalo/cock? Cohen's chapter explores how these animals are chosen to be enmeshed in human leisure and entertainment. These domestic/ated animals are at high risk of suffering the same fate as their factory-farmed compatriots: death. Unless decidedly successful, these animals, bred for human leisure, rarely get to experience leisurely post-competition retirements. Cocks, camels, buffalos and dogs who do not cut it in the fighting arena are highly likely to be culled, akin to unplaced racing horses (Winter and Young 2015) who could also be seen to fit our definition of domestic/ated because of the same teetering between loved human companions and death at the hands of humans.

Domestic/wild

Drummond is a powerful advocate for the rights of small caged "marginalised" animals. She identifies that many of these animals are in fact not domesticated. Domestic but not domesticated. It is not uncommon that they are captured wild animals, removed from their natural, nonhuman environments, to be trapped in human spaces. Alternately they may be the relatively recent generational offspring of captive wild animals, and have not been subject to the genetic and biological processes of domestication that have made other species 'naturally' adjusted to living with humans. Hamsters being an example she provides of a recently captured species (wild), now kept in homes (domestic) but not really domesticated, that is shaped by human breeding interests for many generations.

Recognising these animals as domestic/wild could be one means of raising awareness of their captive positions, and perhaps prompt greater explorations of their needs, particularly for leisure as semi-wild rather than domesticated domestic animals. These animals could benefit from the models of 'enrichment' (Young 2008) that are part of wild animal husbandry in zoos and other captive environments. Enrichment aims to replicate the natural experiences of captive wild animals such as foraging and food sourcing and patterns of social engagement with species peers in order to enhance their lives and wellbeing. As such, the leisure options for these domestic/wild animals may hinge on seeking to replicate wild conditions (e.g. large pens or aviaries as compared to smaller cages) and limiting contact with humans, recognising their innate fear of humans may not have been expunged by generational human breeding control.

Hence there are sub-categories of domestic or domesticated animals that indicate very different responses and awareness's amongst humans with regard to their rights to leisure. Domestic/ated animals – sometimes pets, sometimes simply human leisure competition machines, vulnerable to annihilation at human behests. Domestic/wild – wild animals (often unrecognised as such) brought into human spaces to entertain, soothe and meet human leisure interests without the 'buffering' of domestication breeding control. All of these domestic animals are subject to the inherent power imbalances across the human:animal divide.

Asymmetries of power and leisure

Underpinning any discussions of human:animal relationships sits the thorny matter of power. Humans have power over domestic animals, including the power to define and provide access to even animal-defined leisure. However, power asymmetries do not stop with just humans: animals; there are also differences across groupings of animals. These multiple asymmetries of power are considered below.

Humans:animals

Underlying the rationale for the construction of this book and embedded within all the chapters in it is the play of human power over domestic animals. Postmodern understandings of 'dogs as family' (Blichfledt and Sakacova) and the shared human-animal building of 'equiscapes' (Danby) define them as psychological spaces where positive regard for specific animals is displayed. But this is still at the behest of humans. The horses taken for weekend rides do not have a right or opportunity to resist such human:animal engagement (at least not without negative repercussions), and neither do the dogs who go on family holidays even though in both cases humans may actively seek to identify nonhuman others perspectives. There is a cross-species power imbalance. That said, many teenagers coerced into the same cross-species family holidays might feel that they were in a very similar position of powerlessness within the family (Carr 2006). However teenagers generally progress to a life stage where they can actively choose whether to undertake, or excuse themselves from family holidays. For animals, their participation in these events will continue to be a matter of choice by their human guardians.

However, respectful consideration of power differences can be negotiated. Parents may respond to teenage children's entreaties, animal guardians may perceive and respond to indicators of individual animal leisure interests and wellbeing. The chapters by O'Dwyer, and Brown and Lackova illustrate, from differing stances, that while anthropomorphisation may be seen at times as counter to respect for animals (Francione 2009; Hall 2006) where human and animal leisure lives intersect, human awareness and insights into animal needs may be highly enhanced. In other words, while it can have negative connotations, anthropomorphisation has the potential to be positive for developing understandings of animals, from the perspective of animals, for the benefits of animals (refer to Mitchell (1997), Guthrie (1997) Horowitz (2009) and Carr (2014) for a more detailed discussion of the potential position of anthropomorphisation in animal studies). For example, Brown and Lackova's dog walkers show an alertness to their canine companions likes, dislikes and leisure choices. They do this by observing their dogs' patterns of behaviours both across time (what does the dog usually like?) and in the moment (s/he does not seem so interested today).

Henderson's work builds on ideas of human alertness to animal communication. She critically identifies that there is a need to increase human understandings of animal needs based in evolutionary species specific knowledge in order to improve the lives and leisure experiences of animals, even those to which we may feel incredibly attached. Hurley's explorations mirror Henderson's, identifying that many models of animal behaviour management and control are inherently speciest, presuming and embedding human power and superiority over animals. Some animal training models actively seek to depower animals and remove their opportunities to exercise agency. They may deny domestic animals rights to independent fun and enjoyment; the kind of frivolous enjoyment that the human dog show participants (interviewed by Dabrowsaka) report as inherent to human choices to engage in this form of leisure activity.

Discussions regarding human power over animals and animal leisure hinge on ideas of reconsidering or simply rejecting specicism – that is the presumption that humans are all superior beings to all non-humans/animals, including those to which they feel intensely close. Reconsidering or rejecting speciesism and seeing animals as equal to humans with needs and rights of equal worth implies that individual animals should be recognised as potentially having unique leisure interests. So, for example, such a reconsideration may not simply lead to the banning of dog shows, as some animals, especially those selectively bred for a temperament that adapts most readily to the show environment and demands, may need and indeed thrive in such settings (see Dabrowska). This said, recognition of individualised and genetically construed animal needs for leisure does not mean that there should not be reconsideration of some of the parameters that shape dog showing, dog obedience and the like. But it would mean that a measured approach rather than a blanket one-size fits all approach is taken. Hurley offers insights that could be used to begin to instigate such measured approaches in the field of dog training and beyond. He presents the notion of 'symphysis' where human and animal interests and desires are both recognised, and regardless of species participants are free to engage or disengage in activity as they wish. Hence, rather than seeing animal disengagement or resistance to training (for example) as something to be overcome, such behaviour is seen as indicative of individual animals interests and consideration is given to animals rights to choose to participate or not. This is the same way that ultimately human participants are able to enact rights to disengage, particularly from leisure activities which do not mesh with their individual interests.

Henderson offers a range of ideas that relate to horses that could perhaps be elaborated slightly by inclusion of individualised options as well. For example, walls that can be lowered between individual horses who display 'friendship' towards each other. This idea is expressed with caution as firstly neither editor is an expert in horse understandings, and secondly, friendship does not necessarily mean wanting to be together all the time. The point however is to be incorporating awareness and a willingness to seek to respond to animal interests in leisure, rather than denying them this right.

Arguments for a more equitable understanding of domestic animals' rights to leisure, and engagement in such, sit in opposition to a human-centric animal rights position. Instead an animal obligations position recognises animal agency and human obligations associated with enabling this agency. Domestic animals do not have the privilege of wild or human-independent animals to choose their leisure activities. Domestic animals are dependent upon humans who control their environments to recognise and respond to their needs and wants. This includes recognising needs for rest, recreation and enjoyment as well as taking into account the concern explored by Young and Barker that some domesticated animals selectively bred for labouring over many hundreds of years may suffer a lack of occupation and a burden of leisure in modern societies where their labour is no longer demanded of them. Having bred animals for specific purposes and characteristics, there is a moral obligation on humans as a species to provide opportunities for these animals to experience the activities for which they have been 'designed'. This may include both leisure and work in a way that is akin to the enrichment programmes that have become part of quality captive wild animal plans (Young 2008).

A further complexity to be considered in reflecting on the asymmetry of human power over animal leisure in combination with using an obligations framework arises when thinking about the scenarios explored by Cohen. He alerts us to what can be seen as the very dark side of some domestic/ated animals lives. In this human leisure space of animal:animal fighting the natural capacities and capabilities for defence and fighting of some animals are contained but then strategically 'released' in the interests of human profit and leisure making. In the context of recognising and accommodating the human-designed, now innate desires of some domestic/ated animals, this raises the thorny question of whether having been bred to fight (over generations) some of these animals may have an inbuilt need to undertake combat. Providing fighting opportunities could be a rights recognising approach to fulfilling these animals' leisure needs. This leads to questions of animal:animal power differences.

Power – animals:animals

The authors in this book reveal, challenge and advocate against the multiple asymmetries of power that can be seen to exist between humans and animals. But any sophisticated approach to understanding the leisure needs of domestic animals needs to seek to ensure that multiple layers of complexity and interests are drawn into the analytical framework. The chapters here not only reveal asymmetries in power across human:animal relationships, they also reveal animal:animal power differences. Three key animal:animal power asymmetries, each with implications for animal leisure, can be discerned. Each raise the same core questions of "leisure for who?" and "at whose expense?" The three asymmetries are wild: domestic animals; domestic: domestic animals and "those we love: the rest" (Carr 2015a).

Firstly, wild:domestic animal asymmetries. Wilson, Yoshino and Latkova in particular seek to unpack these animal to animal power differences. When do the rights of domestic animals to experience leisure in natural environments, be these urban, non-urban or wild, clash with the rights of other animals, in particular those animals for whom these natural locations are home? The presence of dog walkers and their pets in these environments may impact on other animal's experiences of leisure and life. They may in fact be detrimental to wild animal's wellbeing. In particular, dogs experiencing high quality off-leash leisure experiences in these places may chase rabbits, birds and any other creatures which live in these environments. Some of these animals may even be killed, as some of Brown and Lackova's dog-conscious, but perhaps less broadly animal-conscious dog walkers note in passing. For wild animals that live in these places, disruption and even destruction of food sources, animal homes and perhaps the importation of disease to fragile wild environments (Banks and Bryant 2007, Smith et al. 2014, Stigner et al. 2016) is an impediment to their rights to wellbeing and indeed leisure. Progressing leisure rights for (some) domestic/ated animals, who it could be argued have more privilege (continued and guaranteed access to food, comfortable safe accommodation) could embed the disadvantage and relative lack of power that other less privileged, more vulnerable wild animals face.

Secondly, there is not just a power imbalance that can be discerned between some domestic/ated and some wild animals. There are also contested rights to leisure and wellbeing that can exist between domestic animals. This can be both within and across species. For example, while some dogs' leisure may be enhanced by off-leash opportunities, this may infringe on the leisure experiences of other dogs (perhaps smaller and less boisterous, or simply on-leash). The freedom to enjoy off-leash leisure in public spaces such as parks and nature reserves, on beaches and the like by large, not even necessarily boisterous dogs, may lead some dog owners to make choices that actually reduce and restrict the leisure options of the canines for which they have responsibility to care. The leisurely freedom of other domestic species to roam in these same spaces may also be impeded by the exercise of freedom experienced by off-leash dogs. The grouping of off-leash dogs may be particularly deadly to other species. For example, the death of a pet cat, cornered and mauled by several off leash dogs appeared in the local paper of one of the editors (Young) while this book was being compiled (Pisani 2017). The complexity of this situation is added to in the case of the homes of both editors as the pet cat is also widely defined as an invasive animal in both Australia and New Zealand. This conflicted position (of pet and pest) feeds into discussions of the appropriateness of cats in public spaces and views of attacks like the one noted above.

The overarching question that arises is when should one group of animals' right to experience leisure be curtailed in the interests of preserving the rights of another group of animals? Often these decisions (human decisions) are made on a species basis. For example, the increasing confinement of cats to human homes, restricting their freedom to roam (leisurely) in order to protect wildlife (Denny and Dickman 2010; RSPCA 2017) is a growing phenomenon in Australia. This restriction on one group of animals' rights to what could be seen as leisure is being portrayed as less important than the preserving of life of other species, especially native birds and marsupials. This is a reversing by humans of the first animal:animal asymmetry noted previously (domestic:wild). Humans have the power to make decisions that restrict or enable domestic animal leisure and this power of choice can in turn impact on the interests of other animals – wild and domestic.

All of the above discussion leads to a final asymmetry that we are very aware of in the book. In the domination of discourses and analyses focussed on dogs and to a lesser extent horses lies the potential to embed a form of animal:animal speciesism. A hierarchy of domesticated animals already exists when comparing the lives of factory-farmed domesticated animals to that of loved pets, and some relatively safe domestic animals in cages. It is clear from the contents of this book that research on domestic and domesticated animals in relation to leisure continues to be, as Carr (2015a) found, focussed on a very limited range of species, particularly dogs and horses. While the importance of these species is undeniable, there remains a clear need to begin to explore issues of leisure in relation to other domestic/ated animals. One of the most intriguing of omissions is that of leisure explorations linked to cats. Research on pet ownership (GfK 2016) across 22 countries found that dogs were the most popular pet in 14 countries. But cat ownership surpassed dogs in eight; and cats were the second most popular pet in all bar one (China where they were trumped by fish) of the 14 where dogs are most popular. Yet there is almost no contemporary academic literature on the role of cats in human lives, and specifically in leisure. Failure to look beyond dogs and horses will only reinforce the privileging of one species over another by humans and damn us to criticisms of failing to truly listen to and pay attention to our obligations to all animals rather than those we happen to like.

Mapping the path ahead

One of our aims in compiling this book was to develop a potential roadmap for future research in the field of domestic/ated animals and leisure, with specific reference to issues of animal and human rights, welfare and wellbeing. Some specific directions arise from the books' content while others come from what is lacking in the content.

Firstly, 'leisure' is a human construction. Indeed 'leisure' can be seen to be a construct that relates to a historically, economically and culturally situated human experience. That said, if we employ Carr's (2015b) very broad defining of leisure as the opportunity to freely engage in activities that facilitate pleasure, enjoyment and a sense of self in individuals, there is scope to explore further and become better at identifying what creates leisure in the lives of domestic animals. After all, we know animals are capable of experiencing pleasure and enjoyment (Berridge and Kringelbach 2008). The question of whether animals have a sense of self beyond the ability to self-recognise and a desire to explore and develop such a self is one worthy of further study. It is an exploration whose answers will have significant implications for the nature of any leisure these animals experience or should have the right to experience.

Domestic animals' closeness to humans can be seen to make fulfilment of their rights to leisure more complicated than perceiving wild animal needs for leisure. This is not just about human abuse of power – it is because human desires to experience leisure *with* these animals can create blindness to animal needs. As described in Danby's chapter, we desire that the horse we ride feels just as fulfilled by hacking across the countryside, and seeing nature, as we (the humans riding) do. Or reflecting on Drummond's analysis, that the guinea pig in the 'Taj Mahal' hutch we have lovingly worked on for the last month can discern the cross-species love and care that drove its construction. While the human aim may genuinely be for this little animal to be able to rest and relax in the 'beautiful' space created, a lack of species specific knowledge may mean that we engender stress in this animal with a structure that does not match their needs. In this regard loved domestic animals can suffer in the same way as human family members in well-meaning but misunderstanding families. For example, the aged parent with dementia who becomes distressed and fearful at a family get together, or the undiagnosed food intolerant child who really is made sick by the food at the same event. Core to these human experiences of leisure not being leisurely for some individuals can be a lack of understanding of both individuals and collective (in the examples given – diagnostic) needs. Meeting the leisure needs and fulfilling a right to leisure for both humans and animals requires understandings of diversity with regard to needs, desires and abilities of individuals and groups. It also requires careful reflection and introspection with regard to human agendas where human and animal leisure intersect. Further research and writing should aim to tease out these complexities of human agendas with regard to animal leisure and ways in which knowledge about diverse domestic animal groups can be better disseminated.

There is a need to link to historical breeding aims and objectives that have created some sub-species and breeds of domestic animals. Understanding biologically based, historically chosen differences within species can enhance animal welfare and wellbeing and indicate what leisure means for the diversity of these animals. This is already quite sophisticated with regard to dogs. For example, couch snoozing for greyhounds, long outdoor runs and competitive activities for border collies, parading for poodles. But this kind of understanding needs to be extended beyond this unique privileged species. Linking to animal researchers in the field of veterinary sciences, ethology and related fields will be important for enriching our understandings of what might constitute leisure for a range of species who share our human lives. This includes the possibilities that some animals, especially those who have been selectively bred to labour, may in fact experience the burden of leisure and have a biologically mapped need for non-leisure or meaningful occupation (i.e. work). These animals may need balance in their lives between rest, recreation and leisure, and work in the same manner that it has been argued that humans do (Sage 2017; Drydakis 2015, Gathergood 2013).

The reality for many of these bred- to-labour breeds is that the breeding of such animals simply ceases given the control humans have over the reproductive lives of these species when they are no longer needed for the job they were 'created' to do (Scherf and Pilling 2015; FAO nd; Hammond nd). From a traditional speciest perspective, this is the economically rational decision. However, it is a perspective that simply ignores any notion of animal agency or human obligations to species. The question is what are the obligations that humans have to individual animals and species in general? Having played God in the designing of these animals, do we then have the right to simply destroy a species by ceasing its breeding? Do we have the right to change the species by more human tinkering with genes, or do we have an obligation to preserve the species in the same way we now seek to preserve wild species and offer them the opportunities to engage in their 'natural' behaviour? These are all complicated, messy questions that bear future exploration inside and outside of a leisure context.

There is a need to continue to explore human:animal relations in leisure from cross-disciplinary perspectives. It is important to remember that biological sciences can only answer so much if we recognise animals as sentient beings. This is especially important when we remember that the vast majority of what we know of animals from the sciences has been gleaned from a position that has regarded animals as automatons – objects capable of movement but incapable of thinking and reasoning. The erroneous nature of this position is only just beginning to become fully apparent as we recognise an increasingly diverse array of animals as sentient beings. Indeed, it can be argued that instead of continuing to identify species as sentient one at a time when sufficient scientific proof has been gathered, we should simply abandon carte blanche the historic position and recognise all animals as sentient beings. Such a shift is arguably being led by social scientists rather than the biological scientists who objectified the animal, a situation that suggests that while we can listen to biological scientists to better understand some aspects of animal leisure, we should also listen to social scientists to better understand animals. The risk with the 'animal turn' across so many fields is that we will hunker down in our discipline-specific comfort zones, reducing the potential to maximise understandings of animal needs and desires by truly engaging in cross-disciplinary work.

This book has covered issues of animal rights and welfare in leisure and of human interests in relation to animal-oriented leisure. Humans and animals exist within the same space (i.e. The Earth) and they do so in an unequal power relation. Humans hold the power, most obviously demonstrated in their ability to decide when and how to kill animals. Based on this recognition, animal leisure and their rights and welfare are, and must be recognised as being, situated within a human-constructed and dominated reality. Given this, it is beholden to humans to recognise their obligations to animals, including their right to leisure and to utilise their power to ensure these needs are met in a manner that ensures the wellbeing and rights of animals *for* animals, not the placating of human emotions. Just as is the case with humans, a better understanding of animals can be gleaned via an understanding of leisure. In this way leisure is not something frivolous and on the edges of society, it is a core component of society and the lives of all (human and animal) who reside within it.

References

Andersson Cederholm, E., A. Björck, K. Jennbert, and A. Lönngren, eds. 2014. *Exploring the Animal Turn: Human-Animal Relations in Science, Society and Culture*. Lund: The Pufendorf Institute for Advanced Studies.

Banks, P., and J. Bryant. 2007. "Four-Legged Friend or Foe? Dog Walking Displaces Native Birds from Natural Areas." *Biology Letters* 3(6): 611–613. doi:10.1098/rsbl.2007.0374.

Berridge, K., and M. Kringelbach. 2008. "Affective Neuroscience of Pleasure: Reward in Humans and Animals." *Psychopharmacology* 199(3): 457–480. doi:10.1007/s00213-008-1099-6.

Brooks, H., K. Rushton, S. Walker, K. Lovell, and A. Rogers. 2016. "Ontological Security and Connectivity Provided by Pets: A Study in the Self-Management of the Everyday Lives of People Diagnosed with a Long-Term Mental Health Condition." *BMC Psychiatry* 16(1): 409–22. doi:10.1186/s12888-016-1111-3.

Broom, D. 2010. "Cognitive Ability and Awareness in Domestic Animals and Decisions About Obligations to Animals." *Applied Animal Behavior Science* 126(1): 1–11. doi:http://dx.doi.org/10.1016/j.applanim.2010.05.001.

Buller, H. 2014. "Animal Geographies I." *Progress in Human Geography* 38(2): 308–318.

Carr, N. 2006. "A Comparison of Adolescents and Parents Holiday Motivations and Desires." *Tourism and Hospitality Research* 6(2): 129–142.

Carr, N. 2014. *Dogs in the Leisure Experience*. Wallingford, UK: CABI.

Carr, N., ed. 2015. *Domestic Animals and Leisure*. Basingstoke: Palgrave Macmillan.

Carr, N. 2015a. "Speaking of the Underrepresented Other: Looking Beyond Dogs and Horses." In *Domestic Animals and Leisure*, edited by N. Carr, 1–13. Basingstoke: Palgrave Macmillan.

Carr, N. 2015b. "Introduction: Defining Domesticated Animals and Exploring Their Uses by and Relationships with Humans." In *Domestic Animals and Leisure*, edited by N. Carr, 1–13. Basingstoke: Palgrave Macmillan.

Carr, N., and J. Young., eds. 2018. *Wild Animals and Leisure: Rights and Wellbeing*. Abingdon: Routledge.

Clutton-Brock, J. 1989. *The Walking Larder: Patterns of Domestication, Pastoralism, and Predation*. London: Unwin Hyman Ltd.

Cohen, E. 2009. "The Wild and the Humanized: Animals in Thai Tourism." *Anatolia* 20(1): 100–118.

Denny, E., and C. Dickman. 2010. *Review of Cat Ecology and Management Strategies in Australia*. Canberra: Invasive Animals Cooperative Research Centre. Accessed June 29 2017. www.pestsmart.org.au/wp-content/uploads/2010/03/CatReport_web.pdf

Drydakis, N. 2015. "The Effect of Unemployment on Self-Reported Health and Mental Health in Greece from 2008 to 2013: A Longitudinal Study Before and During the Financial Crisis." *Social Science & Medicine* 128(March): 43–51. doi:https://doi.org/10.1016/j.socscimed.2014.12.025.

Eddy, T. 2003. "What Is a Pet?" *Anthrozoös* 16(2): 98–105. doi:10.2752/089279303786992224.
Food and Agricultural Organisation of the UN (FAO). nd. "Agrobiodiversity: Th Case for Conserving Domestic and Related Animals." Accessed June 27, 2017. www.fao.org/docrep/v1650t/v1650t0y.htm.
Francione, G. 2009. *Animals as Persons: Essays on the Abolition of Animal Exploitation*. New York, NY: Columbia University Press.
Garner, R., and S. O'Sullivan. 2016. *The Political Turn in Animal Ethics*. London: Rowman and Littlefield International.
Gathergood, J. 2013. "An Instrumental Variable Approach to Unemployment, Psychological Health and Social Norm Effects." *Health Economics* 22(6): 643–654. doi:10.1002/hec.2831.
GfK. 2016. "Pet Ownership: Global GfK Survey." Accessed June 14, 2017. www.gfk.com/fileadmin/user_upload/country_one_pager/NL/documents/Global-GfK-survey_Pet-Ownership_2016.pdf.
Guthrie, S. 1997. "Anthropomorphism: A Definition and a Theory." In *Anthropomorphism, Anecdotes and Animals*, edited by R. Mitchell, N. Thompson, and H. Miles, 50–58. Albany: State University of New York Press.
Hall, L. 2006. *Capers in the Churchyard: Animal Rights Advocacy in the Age of Terror*. Darien, CT: Nectar Bat Press.
Hammond, K. nd. "Identification and Characterization of Domestic Animal Diversity." Food and Agricultural Organisation of the UN (FAO). Accessed June 27, 2017. www.fao.org/docrep/T1300T/t1300T01.htm.
Hart, L. 2003. "Pets Along a Continuum: Response to 'What Is a Pet?'" *Anthrozoös* 16(2): 118–122. doi:10.2752/089279303786992288.
Horowitz, A. 2009. *Inside of a Dog: What Dogs See, Smell, and Know*. New York, NY: Scribner.
Imhoff, D. 2010. *The CAFO Reader: The Tragedy of Industrial Animal Factories*. Healdsburg, CA: Watershed Media.
Markwell, K., ed. 2015. *Animals and Tourism: Understanding Diverse Relationships*. Clevedon: Channel View Publications.
Martin, K., L. Wood, H. Christian, and G. Trapp. 2015. "Not Just 'A Walking the Dog': Dog Walking and Pet Play and Their Association with Recommended Physical Activity among Adolescents." *American Journal of Health Promotion* 29(6): 353–356. doi:doi:10.4278/ajhp.130522-ARB-262.
Mitchell, R. 1997. "Anthropomorphic Anecdotalism as Method." In *Anthropomorphism, Anecdotes and Animals*, edited by R. Mitchell, N. Thompson, and H. Miles, 150–169. Albany: State University of New York Press.
Peterson, A. 2016. "Religious Studies and the Animal Turn." *History of Religions* 56(2): 232–245.
Pisani, A. 2017. "Owner's Outrage as Pet Mauled to Death." *The Messenger*. Accessed June 28, 2017. http://messenger.smedia.com.au/portside-weekly/.
Pręgowski, M., ed. 2016. *Companion Animals in Everyday Life*. New York: Palgrave Macmillan.
RSPCA. 2017. "Identifying Best Cat Management Practise in Australia." *RSPCA*. Accessed June 29, 2017. www.rspca.org.au/facts/science/cat-management-paper.
Sage, D. 2017. "Reversing the Negative Experience of Unemployment: A Mediating Role for Social Policies?" *Social Policy & Administration* (early online) doi:10.1111/spol.12333.
Sanders, C. 2003. "Whose Pet? Comment on Timothy Eddy, 'What Is a Pet?'." *Anthrozoös* 16(2): 114–117. doi:10.2752/089279303786992198.

Scherf, B., and D. Pilling, eds. 2015. *The Second Report on the State of the World's Animal Genetic Resources for Food and Agriculture*. Food and Agricultural Organisation of the UN (FAO), Commission on Genetic Resources for Food and Agriculture Assessments. Accessed June 29, 2017. www.fao.org/3/a-i4787e/index.html.

Schreiner, P. 2016. "Emerging Cardiovascular Risk Research: Impact of Pets on Cardiovascular Risk Prevention." *Current Cardiovascular Risk Reports* 10(2): 8–21. http://doi.org/10.1007/s12170-016-0489-2.

Smith, A., C. Semeniuk, S. Kutz, and A. Massolo. 2014. "Dog-Walking Behaviors Affect Gastrointestinal Parasitism in Park-Attending Dogs." *Parasites and Vectors* 7(1): 1–10.

Stigner, M., H. Beyer, C. Klein, and A. Fuller. 2016. "Reconciling Recreational Use and Conservation Values in a Coastal Protected Area." *Journal of Applied Ecology* 53(4): 1206–1214. doi:10.1111/1365-2664.12662.

The Telegraph. 2017. "Creatures of the Deep: What Lurks in the Depths of the Ocean?" *The Telegraph*. Accessed June 18, 2017. www.telegraph.co.uk/news/earth/earthpicturegalleries/5313918/Creatures-of-the-deep-What-lurks-in-the-depths-of-the-ocean.html.

Winter, C., and W. Young. 2015. "Fatalities and Fascinators: A New Perspective on Thoroughbred Racing." In *Domestic Animals and Leisure*, edited by N. Carr, 241–260. Basingstoke: Palgrave Macmillan.

Wood, L., B. Giles-Corti, M. Bulsara, and D. Bosch. 2007. "More Than a Furry Companion: The Ripple Effect of Companion Animals on Neighborhood Interactions and Sense of Community." *Society and Animals* 15(1): 43–56. doi:10.1163/156853007x169333.

Young, R. 2008. *Environmental Enrichment for Captive Animals*. Hoboken: Wiley-Blackwell.

Index

Note: Page numbers in *italics* indicate figures on the corresponding page.

Acampora, R. 59, 60
Adam's Task (Hearne) 49
Adelaide *see* labour roles of animals
adventure leisure tourism 154
agency: dog 102–104; environment 105–106; human 104–105; of the leash 107–108; multispecies wellbeing and 109–110; of socialities of other dogs and humans 107
alpacas 4
alpha rolls 49
American Kennel Club (AKC) 34, 47, 56–58
amphibians 15
Angus, D. 139
Animal That Therefore I Am, The (Derrida) 60
anthropomorphism 49–52
Antonacopoulos, N. 107
Araújo-Soares, V. 92
asymmetries of power and leisure 213–217
Atkins, P. 129
Audubon Society 68
Aydin, A. F. 194–195

Bauman, A. E. 88
Beck, A. 115
Bekoff, M. 51–52, 60
Belk, R. W. 125
Benhajali, H. 177
Biddle, S. J. 83
Billett, E. 174
biophilia 13
birds 12, 15, 18, 20, 27
Blichfeldt, B. S. 123
Bowes, M. 148, 152
Brandt, K. 151–152
breeding and conformation, dog 56–58

Briefer Freymond, S. 172, 178
Broom, D. 7, 210
Brown, K. M. 100
Buckley, R. C. 154
Budiansky, S. 181, 183
buffalo-to-buffalo fights 196–198
Bulsara, M. 123
Burla, J. B. 177
Burn, C. 23

caged pets *see* marginalised companion animals
Cairngorms National Park 99, 101; *see also* dog walking
Çalişkan, V. 195, 195–196
camels 4
camel-to-camel fights 194–196
Canadian Veterinary Medical Association 24
caravanning: conclusions on 125–126; getting out and going for a walk while 119–120; inclusion and exclusion of dogs in different activities while 120–121; limited space and sociability while 122–123; protective and punitive restrictions while 124–125; research findings 118–125; research methodology 117–118
caretakers, contradictions in expectations and experiences of 23–27
Carr, N. 1, 6, 119, 210, 217; on animals as in a continuum from domestic to wild 3–4; on anthropomorphisation 214; on dogfighting 192; on dogs playing and having fun 60, 110; on leisure 217–218; on professional pet-sitting 116–117
casual leisure: defined 36; dog shows as 36–40; *see also* human leisure

224　Index

children's labour 132–133
chores versus leisure 83–84, 86–87
cities, historical place of animals in 129–131
Clark, D. 117
classroom pets 17
close-bonds and cultural understanding with horses 159–160
Clutton-Brock, J. 3, 211
cock-to-cock fights 198–202
cognitive ethology 35, 41; needs of horses 165–184
Cohen, S. 113–114, 116, 119, 212
Coleman, G. 149–150
companion or family member, marginalised companion animals as 17–18, 21
compulsion training 48
confinement and solitary confinement of horses 169–170
constructions created by the pet industry 21–23
contradictions in expectations and experiences of caretakers 23–27
Cooper, J. J. 176, 179
cows 4, 5
Cozzi, A. 176
"Cropping and Docking: A Discussion of the Controversy and the Role of Law in Preventing Unnecessary Cosmetic Surgery of Dogs" (Broughton) 58
Crouch, D. 148
Cutt, H. E. 88, 90–91

Dabrowska, M. 34
Danby, P. 157
Dashper, K. 152, 155
Davidson, H. P. B. 170
Davis, K. 50, 52
Davis, L. 56–57
Dean, F. 65
Dean, J. 34
Degeling, C. 100, 107, 109
DeMello, M. 28, 152, 155, 161
Derrida, J. 60
Despret, V. 100
de Waal, F. 52
diversion, marginalised companion animals as 15–16
Dog Fancy 47
dogfighting 191–194
dogs 7; agency of 102–104; alpha rolls 49; breeding and conformation 56–58; caravanning holidays and 115–126; dog shows as leisure for 40–44; eating of 3; guard 70; interactions with other animals 73–74; Lexington Attachment to Pet Scale 89–91; as nonhuman family members 113–115; off-leash recreation 63–76; sledding 3; working 138–139
dog shows: as canine leisure 40–44; as casual leisure for humans 36–40; conclusions on 44–45; human leisure and 35–40; introduction to 32–34; play at 36–37; research methodology for 34–35; sensory stimulation at 37–39, 42, 44; social conversation at 39–40; training and 47–60
dog training: anthropomorism and 49–52; breeding and conformation and 56–58; conclusion on 58–60; human-canine relationships and 52–53; human hegemony in 53–56; introduction to 47; literature and practice 48–56
dog walking: agency of dogs in 102–104; agency of humans in 104–105; agency of socialities of other dogs and humans in 107; agency of the environment in 105–106; agency of the leash in 107–108; how perceptions of dog's needs and desires influence practices in 101–108; introduction to 82–84; Lexington Attachment to Pet Scale and 89–91; research discussion 91–93; research methodology on wellbeing and 101; survey respondent profile 84–85; survey results 85–91; towards multispecies wellbeing in 109–110; wellbeing and 98–99; what dogs want from 99–101
domestic animals: asymmetries of power and leisure for humans and 213–217; caged *see* marginalised companion animals; defining 2–4, 210–213; as food 3; human-initiated fights between 190–204; as integral component of human leisure experiences 1; relocation in modern Western society 128–142; rights of 6–7, 132, 209–220; welfare of 6–7, 27
domesticated animals 2–4; in cities, history of 129–131; contradictions in the perceived life experiences of 18–21; defining 2–4, 210–213; human leisure and 4–6; overlooked as part of leisure field 1–2

Donaldson, S. 141
Donlon, J. 195, 199
Dorsey, C. 116
Dotson, M. J. 115–120
Drummond, R. A. 212
Duvall, M. 107

Edington, C. R. 153
Ellis, A. D. 170
Ellson, T. 114, 116
"End of Identity Politics, The: On Disability as an Unstable Category" (Davis) 56–57
entertainment, marginalised companion animals as 15–16
environment, agency of the 105–106
equestrianism 147, 154
Equine Prisoner Model: Circle A and equine stereotypies 168–169; Circle B 169–171; embracing the needs of horses and 183–184; integrative model of 166–183; introduction to 165–166; overlap 171–183; *see also* horses
'equiscapes' 154–160
escapism 156–157
ethography, historical 131–132
ethology, cognitive 35, 41; needs of horses 165–184
eugenics 56–57
Evans, R. 191
"exotic" label 22

Federation Cynolgique Internationale (FCI) 34
Federation of European Companion Animal Veterinary Associations 19
Fenzi, D. 55
Fifield, S. J. 16
fights, human-initiated animal: buffalo-to-buffalo 196–198; camel-to-camel 194–196; categories of 190; cock-to-cock 198–202; comparative analysis 202–203; conclusions on 203–204; dog-to-dog 191–194; introduction to 190–191
fish 14–15, 21
Forsyth, C. 191, 198, 200
Forsyth, D. K. 16
For the Love of a Dog: Understanding Emotion in You and Your Best Friend (McConnell) 49, 50–51, 53
Fraser, D. 166–169
Fudge, E. 26, 29

Gaines, J. 115
Game, A. 148–149, 151
Geertz, C. 198–199
Giles, S. 178
Giles-Corti, B. 123
Gillespie, D. L. 114
Golden Gate National Recreation Area (GGNRA) 63; arguments on 66–74; conclusion on 74–76; contentious process in regulating 64–65; guard dogs and 70; history of 64; and human's recreation, health, and socialisation 69–70; lack of adequate enforcement of existing rules and 71–73; lack of public space and 71; multiple recreation experiences in 66–68; off-leash recreation as part of the San Francisco Bay Area culture and 68; on-leash dogs as more dangerous and 71; promoting preservation and protection of natural and cultural resources 73–74; reducing user conflict and promoting visitor and employee safety 68; research methods on 65–66; user conflict in 68–69; variety of user experiences in 66; violence in 70
Goodwin, D. 175
Granquist, S. M. 178
greyhound racing 4
guard dogs 70
Guest, C. 34
guinea pigs 25
Guthrie, S. 214

Hafeez, Z. 193–194
Hall, C. 174
Hallberg, L. 151
Hama, H. 159
hamsters 4, 12, *17*, 19–20; as teaching tool 16–17
Hannam, K. 157
Haraway, D. J. 100, 102, 104, 109–110, 152
Harding, S. 192–193
Hart, L. 210
Hartman, E. 177
Hausberger, M. 152, 173
Hawley, F. 199
Hearne, V. 49, 51–54
Heitor, F. 176
Helgadóttir, G. 147
Hemsworth, L. M. 149–150
Herzog, H. 13, 18

Hicken, A. 196
Hill, R. P. 115
Hirschman, E. C. 113, 114, 115, 119, 122, 124
historical ethography 131–132
Holbrook, M. B. 115, 125
Honda Motor Company 117
Horowitz, A. 214
horses 3, 7, 160–161; challenges of competition for 171; close-bonds and cultural understanding with 159–160; coping hypothesis and 171–172; cruelty of prevention of adaptation by 172–173; current feeding practices 170–171; embracing the needs of 183–184; environmental challenges for 169–171; Equine Prisoner Model 165–184; in 'equiscapes' 154–160; escapism through 156–157; ethological needs of 165–184; having friends 176–179; and human-equine relations within the leisure landscape 152–154; introduction to 146–148; invisibility of behavioural cues of distress in 173–174; learned helplessness in 174; mirrors for 179–180; nature-based, adventurous encounters with 157–159; post-humanistic approach towards human leisure and relations with 148–149; quantity and quality of forage 175; reciprocal wellbeing with 150–152; reducing concentrates for 175–176; research methodology 149–150; safe sites for cribbing by 181; social bonds 181–183; stereotypies 168–169, 170; tactile contact between 179; weaning of 180–181
horse tourism 154
Howell, G. 122
Hribal, J. 135, 142
Hultsman, W. 4
human agency 104–105
human-canine relationships and dog training 52–53
human-equine relations *see* horses
human hegemony in dog training 53–56
human leisure 1; versus chores 83–84, 86–87; dog shows as 35–40; dog walking as 85–91; domesticated animals and 4–6; human-equine relations within the landscape of 152–154; mapping the path ahead for 217–220; marginalised companion animals and 12–29; post-humanistic approach towards human-equine relations and 148–149; recentring companion species wellbeing in 98–110; rights and welfare 6–7
humans: on the animal spectrum 140–141; asymmetries of power and leisure between animals and 213–217; inter- and intra-species gains and losses for animals and 136–140; reciprocal wellbeing with horses 150–152
Hyatt, E. M. 115–120

Irwin, C. 151

Jarvis, J. 67
Jenkinson, S. 100–101
Jepson, D. 158
Johnson, R. A. 89
Jones, B. 171
Jongman, E. 149–150

Katcher, A. 115
Kawczynska, C. 67
Keaveney, S. M. 155–156, 160
kinaesthesia 151
Koehler, W. 49, 53
Kropp, F. 114
Kymlicka, W. 141

labels 22
labour roles of animals 133–135, 141–142; abuse and 136–137; animals need for labour and 138; history of 129–131; inter- and intra-species gains and losses for humans and 136–140; introduction to 128–129; loss of chances for meaningful cross-species time and engagement and 139–140; new roles for pets away from 140; selective breeding and 137; theoretical and research framework on 131–132; working dogs 138–139
Ladewig, J. 178
Lawler, A. 198
learned helplessness 174
leash, agency of the 107–108
Leffler, A. 114
Lehnertz, C. 66
Lerner, E. 114
Lesimple, C. 173
Lexington Attachment to Pet Scale 89–91
Lim, C. 98
llamas 4

Index 227

MacIntyre, A. 140–141
marginalised companion animals: as companion or family member 17–18, 21; constructions created by the pet industry for 21–23; contradictions in expectations and experiences of caretakers of 23–27; contradictions in the perceived life experiences of 18–21; as domestic/wild 212–213; introduction to 12–13; labels 22; moving beyond the paradigm of 28–29; as ornament, novelty or oddity 14–15; as pets for small spaces 22–23; purposes in human lives 13–18; as teaching tools 16–17; as toy, entertainment or diversion 15–16
Markwell, K. 146
Marx, K. 132, 133
Mason, G. J. 23
Matsyyama, Y. 159
McAfee, L. M. 179
McClure, S. R. 171
McConnell, P. 49, 50–53
McGreevy, P. 171, 173
McKenna, E. 50
Metcalfe, A. 148
Meyer, A. 73
Michael, Y. L. 82
Mikkelsen, M. V. 123
Miklósi, Á. 2
military use of animals 128
Miller, R. 122
mirrors for horses 179–180
Morgan, M. 148
Morris, S. 139
Mosteller, J. 116
mules 4
Murphy, M. 19
Mutrie, N. 83

National Park Service *see* Golden Gate National Recreation Area (GGNRA)
nonhuman family members, dogs as 113–115
novelty, marginalised companion animals as 14–15

oddity, marginalised companion animals as 14–15
off-leash recreation *see* Golden Gate National Recreation Area (GGNRA)
Oliveria, C. 154
ornament, marginalised companion animals as 14–15

Ortiz, F. 193
Other End of the Leash, The: What We Do Around Dogs (McConnell) 49

Park, J. 54, 55–56
Parkinson, J. 194, 195
Parks for People movement 64
parrots 15, 18, 20, 27
Passantino, A. 19
Perlo, K. 132
pet culture 147
pet industry 21–23
play 36–37
Polish Kennel Club 34–35; *see also* dog shows
post-humanism 147; approach towards human-equine relations and leisure 148–149; research methodology and 149–150
Presseau, J. 92
"Procrustean Solutions to Animal Identity and Welfare Problems" (Davis) 50
Pychyl, T. A. 107

rabbits 12, 16, 18, 22, *25*; free-range lifestyle *29*; in small spaces 22–23
reptiles 15, 20–21, *24*
Rhodes, R. E. 98, 99
riding tourism 154
rights, animal 6–7, 132; leisure and wellbeing 209–220; mapping the path ahead for 217–220
Robinson, I. H. 153
Rock, M. 65, 99, 100, 107, 109

Said, E. 2
Sanders, C. R. 41, 113, 115, 124, 211
Sapsford, J. 117
Savishinsky, J. S. 115
Schofield, G. K. 88
selective breeding for labour 137
sensory stimulation at dog shows 37–39, 42, 44
Sharpley, R. 158
sheep 4
Shepard, W. 73
shows, dog *see* dog shows
Sierra Club 68
SigurÐardóttir, I. 147
small spaces, pets for 22–23
Smith, J. A. 19
Sniehotta, F. F. 92
sociable conversation at dog shows 39–40

Stebbins, R. A. 32, 36, 41, 142, 154
Stuart, G. U. 199
Stud Book 33
Stupi, A. 71
"symphysis" 59
Syrian Golden Hamster 19

teaching tools, marginalised companion animals as 16–17
Thomas, K. 14
Thorpe, R. J. 83
Thrift, N. 148
Toohey, A. 65
Torkkola, J. 154
Toth, D. M. 151, 155
toys, marginalised companion animals as 15–16
training, dog *see* dog training
Tuan, Y.-F. 13, 26, 28
turtles 15, *16*

Urbanik, J. 148

Van Reenen, C. G. 170
Van Stralen, M. M. 83
Velten, H. 129
Visser, E. K. 170
Voith, V. 115

walking, dog *see* dog walking
weaning of horses 180–181
welfare, animal 6–7, 27
Wells, D. 70
Westgarth, C. 98, 109
Wilbert, C. 148
wild animals, defining 210–213
Wilson, R. M. 115
Wood, L. J. 123
Woodside, A. G. 115
working dogs 138–139
World Dog Show 42

Yarnell, K. 174
Yilmaz, O. 191
Yogo, M. 159
Young, J. 132